SEVEN BY CHANCE

SEVEN

BY CHANCE:

The Accidental Presidents

BY

PETER R. LEVIN

Farrar, Straus and Company

NEW YORK · 1948

ff

*Manufactured in the United States of America
by The Colonial Press Inc., Clinton, Mass.
Design by Stefan Salter*

ACKNOWLEDGMENTS

Many have a part in the writing of a book such as this. Some by their actions contribute the facts, for better or for worse. Others, by custom consigned to a bibliographical listing, record and interpret these facts. To all I freely state my debt. But as chronicler, compiler and interpreter I add that any error which appears herein is my own.

In most instances, the quotations appearing in the text come from source material. Where copyrighted material is used, the owners have generously permitted its reprinting. The quotation on page 31 is from *Democracy in the Making* by Hugh Russell Fraser, Copyright 1938, used by special permission of the publishers, The Bobbs-Merrill Company. The quotation on page 39 from Vernon L. Parrington's *Main Currents of American Thought—The Romantic Revolution in America* (ed., 1930) is used by permission of Harcourt, Brace and Company. Quotations on pages 28-29 are from the *Memoirs of John Quincy Adams,* edited by C. F. Adams, published by the J. B. Lippincott Company in 1875. The Houghton Mifflin Company granted permission to quote from *The Diary of Gideon Welles* and *The Education of Henry Adams,* as well as the use of materials from Samuel Hopkins Adams's *Incredible Era.* Passages on page 157 from *Chester A. Arthur, a Quarter Century of Machine Politics* by George F. Howe, on page 166 from *James A. Garfield, Party Chieftain* by Robert G. Caldwell, on page 210 from *John Hay, from Poetry to Politics* by Tyler Dennett are reprinted by permission of Dodd, Mead and Company, Inc. The quotations on page 196 from *The Autobiography of William Allen White* (1946) and on page 259 from William Allen White's *A Puritan in Babylon* (1938) are copyrighted by The Macmillan Company and used with their permission. Charles Scribner's Sons, copyright holders of much indispensable material on Theodore Roosevelt, kindly allowed reprintings of passages on pages 189 and 223 from *The Correspondence of Theodore Roosevelt and Henry Cabot Lodge,* edited by Lodge, on page 200 from Theodore Roosevelt's *Works,* on pages 207, 215 and 216 from Joseph B. Bishop, *Theodore Roosevelt and His Time,* on pages 225-226 from Theodore Roosevelt, *An Autobiography,* and on page 228 from H. H. Kohlsaat, *From McKinley to Harding.* Henry F. Pringle granted permission

v

to use both materials and quotations from his masterful biography, *Theodore Roosevelt* (published originally by Harcourt, Brace and Company). G. P. Putnam's Sons permitted quotation on pages 203-204 from Arthur W. Dunn, *From Harrison to Harding.* Lastly, the material on page 316 from Wilfred Binkley, *President and Congress,* published by Alfred A. Knopf, Incorporated, first appeared in the *Christian Science Monitor.*

Two names require special mention. Arthur Orrmont of Farrar, Straus and Company, through patient and persistent editing and uniformly excellent suggestions, contributed much, chapter by chapter, to the shaping of this work. Alice, my wife, was not only burdened by my abstracted presence while the volume was in the process of composition but devoted herself to such wearisome tasks as deciphering the handwritten manuscript, proofreading and indexing. To her, for more reason than her undoubted inspiration, this book is dedicated.

Peter R. Levin

New York, New York
April 18, 1948

CONTENTS

WHEN, on the evening of April 12, 1945, Harry S. Truman, his usually untroubled face tense and his voice muffled by nervousness, was sworn into the presidency by Chief Justice Harlan Stone, he became the seventh in an intermittent line. Like the six before him his elevation was all the more dramatic for its suddenness.

A few hours previously Truman had been a secondary figure on the contemporary American scene. Most cabinet members, the chairmen of several congressional committees, agency heads, a number of generals and admirals had been more important men in Franklin Roosevelt's fourth administration. Leaders of the Republican opposition, state governors, publishers, industrialists and labor chieftains surpassed him in influence and power. As vice-president his duties were few and his responsibilities inconsequential, his major requirement that he be on call.

But as president, Harry Truman became automatically a man of parts. That his accession was the result of Roosevelt's death instead of direct election made him no whit less a president. The Constitution does not differentiate between types of chief executives. They are technically all equal. So far as law and precedent go each is a potential colossus and theoretically there is no higher man in the country.

1. DRAMATIS PERSONAE

If only because each achieved extraordinary position and thus rose far above the average of his countrymen, all thirty-two men within the American presidential gallery command especial attention. There was a time when the lives of presidents, somewhat retouched by legend, were thought the best of examples in educating young boys to the opportunities available in the United States. Though a visit to a store handling juvenile books will confirm the suspicion that this view is not entirely dead, more convincing reasons can be advanced for such study on an adult level.

Because the office is the focal point of the American government, its occupants bear a relationship to the history of the country that other politicians seldom approach. The method by which they are selected renders them unique among American officials. Only vice-presidents are chosen similarly, and they have scant power. All others in the government belong to one of two categories. Where elected they represent constituencies that are state-wide or smaller. Else, where the office is national in character, like a judgeship on the Supreme Court or a cabinet post, its occupant has been appointed. The presidency is the sole office, nation-wide in scope and possessing significant powers, that is filled through election by all the voters.

Seven men, however, stand apart from the main group of First Magistrates. Ascendancy to the White House was, for them, a purely fortuitous circumstance. The public did not choose them to exercise presidential power, nor did their parties. It is paradoxical that a country which practices representative government and prides itself on rule by the people should have one in every four or five of its chief executives chosen by no one at all.

For the seven, as presidents, were more the creatures of a constitutional device than of the popular will. It is the Constitution of the United States, not the people, that demands the vice-presidency. And that office exists and is not considered entirely excess baggage because a presidential term is set flatly at four years while physical survival in office is somewhat less arbitrarily defined. Thus a minor post was created to provide against unseasonal vacancies in a major one. But the uncertainties that attach to its future have caused first-rate politicians to shun it as a more than probable dead-end.

Nevertheless the vice-presidency must be filled, and there have always been men willing to forgo chances of other advancement for the sake of party or empty honor. They qualify for the presidency according to the injunctions of the Constitution, but few consider them as actual heirs apparent. Since Andrew Jackson's day at the very least, party conventions have kept their sights pretty well restricted to the boundaries of the lesser office when nominating a junior partner on their national tickets. The average voter, faced with choosing between those who aspire to head the government, has quite properly devoted most of his attention to first place. It is a question whether he has given sufficient heed elsewhere. At any rate it would seem that his endorsement of a presidential candidate's running-mate is an act of faith, an uncritical seconding of politicians' judgments.

In a general way, this applies as much to the colleagues in accident whose careers are reviewed here as to any others who have been named to the secondary office. What gives the seven importance, in this connection, is that they have gained the presidency; they have escaped from obscurity to power. The others did not. The careers of the seven therefore bring the vice-presidency into focus. Moreover—and from the standpoint of American history and politics—they cast an oblique but nonetheless sharp light on the presidency.

Their first bond appears to be sheer coincidence. Since each of the seven successions was the result of another's death, there is repetition in the manner by which they reached the White House but no rational design. Yet the dominating fact is that John Tyler, Millard Fillmore, Andrew Johnson, Chester Arthur, Theodore Roosevelt, Calvin Coolidge and Harry Truman were all Presidents of the United States. Individually and collectively their careers influenced the nation and its people. An examination of the men and those careers is a partial examination of the presidency. It is a test of the constitutional device that raised these men to the office, of how adequate the system is that produced them.

Their length of service as substitutes is worth noticing. The presidents who died while in office were duly elected to serve an aggregate of twenty-eight years. But the seven who replaced them actually held the presidency for twenty-three of those years or better than eighty per cent of that time. Even more striking are the events that accompanied these changes. Johnson and Truman resided in the White House after America's two severest wars. Tyler made a sizable contribution toward bringing conflict with Mexico. Fillmore's willingness to approve the Compromise of 1850, which would never have become law had his predecessor lived, altered the course of the Union and helped to destroy the Whig Party. Theodore Roosevelt punctured the domestic calm by exploding political and economic firecrackers at superbly timed intervals, meanwhile ushering his country into full association with other nations of the earth. Coolidge sat unknowingly on a powder keg of calamity as its fuse sputtered warnings. Need it be remarked that Harry Truman's years were also those when the United States was forced to integrate its policies at home with the affairs of the world?

Only Chester Arthur's tenure cannot be said to have compassed noteworthy or critical years. Still it fits a pattern with respect to a majority of the other six, a pattern that will be later clarified.

2. THE SETTING: THE WHITE HOUSE

Although this book concerns mainly the lives, efforts and achievements of several presidents, it might be well to list a few of the institutional swatches that clothe the office. For the American presidency is more than what the Constitution says it is. Organically, it controls one major branch of government, the Executive, which is co-ordinate with the Legislative and Judicial branches, independent and in theory merely equal to them. This of course is the idea of separation of powers, preserved by a system of checks and balances that the branches maintain on one another. Beyond this is the system of federal union, of association within a central government by states technically equal in all things except popular representation. Superimposed on three branches the federal system has, with the courts playing a comparatively passive role, produced an unbalancing effect. The presidency, cutting across state lines, has become charged with leadership. In the public mind the chief executive has had fastened upon him a larger share of responsibility for the conduct of affairs than any other political figure. At times this personal burden has been greater than that collectively assigned the entire Congress.

To meet this responsibility a president draws upon his constitutional sources. He has the power to appoint his own subordinates, executive commissions and federal judges who will among their duties pass upon the deeds of his administration. He has the power of recommending to Congress those measures he considers necessary. He may not enact laws, but he shapes their meaning by the way he and his assistants execute them. He cannot require the legislature to do his bidding but he can call it into special session for announced purposes and can veto, subject to the will of an extraordinary majority, almost any bill he deems inadvisable, unwise or unsound. He is named commander-in-chief of the country's military and naval forces, and is granted predominant power in handling its foreign relations. Since these are the areas in which he has greatest independence, it is not surprising that a number of those presidents who established high reputations for strength—Jefferson, Lincoln, Wilson, Franklin D. Roosevelt—were at their most successful in using one or both of these explicit functions.

This, however, only enumerates the threads of power; it does not describe their qualities or the varieties of appreciation by the individual presidents who have held them. Bound together, they have made the office almost infinitely elastic. But how far they may be stretched depends upon many factors, some of which are the requirements of the times, the man serving, the condition of the party system, the make-up and attitude of Congress and its leaders.

Fully as vital to the office are those attributes it has developed outside the scope of the Constitution. Perhaps the least of these is the president's ceremonial position. Socially, all do homage to him. He is no king, but he is covered with the American equivalent of majesty. His reign is temporary, his honors more intangible and his authority in his court considerably less absolute. But his prestige is greater by reason of the power of his office, the range of his activity far broader. So long as he lives in the White House, the privacy accorded him by the people does not compare to that which subjects grant the resident of a palace.

The success or failure of any chief executive is probably determined at those points where the presidency has outgrown the space granted it by the Constitution. In holding him responsible for his administration and, by inference, for the state of the nation, the people have presented to him a more potent leadership than is possible within the limits of his authorized powers. He is not all-powerful. He must be prepared to find disagreement from congenital oppositionists, a Congress jealous of its rights and prerogatives, and those interests adversely affected by his proposals and statements. He may be challenged by others inside and outside the government. Nevertheless he comes closest to being the country's single national spokesman. In international affairs he has no peer in expounding the American position. At home, it is expected that he will pronounce on issues and contribute toward their definition.

More and more, presidents have been required to take a stand, to furnish the leadership that is implicit in the responsibility conferred upon them. Every strong president has attempted to mold public opinion. Through the press and radio, by messages, speeches, reports and the "inspired" activities of their subordinates and supporters, they have laid their cases before the people. On the other hand, public opinion has enforced restrictions on the White House. Here the president depends on those of his trusted advisers whose business it is to sample the popular mind and report on its condition. In recent years independent opinion polls have carried influence in the making of presidential decisions, though to an unmeasurable extent. One difficulty is a lack of clear information by those polled on the question asked. Another is the lethargic attitude which frequently greets important aspects of a program.

After his position as leader of public opinion the chief executive can utilize his place as nominal head of his party. This too is extra-constitutional, for in no instance perhaps did the founding fathers of 1787 display such absence of foresight as in their failure to consider the growth of national political organizations. Thinking in terms of the states, they presumed that presidents would emerge from the fairly complicated electoral system as the "best men" available to the country. In the same optimistic frame of mind they assigned the vice-presidency to the candidate who finished second in the race and could therefore be considered the "second-best man."

Within eight years after the Constitution became operative, the folly inherent in the system produced its first incompatibility. In 1796 President John Adams and Vice-President Thomas Jefferson were the two "best men"; they were also politically and partisanly opposed on every issue. The rise of parties during the next few years further accentuated division and reduced the stature of state electors. By 1800 these were plainly committed to joint candidacies. And when in the tie vote of that year, Aaron Burr disputed Jefferson's election by pressing his own technical claim to the presidency on the basis of the equal electoral votes he had received, the breakdown of the fathers' original concept was at hand. There could no longer be even a show of independent judgment by the electors. Party security demanded explicit candidates for the separate offices. The Jeffersonians pushed through the Twelfth Amendment, thereby writing that security into the Constitution. Henceforth parties would occasionally nominate strong contenders for second place but there was seldom any pretense that one thus selected was a presidential alternate. Today, as for many years past, the office is a plaything of conventions and national committees.

Political organization, however, has increased the breadth of presidential power. On a national level, he personalizes his party. Its victorious standard-bearer and the receptacle of popular confidence, he has a preliminary claim to its loyalty. He represents the unity achieved by the many elements that elected him. The circumstances of his rise to the post and his ability to preserve a supremacy over the organization through such agencies as the patronage may determine whether his leadership is actual or merely titular. How stern are the needs of the various factions and how harmoniously they work together will partially condition his success. So too, the willingness of party subalterns to labor enthusiastically and of other chieftains to follow his guidance.

Yet the party is the president's engine. He cannot move without it. Its congressional leaders enact his program; its committees and conventions nominate those who will support him—if he is to receive any formal support. It defends and publicizes his policies; it carries a considerable part of his fight against the opposition. In consequence strong presidents have always been adept party leaders. Where such leadership has been lacking, especially in peacetime, chief executives who would not surrender to those with positive strength have found themselves confronted with an antagonistic bi-partisan bloc.

Mention should be accorded one last resource of the president. This is his relationship to those who work for him. Though in him responsibility is centralized, his job is so broad that he can approach its many particulars in only the most general way. As he is dependent upon party and congressional chieftains and subordinates, so he requires competent assistants. His cabinet need not mirror his will completely, but its members should devote themselves to the administration's interests and be prepared to assume initiative where they can relieve their superior. His other administrators should be cut of the same pattern. Advisers, official and unofficial, must understand the peculiarity of their function: that they are responsible to the man but not the people.

Over all of them the president governs through a number of intangibles. Skill in selection is a necessity, though his field of choice is usually restricted by political and geographical considerations. He has to take what Congress and the party offer him. His cabinet is usually a compromise between exigency and personal desire. He may rebuild to fit his needs and wishes. Nevertheless, whether he is building or not, the United States is a going concern at all times and the presidency must be active continuously. Thus the chief executive must use and get the most of what is supplied him. By dint of personality and through application of his constitutional and customary powers, he attempts to pull together those under him toward a common goal and the creation of a successful administration.

*   *   *

But there is in the case of the seven an unusual problem. They were not elected to the presidency; they were thrust into it. They were not asked to create administrations; they inherited them. The machinery was already installed and in good working order. Their right of title was nominal at best.

BY THE late 1830's, the generation of political leaders that had created the republic and grounded its institutions was gone. A second generation had arisen, and a third was beginning to make itself heard. Coming as they did from the lifestream of a people expanding its settled area and increasing its numbers, developing new economic patterns, becoming ever more conscious of a new nationality, continually re-evaluating its ideals, most of the men who succeeded the founders were new in name and outlook. But among them were a few with the older names, men like John Quincy Adams and John Tyler—men of intelligence, strong opinions, a high sense of public duty; men powerfully influenced by the dreams of their fathers. In the careers of both are the epilogues of the cultures each represented, Adams' puritanism and Tyler's patrician agrarianism.

1. VIRGINIA EXPOSURE

In March of 1841, John Tyler was facing four years of quiet and prestige as the eleventh vice-president of the United States. For years, his inflexible convictions had pushed him into political battles, and from each one it seemed that he had emerged a little further removed from the inner party councils, a man less likely either to lead or to be trusted by party leaders. Yet the amorphous opposition to Jacksonian democracy which created the Whig Party and devised the harlequinade of the 1840 campaign had raised him to what was, nominally at least, exalted office.

John Tyler's brand of Whiggery differed from that of Henry Clay or Daniel Webster, the "giants" of the party. Its ingredients were of another sort from those of his Virginian fellows. But, to all who thought about it, the factor of variation had little significance; though Tyler might now have title, he had little real power. And Tyler himself was satisfied. His deteriorating political fortunes had received a sudden boost. His new position would hardly require arduous labor. Even his virile conscience could rest in silence, except for those unlikely occasions when an equal split of the senatorial yeas and nays required his casting-vote. The President, old General William Henry Harrison, and the presidential advisers and the congressional leaders could guide this first Whig administration in American history; Tyler would do justice to his few duties and enjoy the social life of Washington. More important, he would spend the long vacations between congressional sessions with his family and friends in Williamsburg.

Inauguration Day passed easily, almost quietly. In the Senate chamber, Tyler received the oath of office and followed it with a speech of small distinction. For his text, the Vice-President contented himself with paying tribute to General Harrison and to the doctrine of states' rights, the latter a somewhat distasteful philosophy in many Whig quarters. Then, the assembled Congress and its guests moved on to the eastern portico of the Capitol for the main event, the inauguration of the first Whig President.

While the new officialdom sat around him, and a multitude of office-seekers and the merely curious looked up at him, the old General unrolled a sheaf of foolscap and read his address. Where Tyler's speech had been mercifully short, Harrison's went on for more than an hour and a half, replete with generalities and classical allusions. Daniel Webster's previous revisions on it had "killed seventeen Roman proconsuls dead as smelts," but the audience still received more an exposition on the functions of the Executive branch, together with a lesson in ancient history, than an enlightenment in future policy. Eventually, however, it was over; and the formalities done with, Washington settled down to entertaining the new administration. President Harrison moved into the White House to save the nation from the aftereffects of Jacksonism, and John Tyler departed for tidewater Virginia and home.

It was not that the new Vice-President had a pronounced aversion to the nation's capital. He had a choice of residence, and he was making it. Washington itself lacked the attractions other places had. Only slightly over forty years old as a settlement, it was home to 25,000 people, but a source of criticism and jest to outside observers. Houses were scattered over its spacious blocks, but the streets, according to Charles Dickens who visited a year later, led nowhere. From the Capitol, if one gazed up Pennsylvania Avenue—the single fully paved street—he saw the White House. Looking in other directions, the view was less inspiring: an undrained swamp, a slaughterhouse and its animal pens, jerry-built houses, and a cow pasture. To the French minister, doubtless dreaming of Paris (his center of civilization and of the universe), the seat of the government of the United States was "neither a city, nor a village, nor the country"; it was a "building-yard placed in a desolate spot."

To Tyler, Williamsburg was more desirable. A genuine family man, he felt a strong call to be with his paralyzed wife. A Virginian by conviction, he preferred the comfortable atmosphere of an Old Dominion city to the crude tyro on the north bank of the Potomac. And the actual distance between the two places was comparatively small, though the journey was not as short as it might have been. Railroads were still a Northern experiment; good roads were being worked out in the North and demanded by the West; the traveller going more than a few miles in Old Virginia depended upon the waterways of Chesapeake Bay and the rivers that emptied into it.

Lying on the historic Yorktown peninsula, Williamsburg existed on its memories of great days long past. Once it had been the capital of the British province of Virginia. At times, the court of the colonial governors outshone even the mother Court of St. James. While the legislature was in session, the town was filled by tidewater planters and their families—the men to look after their interests both economic and political, the entire family to participate in the brilliant social season. In 1693, the College of William and Mary was built, patterned after Sir Christopher Wren's plan for Chelsea Hospital in London. Through the years, the school had maintained an excellent faculty and from its small student body had given the country great men. It had also started Phi Beta Kappa, that good if honorary company of scholars. The Governor's Palace had once housed the titans Patrick Henry and Thomas Jefferson as well as others less illustrious like the Englishmen, Dinwiddie and Spotswood. All in all, Williamsburg had been to the Upper South what Boston was to New England, Philadelphia to the Middle Colonies, and Charleston to the Carolinas—a hub for those immersed in politics, those given to developing the intellect, and those athirst for the exercise of the social arts. It was, in short, the part-time metropolis of a tobacco-wealthy agraria.

But before John Tyler's birth, the world that made Williamsburg the symbol of colonial achievement had fallen away. The once rich tidelands lay exhausted and poor, the wealth of their soil mined by too many tobacco harvests. Profitable agriculture moved west into the Piedmont and upland country. And with it went Virginia's real strength. When, during the Revolution, Governor Jefferson moved the capital up the James River to the village of Richmond, he gave the *coup de grâce* to an already dying region. Creative wealth, the will to progress, and opportunity had gone; prominence followed them.

Something of the old town remained. The college kept it alive. The mansions still stood and their inhabitants retained stubborn loyalties to family dynasty and the aristocratic tradition. Yet the old spark was gone: the clashing revolutionary and tory ideologies belonged to the past; the ferment which gives diversity of outlook had moved elsewhere. In the great debates between Jefferson's democracy and Marshall's federalism, Williamsburg gave adherence to both causes and believed in neither. Instead, it held to an older feudal ideal, the ideal of planter rule. From Jefferson it borrowed the supremacy of local rights; but where he had established the concept as a protection of individual freedom and as a base of broad humanitarianism, Williamsburg took it as a defense against change. From Marshall, it borrowed the precedence of vested interest; but it ignored his nationalistic views and his broad interpretations which upheld privilege everywhere, inside *and* outside seaboard Virginia.

*　　*　　*

In 1837, while temporarily without political office, Tyler was able to exercise one of his few romantic tastes by moving to Williamsburg. Though he had not been born there, three generations of Tylers before him had. Like him, those who had received advanced schooling had gone to the college. The county itself had been the first Tyler home in America. A family aura hung over the old town; and Tyler, so unsentimental in other ways, was strongly attracted by his heritage and his college.

The Williamsburg of 1837 had been going its tangent way for fifty years. It had been singularly unaffected by the deepening humanitarian stream that was running across the country. It had repudiated the nascent commerce and industry of the North. Its horizons were narrowed; its mental climate was plainly sectarian. Its standards were rigid: the old aristocracy had to be preserved; the Virginia tradition had to be glorified as the epitome of high culture; the South as a section had to be justified and exalted. Among the town's citizens, those few men of capacity who chose to reside there betrayed, by that very choice, an insular state of mind.

There, Thomas R. Dew, President of the College of William and Mary, had gone to the realms of political economy, history and Scriptural command to prove the new truth that human slavery was morally sound. His ethical discovery gave John C. Calhoun and others the framework upon which to build an entire southern philosophic defense. There, Nathaniel Beverley Tucker, sometime embittered judge in Missouri and now professor of law, fought his personal crusade against things Yankee and Jacksonian. A retiring man in his personal habits, Tucker on paper was a vitriolic hater. As early as 1820, his conflicts with northerners in Missouri convinced him that the South's future lay in secession. By 1836 he had restricted his outlook even further. The future of Virginia, and Virginia alone, was of uppermost importance. As a sovereign state of the Union she was being ruined in the trail of excesses left by Jeffersonian democracy. For to Beverley Tucker democracy meant the power of Jackson's rabble and the cry for abolition that was spreading through their northern ranks. If planter Virginia was to be saved, she must follow Calhoun and his South Carolinians; she must reject her own heroes Jefferson and Madison; she must certainly have no traffic with the egalitarian Democracy of Andrew Jackson and Martin Van Buren. Thomas Dew could provide suggestive directions to Calhoun's thought; Beverley Tucker would set out the lead-strings for John Tyler's policy.

A later entrant into the circle was Judge Abel P. Upshur of the Virginia Supreme Court. His northern education had done little to temper his planter background and studies in Virginia law; he remained southern to the core—and thoroughly antidemocratic. Numerical majorities, in his belief, had no place in government. A government of laws—that catch-phrase used as much today as in the past to cover devious political concepts—was one which suited the needs and interests of the people. Yet the people were, by no means, the necessary and proper sovereigns of their government. Rather, the "law of force" was the only determinant of who should rule. That liberty might be an existing condition of governments of law was, to the judge, all well and good. Liberty was, however, never basic to such governments, and was, in his own chaotic times, committing "suicide" and would linger on if at all "in the slave holding states."

If this climate of opinion irritated the Jeffersonian credo John Tyler professed to hold, he gave few such indications. His father had been a friend and follower of the Monticello sage, detesting slavery as a state of man and as a bulwark to southern economy. In 1787-88, he had fought ratification of the Constitution because that then unhallowed document permitted a continuation of the slave trade for twenty years. His life in Virginia politics as legislator, governor, and judge had been marked by a democratic outlook and the promotion of democratic practices fully in harmony with those of his leader. During the years of the younger Tyler's ascendancy, however, adherence to the Jeffersonian line was becoming more difficult for the planter aristocracy to which the Tylers belonged. Turning somewhat away from the battle with federalism abroad, the old ex-President-philosopher was, from retirement, issuing uncomfortable remarks about basing Virginia's government on numbers rather than wealth and property. In a way that rankled he was pointing out certain distasteful things about slavery and methods for ending it. Though the news of his death was received with sorrow, the feeling was accompanied in patrician quarters, and probably in John Tyler as well, by a sense of relief.

In Williamsburg the younger Tyler found ease and companionship, but he also found nice areas of disagreement with the philosophic pattern of the town's recognized thinkers. Something in the memory of his father's enthusiasms prevented his accepting the school of thought around him. He could not hold with Professor Dew that the ownership of slaves was necessarily glorious in the eyes of God. Nor did he assert with Calhoun that "the relation now existing in the slaveholding states between the two [races] is, instead of evil, a good—a positive good." In principle, of course, Tyler opposed anything that emanated from William Lloyd Garrison's abolitionism or the more moderate northern proposals for gradual extinction. Steering between the extremes, he set himself a course dedicated neither to attack nor defense. Legislatively, he favored ending the domestic slave trade (though not slavery) in the District of Columbia; in the sphere of social action, he contributed some of his time to the Virginia Colonization Society which made fainthearted efforts at gradual emancipation and meanwhile hoped to settle freed Negroes in Africa, distant from whites and enslaved blacks alike. Philosophically speaking, the institution troubled him; practically speaking, it had to be retained until that as yet unperceived day when all men were enlightened enough to live without it.

In his thoughts on government, Tyler was on more confident ground—the ground that the states had created the Union and were, therefore, sovereign. From his father he inherited a fear of federal power—a power that elder Jeffersonians believed was dangerous because it could be used in suppressing individual freedom and cementing privilege. With Tyler the fear persisted. His worry, however, was not for the individual nor at the possible aggrandizements of the privileged. It was, rather, for the defense of what he considered the absolute rights of the states, particularly of Virginia and her southern sisters. Should federal power be used in ways beneficent to the people as a whole or the nation at large, if it infringed states' rights or adversely affected the established custom of the South, its use was wrong. Logically, one might suppose, he should have carried his argument to its conclusion and advocated government by and for those standing to gain most from enforcement of the states' rights doctrine, the planter class. But unfortunately for logic, Tyler was a politician. On that point, he was silent. Any words favorable to planter domination would lose him the considerable vote of the small farmers and the common folk temporarily under the spell of the Jacksonian appeal. To plump for southern supremacy would blacklist him from the northern Whig support he needed if he was ever to come to Washington in high office.

2. "TIP AND TY"

Exactly one month after Harrison's inauguration, young Fletcher Webster was on his way from Washington to Williamsburg. Never matching his father Daniel's abilities as an orator, vote-getter, or advocate of the due to be paid the old-style New England federalism or the new-style conservative nationalism, the younger Webster's security was a perpetual worry to the older one. At the moment, the Webster family, though feeling as always a certain financial strain, was running the State Department, Daniel as its Secretary and Fletcher as its chief clerk. Nepotism perhaps accounted for Fletcher's presence in the government, but his mission to Williamsburg was one of extremely official business.

In the penetrating chill of the early morning of April 5, 1841, he sought Vice-President John Tyler. Arousing him, Fletcher wordlessly delivered a note from Harrison's cabinet. The sixty-eight-year-old General was dead. After forty years of public service in and out of military life, one month of the presidency had killed him. The half-awake Virginian was now the Chief Executive.

*   *   *

William Henry Harrison had, in his opinion, served his country well and felt it was the country's duty to repay such service. That others agreed with him on occasion was, for him, a fortunate meeting of minds. For alongside the records of those who preceded him in the presidency his own contained nothing to mark him the equal of any of them. While he had demonstrated military aptitude and a potent thirst for any public office, his ability to handle the entire complex of national affairs was questionable at best. Yet, he had ambition. And compounded with luck, some fairly astute politicking, and a judicious exploitation of the early part of his career, this was sufficient to bring him to the White House.

During the first decade of the century Harrison had been both Governor of the Indiana Territory and superintendent of the Northwest

Indians. By the white man's standards his administration had been successful. Superintending was a relatively simple matter: one invoked enough long-winded oratory and distributed sufficient whiskey until the aboriginal owners signed a treaty deeding away their hunting grounds to the United States; then one saw to it that hindsight and sobriety did not bring Indian efforts at abrogation. Through this method—condoned, it must be said, by Jefferson and Madison—the vigorous Governor opened millions of Indian acres to land-hungry whites and won himself a strong local popularity.

Popularity became reputation when the Indians revolted, led by two particularly able men, Tecumseh and his brother, the Prophet. Their gospel was not so much military retaliation as a spreading of new ideas —a deadly form of revolution anywhere and one especially so on the frontier where Indian complaisance in the established pattern of settlement was a condition of peace. In a great wave of reform the brothers stirred the tribes to a puritanical renunciation of both intoxicants and white men. A confederation was organized and a major settlement made at the junction of Tippecanoe Creek and the Wabash River. Harrison, forced to act, provoked Tecumseh into battle and destroyed the village. How successful he was in crushing the confederation may be judged from the fact that four months later the Indians returned to the same lands and Tecumseh was driven into concluding an alliance with the British.

Two years later, during the War of 1812, however, he gained real stature as a military commander. In a war marked by few American victories, Harrison met the allies at the Thames River in Ontario, defeated them, broke the Indian power, and saw Tecumseh killed in the battle.

Making his home on the Ohio River, he merged with the growing West. His birth and antecendents among Virginia's patrician aristocracy were forgotten, brushed aside by the frontier legend of the Hero of Tippecanoe and the Thames. He farmed his land as a true westerner. His grateful neighbors sent him to Congress as their representative. But there the progression stopped. His record as a legislator was minor. Eclipsed by the lustrous young generation of politicians rising to fill the void left by the retirement of Jefferson and the downfall of the Federalists, he returned to private life. There, dissatisfaction and financial reverses led him to remember the debt his country owed him; and, after much cajoling, John Quincy Adams appointed him minister to the new republic of Colombia. Though on the face of things he returned to his Ohio farm, a casualty of Jackson's spoils system, he had, during his short tenure in the post, estranged the two countries by most undiplomatic references to Bolivar's dictatorial methods.

The Jacksonian days were bad ones for Harrison. Not only were offices denied him; his farm was losing money and his children were a disappointment. Campaigning for the presidency in 1840, his official position was Clerk of the Court of Common Pleas of Hamilton County, Ohio. Nevertheless, by that time he minimized those questionings of his abilities that might be raised from his uneven career. His appeal was not as a solon, but as a war hero, a frontiersman, a simple western farmer doing his duty by the West. His appeal made him the "available" candidate of his party. It gave the Whigs an answer to Andrew Jackson in the form of another hero of the same war, another westerner, another general.

And in addition to personal appeal, Harrison gave assurances. His Virginia birth still counted with those planters who gave allegiance to the Whig cause, while his Ohio residence freed him from the "taint of slavery" now beginning to repel northern laborers and farmers from southern hopefuls. He was a farmer, it was true; but his connections were with large land speculators, his dealings with the men of the Bank of the United States were more than social, and his most recent economic savior and political mentor was Abbott Lawrence, a prince among New England manufacturers and an apostle of conservatism. If proof were needed that he could pull votes, in 1836 he had run a stronger race against Martin Van Buren than the other Whig candidates in the field.

If Whiggery were to win in 1840, who else was there? Daniel Webster, who had run fourth in 1836 and was not, according to Lawrence, a candidate? General Winfield Scott, who had a good military record and Virginia birth, but who opposed slavery and lacked political experience of any sort? Henry Clay, who had twice before been beaten, who was too openly identified with the Bank "octopus" the West dreaded, who had been on both sides of most questions during the past thirty years and had strong enemies in both parties? Who else, now that Hugh Lawson White, the third place contender in 1836, was dead, and now that Calhoun had made his peace with Van Buren and the Democrats? Who indeed, but General William Henry Harrison, the man who could find something in himself for each section of the country. Who indeed, but the Clerk of the County Court, whose career had made him no enemies in politics and who had never been required to take a stand on any of the issues brought forth by the advent of Andrew Jackson.

The magical potion of folk heroism and political obscurity worked. A campaign of noise and nonsense by the Whigs and a popular protest against the hard times turned out the Democrats. To the Whigs, the victory was gratifying after twelve years of conservative hunger. To President Harrison, it was a personal triumph, though he had no certainty of what he would do with it. His death ended the triumph; the uncertainty passed over to the party as John Tyler prepared to succeed him.

*   *   *

Like Harrison, John Tyler had a long record of public service; but unlike his predecessor, Tyler had accumulated both enemies and as definitive a record as a politician dares be saddled with when he takes office. If Harrison, on carefully built appearances, had been all things to all men, Tyler presented but one face—a thoroughly southern one. From 1811 to 1841, his career had been identified with the divergent currents that swept Virginia politics, with the issues that had continually churned up the country. He had participated in the many party battles which made, destroyed, and reconstructed coalitions, and which ballooned men to prominence and power or dropped them to obscurity.

Virginia knew him well. On three well-spaced occasions, its House of Delegates provided him a springboard to higher office. The first leap was small—election to the Council of State, an advisory body to the governor. The second leap was higher, to the governor's chair itself. The third leap, in 1839, was furthest of all. At that time, his aim had been the United States Senate, but his failure to reckon the true velocity of the prevailing political winds resulted in his vice-presidential candidacy.

For those who were interested, Tyler's eleven years in Virginia's government rendered clear evidence of where his sympathies lay. That he announced his actions to be Jeffersonian, and probably believed they were, was a tribute to the efficacy of slogan thinking. Whatever his doctrine actually was in name, it coincided most closely in fact with the conservatism of the tidewater. As a young state legislator, he had led the demand to censure Virginia's senators when they chose to ignore instructions from home and vote according to their own lights.[1] To a

---

[1] In those times, state legislatures eyed the federal government and the state delegation in Congress far more closely than they do today. The reasons were many, some associated with the traditional fear of central government, others with the relatively greater power of the states. The election of senators by the state legislatures made the former at least partially responsive to pressures from home, and made the latter interested scrutinizers of senatorial careers.

man so aware of his own conscience, the extension of the same privilege to others seemed beside the point; "the said Richard Brent and William B. Giles did, on that occasion [i.e., in voting to renew the charter of the first United States Bank], cease to be true and legitimate representatives of this State."

Interpreted alone, it seemed an insignificant matter in John Tyler's stormy public life. But viewed in retrospect, it was a preview of his steady adherence to the strictest interpretation of the states' rights creed, the first sign in a mass of evidence that he thought northern capitalism antithetical to southern interests. In the next few years, he was to prove his alignment with the tidewater against the developing commerce and industry of the North and the rough democracy of the common man. In 1823, he tried to fasten Virginia's prestige to the fading strength of "King Caucus," that unpopular means of selecting a presidential candidate behind closed Congressional doors and then presenting him full-blown and unchallenged to the electorate. Back of the act was the purpose of insuring William G. Crawford of Georgia, the friend of the planters, as Monroe's successor, and of stifling the drives of New England's John Quincy Adams and the West's Henry Clay and Andrew Jackson. In the Virginia state constitutional convention of 1829-30, Tyler quietly supported all tidewater efforts to keep the more populous upland sections of the state under-represented in the legislature.

Washington, too, knew John Tyler. During the years anomalously known to history as the "Era of Good Feelings," he had sat in the House of Representatives, opposing anything that might transcend the supremacy of the Old South. The wounds of the War of 1812 which left the Treasury gouged and the nation's financial structure gasping; the demands from over the mountains of both the Southwest and the Northwest for spurs to settlement in the forms of cheaper lands and internal improvements at Federal expense; the call of the Northeast for encouragement to its rising manufactures—all these he tried to subordinate to the planter interest. Solution had to come, if at all, he held, from within the framework of the individual states. The doctrine of states' rights, hallowed and cherished in Richmond, applied with equal force in Washington.

In 1819, the second Bank of the United States which had been chartered by Virginians Madison and Monroe to help cure the nation's monetary and financial ills was, as yet, far from the dominating force it later became. But for Congressman Tyler the Bank was an illegal instrument, chartered in violation of the strict construction of the Constitution. He was ready to vote its repeal "without awaiting a judicial decision"—an interesting viewpoint for one schooled as a lawyer and an impractical one so long as John Marshall guided the Supreme Court.

Tariffs for the protection of northern manufactures were an abomination. They would not only force agriculture to pay the bills of industrialization and the cost of building northern cities, they would make the nation dependent upon Europe. Internal improvements at national expense were not only unconstitutional, they were degrading. Virginia required no "charitable donation" from Congress. In the great debate on the rights and prerogatives of slavery—the question of Missouri's admission to the Union with a slavery constitution—John Tyler became a mouthpiece for the extreme in southern thought. Slavery, he said, was an institution of the states; its spread could not be limited by federal imposition. If he thought inwardly that slavery was morally wrong or that it was a hindrance to progress, whether spiritual or economic, he was silent. On the contrary, his argument presumed that it would exist into all the future then discernable, a cornerstone to the plantation economy and an inalienable right in southern politics.

As a senator, John Tyler was even better known in Washington. He had replaced John Randolph, the bitterest states-righter of them all. His election had been made possible by Adams-Clay men, but Tyler, shortly afterward, chose to support their rival, Andrew Jackson. For four years he followed the Jacksonian line, with only minor defections, considering himself a Democrat and happy in the general's apparent devotion to states' rights principles. If Tyler had a political antagonist in the Senate, it was Henry Clay, whose affections for high tariffs and Nicholas Biddle's Bank were contrary to all southern doctrine whether patrician or plebian.

But the break was inevitable. Jackson demanded loyalty of his followers, and expected that the loyalty be directed toward the preservation of the Union and the destruction of entrenched privilege. And Tyler, never one to follow any dictations but those of his own conscience, refused. South Carolina's emphatic threat to leave the Union rather than obey the tariff laws won his sympathy. Jackson's answer— a firm promise to use force if the state carried out its announced intention—provoked the Virginian's hostility. In the Congress that passed Old Hickory's Force Bill, Tyler cast the sole "nay," Calhoun and the other southerners tactfully abstaining.

When Jackson and Roger Taney opened war on Biddle's citadel of privilege, Tyler's break with Democracy was complete. In theory, he still considered the Bank unconstitutional; but in contrast to his fire-brand opinions of 1819, the administration's policy was now a violation of contract, a breach of faith. In 1834, he led a floor fight together with Clay and Webster censuring the old warrior and whitewashing the Bank of all charges. In his politics and his person he had embraced the Whigs.

This retreat to more rewarding companionship was no better received by Jackson men in Virginia than were the attacks silently accepted by the President's defenders in Congress. Jacksonians began action to expunge that censure from the Senate's journal. Back in Richmond, Democrats in the legislature instructed Tyler and his junior partner, Benjamin W. Leigh, to cast their votes for removing the "slur." Tyler characteristically refused to compromise: he would not reverse his first vote and he could not defy Virginia's instructions, no matter how erroneous he thought them. He consulted his conscience and in a burst of righteousness resigned his seat. Leigh, with feelings less acute, voted against Jackson and stayed on, oblivious to orders and the stern demands of states' rights. . . .

The next time John Tyler held office in Washington he would be vice-president. First, however, must be told the story of a party's rise to power.

3. WHIGGERY, AMERICAN STYLE

The revolution that came to American politics with Andrew Jackson's ascendancy was not, as in all such upheavals, without its dissenters. In its beginning, it appeared to be a mere regrouping of strengths within the Jeffersonian Republican party; one group had taken power from another. In reality, the party system of the country had been brought to a new turn. The myth that had prevailed since the death of the Federalists, that America needed but one party to reconcile all differences and recognize all points of view, was dead. Andrew Jackson and Martin Van Buren, in their jockeying for position, had destroyed it.

Two parties sought control of the government; two parties appraised the social order. One defended the old ways and the time-honored methods; the other breathed a wild new spirit and demanded a redistribution of favors.

The basic defenders were a well-defined group of one-time Federalists and new conservative nationalists, the New England partisans of President John Quincy Adams. To them were added the Ohio Valley followers of Henry Clay, the heir-apparent to Adams' presidential chair, and a diverse conservatism from the Middle States, Maryland, and southern Louisiana. Theirs was a cohesive amalgam of wealth, commerce, large-scale enterprise, manufactures, and privilege.

The Jackson men were united only in their unrest; their one aim was the overthrow of those "corrupt bargainers" Adams and Clay who had frustrated their hopes and apparent victory in 1824. The common men—the small farmers over the mountains, the debt-ridden farmers of the North and South, the workingmen of the cities—gave the revolution its backlog of strength, provided its inchoate demands, elevated its leader. Jackson—the humbler of the British before New Orleans, the punisher of the Indians, the opponent of the banks, the questioner of privilege—was their idol. He understood their needs, shared their hatreds, promised them solutions. They came to his banner naturally, easily, happily. In the new temple of egalitarian democracy that was to arise, their votes were the bricks which gave an overpowering massiveness to the edifice. But until the common men could find within themselves the mortar of secondary leadership, power, wealth and prestige, the movement had to borrow it from the rival political sect. How conservatives were led to the Jacksonian temple is an explanation of Van Buren's right to be called "The Little Magician."

To the conservative wheat growers of the Northwest, who could have been expected to follow Henry Clay, he intimated that canals and roads would be constructed to move their produce to market. To the protectionists of New York and Pennsylvania, he murmured of tariff laws which would promote their interests over the industries of New England. The planter fear of the rising northern capitalism received his assiduous exploitation: tariffs—that bane of agriculture—would be reduced; Jackson, the Indian fighter, would open new lands in the Southwest for the extension of the plantation system; Jackson, the Tennessee slaveholder, would buttress the South's labor system against New England's blue-nosed unfriendliness; and Calhoun, the new philosopher of slavery and particularism, would succeed the sickly old warrior if for the time being he postponed his presidential aspirations. And thus placed under the spell of Van Buren's soft persuasion, conservatives too shouted for the Hero, perhaps less happily than the wearers of homespun, but shouted nonetheless.

The coalition deposed Adams as a national leader. In his conservatism, he was unable to comprehend the vitality of the new democracy; in his honesty, he was incapable of using the methods of the Van Buren political school. During the last twenty years of his life, driven by his Puritan conscience, he preached the heresy of abolition, questioning and threatening the doctrine and the fact of slavery. The task of directing national conservatism fell to men more willing to compromise with principle, more adept at trafficking in votes. And New England being suspect, as always, outside its borders, guidance and strategy passed to Henry Clay rather than Daniel Webster.

Still, Clay had the same problem—the conquest of Andrew Jackson. For years, Clay had advocated his "American System," a latter-day version of Hamilton's program. But where Federalism had been coolly intellectual in both its exposition and its exponents, its sequel was sparked by a man whose personal warmth made him "Harry of the West" rather than "Mr. Clay" to those who believed him. Virginia birth and a Kentucky plantation, he felt, were enough to recommend him to the plantation aristocracy. The "American System" was for the North and West. These he conceived to be one huge region, each section supplementing the other. By his plan, the West, so anxious for internal improvements and a "home market," would receive its roads and canals at the expense of the federal government. The North, though unhappy at the spending of the country's moneys in the West, would have its industries encouraged by frankly protective tariffs; and, in perfect consequence, its booming cities would take the transmontane produce.

When the West inclined to view internal improvements as too paltry an offering, Clay, mindful of eastern antagonism to cheap public lands, developed what he was convinced was the happy satisfaction to all. Land sales brought money into the Treasury. Why not distribute the incoming funds among the states for public works and educational subsidies? Since most of the lands sold were western, let the states from which the money came receive the lion's share of the bonus. Thus, in one way or another, the one section would have its improvements at no expense to anyone; and the land payments, which gave the Treasury revenue and proved so embarrassing to those protectionists who argued for high tariffs as a source of government income, would be eliminated.

One more device. Jackson's suspicion of banks in general was focused in his hate for Nicholas Biddle's giant. The Bank's charter was to expire in 1836; but 1832 was Clay's presidential year. Even if it was premature to raise the question of the Bank's future, the alert Kentuckian stood ready to make its continued life rest on a test of politics instead of on the nation's economic requirements four years hence. As Clay saw it, if Jackson's hostility were forced into the open, the entire

Ohio Valley and the Northeast would turn on the old man and send Henry Clay to the White House.

Accounted by himself and others an expert calculator of political odds, he played his cards exultantly. He hammered through a high tariff that included the distribution scheme. Undoubtedly, the old man would veto it, and eastern protectionism and the bankrupt West would wrathfully rebel. Jackson double-crossed him and signed. Vague stirrings were heard among some of the planters, but only in South Carolina, domain of the now isolated John C. Calhoun, were collars warm.

Clay played his trump. Both houses presented the President with a bill to recharter the Bank. This time, Jackson did not disappoint; his veto came back bristling with objection. Clay had his campaign issue, and eastern money rushed to his support.

The election returns came in—a landslide for Old Hickory, an overwhelming defeat for Henry Clay. The South, so dear to his rhetoric, where it had not gone for the General, preferred Governor Floyd of Virginia. Deftly outmaneuvered, Clay had too obviously walked the path of entrenched privilege; and once there, the people rampant had steamrollered him. Even John Tyler, planter and aristocrat, had preferred Jackson.

* * *

The electoral beating failed to persuade Clay that the presidency was out of his reach. It did convince him that something else was necessary. He found circumstances still propitious. The eruption in South Carolina and Jackson's brusque rejoinder won Democracy a temporary gain of northern nationalists but permanently lost it the uneasy planters. To the feudal aristocracy, the states' rights doctrine was far too sacred a thing to be kicked around by a western democrat. In the exodus went John Tyler and the Virginia set, and not a few other big names like Hugh Lawson White and John Bell of Tennessee. For sweetening, Tyler and Clay sponsored the Compromise Tariff law of 1833 progressively lowering those duties that had so exacerbated South Carolina. Jackson's signature on the bill, together with his stepped-up war on the Bank, further infuriated the northern money power.

As if this were not enough, the very presence of laboring men, small farmers, minor planters, the poor and the debtors within Democracy's ranks bred an attitude in manufacturers, bankers, the great planters and grain-growers that the other party offered better consanguinity. One more group, the Anti-Masons who had voted for Wirt in the

South and who represented a sizable rural bloc of anti-Jacksonism in the Northeast, was pulled into the coalition. From them came a base of common men and three accomplished politicians—Thaddeus Stevens of Pennsylvania, and Thurlow Weed and William Seward of New York.

To receive the heterodoxy, Clay and his companions made admission easier by jettisoning the "National Republican" name that dated from more exclusive days. There was no need, they reasoned, to jolt memories of Adams' nationalism or Jefferson's republicanism. Rather, they took a new name, short, palatable and, in American terms, meaningless. The new party simply knew itself as "The Whigs."

Immediately there were difficulties. No positive platform could be created without alienating one or several groups. Worse yet, torn between seething doctrines and implacable ambitions, the party failed to agree on candidates. Henry Clay, for all his ability as the architect of the party, was distrusted by the states' rights wing. Daniel Webster, another quadrennial seeker of nominations, gained no southern confidence by his too patent record of neo-Federalism and his New England residence. In the dilemma, sectional candidates ran separate races against Martin Van Buren in the hope that no one man would receive a majority and the final determination, therefore, would be thrown to a Whig House of Representatives. North of the Mason-Dixon Line, William Henry Harrison was teamed with Francis Granger, the son of Gideon Granger who as Postmaster-General had once earned the misgivings of President Jefferson. Massachusetts violated party regularity by standing firm for Webster. In the South, Hugh Lawson White, calling himself a "true Jackson man" in defiance of the General, campaigned with John Tyler as his mate. Here, too, there was irregularity. South Carolina, in a thorough repugnance for things Jacksonian whether enunciated by the namesake or an erstwhile, disgruntled henchman, backed Willie P. Mangum, a favorite son.

What Clay could not do in 1832, the four almost accomplished in 1836. Among them they amassed more than forty-nine per cent of the popular vote and aggregated 124 electoral votes to Van Buren's winning 170. Harrison had done surprisingly well. And Tennessee, the cradle of Jacksonian democracy, had gone for White.

Henry Clay read the returns and planned for 1840. If one more unhappy group could be intrigued into the coalition, Whiggery would ride in on the protesting tide.

As for Jackson's heir, luck turned against him almost from his inauguration. Economics caught up with him. Before his administration could get its bearings, a panic engulfed the country. While bank doors closed forever, businesses crumbled. Constriction of the currency placed new hardships where they always come first, on the poor in the cities, on the small farmers, on the West. When the pyrotechnics were over, the country settled down to a depression that lasted through his term. Either unable or unwilling to find a daring solution, Van Buren's inner circle offered no salvation but the exceedingly limited Independent Treasury plan. In itself, it was a good measure, designed to free government finance from the spasms of an uncontrolled banking system. But it also placed a brake on the easy money heretofore obtainable for speculation and business credits. Conservative Democrats took alarm; their congressional counterparts formed an entente with Clay's sniping Whigs to hold up passage until 1840, too late for any amelioration of the "Little Magician's" promised woes. The last dissenters were safely in camp.

* * *

In the Virginia legislature, another partisan storm was brewing. On March 3, 1839, the senatorial term of William Cabell Rives, a conservative Democrat and opponent of Van Buren's financial policies, would end. Originally the seat had been John Tyler's until that gentleman's conscience had caused him to resign. Tyler stubbornly wanted his seat back, or, at a minimum, believed he was entitled to the Whig nomination. Rives also wanted the seat.

In the cause of unity, the Democrats were willing to overlook Rives' strayings if he promised to endorse the administration in the coming national election. But Rives was cold, an attitude he had first developed in 1836 when Van Buren had preferred Colonel Richard Johnson as a running-mate. Rebuffed, the party regulars put forward Judge John Y. Mason. Meanwhile, the Whigs serenaded Rives with promises; for in the delicate balance of the state's politics his small bloc might swing the 1840 election to Henry Clay.

The legislature took up the question. Regular Democrats stood solidly for Mason; the Whigs, after a complimentary gesture toward Tyler, joined the conservative Democrats behind Rives; twelve fighting "Impracticable" Whigs held out for Tyler—and stalemated the election. The angry Tyler men turned to Henry Clay for an explanation: Rives's term having expired, Virginia was without one senator in Congress, and here were the Clay men voting for a Democrat! The amiable Kentuckian hedged, then proposed one of his famous compromises, more fateful in results than he ever dreamed. Rives, the opponent of "Van

Burenism," to be senator; Tyler, the Whig, to be Clay's vice-presidential candidate.

Tyler seems to have played no part in the negotiations or to have furthered the proposal. Perhaps he recognized in its fatuous nature that Northern Whigs would never permit a Kentucky-Virginia ticket in a national election. In any case, his "Impracticables" deadlocked the legislature not only until Rives had announced Whig sympathies but until Tyler was nominated and elected, almost two years later.

*   *   *

The Whig national convention met at Harrisburg, Pennsylvania. Once again, out of respect for the sensibilities of its diverse elements, it refused to draw up a platform. Under the skillful handling of Thurlow Weed and Abbott Lawrence, the nominating committee by-passed Henry Clay's controversial brilliance for General Harrison's anonymity. Then, having enraged the party's politician par excellence, the committee moved to placate him, as well as the South, with John Tyler's nomination for second place on the ticket.[2] In no sense was the nomination a popular one. Because of his unyielding stand against Rives, the Virginia delegation refused to sponsor his candidacy. When his name was presented by Massachusetts, it silently repudiated him by casting a blank ballot.

Nevertheless, the Whigs were able to campaign with more harmony than they had in 1836; at least they had only one set of candidates. And unhampered by a need to expound principles, they concentrated on entertaining their audiences and lambasting the Democrats. An unlucky slur in the Baltimore *Republican,* which was quoting a disgusted Clay Whig, took the campaign out of the field of reasonable discussion. Reported the paper: ". . . Upon condition of his receiving a pension of two thousand dollars and a barrel of hard cider, General Harrison would no doubt consent to withdraw his pretensions, and spend his days in a log cabin on the banks of the Ohio."

Wealth and aristocracy suddenly discovered the common man. He had been insulted; the Whig Party belonged to him; the Democrats were the party of his defilers, and Martin Van Buren (in spite of his extremely humble origin) was a Bourbon. Lavish spending of the pub-

[2] Since the committee sessions were secret, the exact names of those also considered for the vice-presidency are not precisely known. It seems clear, however, that the position was first offered to Benjamin W. Leigh, head of the Virginia delegation to the convention, who disdained it. N. P. Tallmadge, a conservative Democrat from New York, J. J. Crittenden of Kentucky, John Bell of Tennessee, and J. H. Clayton of Delaware may also have been thought possible nominees.

lic funds by the administration had turned the White House into a Roman "Palace." Whiggery, preached its orators, was the quintessence of simplicity. Log cabins became the party's symbol; cider, not infrequently mixed with more stimulating liquids, its beverage. Political rallies were transformed into huge barbecues. General Harrison, supervised by his "conscience-keeping committee," set the note. He damned "executive usurpation" of congressional authority; he deplored the use of patronage for political ends. Then he regaled his listeners with anecdotes of the War of 1812. In one particularly touching speech, he expressed bucolic longing for the "peace and quiet" of the family's "log cabin at the Bend"—this cabin being a fine two-story home.

John Tyler, whose more pronounced views could only bring discomfort to the party, kept sensibly to home. He attracted little attention and returned about the same amount. Only once did he make a tour, and then he followed the non-committal party line. Pressed for answers, he referred his hecklers to his record. The answer was there if they wanted to find it; he was making no statements other than that he was a "Jeffersonian Republican." In lieu of a faith in the log cabin, he pointed with pride to the Virginia ancestry he and Harrison had in common, and how closely their fathers had been associated, not in the War of 1812, but in the Revolution, sixty-odd years ago.

In trying to conduct the debate along intelligent lines, the Democrats were helpless. Songs, slogans, jokes and the hard times turned the people against them. The electoral landslide gave "Tippecanoe and Tyler Too" 234 votes while "Van, Van, the used-up man" received a bare sixty. Yet the popular vote was close enough to cause examination before anyone spoke of a mandate. And Tyler's Virginia had preferred the Democrats.

4. TYLER'S INHERITANCE

It was dawn when the river boat brought John Tyler and Fletcher Webster back to Washington from Williamsburg. The young chief clerk had slept soundly after his two days of exertion. The older man had paced the deck through the night, thinking.

General Harrison was the first president to die in office; no precedent existed to explain what happened now. Tyler had already taken an oath as vice-president to uphold the Constitution. He considered that oath broad enough to be binding on him in the exercise of his new office. . . . He would not press the point if it was thought necessary for him to be resworn. But of one thing he was certain: he was the actual president, no mere regent or *ad interim* administrator. . . . Another matter troubled him. From the crazy-quilt that was the Whig party, Harrison had fashioned a cabinet of "constitutional advisers." They were not the men Tyler would have chosen . . . but it was better to keep them than to split the party by demanding their resignations. . . . Still another disturbing thought. The old man had renounced all claims to a second term, partly as a matter of conviction, partly in deference to Clay. But why should Tyler be bound by Harrison's words? Surely, if Tyler created a notable administration, he would deserve nomination in his own right.

*　　*　　*

Washington's Indian Queen Hotel swarmed with politicians and office-seekers. They filled its lobby and overflowed its bar. In a parlor away from the tumult, Chief Justice William Cranch of the Circuit Court of the District was swearing in the new president. Perhaps it was inappropriate to beset Tyler so soon, especially after the way the Whigs had hammered at Jackson's and Van Buren's patronage policies. But the campaign was over, and a job was a job. Something had to be done soon; a month had already gone by and too many Democratic appointees still remained in petty offices that rightfully belonged to Whigs in recompense for their contributions to the glorious victory. What had been the use of electing a Whig President? Harrison had often gone out into the damp March night rather than face the importuning horde at the White House. On one of those escapes from reality, he had contracted the pneumonia of which he died. No, Tyler would not get out of the hotel until a few men at least got his ear.

Meanwhile, the oath administered, Judge Cranch prepared a certificate at Tyler's request: "I . . . certify that the above named John Tyler personally appeared before me this day, and although he deems himself qualified to perform the duties and exercise the powers and office of President on the death of William Henry Harrison, late President of the United States, without any other oath than that which he has taken as Vice President, yet as doubts may arise, and for greater caution, took and subscribed the foregoing other [oath] before me." Tyler, the lawyer, was leaving no loopholes his enemies might use.

Yet all were not satisfied. A few days later, the chilly Representative of Massachusetts, John Quincy Adams, told his diary: "I paid a visit this morning to Mr Tyler, who styles himself President of the United States and not Vice-President, which would be correct style. It is a construction in direct violation both of the grammar and context of the Constitution which confers upon the vice-president, not the office but the 'powers and duties of said office.' " "Mr. Tyler" himself, Adams had already decided, was "a political sectarian of the slave-driving, Virginian, Jefferson school, principled against all improvement, with all the interests and passions and vices of slavery rooted in his moral and political constitution—with all talents not above mediocrity, and a spirit incapable of expansion to the dimensions of the station upon which he has been cast. . . ." Only vitriol could appease the ex-president's bitterness. His feelings boded hard exchanges of thoughts and words during the years to come between the sections each represented.

* * *

Shortly after the inauguration, Tyler met with the cabinet he had inherited. Like so many others, before and since, this one owed its constituency more to contemporary politics than to the undoubted capabilities of some of its members. Daniel Webster, the Secretary of State, was obliged to Abbott Lawrence, the financier of Harrison's debts, for his position. Though most conceded he was the finest orator of the era, time and again the more agile Henry Clay undermined his efforts at advancement; and, though his qualities as thinker and politician made him New England's first statesman, they earned him nothing but distrust in his western and southern colleagues. It was best for him to be in the cabinet. There, his magnificent presence could lead weaker presidents in ways beneficial to New England; there, he could enhance his own presidential chances.

Secretary of the Treasury would have been Nicholas Biddle if Harrison had had his way. But Biddle preferred a powerful bank over a weak governmental till, and the post went to Thomas Ewing of Ohio, a Bank man and Clay partisan to the last breath of his conservative loyalties. Another Clay man was John J. Crittenden who had resigned his place as junior senator from Kentucky to become the Attorney-General. John Bell, in the War Department, was also reputed to look Kentucky-wise for guidance, though he once possessed affinities for Jacksonism. An obscure politician, George E. Badger of North Carolina, was given the Navy portfolio after Harrison tossed the office to the southern senatorial clique for decision. Rounding out the numbers was Postmaster General Francis Granger from New York, cunningly placed where patronage could best serve Thurlow Weed and William Seward.

The meeting revealed surprises to both Tyler and his "constitutional advisers." The old General, it seemed, had permitted himself to be bound by majority decisions of the cabinet, in which he was allowed *one vote.* Would Mr. Tyler follow this policy? Eyebrows raised at the answer: " . . . I shall be pleased to avail myself of your counsel and advice, but I shall never consent to being dictated to as to what I shall or shall not do. I, as president, will be responsible for my administration. I hope to have your co-operation in carrying out its measures; so long as you see fit to do this, I shall be glad to have you with me—when you think otherwise, your resignations will be accepted."

*   *   *

Three days later, President Tyler released a statement to the nation as a sort of inaugural address. Paraphrasing Jefferson, his foreign policy was summed up as "justice on our part to all, submitting to injustice from none." Economy and a war on patronage were promised; the Independent Treasury would go. But his other financial policies were hazy; he would accept a "constitutional" act of Congress to restore a "sound circulating medium." And where a question of the meaning of "constitutional" arose, he would turn for advice to the "fathers of the great republican school."

On the whole, the Whigs were publicly happy over the message. Yet certain things were left too indefinite. Exactly where, ran the private questions, did Tyler stand on higher tariffs and a bank?

In Democratic quarters there were also doubts. The doughty Thomas Hart Benton thought the "fathers" might mean Washington and John Adams as easily as Jefferson and Madison. Others felt Tyler was simply Clay's tool. But Andrew Jackson was confident in the extreme. The succession was a happy one. "A kind and over-ruling Providence has interfered to prolong our glorious Union which Harrison and his Cabinet were preparing to destroy under the dictation of that profligate demagogue, Henry Clay." Tyler was a true states' rights man who, unless he abandoned all past principle, would save the United States from the unregenerate Whig gang. "'The Lord ruleth, let our nation rejoice!'"

That profligate demagogue was, meanwhile, frankly worried. At "Ashland," his Kentucky acreage where he played the gentleman planter, he wondered about Tyler. Harrison, an easy-going man, had bridled at dictation on the matter of a special session of Congress. In fact, though Clay had won the point and the call had gone out for May 31st, he had broken with the old man. Yet it had been necessary. To have waited for the regular session meant leaving Webster eight full months to establish a rival hegemony over the administration and the party. The 1844 nomination was at stake; Clay needed an undisputed title as chief of the Whigs. Enactment of his "American System" would end the claims of all pretenders.

Now, Harrison's death raised doubts. Tyler was a stubborn man. Those tidewater men looked differently on high tariffs and a United States Bank. Judge Tucker had sent him a plan for a bank owned by the states, without private subscribers to its stock. It was an impossible mechanism to one who had been an attorney for the old Bank and who looked to private finance for guardianship of the country's monetary and credit system. Next, there had come a letter from the President suggesting postponement of all discussion on a bank until the administration was ready with its own proposal. Else, Tyler strongly implied, any bill of Congress would have to meet the test of constitutionality or be vetoed.

To Clay, the mail demonstrated a challenge. The Virginians were asking that he set aside the victory for legislative supremacy he had won over Harrison and Webster, that he surrender the sword of leadership to a lesser politician accidentally ensconced in high power. But he would not; the Virginians had less right either to formulate policy or to hold the party reins than he. Hadn't the 1840 election result been a mandate for a Bank and the "American System," as the Whig press was editorializing during these past few months? Hadn't the "republican father" James Madison signed the 1816 bill that created the Bank? And, if these weren't sufficient arguments, hadn't Virginia negated Tyler's claim to leadership by going Democratic in the election? [3] Surely, it was Tyler's duty to follow the Clay line the voters had upheld. . . . Well, maybe this President listened to reason, or possibly, like the last one, retreated under pressure. . . . Clay prepared to leave for his command. "I repair to my post in the Senate with strong hopes—not, however, unmixed with fears."

5. HISTORY OF A DIVORCE

Beverley Tucker was unusually cheerful. As a thinker, he knew that of all man's achievements on earth, tidewater Virginia was the worthiest. As a judge and lawyer, he devised proposals to support his *desideratum*. It was his moment; Virginia's aristocracy had its man at the federal helm. No sooner was his friend and fellow-townsman in the White House than Tucker was writing him voluminous letters, urging actions, giving advice, seeking to lead by sheer weight of intellect.

[3] Whatever the dubious validity of the last two arguments, the first had none. The Whigs, be it remembered, had presented no platform to the electorate. During the campaign, Clay had been reticent about a Bank or any other part of his program. The other party orators had carefully said nothing.

The recipient of the letters was, in his turn, cordial. The law pro-
[fess]or had interesting ideas on banks, the preservation of the federal
[deb]t and the controlled disposition of the public lands. Tyler had to
have a program—had to have one, that is, unless he was prepared to
accept everything Henry Clay's Congress sent over for signature. That
he refused to do. Such subordination could give only two results, each
bad in its own way: the nationalism of the North would be fastened on
the country, damaging the plantation economy even further than it already was and ending forever the political power of the Old South;
Clay's nomination in 1844 would be a certainty, and Tyler, at fifty-four,
would be consigned to limbo. Decidedly, if his conscience and his
ambition were to be served, he had to create his own policies and he
had to build his own circle of advisers and strategists.

His cabinet did not measure to the demand. Of the six, only Webster respected him, and even the "godlike Daniel" was ultimately in the
debt of those New England capitalists who supported him financially.
Yet, Webster's small following contained a valuable man. Representative Caleb Cushing of Newburyport, who was expected to succeed Webster and Governor Edward Everett as the leader of Massachusetts
Whiggery, had the ability and intelligence Tyler wanted. A historian
and a lawyer, an authority on international law and chairman of the
House Committee on Foreign Affairs, his knowledge and station made
him eminently desirable as an inner councilman. Furthermore, his
conservatism was unimpeachable; for, while his fellow-Congressman
J. Q. Adams agitated for action on slavery, Cushing maintained that,
despite the moral evil of the institution, the North was without right
to influence its ultimate fate.

But after Cushing, Tyler all too naturally selected his lieutenants
from the South. Henry A. Wise and Thomas Gilmer, both of Virginia,
joined Cushing to operate on the House floor or more preferably in
its cloakrooms. In the Senate, William Cabell Rives, singularly free of
enmity, became the President's spokesman. It was a small group, so
small that it was soon referred to as the "corporal's guard." It lacked
the thinkers, the political analysts, the undercover men a president
needs to carry on all aspects of his work.

Once again Tyler looked south. Tucker and Dew were there, of
course, with objectives and plans. From Virginia also came the advices
of Judge Upshur and Littleton W. Tazewell, a man, as Tyler phrased
it, "thoroughly at home on all subjects." Working surreptitiously in
the Senate was the diminutive Robert J. Walker from Mississippi, not
a Whig at all but a Democrat. And, not infrequently, if a White House

visitor glanced curiously around the half-closed doors, he saw Duff Green stretched out on one of the sofas. Duff Green, a man whose name was synonymous with treachery to good Jacksonians, the editor who had deserted Old Hickory to become Calhoun's apologist and sounding-board, the publisher of Tucker's novel *The Partisan Leader*, which diatribe against Van Buren had contributed to the general assassination of the "Little Magician's" character in 1836.

In the Executive Mansion, in the law offices and studies of Virginia, Tyler now had his own Kitchen Cabinet feverishly seeking a program to counter both the "American System" and the recently defeated but still vocal Jacksonian democracy. When Congress met on May 31st, there would be at least a covert struggle for control of the Whig Party. Senator Henry Clay obviously presumed his own authority, but President John Tyler was not recognizing the claim.

* * *

As the session opened, Congress was organized according to Clay's specifications. Southard of New Jersey, president pro tem of the Senate and next in succession for the presidency under the existing law, was his man. The leader himself headed the important Finance Committee, and a trusted follower controlled the Public Lands Committee which would handle the distribution bill. At the other end of the unfinished Capitol building Clay's forces also ruled. Twenty-six-year-old John White of Kentucky was the Speaker of the House; Millard Fillmore of western New York chaired the Ways and Means Committee; stalwarts ran the Committee on Public Lands and the special one on currency. Whig majorities were substantial in both Houses. If the "corporal's guard" was kept down to just that size, Clay faced the President with an army.

Tyler's opening message to Congress was cautious; it was evident he so far had no definite program to recommend. He pointed to the deflated Treasury and suggested that provision be made to end the deficit. He warned, however, that in solving the problem the careful balance of the Compromise Tariff of 1833 must be left undisturbed. Land-sale receipts would be distributed to the states only if the duties remained at the low level set eight years before. Otherwise, they would be applied to the federal debt. As for the bankrupt western states and their plea that the central government assume their debts, the present deficit of the Treasury spoke strongest against taking on the deficits of others.

Tyler then unwittingly helped prepare the road to his future hell. Van Buren's "Subtreasury system," he announced, "is unsatisfactory and has been plainly condemned by the voice of the people. No other financial scheme has been agreed upon, and so it is incumbent upon Congress to devise a plan." A "suitable fiscal agent" to handle the government moneys and establish a "currency of uniform value" was in order—if it did not meet with constitutional objection or threaten the nation's prosperity.

Conciliatory as the message was, Clay, the Great Compromiser, was making no compromises. He arose to present a series of resolutions on what he deemed was the business of the session. "First, if not exclusively," Congress had gathered to consider "the repeal of the sub-Treasury; the incorporation of a bank adapted to the needs of the people, and of the government; the provision of adequate revenue for the Government by the imposition of duties, and including the authority to contract a temporary loan to cover the public debt created by the last Administration; the prospective distribution of the proceeds of the public lands. . . ."

Marching in tempo, Congress repealed the Subtreasury law. Until some new legislation was passed, government funds were thus returned to the hands of the sporadically regulated and completely unco-ordinated state banks.

With the need for a new agency apparent, capitalism and nineteenth-century feudalism prepared to fight through the bank issue. Tyler and Clay had met at the White House. The President had offered a middle-ground plan which satisfied government requirements but precluded the setting up of a monopoly such as the old Bank of the United States had enjoyed. Clay would have none of it. And Tyler, having gone the limit of his conscience, rose from his chair, shouting his anger with precise earnestness: "Then, sir, I wish you to understand this—that you and I were born in the same district; that we have fed upon the same food, and breathed the same natal air. Go you now, then, Mr. Clay, to your end of the avenue, where stands the Capitol, and there perform your duty to the country as you shall think proper. So help me God, I shall do mine at this end of it as I think proper."

The break was irreparable. The contest of the legislature versus the executive began. Clay cracked the whip and his followers responded. Secretary of the Treasury Ewing benignly watched the administration's proposed bank measure emasculated and then rebuilt to near-monopoly dimensions. In party correspondence, the President was maligned and ridiculed. Webster men were deliberately misled on Tyler's intentions through contrived, double-faced statements by Clay's intermediaries. Compromises which compromised nothing but personal scruples were added to the bill. Then, silence. The opposition talked itself out and the administration's amendments were defeated. Clay had the votes; and the bill passed. To the pretended surprise of the Clay faction and the genuine surprise of no one, Tyler resisted the pressures of his cabinet and sent Congress a veto, carefully worded in all respects but the most important—what kind of bank he would find acceptable.

In the Senate, two men watched and calculated. John C. Calhoun awaited the crackup of the Whig Party on the rock of presidential vetoes. When that day came, he believed, the states' rights men, including Tyler, would again become Democrats, and Calhoun would capture his party from Van Buren. Henry Clay controlled his wrath for a shorter-run development. Tyler had to be made to *appear* to have consented to the new "Fiscal Corporation" bill that was soon to be introduced. Clay's emissaries were at the White House preparing the ground.

During the interval, Tyler himself vacillated: he doubted that he would sign any bank bill; he gave advice on what kind of bill he would sign; he asked influential friends to work for postponement. Ewing and Webster prepared a supposedly acceptable bill but neglected to secure its approval by Tyler. Worse still, they somehow failed to include a proviso against his pet abomination—local discounts to private individuals. Clay's White House visitors came from their conferences with the President in possession of a piece of paper which could be alleged to have his blessing. . . . The trap was sprung. . . .

Then Clay stopped waiting. On the Senate floor, he delivered a philippic, avoiding no materials for insult in his attack. Tyler was a turncoat, a dishonest states' righter, an irreconcilable, a would-be dictator, a narrow-minded politician disregarding the mandate of 1840. If he could not administer the presidency in compliance with the popular will, he should resign as he had once resigned his senatorship. If the forthcoming bill and the other important measures were thus nullified, the Whigs would move to amend the Constitution and free the country from the obstruction inherent in the veto power.

The hot summer days of the end of August were sad ones for the bedeviled President. While the Whig press pounded at the veto of the first bill, he saw the painful fiction spread that the second had been drawn with his concurrence. He saw the cabinet restive but still obedient under the lash of party discipline. Almost stoically, he received the bill. Signature meant inglorious defeat, a veto practical excommunication. Calmly and patiently, he and Caleb Cushing wrote the veto. . . . The trap snapped shut.

This time there was no waiting. From the hinterlands came the cry so often shouted at Jackson and Van Buren—"EXECUTIVE USURPATION." Whig Representative John Minor Botts of Virginia was livid: "The President betrays, as the nation will discern, a destitution of sincerity and candor. . . . It is impossible to serve God and Mammon both, so I conceived it impossible to serve Mr. Tyler and my country at the same time. . . . They say the President has differed with us on one point only [the discounting feature], but Benedict Arnold and Commodore Hull differed on only one point—and that was whether they should fight for or against their country."

Angry Whigs built a fire under the cabinet. If it resigned as a body, John Tyler's fate was sealed. He could not operate the departments by himself, and he would be unable to find a new cabinet before Congress adjourned. He, also, would be forced to resign, and his successor would be Samuel P. Southard, the reliable Clay Whig. In the rush from Tyler's floundering ship of state, the Clay men—Ewing, Crittenden, Bell and Badger—gave up their portfolios, each with a blast at their former chief. On consultation with the New York delegation, Granger followed suit, giving Tyler's slowness in properly redistributing the patronage as his reason for leaving.

But the plot ran afoul on Webster who was admitting no master. The godlike Daniel saw "no sufficient justification for the dissolution of the late cabinet"; secondly, he was convinced vital diplomatic negotiations going on with England required his continued presence. With misgivings, even John Quincy Adams accepted the explanation.

On the night Congress adjourned, the Whig caucus met to settle accounts with John Tyler. Resolutions of condemnation had been prepared. Of the bounteous feast the party had planned for the country, it had been able to throw only a few bones. Tyler's recalcitrance had destroyed the rest. For this, the caucus, in its manifesto, apologized to the people. It hoped, however, to gain its ends in the near future by securing large Whig majorities. Failing that, it sought curtailment of the veto power "which has ever been regarded with suspicion, and often with odium." Future co-operation with the President was impossible, made so by himself. Further relations with him would not be required; "all political connection between this Party and John Tyler is at an end."

❦ III : A LEADER WITHOUT FOLLOWERS

THE bill of divorcement that separated John Tyler from Whiggery terminated what had been a marriage of convenience. So long as the marriage lasted, the convenience had been mostly on Tyler's side. With dissolution, he lost more than companionship. As a Whig, he had been pulled bodily into the stream of events. The challenges of problems provoked the party to responses, and Tyler had been carried along. But as a maverick, he was forced to depend upon his own resources and his own creed. The lore of Williamsburg and tidewater Virginia was all he had on which to draw.

Tyler's rustication by Henry Clay's Whigs did not split the party. A few men, mostly Virginians, followed him out. Their total number was so small that they cannot be said to have constituted a rump force, but merely a group of retainers who, for conviction or political expediency, found it desirable to abandon Henry Clay. Tyler's inner circle, both at Washington and in the tidewater, stayed loyal to him. But not even the South rose to his defense. His brand of southern supremacy was too specialized. Jacksonians saw nothing in the schism that attracted them to the schismatics. Calhoun, building more and more of his philosophy on the slave interest, seemed to the other Democrats a far better champion.

Outside Virginia, the planter aristocracy—perhaps more alive to contemporary currents and unimpressed by the narrowness of the Old Dominion's exclusive tradition—preferred to recognize Clay's leadership. A large measure of their Whiggery was a reaction against the common folk in the Democracy. But in the South, where Democratic state banking laws and currency rulings had created economic disaster in the late 1830's and where the party of Jackson now advocated a repudiation of state debts, conservatives—both plebs and aristocrats—gravitated toward the regular Whigs. By advancing conservative financial policies, Whigs posed as reformers, though their proposals were nothing but the old solutions dressed in new words. By flatly opposing repudiation, Whiggery posed as the party of honesty. And because conservative finance and a recognition of "honest" obligations were more the expressions of Clay's program than of Tyler's, southern conservatives looked to Kentucky for leadership rather than to Virginia.

37

Indeed, Clay's worst threat in the South came not from Tyler but from Calhoun. But, as yet, the section's conservatism was not ready to embrace the South Carolinian wholeheartedly. The plantation system was still growing. There was wide and cheerful talk of establishing a southern cotton manufacturing industry. Henry Clay's tariff could protect this dreamed-of infant from English competition. His Bank of the United States could provide the substance to bring it to a strong manhood. Tyler's rigid localism forbade these dreams. Even Calhoun's stern states-rightism took a sour view of tariffs and central finance. Only slavery might be a stumbling block to southern conservatives, for Clay was known to favor gradual emancipation and northern Whigs like William Seward and Thaddeus Stevens, as well as Millard Fillmore and Joshua Giddings, either courted or spoke the words of abolitionism.

But in the 1840's, though pro-slavery sentiments were considered a tasty and altogether appropriate dish, they were not the safe food on which southern political and social appetites subsisted. And Henry Clay, a master at the straddle, took a comfortable and seemingly impregnable position on the fence. Immediate abolition, he told the planters and dreamers, would cause a "contest between the two races, civil war, carnage, conflagration, devastation, and the ultimate extinction or expulsion of the Blacks." Southern conservatives needed to hear no more. John Calhoun might put the defense in stronger terms and might exclaim on the actual virtues of serfdom. But the implications of Calhounian states-rights on economic expansion were a twilight gray; Clay's evangelic heralding of industrialism as implemented by his "American System" had the fresh glow of a roseate morning.

1. TYLER REORGANIZES

It was a wishful belief that Tyler would be unable to find lieutenants after the mass resignation of General Harrison's ministry. If Webster's decision to act independently of his party splintered Whig hopes, the success of the Chief Executive in rounding up a group of men thirsty for high office and power atomized any possibility that he would step out and make room for a new administration. Helpless as the Virginian appeared during the first assaults of Clay's army of congressional Whigs, he skillfully marshalled sufficient men from his "corporal's guard" to replace the deserters and man the Executive bastion.

A part of Tyler's salvation lay in his having partly anticipated the exodus. Before the sudden avalanche of withdrawals hit the White House, Duff Green had been dispatched to Kentucky where a politically down and out enemy of Clay, former Governor Charles A. Wickliffe, hoped for a comeback. The terms of alliance are unknown, but Green was as facile with his tongue as with his pen, and probably promised Wickliffe the state of Kentucky in the form of offices and patronage in exchange for adherence to the administration. Wickliffe—who had little to lose, considering Clay's grip on the state—readily accepted. When opportunities opened in Washington, he received the Postmaster Generalship vacated by Francis Granger. In some of the correspondence of the period are letters of well-informed men suggesting the President wished to rid himself of the old entourage. The Virginia coterie was advising the move, and, during August, newspaper reports said that his attitude toward the Harrison holdovers was distant. Given the fact that Tyler was, over two week-end days, prepared with a new slate, it is clear that advance preparation had been made.

Nevertheless, there were difficulties in the reorganization. Associate Justice John McLean, of the Supreme Court, was approached to transfer the prestige of his name to the War Department. He refused. Henry Wise, though still loyal to his friend in the presidency, played practical politics to the limit by choosing to remain in the House after he was offered the Navy portfolio. John C. Spencer of New York had to tear up a speech in which Tyler's "treachery to the Whig party" was to have been denounced with searing fire. For Spencer received unexpected promotion. He was the Federal District Attorney for western New York; he was asked to become Secretary of War for the United States in place of McLean. Without apparent emotional or intellectual twinge, Spencer accepted. Finally, Walter Forward, a high-tariff man from Pennsylvania, took the Treasury and Judge Upshur crossed the Potomac for the Naval ministry. From Charleston, the real intellectual center of the ante-bellum South—whatever the pretensions of Williamsburg—Tyler drew his Attorney General, Hugh S. Legaré.

In this form, the new cabinet received the polite acclaim of critics who were expecting much worse. The most influential Whig organ, the *National Intelligencer,* which had had few reasons to speak kindly of the President, editorialized in happy incredulity: "They are all gentlemen of honorable repute, of intelligence, and, we believe, of business habits." Possibly, in quality, Tyler chose better men than he lost. Legaré has been pronounced by Vernon L. Parrington, the literary historian, "the most cultivated mind in the South before the Civil War." In 1841, it is doubtful if any other man in the country, including the judges on the highest bench, had thought so deeply on legal theory or knew so much

of the history of law. Forward, too, however much his protectionism
conflicted with his chief's suspicions of industry, had a sharper mind
for economics than Ewing, his predecessor.

Yet, the cabinet betrayed weakness. All its members were Whigs;
but only Webster had party status. Geographically, three were from the
North and three from the South, maintaining a desirable balance. But,
by location, they were drawn, contrary to the course of empire, from the
East. Wickliffe alone came from over the mountains, and his extremely
conservative views could not be classified as western.

Moreover, all were Harrison men who had renounced Clay's leadership and all except Webster had once been Jackson men who revolted.
By that token, they were deemed unreliable by the believers in regularity. But to Tyler, they appeared a nucleus around which he might
appropriate leadership and build a new coalition by encompassing Webster and anti-Clay Whigs and anti-Jackson and anti-Van Buren Democrats. Here was the slenderest of hopes. Aside from the Secretary of
State, none of the advisory board was a leader. And his New England
following would not ally itself to Tyler's southern standard. In the contest between the President and Clay, Webster Whigs decided on neutrality.

With the Democrats, the story was the same. Calhoun, as the general of the largest political force after those commanded by Clay and
Van Buren, determined to act independently of the new faction being
born in the Executive Mansion. Balancing numbers and power, the
apostle of particularism was sure he saw failure in Tyler's efforts to
construct a new coalition. Further, he saw no advantage in joining the
White House alliance as a junior partner. By waiting, he believed that
repeated frustrations would ultimately force Tyler over to the Calhoun
Democrats, with John C. Calhoun retaining his full seigniory—or even
increasing it—in the addition. Always a better reader of the future than
the past and present, the South Carolinian was correct in his specula-
tions.

Thus, Tyler's program for gaining adherents was bound to fail.
What even Calhoun did not perceive, however, was a deeper absence of
clarity in Tyler's political thinking. For Calhoun, in 1841, was making
the same mistake himself. Both saw themselves as occupying the middle of the road between Whiggery and Jacksonianism. In a partisan
sense, the notion had a certain validity. As Tyler hunted for states-rights
Whigs, so Calhoun searched for states-rights Democrats. These, in combination, would undeniably compose a third group. But the error arose
when both men conceived their third group to be the political center

between extremes. In actuality, it was not. The faith in states' rights was a third way, just as extreme as the nationalism and agrarian democracy against which it competed for attention. Its interpretations of the proper organization of economic and social life no more represented a compromise between Clay and Van Buren than did Aaron Burr suggest a middle position between Hamilton and Jefferson. The substance of the Tyler-Calhoun thought was an appeal to dissatisfied minorities in both parties.

* * *

To give character to his reorganization, the ostracized President polled his advisers and scanned the horizon for the makings of an independent program. Caution sided with principle in bidding him go slowly. But move, he did. Tazewell, though a Democrat, was sounded out on a new kind of bank the Chief Executive thought of creating. Webster, vacationing from the cares of state and also the attacks upon him for remaining with the administration, was felt out on a "simple" financial agency. Playing on the New Englander's vanity, Tyler delicately asked about acquiring Texas by treaty. "Could the North be reconciled to it, would anything throw so bright a lustre around us?" Slavery, continued the anxious Virginian, was not a real objection, for did it not "already exist around us?" Really, he said, if laws against the slave trade were enforced, Texas would cause "as many free states South" as the territory would add slave states. "And then the future, distant as it might be, would present wonderful results." This, of course, was included to comfort Webster's known antislavery feelings. But furthermore, it was what conscience-stricken men of the South told themselves because they could not escape the philosophic heritage of Jefferson and John Tyler's father. Rather than espouse a moderate abolitionism, they advocated "dispersion" as the process that would surely, though slowly, end the shame.

Webster had nothing encouraging to say on Texas. The central bank or Exchequer—the descriptive word given it by the President—was a project more harmonious to the business mind of a man who represented the industry, trade and commerce of New England in Washington and in the courts. The Whigs of "business habits" in the cabinet also gave their heartiest approval. With zest, the Secretary of State turned to painting it in bright colors for the benefit of the Clay Whigs who would first hear the plan in Tyler's Annual Message to the regular session of the Twenty-seventh Congress in December. Because the idea was merely recommended and died a cruel death under Millard Fillmore's executioner's axe, its details are unimportant to history. But the gusto, the language and the arguments with which it was advanced are for the capitalist rather than the planter mind. According to Abel Upshur, that part of the message was the work of Webster's hand. It reads as if it were: "It [the Exchequer bank] . . . produces no dangerous redundancy of circulation; affords no temptation to speculation; is attended by no inflation of prices; is equable in its operation. . . . If all these assurances are not sufficient, then the idea, it seems to me, of furnishing a sound paper medium of exchange may be abandoned. . . . To argue against any proposed plan and its liability to possible abuse is to reject every expedient, since everything dependent on human action is liable to abuse."

One other proposal sought to tear Whiggery from the reins of Henry Clay. It was suggested that, in view of the depressed state of the Treasury, a revision of the tariff for revenue purposes would be acceptable. Hastily, words were added to imply that protection was not to be considered. Yet it is difficult to raise tariff duties without granting advantages to some domestic producer.

So long as the "godlike Daniel" held the foreign ministry, Tyler's ambitious ideas for Texas were consigned to the file reserved for tentative plans. Urged on by his friendly minister to Mexico, however, he thought of joining the annexation of Texas, which Mexico had not reorganized as an independent republic, to the acquisition of California, which Mexico owned but was thought willing to cede in order to wipe out American claims against her government. If Webster shrunk from Texas, he was alive to the value California offered Yankee shipping and trade. One further interested party, England, was to be drawn into the bargain for a price. If it took a complacent view toward American expansion where the British also had interests, and if England's minister in Mexico pressed for acceptance of the American plan, repayment for the services rendered would be made by admitting Britain's claims to all the disputed Oregon country north of the Columbia River line.

As insurance in consummating all pieces of the arrangement, especially the Texas phase, Tyler worked to remove Webster in a gracious manner. His first thought was a special mission to London where the Secretary could negotiate on the Oregon phase. The House Committee on Foreign Affairs refused to vote the necessary funds. His second thought was to appoint Webster as the representative of the United States at the Court of St. James. Edward Everett, the current minister, was to be transferred to a post in China created to effect the shuffle, thus leaving jobs for all. But Everett found this demand too much even to accommodate a fellow statesman from Massachusetts. London, not China, was where he wanted to be, and so the President was informed. Reluctantly, Tyler again closed the file.

2. THE LONELY YEARS

A Congress that lived under the spell of Henry Clay was unreceptive to John Tyler's bid for leadership. A Whig party that idolized its "Harry of the West" had only the coldest feelings toward the man who had halted its hero's program. A Whig press, firm in its allegiance to the regular politicians that provided its inspiration and public printing contracts, tirelessly reminded the faithful that the President was "His Accidency," "The Accident of an Accident" and "a vast nightmare over the Republic." At one point, an influenza epidemic struck the country; the people called it the "Tyler Grippe."

The hostile Twenty-seventh Congress that witnessed the Chief Executive's first attempts to recover a state of grace needed no fiery oratory from Clay to keep it in line. It sneered; it called names; it ranted; and it denounced. It proved remarkably uninterested in passing legislation. Apparently bored and certainly with nothing on which to focus his attention that was not already well handled by his subordinates, Henry Clay spoke seldom. Still, embarrassing entanglements were possible while Tyler hung on and plotted at the other end of the Avenue. So, the Kentuckian introduced a few resolutions that could easily be his platform for 1844. The veto power had to be curtailed, the Treasury controlled by Congress, more economy practiced in government, distribution of the land funds continued, the tariff raised to provide revenue and "incidental protection." Then, on March 31, 1842, while an overflow audience listened and snuffled and wept unashamed tears, he announced his "retirement" from public life. With his flair for the dramatic, he quietly explained that his motives were ever honest, never dictatorial. Recalling that his statements may sometimes have been harsh, he pleaded for forgiveness. Only Clay could have saved the following, his closing words, from a ludicrous connotation:

"May the most precious blessings of heaven rest upon the whole senate and each member of it, and may the labors of everyone redound to the benefit of the nation, and the advancement of his own fame and renown. And when you shall retire to the bosom of your constituents, may you receive that most charming and gratifying of all human rewards—their cordial greeting of 'Well done, good and faithful servant.'

"And now, Mr. President and senators, I bid you all a long, a lasting, and a friendly farewell."

Only the hypnotic quality of the man's voice and personality could have made them believe him, as they sat there. It was inconceivable that Henry Clay, who had fought Andrew Jackson and Martin Van Buren, should retire before the challenge of John Tyler. It was beyond belief that Henry Clay, still of sound mind and bright eye, had surrendered his dream of the presidency. In the next weeks and months, dinners, mass meetings, state legislatures and local conventions hysterically endorsed him. Philadelphians raised a banner, "Betrayed but not dismayed." That summer, he exhorted his congressional lieutenants to stand firm to keep the tariff and distribution in a single package, whether or not the government had enough money to pay its bills. The retirement was all sham; but nearly everyone except John Tyler loved it.

By June of 1842 the Whigs thought they had found their issue. The bank issue was dead; in Philadelphia Nicholas Biddle stood in the criminal dock charged with corrupt management of his onetime monopoly. But the Compromise Tariff of 1833, which Senators Tyler and Clay had jointly sponsored, was to expire on June 30th. Under it, duties were to be reduced to a final twenty per cent figure. Another law stood on the statutes to make conditions intolerable for protectionists who were also friends of Henry Clay. One of the few bills passed by the special session of 1841 and signed by the President was a Land Law. Included among its provisions was a prohibition on distribution if tariff rates rose above the twenty per cent level. And since the Treasury panted for funds, increased duties were a necessity. In short, the Whigs faced either a lower tariff (non-protective) and distribution or a higher tariff (protective) and no distribution. In a maneuver similar to that which northern Republicans and southern Democrats tried on President Harry S. Truman one hundred and four years later, Clay men held back passage of a new law until June 27th. They were assisted by Treasury Minister Forward's unofficial opinion that unless something were done before the month closed, the starved government would be unable to collect duties.

The two sides joined in battle. Tyler would permit distribution only if duties remained low; but in the need for revenue he had asked for an increase that would at once provide increased funds and cut out distribution. Whig regulars, more alive to the demands of the bankrupt western states, wanted distribution continued together with a higher tariff.

The bill they sent the President three days before the end—the so-called "little tariff"—postponed the date of final reduction established by the 1833 law for one month and decreed that distribution could not be suspended for two months, no matter what the level of the rates applied on imports. It looked like another trap; but Tyler was armed with his consistency and a ruling. Attorney General Legaré showed himself a more acute lawyer than Secretary Forward. To Tyler, he gave his opinion that unless a new law were approved, the government could hold duties at the old rates. Revenue would come in; distribution would still be suspended. On June 29th, within two days, Congress received its bill back, under the cover of a presidential veto.

Quite reasonably, Tyler told the legislators that their measure had not only violated the letter of the Land Law of 1841 and the spirit of the compromise of 1833, but also required a federal government strapped for money to impoverish itself further by paying out funds to the states. The Whig regulars, however, were beyond reason. In early August, they presented a second bill at the White House door. It contained the same provisions as the first, with a single difference; this time the law would be permanent. But what was applicable to the short run was, in the President's mind, gospel for the long run. Again, Congress was treated to a veto.

The Whig majority, led by John Quincy Adams, could not override the veto, but it had the strength to make its feelings known in censurious terms. Tyler's "repeated and daring assumption of both legislative and judicial power presents anomalies of character and conduct rarely seen on earth. . . . The power of the present Congress to enact laws has been struck with apoplexy by the Executive hand." Now, John Tyler, who had once led the Senate in its censure of Andrew Jackson and who had resigned rather than vote to expunge that work from the record, discovered that he was himself gazing at Capitol Hill through the eyes of Old Hickory. "I have been accused," he protested to the House, "without evidence and condemned without a hearing. . . . I am denied even the boast of a good name. . . . I am charged with violating pledges I never gave. . . ." Adams, Botts and Fillmore sent him his answer. They returned to Tyler a copy of those resolutions he had once sent Jackson.

At last, on August 22nd, Congress faced facts. It passed a law generally raising tariff rates. A separate bill pronounced for distribution. Tyler approved the first; no one was surprised when he pocket-vetoed the second. The disgruntled Whigs had already adjourned the session.

Nevertheless, if Tyler had again defeated the Clay program, he lost rather than gained in his personal victory over Prince Hal. The tariff law had won by a single vote in each house. Southerners—Whigs and Democrats alike—and western Democrats had opposed it; northeastern Whigs and Democrats and western Whigs forced it through. Southern and western Whigs, representing states unconcerned at the central government's financial difficulties when they had so many of their own, bridled at the vetoing of the distribution bill. In John Tyler, the man hunting materials for a third party, they saw little in which to place their confidence.[1]

*　　*　　*

For the next session of Congress, the still isolated Chief Executive returned to his Exchequer plan. Once more, the corporals in command of Tyler's palace guard—Caleb Cushing and Henry Wise—tried to get a hearing. Once more, the Whig majority was deaf. It thought of the scheme as a "government bank"—a type of institution that had twice been refused Jackson in the 1830's.

But the bitterest in the President's not too loyal opposition were not satisfied by merely holding from him his pie as he held theirs from them. At the time of the second tariff veto, Adams spoke longingly for impeachment. Because, "resort to that expedient might—in the present state of affairs—prove abortive," however, he declined to make specific accusations. Four months later, John Minor Botts had had enough. The day before Fillmore's Ways and Means Committee had reported the Exchequer plan unsound. Botts exceeded all previous diatribes when he proposed his "charges of corruption, high crimes and misdemeanors committed by the *acting* President of the United States." In all, there were nine counts. Their verbiage would easily have come from the most vitriolic columns of the Whig press. "Wicked and corrupt abuse of the power of appointment . . . ," "exciting a disorganizing and revolutionary spirit . . . ," "arbitrary, despotic and corrupt use of the veto power . . . ," "gross official misconduct and shameless duplicity, equivocation and falsehood . . . ," "illegal and unconstitutional exercise of power . . . ," "withholding from the representatives of the people information called for . . ."—nothing was too strong for the speaker.

[1] South Carolina hotheads provided the partial reply of states-rights Democrats. Intoxicated by the feverish urging of Robert Barnwell Rhett, they inaugurated another movement to nullify the tariff. By 1844, they had affianced nullification to the extension of slavery into Texas. John Calhoun and Langdon Cheves, however, their nullification thoughts diluted by political considerations, counselled moderation. There was victory in the air for the Democratic party.

There was no discussion. On the immediate vote, 83 Congressmen sustained the Virginia Representative; 127 Democrats, Tyler Whigs, scattered abolitionists and neutrals upheld the Virginia President.

In March, the Clay Whigs took their revenge. Forward had resigned the Treasury and Tyler had named Caleb Cushing for a long deserved reward. Again, discussion was kept at a minimum. The Whigs knew their duty, and they performed it. Cushing was rejected, 27 to 19. Dissatisfied at the close vote and stubborn as always, the Chief Executive sent back the same nomination. The Whigs delivered their second response; Cushing went down 27 to 10. Now the finance ministry became a ball tossed back and forth down Pennsylvania Avenue. A third time, Tyler proposed the Representative from Newburyport. A third time, the Senate voted him down. With only two senators supporting him on the last trial against the steadfast twenty-seven, the President quit the game. Drawing on his meager resources, he moved John Spencer over from the War Department, and filled that vacancy with James Porter, a Democrat from Pennsylvania.

* * *

If the atmosphere around the Executive Mansion was gloomy in most respects, Daniel Webster's diplomacy afforded the administration a few bright shafts of sunlight. A number of minor altercations with England were settled. An agreement between the Secretary and Lord Ashburton, the British minister in Washington, bound the two countries to station naval squadrons off the African coast as a means of preventing the illicit slave trade. This appeased New England, both for the blow at slavery and because American ships would now search private vessels instead of leaving that ticklish procedure to the discretion of Albion's sea captains. The South received satisfaction when Ashburton apologized for his country's "necessity to act" in freeing a load of slaves, who had successfully mutinied on shipboard and brought their craft to the Bahamas. Webster's largest service was the conclusion of a treaty with London's representative after a year and a half of conversations. The work ended the long-standing dispute over the Maine-Canada boundary on approximately even terms.

The treaty was signed on August 9, 1842, and ratified by the Senate eleven days later. With that, Webster's usefulness to Tyler ceased. The last excuse for giving his name to the pro-southern policies of the administration was gone. His sometime Federalist and latter-day Whig adherents first grew restless and then sharply critical. A Boston editor put it decorously, but the disapproval was there: "We say then, most

unreservedly, that we are not satisfied with Mr. Webster's position."
Yet Mr. Webster hung on, even after Congress knocked out his special
mission and his friend Everett declined to make room for him in London. Probably, he remained because he needed the job. A Massachusetts senatorial seat would not be open until 1845, and his law practice
was practically gone. Although he was heavily in debt and living beyond his income as Secretary, the State Department nonetheless provided some salary where he had no immediate prospects of being able to
secure any other. Furthermore, a new foreign minister would certainly
select his own chief clerk, and Webster would have to worry about his
son Fletcher, also made jobless by the change.

At one point, the Secretary defended himself before Boston Whiggery by proclaiming, "I am a Whig, I have always been a Whig, and I
shall always be one. . . . I am a Massachusetts Whig, a Faneuil Hall
Whig. . . ." But the longer he stayed, the harder matters got for Tyler,
who was champing for Texas. Finally, in an exchange of complimentary letters, he parted with the office and the President on May 8, 1843.
From then on, Webster gradually pushed himself back into Whig affections by endorsing and working for Henry Clay.

Webster's resignation gave Tyler the chance to alter political direction and display his ingenuity in shuffling men. Legaré moved briefly
into the State Department, to be followed on his death by Judge Upshur. These events provided two cabinet openings, and the Chief Executive selected David Henshaw of Massachusetts for the Navy post
and John Nelson of Maryland as the administration's law officer. Both
were Democrats, but apostates to the Van Buren cause. When the Senate refused to confirm Henshaw, the President scoured the Virginia
landscape, and brought back another old friend, Thomas W. Gilmer.
The significance in all this was inescapable. Tyler was not only running
out of loyal Whigs; he was starting to direct his ambition toward the
Democratic party. For one so proud of his consistent stand on principle, he was demonstrating, by his appointments, a remarkable agility
in jumping from creed to creed.

Nor was this all. Around the turn of the year, Tyler showed himself
willing to do business with everyone—except perhaps, Henry Clay—by
asking Van Buren and, when he declined, Silas Wright—another New
York Jacksonian—to fill a vacancy on the Supreme Court. Shortly afterward he invited Jackson's heir in Tennessee, James K. Polk, into the
cabinet. That implacable westerner, Thomas Hart Benton, was courted
by placing his son-in-law, John C. Fremont, in command of an expedition to explore the Oregon country. Each was a frank bid to buy off

the opposition. All but the last gesture were disdained, and that one was ineffective.

One further disaster struck the administration. On February 22, 1844, a presidential party of holiday celebrants boarded the new warship *Princeton* for an inspection and cruise down the Potomac to Mount Vernon. The ship, designed by John Ericsson, was, with its speed and firepower, supposed to be the most modern and efficient naval vessel afloat. For reason and for no reason, her guns saluted the passengers and the shoreline, as the day passed. On the return voyage, just as the final toasts were being said over dinner below decks, Navy Secretary Gilmer asked that the ship's biggest gun, the "Peacemaker," be discharged one last time. A number of spectators came on deck for the firing. The gun exploded. Among the dead were Gilmer and Abel P. Upshur.

3. TEXAS

Judge Upshur's death awoke ideas in the mind of a man who heretofore had been a trusted aide to the President. But Henry Wise, seeing the dead-end of his Virginia friend's course, had been veering toward Calhounian democracy. Now that the State Department was free, the Representative believed the South's best interests demanded the presence there of John C. Calhoun. Thus far, Tyler's efforts to make Texas a part of the United States had been principally words. And though Upshur's expansionism in ways beneficial to the South was above reproach, his deeds had been unsuccessful.

Ever since Texas had won its unrecognized independence from Mexico in 1836, there had been some American sentiment for annexation. It was a Texan expectation that, one day, the United States would willingly take its former citizens and their new territories back into the Union. Meanwhile, they did their best to go it alone, though threatened by Mexican hostility and encumbered by an enormous public debt. But Jackson had decided to delay; and Van Buren, fearing alike a war with Mexico and the brickbats of the abolitionists, stifled congressional talk of adding the young republic.

But in the forties, sentiments intensified. The North and Northwest sped ahead in the population race. The reapportionment of Congress in 1841, in accordance with the census reports of 1840, cost the South seats. Her political strength slipping, she seemed to think that in Texas lay her future safety. Out of its territory could be carved five states, each sending two senators and a minimum of one representative. Furthermore, in the early years of the decade, Texas appeared the ground on which slavery would live or die. In the cold draft that blew down from the north so long as Van Buren and Webster expressed antislavery thoughts, the new republic commenced flirting with England and France. Sam Houston, her president, was not a last ditch defender of serfdom. He was known to be willing to ally his country with European powers on mutually advantageous terms. If they aided him in cleaning up his financial messes and guaranteed protection against Mexico and the United States, he was ready to abolish slavery and provide a market for European manufactures.

How this intelligence was met in the American slave states can be imagined. A free and independent Texas could become a haven for fugitive slaves; a strong Texas could expand to the Pacific across lands that farsighted slaveholders had already earmarked for the extension of the plantation system. To counter the prospect, Virginia and South Carolina expansionists organized an informal axis. The reluctant and antipathetic North, and particularly the wavering Northwest, were bombarded by propaganda. Oregon was held out to expansionists who dreamed of Manifest Destiny on a free soil basis. Bondholders of the Texas debt were promised that the federal Treasury would assume the defaulted obligations. Some headway was gained in the South. But the North was the scene of a rapidly growing antislavery movement. For every convert to annexation, there was a convert to abolitionism.

Fears compounded. In 1843, England secured a truce betwen Mexico and Texas. According to diplomatic reports, the King's minister was attempting to secure Mexican recognition of Texan sovereignty if slavery were ended. From London, Duff Green wrote confidentially that Lord Aberdeen's government was prepared to guarantee the Texan debt in exchange for abolition. In his Annual Message of December, Tyler denounced the Latin American republic for its belligerent attitude toward Texas, for its threats of war if annexation came about, and for its responsibility in bringing European intervention to the western hemisphere. Upshur divided his time by bargaining with Houston's ministers and lobbying among senators. The first were causing him trouble by demanding an American guarantee of protection if Mexico attacked before annexation was completed. Of course, this could not be given where the Constitution permitted only Congress to declare war. But Upshur kept trying. Ratification of the expected treaty was urged on the senators for a plethora of reasons—for the glory of national expansion, to free the border of foreign influences, to increase the commerce of the Mississippi Valley, to give the United States a monopoly over cotton production and export. Everything was stressed, in fact, except the pro-slavery argument. And, by this technique, the Judge believed he had his needed two-thirds majority.

Henry Wise was familiar with—indeed, had been a maker of—this history when he hastily offered the State Department to Calhoun. But he neglected one aspect of the appointive process; he did not consult Tyler. And Tyler, aware of Calhoun's inability to subordinate himself, had no wish to include the South Carolinian in his ministry. Yet Wise, by his meddling, had forced the President's hand. Calhoun had accepted the indirect invitation. To rebuff him would, after Tyler's failures to align the states' rights Whigs and the Van Buren Democrats, be to drive the last sizable faction into overt opposition. Tyler's isolation would then be splendid and perfect, but it would be impractical.

Thus John Calhoun entered the administration. Moreover, he entered it without commitment on his part. Unhesitantly, he picked up the Texas negotiations. Tyler still balked at an absolute guarantee of protection. In Texas the republic's Secretary of State spoke to the American chargé about British and French designs, and the terrified chargé repeated the words to his superiors in Washington. An alarmed President agreed to the pledge. Calhoun signed a treaty of annexation on April 12th. Ships sailed into the Gulf of Mexico and troops marched to the Texas border.

Calhoun, however, following diplomatic success, chose the most questionable of political tactics. Throwing away the arguments Upshur had so carefully fashioned, he declared flatly that the treaty was necessary to the security of the South and the extension of slavery. Whether this was for the record or a device to separate southern ducks from southern drakes, it was a singularly inept move. Tyler disapproved his minister's method of salesmanship, but had to permit him his way. Calhoun was, after all, the greater leader. But the high priest of slavery had not considered Henry Clay. That master of Whiggery opposed immediate annexation. As a result, the treaty was overwhelmingly defeated in the Senate. Twenty-eight Clay Whigs and seven Democrats voted against it; one brave Whig and fifteen Democrats upheld the Secretary of State. Pessimistically, Calhoun suggested that the President abandon Texas. But Tyler, often beaten yet never discouraged, planned another attack.

* * *

Meanwhile, the Texas issue had transcended the internal questions on which Henry Clay, as far back as 1841, had hoped to conduct his 1844 presidential campaign. In 1842, shortly after his "retirement," he had received Martin Van Buren, his supposed rival in the next assizes, at Ashland. Together, they had agreed to keep annexation out of the canvass. On that basis, the Kentuckian had persistently shied from expansionists and antislaveryites in building his nomination. On April 27, 1844, the *National Intelligencer* carried a letter from him, and the *Globe* a letter from Van Buren. Both opposed annexation "at this time."

Yet Clay had built a house of cards. He won his party's nomination easily, and pulled southern Whiggery along on Texas. But the Democrats selected James Polk instead of Van Buren. Because Jackson was plumping for annexation, and because Polk was his man, the Texas issue reappeared in a dangerous light. Polk made it the center of his campaign, promising the North compensation in the "re-occupation of Oregon."

A third convention, manned mostly by government officeholders, met while the Democrats were debating the comparative virtues of Van Buren, Lewis Cass and Polk. Its purpose was twofold: to nominate John Tyler as the defender of the Constitution and "savior of the Democratic Party," and to embarrass Van Buren's supporters. Naturally, it acclaimed the President's policy on Texas. It is possible that the Virginian tolerated its efforts because he hoped, first, to prevent the Little Magician's nomination, and second, to insure Clay's defeat. Perhaps optimistically, he estimated that he could attract 150,000 votes over the country. He accepted the tribute and settled back comfortably. In due course, Robert J. Walker, representing the nervous annexation forces of Polk, called at the White House. He pointed out what Tyler knew, that two Texas candidacies would neutralize each other to Henry Clay's advantage. After the interview, arrangements went forward to welcome Tyler Whigs into the party of Manifest Destiny. On August 20th, the Chief Executive announced his withdrawal from the race.

The campaign was 1840 in reverse. Clay's sins of forty years in public life were exhumed by the Democrats and given renewed currency. His straddle on Texas caused him trouble everywhere. In the South, he was painted as abolition's champion; his "American System" helped label him the protector of northern industrialism. In the North, his mild emancipation beliefs were turned into accusations of pro-slavery sympathies; his refusal to announce a clear negative on expansion was imputed to mean tolerance of the "conspiracy of the slavocracy." His running mate, a nativist, lost the Catholic and foreign-born vote in the cities. As Martin Van Buren had been unable to answer the Whig slogans of 1840, Clay now found no words to reply when Democrats yelled, "Fifty-four Forty or Fight." His opponent was not quite the obscure man the Whigs sought to imply when they asked, "Who is James K. Polk?" But Polk, a methodical toiler in the vineyards of political regularity, did not have to contend with Henry Clay's record.

Texas won for Polk in the South; antislavery defeated Clay in the North. In New York, the independent Liberty party, a forerunner of Republican abolitionism, lured enough Whig votes to force the state into the Democratic column. Its thirty-six electoral votes spelled out the country's final repudiation of the glamorous Old Prince. The count stood Polk 170, Clay 105. Of 2,600,000 popular votes, Clay was behind by fewer than forty thousand. The contest was close; but the victory was for expansionism.

* * *

With deep satisfaction, John Tyler recommended that the "lame-duck" Congress accept Texas by joint resolution. "A controlling majority of the people and a large majority of the States," he argued, "have declared in favor of immediate annexation." [2] In other respects, Tyler intimated that his unpopular administration had performed great works for the country. He reported that government credit was restored, the Treasury healthy, the currency stable, "commerce and manufactures . . . revived, and the whole country exhibits an aspect of prosperity and happiness." "[The] rapid growth of our cities in every direction bespeaks most strongly the favorable circumstances by which we are surrounded."

The legislature listened wearily to the self-praise and unwound for action. Tyler did not think Mexico would fight, although her government had given abundant indications that it would. Congressmen accepted the rationalization. On January 25th, the House passed its resolution favoring the annexing of Texas as a state. The Senate, however, was impressed by Thomas Hart Benton, a lukewarm friend of the proposal who wanted credit for the deed—if ever accomplished—to fall upon a Democratic president. He asked, therefore, that a new treaty be negotiated, assuming that Polk would be in office before details were set down in finality. Robert Walker advanced a compromise, a resolu-

[2] The Presidential arithmetic was here awry. Adding the Liberty party's 62,300 to Clay's 1,300,000, the anti-expansionists emerge about 25,000 ahead of Polk's total vote. Similar juggling of the New York electoral figure puts anti-expansionism ahead in that category. Actually, Polk was a minority president.

tion embodying both the House plan and Benton's scheme that authorized the president, whoever he would be, to choose between the alternatives. By a narrow margin, the Senate sided with Walker; by a wide margin, the House concurred.

On March 1, 1845, Tyler received the resolution. Knowing that a treaty would never meet the approbation of two-thirds of any group of senators, the Virginian decided on the House alternative. Working against time, he sent Calhoun to discover Polk's views and intentions. The President-elect declined to commit himself. Tyler saw more delay, and possible loss, if the delay moved Texans to permanent independence and closer alliance with France and Britain. At the moment, Mexico was in the process of ratifying a treaty recognizing the Texas Republic on the condition that it would never become part of the United States. Inactivity would have been fatal to the South's interest. On the last day of his term John Tyler finally scented triumph. He dispatched instructions to the American chargé in Austin to offer Sam Houston annexation and statehood.

* * *

After Polk's inauguration, Tyler returned to Virginia, but not to Williamsburg. His circle there was gone. Upshur and Dew were dead; Tucker, bitter that his townsman had not utilized all that was in those first letters of advice, no longer spoke to him. During his years in Washington, Tyler had purchased a plantation in Charles City County. There he retired, farming in the tradition of a Virginian aristocrat and searching for signs of a revival in his empty political future. In 1856, there was some excited talk that the Democrats might take him as a compromise candidate; and four years later, hopes were higher. But these were, in part, fragments of the unreality that had surrounded him all of his life.

In 1862, the careers of the two men, who had stood that April 5th of 1841 in the chilly morning air of Williamsburg while the younger delivered his message, came to an end. Fletcher Webster fell, a colonel in the Union Army, at the Second Battle of Bull Run or, as southerners called it, Manassas Creek. John Tyler died, a member of the House of Representatives of the Confederate States of America.

JOHN TYLER'S annexation of Texas opened the way to conflict with Mexico and it merely remained for James Polk to remove the collars from the dogs of war. But once the struggle commenced, Polk bitterly discovered that neither politics nor sectional interest receded to give place to the task of winning a victory. Prophets of America's manifest destiny agreed neither on how much territory should be acquired at this one sweep nor to what use the conquered area should be put. Some, particularly southerners, saw the feeble opposition of the Mexican army, and envisioned an incorporation of all the enemy country under the Stars and Stripes. More restrained advocates thought ambitions and needs would be sated with New Mexico, California and the ⬛⬛⬛⬛ims. On the other extreme, northern abolitionists condemned the entire adventure as a "conspiracy of the slavocracy."

Part of Polk's trouble derived from his announced intention of serving only one term. Because of that statement he never got full control over his own party, nor did he tie its politicians to the policies of his administration. In consequence, diverse programs blossomed to divide the Democrats, as they could not divide the Whigs. Thus, the resolution of David Wilmot, a Pennsylvania Democrat, that none of the new territory be open to slavery, affronted all southerners and split the party. But while plenty of northern Whigs agreed with Wilmot, the Whig party had a primary interest which preserved unity in the face of this explosive doctrine—it was out of office and it wanted to get in. To its politicians, therefore, the wish to possess the governmental machinery was superior to any discussion of the principles under which the machinery was to be operated.

Democracy, however, being in the last throes of Jacksonism, still felt the need to argue out its partisan credo in fairly explicit terms. But the Jacksonian philosophy, in its brightest years, had not come to grips with the slavery problem. In the declining years, Wilmot's shaft transfixed both the philosophy and the party. Until Jacksonian democracy could answer the question—should or should not slavery be permitted to grow—its future was arid, its promises were unattainable. On the other hand, the Whigs, having for all practical purposes never held national power, were untroubled by fundamentals. Internally, the Wilmot

Proviso might provoke them into debates over its rightness or wrongness; but officially and publicly it belonged to the Democrats, and with that party it was studiously left. Rather, accepting the tenet that the task of the opposition is to criticize, the Whigs maintained solidarity by snipping at every possible thread in the fabric of "Mr. Polk's war." Praise, if any, went to the glorious passages at arms by the Whig generals, Scott and Taylor.

In 1848, when Whig unity met Democratic dissension at the polls, the obvious happened and unity won. But faced with responsibility for policy and government, Whiggery likewise proved unable to escape fundamentals. The slavery issue forced itself upon the country, superseding party preferences. And Whig elders and Whig junior statesmen wrestled with what they would rather have ignored.

1. A RELUCTANT OFFICEHOLDER

The Thirty-first Congress of the United States was as illustrious a body of statesmen and politicians as had ever sat in the legislative halls of the Capitol. Day on day speakers debated, forging and endless chains of argument. Sometimes the orators talked calmly, passionately; sometimes they breathed fire and the air crackled ominously; but almost always they spoke with deep conviction. Taken in comparison with the remarks made for the record during other sessions, the quality of those uttered on the floors of either house in 1849 and 1850 is among the highest. And evidently the men and women in Washington during that time realized it. They filled the galleries constantly. On days when particularly noteworthy addresses were anticipated, men balanced themselves on tiptoe behind the seats filled with ladies, cupping hand to ear to gather in the rich flow of words, straining to catch a glimpse of the speaker below, or the flash of expressions on the faces of one or another legislator as a cogent phrase rang out. Often, to accommodate dignitaries, friends and wives against the overflow crowds, the rules against visitors on the floor were relaxed and closely packed audiences listened rapt while Representatives or Senators spoke on for hours, and even days.

For the issue under consideration was, of course, the fate of the new western territories detached from Mexico and, with them, the fate of slavery. And bound to the decision of Congress, so the listeners felt, was the destiny of the Union.

There were wholesale anomalies in the situation. By the end of January, 1850, two Whig plans had been advanced for discussion—one by President Zachary Taylor, another by the party's Old Prince, Senator

Henry Clay of Kentucky. The plans were inharmonious, and their inventors were beginning to hold intemperate opinions of each other. The incipient fissure in the party ranks presaged an open rupture as the debate toiled onward.

Added complications presented themselves. Though a Whig Chief Executive headed the administration in power, the Congress elected at the same time as the President belonged to no party. Unsteadily, 105 Whigs faced 112 Democrats in the House, but holding the balance was a minority of thirteen northerners of the newly formed Free Soil Party. Their position they summed up in their campaign slogan: "Free Soil, Free Speech, Free Labor, and Free Men." Although not all of them were obdurate abolitionists, they were in favor of the Wilmot Proviso to a man; on each roll call, their votes would be cast against slavery. Because they abjured common cause with their southern Whig or southern Democrat, because they united readily only with northern antislavery men, sixty-three ballots had been necessary before Howell Cobb, a Georgia Democrat, was elected to the Speakership. Even then Cobb was a slavery expansionist who could count on his unpopularity with the majority of Representatives from the North, whose numbers outweighed the total from the slave states by some forty members.

The Senate was similarly outside Whig control; thirty-four Democrats held seats against twenty-four Whigs and two Free Soilers. Nevertheless, on a question like slavery, section bulked larger than party in determining the vote of an individual solon; on any test of that issue, there were senators from fifteen free states and fifteen slave states—thirty potential votes on either side. Still, this analysis is a rude oversimplification. None knew how old Thomas Hart Benton of Missouri stood. His state was southern, but he was a fighter for free homesteads in the West and an opponent of serfdom. Nor could predictions be made in the courses of Stephen Douglas of Illinois or Lewis Cass of Michigan, each grinding his axe of presidential aspiration, each known to possess a certain friendliness toward the South. These men were Democrats. So too could one speculate on elasticities in the Whig consciences of John Bell of Tennessee and Daniel Webster of Massachusetts and the New Englanders he influenced. In short, the Senate was a body indefinable on the great issue before the country. A political mathematician, searching for a pre-tested answer, would find his task impossible; there were too many unknowable quantities in his equation.

Not the least of these was the presiding officer, Vice-President Millard Fillmore of New York. Sitting on the dais as he swung his gavel and handed down his parliamentary rulings, he looked and acted his office to near perfection. His six-foot frame was approaching the stout-ness of middle age without taking on flabbiness. A round face, un-adorned by the side whiskers or chin beards some of the senators were starting to affect, blandly and attentively surveyed the proceedings for bad tempers and insults. Then a peaceable voice suavely quieted the uproar, and returned the discussion to its proper ways of dignity. As chairman, the Senate had a man who respected its members and its tra-ditions, and who treated both with a fairness that did much toward ele-vating its deliberations above the level of petty bickering over party and personality.

But Millard Fillmore, presiding, was also Millard Fillmore, politi-cian and man. According to the rules, he was forbidden to speak offi-cially on the public matters the Senate took up. Yet there were strong likelihoods that the slavery and territorial issues would produce tie bal-lots, and it was in the power of the presiding officer to determine leg-islation by his casting-vote. Where did he stand?

On the one hand, by virtue of his election as the tail on the ticket of which Zachary Taylor was the head, Fillmore was more or less bound to the administration. On the other hand, he was also known to have been a Clay Whig, and one who rather admired the old man after his power began to fade. He had, at one time, been listed in abolition's ranks for having supported John Quincy Adams and Joshua Giddings when they introduced petitions into the House demanding the end of slavery in the District of Columbia. Yet in the 1848 campaign, the vice-presidential candidate had apparently satisfied the southern Whigs who voted for him by explaining that he upheld the right of petition, not what the petitions said. And how would he cast his tie-breaking vote? Only Millard Fillmore knew. He was keeping that vital information to himself.

*   *   *

Consider this close-mouthed politician. Fifty years before he had been born in the western forest of New York State of a father from Bennington, Vermont, and a mother from Pittsfield, Massachusetts—rural Yankee stock. In boyhood, he worked with his father on the farms the family chopped out of the wilderness. But despite good soil the Fillmores remained poor. They fought the elements, tax-gatherers and uncertain economics; and by the time young Fillmore was fifteen, his father had decided that agriculture was an unfortunate calling for his sons. So, to free Millard from the land, his father apprenticed him to a clothmaker in the hope that here was a trade unsubjected to the vagaries of weather and overproduction, where a man was paid in gold and unencumbered by debt.

The experiment lasted three months during which the bound boy was given the exclusive duty of chopping wood—something he had learned well at home—and taught nothing of the clothier's art. Being endowed with a Yankee respect for contracts, he protested the one-sidedness of the curriculum. But his employer was evidently too impressed with the quantities of wood the apprentice cut. Finally, in fury, Fillmore threatened to use his axe on employer instead of wood, and the contract was abruptly terminated.[1] Another apprenticeship was soon entered upon, but it was also unsatisfactory. At eighteen, he spent a short time teaching. That he could have done so is a commentary on both Fillmore and the educational system. For he had little formal schooling. He had painstakingly read and nearly memorized what few books were available in his frontier community; but he was, by his own admission, appallingly deficient in many subjects. It is not unlikely that, in a few months of instructing, he spent more time inside a school-house as a teacher than he had as a scholar.

In 1819, the family moved again, and Fillmore severed his relation-ship with clothmaking to read law with a local judge. Four years later, he moved to Erie County and opened his own office in East Aurora—which, unaccountably, is west of Aurora—a village near the frontier town of Buffalo. Once established there Millard Fillmore felt something of the promise of American life. He learned more law, developed more confidence in himself, orated locally and scraped along. In 1830, he moved to Buffalo—now growing into a booming lake port from the commerce between the Ohio country and the East—where he formed a partnership with one Nathan K. Hall, to begin his rise as a metropoli-tan attorney.

Meanwhile, the year previous, Erie County had sent him out, an as-semblyman to the state legislature. It did twice again in the next two years. The experience was productive of good works, for Fillmore la-bored successfully to abolish several relics of a less enlightened age—imprisonment for debt, and the requirement of religious tests (i.e., Christianity) for legal witnesses. More productive still were the ac-quaintances.

For in Albany he met two men, one a gentleman, the other not. The

---

[1] Writing an autobiographical fragment in later life, Fillmore said of the incident: "It made me feel for the weak and unprotected, and hate the insolent tyrant in every station of life." In directing this hatred, two of the men he found tyrannous were Jackson and Lincoln.

gentleman was William H. Seward, a lawyer from Auburn; the common clay was Thurlow Weed, editor of one of the state capital's newspapers. The two were working in anti-Masonic circles, which meant, in national politics, alignment with John Quincy Adams against Andrew Jackson, and, in state politics, opposition to Martin Van Buren's and William Marcy's "Regency" domination of New York. Fillmore's New England background and predispositions were comfortably attuned to the Seward-Weed brand of partisanship, and he became the faction's leader in his section of the state. When Antimasonry lost its individuality in Henry Clay's coalition Fillmore continued a Seward-Weed outpost in western New York. Thus in 1832 while Clay lost, Fillmore was elected to Congress. Again, after skipping a two-year period, he returned in 1836, while General Harrison was bowing to Van Buren.

During those congressional years, the Buffalo attorney sedulously pursued his golden fleece. In the existing mythology of that day (and not entirely dead in this) that the office should seek the man rather than the man the office, Fillmore faithfully issued disclaimers of ambition to his constituency, but was happily incapable of staying their votes. In 1834, he actually convinced himself that he preferred the law and refused to run; but two years later he was back. After that he was a regular candidate, writing his reluctancies but thirsty at the public trough. From Washington, he dutifully wrote Weed private missives, reporting trends, offering suggestions, requesting advice. He had not grasped the fact that his addressee and William Seward were two humans with but a single self and a unified purpose—Seward for office, prestige, and reputation; Weed for backstage power, wealth, and the pleasure of maneuvering destiny. Thus, in 1838, Fillmore thought he deserved New York's governorship, but Weed arranged the nomination and election for Seward, and the Buffalo lieutenant had to be content in Congress. This was the beginning of a rift between Seward and Weed, on the one side, and Fillmore, on the other. Though its origin lay in conflicting political ambitions, it would grow to include antithetical ideologies, disparate interpretations of the correct application of statesmanship, and finally war for the control of the Whig party.

At first, estrangement developed gradually. The Representative took issue with the state boss over selections of nominees for several posts and chaffed while less deserving Whigs received Weed's benedictions. More serious to the growing division were Governor Seward's attempts to steal the urban Catholic vote from the Democrats. This, a quite usual political move, was to be done by apportioning part of the state's education funds to parochial schools, or, as eventually happened, to improving the common-school system in the heavily populated immigrant sections of New York City where most Catholics lived and where educational facilities were inadequate. To Millard Fillmore from western New York State, the plan bordered upon heresy, political and religious. Recent settlements in the backwoods and the towns by German farmers and tradesmen coincided with a wave of Protestant revivalism and a surging nativist movement. Fillmore sympathized with the feelings of the "American" elements of his constituency, and, therefore, registered horror at Seward's activities in behalf of the "foreigners."

Meanwhile, in the House, Fillmore loyally championed Clay's "American System." His regularity and his tenure earned him the chairmanship of the Ways and Means Committee under the Kentuckian's dictatorial organization of Congress after the rousing victory of 1840. Tyler's discouraging course oppressed Fillmore fully as far as it oppressed the Whig general staff. He joined willingly in the efforts to "head Captain Tyler" and stood somewhat in the background while the denunciations went on only because he lacked ability as a firebrand orator. Skillfully, he rolled logs to secure internal improvements for Erie County at federal expense. Diligently, he constructed the increased tariff schedules of 1842—both those vetoed and those accepted by the intransigent President. Then he announced his retirement from Congress, again ostensibly to devote full energy to his comfortable law practice.

Behind his expressed desires were the political exigencies of the next presidential election. Clay appeared a certain candidate and strong sentiment existed to name Fillmore his running mate. Clay, it will be remembered, had withdrawn from the Senate earlier in the year, the better to promote his White House ambitions. That Millard Fillmore adopted the same technique of "resignation" to himself may be assumed from his parting blast at Tyler. His explanations to Buffalo's citizenry on his decision to quit the House bore close relationship to Clay's valedictory at leaving the Senate. "We have struggled hard under every discouragement to carry out the true Whig principles of 1840, and give relief to the country. Our progress has been opposed and our efforts thwarted at every step by the peculiar friends of the Executive on the floor of Congress. . . . I . . . cannot but regard it as an awful warning to select no man, even for a contingent station of such vast power and responsibility, whose talents and integrity are not equal to it." What lay unsaid was that Fillmore, like Clay, was stepping out of public office to avoid being trapped by any of Tyler's controversial measures. Theirs was the time-honored device of allowing themselves freedom to criticize while forswearing responsibility.

But, though the Whig convention nominated Clay, to run with him it chose not Fillmore but someone else. Chagrined but undaunted, the Buffalo politician listened to the siren voices of his partisans singing of his availability for the governor's chair. To Weed, he wrote—for publication—of his indifference to office. It was the kind of reluctance that shivers for fear it will be taken seriously. The wily editor-boss so recognized it, and out of an array of unsatisfactory aspirants, he phlegmatically endorsed the writer. He had little confidence that the candidate would win; he had few hopes for his party's chances. He was correct; Clay's mistakes in the campaign lost New York and the election. Fillmore's weakness at the polls was demonstrated when he ran behind the national ticket.[2]

In despair, he wove his own excuses for the defeat. "The Abolitionists and foreign Catholics," he told Clay, "have defeated us in this State. . . . A cloud of gloom hangs over the future. May God save the country; for it is evident the people will not."

* * *

Four years later, when the party gathered for its convention, the breach between Weed and Fillmore had widened appreciably. While their letters to each other still continued friendly, Fillmore's men indignantly accused the Albany "Dictator" of trying to submerge their leader. Certainly, he had made scant progress. Though no documentary evidence exists to support the thesis, it is reasonable to assume that these statements were made on Fillmore's inspiration or with his approval. Such a strategy of attack through subordinates was the best method of challenging Weed's supremacy; at the same time, it best promoted the Buffalo attorney's future in politics. The cordial letters provided a not very cordial mask to Fillmore's desperation for office and advancement. Probably he had begun to understand the indissolubility of the Seward-Weed relationship. Having broken with Seward years before, he had deceived himself into thinking that Weed would continue to treat both of them on equal terms. By 1848 the dimness of this hope had become clear; the editor-boss seemed not merely to doubt Fillmore's capabilities as a politician, he appeared to be moving

[2] The victorious Democrat was Silas Wright, a man of great capacities never fully realized. Probably his strength on the ticket was as influential in carrying New York for Polk, and Polk into the presidency, as were the defections of those normal Whigs who were diverted from Clay by the abolitionist Liberty Party for, where Polk's plurality was 5,100, Wright won over Fillmore by 10,003 votes.

in directions that would cut out any Whigs not ready to follow his and Seward's leadership. Strong differences were showing themselves. Weed increasingly filled his columns with sharp antislavery editorials; Fillmore, still holding to his dream of the vice-presidency, was, meanwhile, soft-pedalling his old associations with Adams and Giddings.

More serious in its political implications was Thurlow Weed's direction of the movement in New York for Zachary Taylor; this, when the Fillmore camp wanted Henry Clay. For second place on the national ticket, Weed favored Daniel Webster. When New England's Whig spokesman refused the shadow in his everlasting quest for the substance, the scheming boss hoped to convince the convention that Abbott Lawrence, who himself needed no persuading, would make an admirable vice-presidential candidate. Here was the heart of the threat to Millard Fillmore. It opened the possibility of his political extinction. By the letters, he sought to preserve an atmosphere that contained a semblance of the harmony in which politicians find it most congenial to work. He shrunk from the idea of an outright fight until all other efforts were exhausted. The challenge through his partisans was such an effort. But, if necessary, he would have pulled Whiggery apart in the Empire State if that was the only way to secure the nomination, so hungry was he for office.

In the convention, Clay men grew dangerously angry after watching their hero casually pushed aside by Weed and his allies. Lawrence, they recalled, had given considerable effort in elevating General Harrison over Henry Clay eight years before. Now, they shouted that with Taylor, a planter, and Lawrence, a cloth manufacturer, running together, cotton would be at both ends of the ticket. For their satisfaction, they said, they must have a loyal follower of the Old Prince; and swayed by the enticing appeals of certain New York enemies of Thurlow Weed, they averred that Millard Fillmore was the man. Weed read the signs and saw local disaster if he held out against this unwelcome selection. In what promised an extremely close campaign, he understood the necessity of appeasing every possible faction. He tolerated the revision of his plans, permitting a temporary unity for the purpose of national victory. Perhaps he also thought that the vice-presidency would end Fillmore's career and that a particularly obstructive local leader would be permanently removed from the New York terrain.

2. THE GENERAL VS THE POLITICIANS

Each of America's military adventures has usually produced a popular hero—or several heroes—whom the politicians have been able to deny only with difficulty. Nor are politicians always anxious to deny the hero, for they are awake to the possibilities inherent in running him for public office. Because the average candidate for a governorship, the Senate, or the presidency has had to serve his time for one or another interest, one or another political faction, one or another section of the electorate, he has created a record of acts, of backs and fills, and of equivocations that arouses a measure of opposition here and a degree of coldness there. But the man who has won glory on the battlefield is often above criticism. Where his name has been associated with an epic event like a Yorktown, a New Orleans, a Tippecanoe, an Appomattox, or a San Juan Hill, he may become in life a legendary figure. And few will gainsay the persistant strength of a legend even after it has been subjected to scientific examination. That he may have indicated few capacities for civilian pursuits is an objection that vanishes in consideration of his fame as a soldier.

Such was the case of General Zachary Taylor, born a Virginian, bred a Kentuckian, a resident of Louisiana, but above all a soldier who had spent his lifetime at army posts on the Indian frontier and in fighting his country's wars. Known among the military caste as a competent administrator, an excellent leader, and a bluff and obstinate man once his mind reached a conclusion, it was expected that he would retire to a comfortable obscurity once he became too old for active service. It was also known that he had a cotton plantation in Mississippi on which labored several hundred slaves and which would, therefore, after he retired, provide him with a limited area to exercise the command he loved.

But outside General Taylor's ken, and certainly outside his interest, political forces culminated in war with Mexico. And the General, being the first commander of consequence on the scene, quickly rang up popular victories at Palo Alto and Resaca de la Palma, on the road to the Rio Grande. Succeeding triumphs at Monterey and Buena Vista added to the wide acclaim already given him. By the time of that last battle, Winfield Scott had been sent down to Mexico to divide the laurels of glory with Taylor and had superseded him in command of the armies in the field. Militarily speaking, the move was sound, for Scott was a talented strategist—something Taylor was not—and major operations against the invaded country's cities were about to start. To carry out his plan for subjugating the enemy, Scott appropriated most of Taylor's troops and ordered his subordinate commander to defend Monterey and hold off from further offensive action.

Politically speaking, however, this looked like the purposive casting down of a hero. There resulted, to the delectation of the Whigs, an airing of ugly charges that President Polk and Secretary of War Marcy were seeking to neutralize Taylor's popularity by building up Scott. That Polk had recently reproved Taylor for the easy surrender terms granted at Monterey seemed to sustain the accusation. Indisputably, it evidenced an administration at outs with its captain.

On his part, Taylor was convinced that "Scott, Marcy & Co." were plotting to halt his success, that they were more interested in containing him than in winning the war. Scott needlessly affronted the man he had supplanted in command by dealing through Taylor's staff when etiquette dictated direct conference with him; the War Department delayed in sending Taylor full information. In this atmosphere, he disregarded the instructions of his commanding general and took his depleted force in search of Santa Anna, the Mexican leader. He found his quarry on the field at Buena Vista.

Had Zachary Taylor lost the battle, the consequences of his disobedience would undoubtedly have been court-martial and disgrace. But having won and having had his triumph once more acknowledged by the administration in extremely bad grace, he was easily portrayed as a wronged man. In the partisan public mind, sympathy for his persecutions commingled with the majesty of his victories. His appeal grew enormously.

Already that appeal was being put to use. As early as 1846, discreet inquiries by Thurlow Weed revealed that the General hated Andrew Jackson profoundly, and so detested European manufactures that his uniforms and apparel were made only of American cloth. To the New Yorker, that made Taylor enough of a Whig to counteract Henry Clay's quadrennial bid for the White House. Other politicians, no longer bemused by Prince Hal's glamour, soon arrived at the same conclusion. John J. Crittenden, once Clay's protégé and a senator and former cabinet officer, brought the Whig machine of Kentucky into the Taylor fold, and thereby dealt his benefactor and the state's favorite son a blow he never quite forgave. Alexander Hamilton Stephens, Whig Congressman from Georgia and a proslavery leader, scurried among his colleagues from the Lower South thumping the tub for the planter General. In paradoxical alliance with Representative Abraham Lincoln, he organized a congressional club, styled the "Young Indians," to orate on Taylor's virtues and circulate these encomiums systematically under their franking privileges.

Meanwhile, the busy politicians advised Taylor to write no letters, give no speeches, and focus his eyes exclusively on Mexico. But the hero of Buena Vista was too guileless a man and too straightforward a character to maintain silence. Before the embargo was placed on his words he had freely admitted his past inattention to things political, but ventured that had he been even so active as to cast a vote—which he never had—it would have been Whig. Now, when letters came respectfully or trickily asking his opinions and his party preferences, he felt that good manners required the questions be answered. In the published replies, his picturesque spelling and the defeats he suffered in his tilts with syntax disturbed those who thought a president should have reasonable facility in the formalities of the English language. More serious still was the freeness with which he confessed ignorance on many of the issues that were the warp and woof of politics. Most serious of all was the childish innocence of his expressed desire that he be nominated, if at all, as a nonpartisan, that his nomination come directly from the people instead of a convention, and that he would accept Democratic as well as Whig endorsement.

Eventually, however, Weed, Crittenden and Stephens got Taylor's pen under partial control. In careful phraseology and with improved grammar, they worked out missives for his signature that, when published, covered the General's apoliticality with a veneer of Whiggery. By convention time, they had mitigated the damage done by their candidate's inept tactics. His popularity with the common man easily overcame the resistance put up by the supporters of Clay, Scott and Webster. As important was the indefiniteness of his position. On the all-consuming question of slavery and the territories, Taylor offered no hint of his beliefs. In the South, his cotton planting was dangled as a guarantee of his loyalty to the peculiar institution; in the North, his avowal that he would use the veto power very sparingly was interpreted to mean he would accept the Wilmot Proviso if Congress passed it.

Reviewing the wisdom of 1840, the party again sent out its standard-bearers untrammeled by a statement of principles. The campaign was dull, tinged with excitement only in a few northern states. There, a third party composed of Abolitionists from both parties and of Democrats disaffected by Polk's patronage policies and expansionism united behind the Free Soil candidacy of Martin Van Buren. In retrospect one wonders what led the Little Magician into a hopeless canvass, unless it was his antislavery convictions or a desire to revenge himself on a Democratic Party that had twice since 1840 rejected him as its nominee. Yet no doubt attaches to the consequence. In New York, Van Buren drew more votes than did Cass, the Democratic choice, and the state went to the Whigs. With it went the election.

* * *

Zachary Taylor's academic schooling had been haphazard and, in earlier years, no one had much cared that he improve it; but from the day of his election, his political education was the immediate concern of many. Would-be instructors recognized in him a field that had lain fallow through forty years of soldiering; they dreamed of sowing a seed and reaping the harvest. While he prepared to leave Louisiana, office-seekers bribed his tailor that they might leave notes in the pockets of the suits being made for him. Those out of reach of the New Orleans shop or the General's cabin in Baton Rouge sent him letters. Others readied themselves for his tour to Washington when Taylor, passing triumphantly through their sections, would be receptive to their bland-ishments.

Yet those who thought him confused and malleable grossly under-estimated him. His long military career had been active and unstulti-fying. Trained for command, Taylor had developed a habit of inde-pendent judgment that he refused to surrender merely because his oc-cupation was no longer the same. Whatever his linguistic idiosyn-crasies, he was well read and a strong believer in the simple virtues of directness and honesty. The smell of patronage he abhorred. More than any other aspect of the office, the squabblings incumbent upon the dis-tribution of loaves and fishes had caused him to doubt whether he really wanted the presidency. Now perforce, he listened glumly while men extolled their own abilities and begged for a place.

Among the pre-inauguration suppliants was Vice-President-elect Millard Fillmore. His manner, however, was that of a friend offering the helping hand of experience, and generous relief from a repugnant chore. From him, Taylor expected the invaluable support and advice of a politician highly ensconced both in party circles and the govern-ment. In exchange, the new President willingly agreed to divest him-self of the worry over New York's share in the new Whig pie by giving the entire cut to the Buffalo statesman. It seemed a happy arrange-ment. Fillmore spun visions of a Whig organization cleansed of Seward and Weed, and doing homage to Buffalo instead of Albany.

But Thurlow Weed had anticipated Fillmore's plans. He jammed the nomination of Seward to the United States Senate down the throats of the Fillmore bloc within New York, and ruthlessly dictated the elec-tion in the legislature. Taylor, brought up to date on Whig politics in the Empire State, received Seward graciously and was rapidly won away from the Vice-President by the Senator's more captivating personality. Fillmore sulked over the loss of his opportunity and closed the gate of reconciliation with Weed in an angry letter. He attempted to enlist the General's cabinet only to find that his rival had beaten him in that quarter also. In a few short months, Millard Fillmore had been forced deep into the hollow shell of the vice-presidency; he was powerless, his tendons cut by the knife he had prepared to use on the Albany publisher and the Auburn lawyer.

Nevertheless, Seward's ascendency over Fillmore did not mean his domination of the President. Zachary Taylor believed himself Chief Executive of all the people, and therefore above faction. He received suggestions and consulted those he trusted; but his will was his own, and his decision, once arrived at, he considered right and patriotic and beyond the pale of argument. The New York Senator intelligently grasped this facet of the General's character, and treated him deferentially and kindly. This, more than any other factor, made Seward welcome in the White House. It gave him an undefined power and protected Taylor from some of the factional strife breaking out in the party. But it also produced an illusion that the President was a prisoner of Seward's agile mentality and mercurial schemes—an illusion that was false, yet sufficiently credible to those less familiar with the personality of the sixty-five-year-old man.

No one dominated Zachary Taylor. No one could have. Any president must have advisers and, if not friends, at least some people with whom he feels comfortable. These may or may not influence his decisions, but because of their closeness to him, they invariably are gossiped about as the "hidden powers" or as a segment of the "invisible government." Taylor came to the White House without a predetermined circle. If anyone held his confidence as well as a first mortgage on his administration it was Crittenden, who had perhaps contributed more toward bringing the General to the presidency than had any other man. Taylor had appreciatively tendered Crittenden a choice of any cabinet office he wished for himself, but the rising Kentucky leader decided to take instead the governorship of his state, to which he had been recently elected. This decision carried a double result. First, it created a vacuum around the General, and it deprived him of an able councillor. It was into this vacuum that Seward so naturally slid. The second result had larger significance. With his imperfect education in politics the President announced independent judgments and policies for which his party had not been prepared. Here, Crittenden would have been valuable; with his acuteness, he could have planed down the crudities of the old soldier's platform; with his national reputation, he could have brought some harmony where lack of understanding soon caused dissension.

How much Crittenden could have done for Taylor, and how closely Taylor would have followed him is, of course, debatable. But, in keeping to Kentucky, he left the President with a cabinet of second- and third-rate politicians. He also left an inexperienced man to deal with the ambitions, rivalries and suspicions of an unsteady, unmanageable coalition that called itself a party. Though Taylor was its nominal leader, important men held back their allegiances. Henry Clay, disgusted that he had lost the nomination, had issued no word of approval during the campaign. After the election, he maintained a distant relationship with the General. Stories spread that Clay was bent upon "rule or ruin," and he did nothing to correct the impression. In the face of this abnormal show of dignity on the part of an elder statesman, Taylor believed the stories. Daniel Webster was also cold. In 1848, his eleventh hour endorsement of his party's candidate had constituted damnation with faint praise. In 1849 and 1850 he appeared more concerned with securing the 1852 nomination for himself than in assisting the incumbent administration. Southerners as a group were soon alienated by Taylor's sympathy for nationalist rather than sectional aims.

Division of the spoils drew immediate repercussions. In his distaste for patronage problems, the General turned over most of the petty selections to his cabinet members. Wiser men would have used such broad powers with a sense of discretion. These, however, were products of years of internecine fighting among the Whigs; they removed Democrats pitilessly and doled out their bounties along rigid factional lines. Incontinently, they rewarded their friends too often and their acquaintances not often enough. It was this situation that Seward turned to his personal advantage when he established cordial relations with all but one of the ministry. While forestalling Fillmore, he also shut out a number of other politicians, North and South. Not only did he have more influence than is usual for a freshman senator; he was, in the matter of appointments, stronger than any member of the upper house, where the senatorial privilege of distributing offices among the faithful is a fetish.

In hostile eyes, he had taken control of the North and "sacked the South." This somewhat overstated the case. But it mattered not. Those whose backs remained unscratched during this, their first genuine opportunity in twenty years, were too bitter to analyze things rationally. The abuse of disappointment heaped upon the cabinet; its members, never well liked or respected by the congressmen, lost whatever standing they had. Rumors of their resignations—the wish being father to the thought—circulated through the capital city. Secretary of State John M. Clayton's sword-rattling diplomacy with France, Portugal, Spain and the German Confederation got him perpetual criticism.[3] Plots simmered to remove Interior Secretary Thomas Ewing—if necessary by abolishing the entire department. A noisome scandal over an ancient land claim engulfed three other cabinet officers; and, although no turpitude was involved, certainly one member was too secretive about a fee he was to receive from the settlement, while the other two were too complaisant in granting seventy-five years of back interest.

These assaults on his trusted advisers hurt the General deeply. He interpreted them to be veiled personal attacks, as some were. He was perhaps too sure of his own wisdom to realize that his first appointments were mistakes. But just before his death, he and Weed had drawn up plans for a sweeping revision. In that respect, his education was taking root.

For his other troubles, however, there was no ready solution. Turn out as many Democrats as he might, there were insufficient offices to satiate all thirsts. Magnificent as the Whig renaissance appeared, too many wanted to lead him by the hand; too few would grant him the luxury of independent thought or credit him with the ability to guide himself. His party smiled at his simplicity when he pastured his favorite horse on the lawn of the Executive Mansion; it became angry when he applied his hastily crammed political education without finesse. It was almost a corollary in Whig doctrine that the president

[3] With Britain, Clayton was more conciliatory. The gold discoveries in the West and the prospects of Far Eastern commerce had raised demands for a canal across the Central American isthmus. Cutting athwart these demands was British domination over a part of Nicaragua, whose lakes and waterways made it the logical country across which to build the canal. After protracted negotiations during which each country tried to persuade the other that it held the upper hand in the region, an agreement was signed and later ratified (under Fillmore) binding both countries to co-operate in building a canal *anywhere* on the isthmus, and enjoining them from fortifying or exercising exclusive control over it. Known to history as the Clayton-Bulwer Treaty, its unpopularity grew as the restrictions it placed on American expansion became apparent. In Chester Arthur's time, an effort to abrogate it was unsuccessful. By McKinley's day, the terms were considered intolerable. Yet, in 1850, when Britain was expanding her Caribbean interests, by signing the treaty, she voluntarily restricted her own sphere of activity. In this sense, the final conditions agreed to represented, at the time, something of an American diplomatic triumph.

is a creature of the party. As Taylor grew with his office, he discovered that the presidential power is great in its own right. The Whigs, in seeking a figurehead, set up a man who had spent a lifetime in issuing orders. When he sought to use his place as a commander would, they squirmed restlessly and muttered their old catchwords about "usurpation."

3. THE COMPROMISED IN 1850.

Underlying all other considerations was slavery and its disposition in the territory taken from Mexico. The debates on the Wilmot Proviso had sketched out the lines of argument for the North and South. But so long as there remained southern equality in the Senate, its passage into law would be prevented, regardless of the number of times northern majorities pushed it through the House. Meanwhile, gold was pulling people into California, making organization of that far western country imperative. Some decision on the other territories—ungoverned except for the rule of the army or the Mormon church—was advisable. Back east, where government existed, abolitionists and milder antislavery men grew increasingly wrathful because the House refused to hear their petitions for the abolition of slavery in the District of Columbia. Southern indignation mounted while emancipation sentiment in the North heightened and fugitive slaves moved to freedom across the Ohio River and the Mason-Dixon line. Mere repetition of the charges and arguments from either section drove men into embracing the positions of the extremes.

In the agitation, some form of settlement of several, if not all, of the issues was clearly necessary. Stormy prophecies of disunion oppressed those not ready for so drastic a step. Yet, the politicians were loath to jeopardize their careers by advocating any but a solution beneficial to their own sections, of which David Wilmot's northern contribution was an example. The Polk administration, which, in its war, had presented the nation with the territorial problem, had purposely avoided making an effort to deal with it. Cognizant of the factors likely to promote a party split, it left office deeding the consequences of expansionism to the Whigs and Zachary Taylor.

Taylor was more of a nationalist than men suspected and southerners thought proper. He was also a realist. Believing that the country would be better served without the acrid debate on slavery he knew must come if any territorial bills were introduced in Congress, he attempted to avert the entire subject by bringing the Southwest directly into the Union without an intervening territorial stage. Before Congress met, he dispatched messengers to encourage the people of California and New Mexico to draw up constitutions and apply for statehood.

Californians responded. In a fever of activity, they met, drew up an organic law, ratified it and were ready to ask for admission by the New Year. Meanwhile, the President had advised the Thirty-first Congress of the impending request and of another likely to come from New Mexico. He recommended that the new states be received. To preserve "confidence and kind feeling," he suggested that the national legislature peacefully await developments, that its members hold their feelings in abeyance, anticipating nothing, until the new constitutions were presented. On the other slavery matters, he asked that members "abstain from the introduction of those exciting topics of a sectional character which have hitherto produced painful apprehensions in the public mind." In other words, he wished the North to forget about the District of Columbia and the South about fugitive slaves. Those problems, he felt, rightly or wrongly, were best left to the solutions of time.

It was a delusory hope. To the South, Taylor's action appeared a sellout. His sin was all the greater because he, a southerner, was for presenting to the North what it wanted. The Wilmot Proviso was now unnecessary. Because the frontier communities the General urged upon Congress had no slaves they would come in as free states. And once in, their votes in the Senate would settle the fate of slavery. So ran the reasoning. Behind it, of course, rested the southerners' full acceptance of Calhoun's dictum that the slavery institution was a "positive good."

One after another, southern orators raised their cries. "Secession" and "disunion"—words once so terrible that they were uttered in furtive, deprecating tones—rang their alarums in both Houses. John Calhoun rasped that the South had "borne the wrongs and insults of the North long enough." More vitriolic critics upbraided Taylor for having committed a "crime against the constitution" and for encouraging "revolution." His peaceful motives were distorted; the slavery bias transmuted them into meaning nothing short of aid and comfort to abolitionism and Free Soil. Few Whigs came to his defense. Northern Democrats, jumping at the opportunity to throttle the administration, joined the southern clamor. In the White House, the General painfully absorbed these lessons of political life, and rued the weakness that had allowed him to consent to serve in public office. The crossfire, however, stiffened his backbone. He believed he had offered a program for national peace; now that he heard the objections of sectional prejudice, he was certain that his policy was right.

* * *

In late January, while imprecations still rained on the President's head, Henry Clay arose in the Senate to present a series of compromise resolutions. After nearly eight years, he was back, filling out Crittenden's unexpired term. As he stood, his colleagues saw an enfeebled old man; but while he talked on, they wondered whether he was contesting General Taylor's nominal leadership of the party or whether he was throwing himself into one last battle, sincerely sacrificing his life for a group of measures he believed would preserve the Union.

There was nothing new in what the Old Prince said. He simply took the demands of both sections, said they were all just, and lumped them together. The administration group and the North he sought to placate by California's admission as a free state. Southern sensibilities he hoped to calm by organizing the other territories without reference to slavery. That question, he felt, the future would determine; and geography—if nothing else—insured them for antislavery. Thus, the North would get the land; the South would preserve its principle—that Congress could not legislate on slavery in the territories. A boundary dispute between Texas and New Mexico was to be settled in the latter's favor, thereby cutting off the last area to which slavery could be extended; but holders of the Texas Republic's depreciated bonds—mostly southerners—were to be compensated by the United States Treasury. For the North, the slave trade in the District of Columbia was to cease; for the South, slavery in the District was not to be abolished without compensation or without the consent of the residents and the state of Maryland. As an open concession to the slave states and to balance California, a strict federal fugitive slave law was to be enacted, and a resolution adopted by Congress that it had no authority to regulate the interstate slave trade.

Balanced one against the other, Clay thought that the heterodoxy of his proposals would attract votes from both sections so long as the measures were neatly packaged. If each item of his compromise was introduced separately and independently he felt the northern group of demands might pass by sheer weight of numbers, the southern group surely lose; but if only one or neither section was satisfied, the Union would suffer.

Whatever Henry Clay's motives—and on his 1850 resolutions most historians are inclined to treat him charitably—his propositions further isolated the President and set off a new debate. Senators explored the ground already well covered. Taylor pressed the issue by submitting the California constitution and again asking its acceptance; but action was halted. Congress was stalled in argument, anxiously awaiting the opinions of its other leaders.

On March 4th, John C. Calhoun was carried into the Senate Chamber. It was his day to speak, but a catarrh muffled his voice to a hoarse whisper. The pallor of his face and the flannel wrappings around his long, emaciated body were ghastly to look upon. Only his eyes burning in their deep-set sockets showed the invalided body still fought for life. While Senator Mason of Virginia read the South Carolinian's manuscript to the hushed chamber, those eyes fiercely punctuated each point of the logic. For Calhoun, near death, was making peace with no one; he was once again driving home his thesis of the shames and injuries done his beloved South. Taylor's plan, Clay's plan, the Wilmot Proviso —he found them all impossible. The whole trend of government, he said, had gone on unconstitutionally and at the expense of the southern section. The "Federal Republic, as it originally came from the hands of its framers . . . has been changed into a great national consolidated Democracy." The North had seized "absolute control," and, in her antagonism to slavery, was causing a gradual disruption of the Union. While Mason read Calhoun's defiance, the cadaverous man snapped his eyes. "The South asks for justice, simple justice, and less she ought not to take." Then came the challenge. The North must demonstrate her fidelity by giving the South "equal right" in the territories, by returning fugitive slaves, ending abolitionist propaganda, and accepting a constitutional amendment that restored the South her lost position of equal power. Else, the alternative for the South was subjugation.

Three days later, Daniel Webster delivered his answer. But it was less an answer than an appeal. He essayed little logic in refuting Calhoun's charges and he entered into no dispute on the meaning of the Constitution. Instead, he played upon his once magnificent voice as though it were still an organ, laboriously rolling out rhetorical cadences for the preservation of the Union. In general, he seconded the suggestions of Clay, his rival of decades. He condemned extremism, North and South alike, and overnight lost his antislavery following at home. To New England, it seemed that Webster was defacing his past record and scorning his own section in order to appease southern proslavery moderates with soft words and Henry Clay's concessions. His hard remarks about abolition lent themselves to the conclusion that this Senator—another grown old and perhaps engaging in his last fight—believed compromise was more possible with the South than the North. Whether or not this was true, his speech had just such an effect; talk of secession momentarily halted. The unity of these two elder Whig statesmen temporarily opened the door for a compromiser's peace.

Four days later it was again slammed shut. William H. Seward, the youngish freshman Senator from New York, delivered his blast at Calhoun and Clay. He did not explicitly defend the President, but in speaking for the admission of California unadulterated by compromises with slavery, he in effect concurred in the administration's position. In adjuring Clay's compromise, Seward said things that fell unkindly upon his listeners, but which were nevertheless true. Aside from his critical remarks on the moral obliquity of compromises in general, the whole tenor of his speech emphasized the point (the obverse of which was equally plain to Calhoun) that certain issues based on moral convictions are impossible of adjustment through bargaining. That antithetical principles were linked in the same bill made them no more acceptable. In a famous declaration for morality, and for the fundamental justice of the antislavery position, Seward exclaimed: "But there is a higher law than the Constitution, which regulates our authority over the domain. . . . The territory is a part—no inconsiderable part—of the common heritage of mankind, bestowed upon them by the Creator of the universe. We are his stewards, and must so discharge our trust as to secure, in the highest attainable degree, their happiness. . . ."

The statement was one of the high watermarks Seward left on the antislavery beach. Another was his address eight years later on the "irrepressible conflict" between the sections. Yet, as war moved ever closer—inevitably, if the New Yorker believed his own speech—and after fighting broke out, Seward was to show his unpredictable instability by trying to do business with the South. In 1850, however, he spoke for a North awakening to a new idealism—not necessarily the fanaticism of abolition, but the determination that slavery must somehow give way to free labor, that neither Calhounian sophistries nor southern truculence nor the special privilege demanded by slavery for its survival in an antagonistic world would deter the North from the greatest possible advance of its population and resources.

*   *   *

Over the senatorial discussion, Millard Fillmore continued to preside impassively. Though he concealed his feelings, he had been swayed by Clay and Webster and had privately decided to cast his valuable vote in behalf of compromise.

By May, the resolutions were given to Congress for its consideration in the wrappings of an "Omnibus" bill. The arguments ground on, now made more exacerbating by their repetition and all the twists and turns of parliamentary maneuvering permitted by the rule book and the chairman of each house. By then Calhoun was dead and his scepter of leadership over southern Democrats taken up by Jefferson Davis, the President's son-in-law. Henry Clay still defended his measures and Webster helped him, but the months were wearing them down. Much of their burden was being assumed by two northern Democrats, the elderly Lewis Cass of Michigan and the young Stephen Douglas of Illinois.

In the White House, however, the President was living up to his nickname of Old Rough and Ready. His distrust for Henry Clay increased as each week showed the California bill and the presidential solution to have smaller possibility of coming to a vote, much less passing. He watched while his Vice-President's newspaper spokesmen praised the compromise even if their inspiration kept his official silence. He suffered under the attacks upon his policies and his cabinet. But he gave no ground. He was convinced of the efficacy of his plan, and when his chief defenders turned out to be Seward and the Free Soilers, he re-examined his prejudices about the North. In this soul searching, he became certain that his southern advisers had misled him, that the *South* was the aggressor and the danger to the Union.

The growing tension on the New Mexico border brought on angry threats that Texans would march and sons of the South would enlist under their banner to help them. Representatives sent to sound out the President found him prepared to lead an army, if necessary, to suppress any uprising. Once again, the shade of Andrew Jackson hung over Washington while General Taylor leveled his curses at "traitors" in Congress and talked of "hanging rebels." But most of all, he made it plain that Clay's "Omnibus" was unacceptable, that California was entitled to admission without "bringing the Territories [in] on her back." To others, he let it be understood that he would not veto the Wilmot Proviso.

By July, 1850, seven months of discussion on slavery had contributed a host of resolutions and columns of debate in the *Congressional Globe*. The middle ground of the compromisers shook with every speech from the extremists of both sides. On a test vote, proslavery and antislavery men would combine in the negative to invalidate progress by the Clay forces. More federal troops reinforced the garrisons in New Mexico, and Alexander Stephens excitedly talked of impeaching the

President. Yet, if anything, Taylor's program was beginning to be better engineered on the Senate floor. John Bell of Tennessee—who had once resigned a cabinet post when President John Tyler stood against Clay's leadership—and Hannibal Hamlin, an abolitionist Democrat from Maine, joined Seward in replying to the bitter attacks. The General's faith in his plan deepened; threats of secession and civil war convinced him that Union through compromise was impossible.

On the Fourth, he delivered a short address at one of those myriad ceremonies a president must always attend whether or not he is enmeshed in work or in need of relaxation. The occasion was the cornerstone laying for the Washington Monument. The day was hot and the other speeches long. The General sat through the afternoon on a platform unprotected from the sun's direct rays. Without thought, he tossed off glasses of ice water and afterwards at the White House wolfed cold cherries and iced milk. In the evening, he suffered violent cramps. His doctors diagnosed the illness as "cholera morbus"; as days passed without his recovery, they announced he had a "bilious remittant fever." On the night of July 9th, Zachary Taylor spoke his last fighting words: "I have endeavored to discharge my official duties faithfully. *I regret nothing,* but am sorry that I am about to leave my friends." [4] In a few moments, he was dead.

*   *   *

Millard Fillmore was sworn in the next day before both houses of Congress. The eulogies on the dead President were said by Daniel Webster and Representative Conrad of Louisiana, both of whom had, a few days before, tried to get Taylor to alter his firm position on the territories. It is interesting that they dwelt on his simplicity and his ingenuousness, his sense of duty and his honesty and integrity. Only in passing did they speak of those stormy years when he was a soldier at odds with his superiors and a Chief Executive at lances with his Congress.

The new occupant of the White House said nothing of carrying out the General's policies. He kept the Taylor cabinet only long enough to draw up a slate to replace it. Intimations went out that he would sign the compromise measures whether they came to him in the "Omnibus" or, so the expression felicitously described it, in a "Cab"—that is, individually. Early in August, he sent the legislature a special message calling its attention to Texan military preparations and designs, and to

---

[4] Significantly, Millard Fillmore's announcement to the Senate and the country showed careful editing of the General's words and, therefore, gave them a shading which, in differing with the original, fitted the successor's political aims: "I have always done my duty. I am ready to die. *My only regret* is for the friends I leave behind me."

the unrest on the New Mexican border. The gist of his paper was that he would be forced to use troops unless Congress gave him a law organizing the territory, drawing the boundary, and indemnifying the overwrought state for the loss of its claims. He pleaded for a law; he clearly wanted to avoid using force.

Stephen Douglas took over leadership from the faltering Henry Clay. With his lieutenants, the Illinois Democrat fed the compromise provisions one by one into the legislative mill, from which they emerged to be signed by Millard Fillmore and become the law of the land. It was the compromiser's peace.

But the central issue of slavery had been left unsettled. Its fate in the territories lay outside the purview of the law, undetermined but still hotly contested. The new fugitive slave law improved few northern tempers, and northern resistance to its enforcement raised southern tirades of protest and recrimination. If the accession of Fillmore and the passage of the compromise were supposed to bring peace, they failed in their objective. For the peace they marked out was one of politicians averse to facing a problem squarely. Neither Wilmot nor Calhoun received frank answers to the solutions they had propounded. And faith in these solutions was already lodged in northern and southern consciences.

Thus, too many were compromised in a fate they did not want—Wilmot and Calhoun, Seward and Jefferson Davis, Zachary Taylor, abolitionist and slaveryite. If Henry Clay's resolutions had been drawn for the purpose of chastening Zachary Taylor as he had chastened John Tyler, or if they were given out of concern for the Union, they were unsuccessful at bottom. Basically, they scratched at the problem and opened old sores not easily healed. Taylor's proposal had, at least, the virtue of doctoring only what screamed for remedy while permitting the remainder to seek natural cure.

4. A POLITICIAN IS NOT ENOUGH

Even Thurlow Weed was compromised, if such a thing were possible. He and Seward had used their artistry too fully when Taylor was alive. They had built a spectacular patronage machine, but they had worked on the assumption that the General would live to succeed himself. The shock of Millard Fillmore's succession tottered their empire, preliminary to a crash.

First came the cabinet and the mass exodus of Seward and Weed allies. Most portentous of the replacements was the new Postmaster General, Nathan K. Hall of Buffalo, Fillmore's old law partner. The other appointees to ministerial posts manifested independence of Seward rule, if not latent hostility to it. They were all Whigs who favored the compromise, and, by the inclusion of Webster and Crittenden, undoubtedly possessed more talent as a body than did their predecessors. Next came Fillmore's effort to take actual as well as nominal leadership of the party. For Fillmore who had been disposed to compromise on moral issues showed no inclination to compromise on politics. He concentrated upon pinioning or stifling all opposition within Whig ranks and on insuring his nomination by the national convention in 1852. The glove of power having fallen into his hand, he began its employment by slapping at the Seward-Weed domination of New York State. His friends toured back and forth shouting maledictions at the followers of the men from Albany and Auburn. His press published scathing editorials damning the established machine. Seward was banished from the White House. In a warfare as open as politicians of the same party dare to indulge, the President attempted to take control of his home state in preparation for taking over the party.

His task was hard, his chances of success few. The majority in New York Whiggery opposed slavery and heartily applauded Seward's "higher law" doctrine; the Fillmore minority was pledged to the compromise. The President's faction quickly decided to make Seward the issue. In the 1850 state convention, Fillmoreites worked to withhold a party endorsement of Seward's course and thereby discredit him before the rank and file. This was to be the first in a series of moves to convert northern Whigs to the compromise and thus commend the party to the South. Weed perceived in the maneuver not only a threat to himself and his *alter ego* but an imprisoning of the party under southern jailers. He foresaw a junking of the Whig creed—the tariff, internal improvements, distribution, a conservative fiscality—merely to placate slavery by committing the party to its cause. He foresaw, in the process, the gradual destruction of antislavery Whiggery and the evanescence of the party's strength in the North. Conscientiously, he labored to prevent an open break, to preserve his power over the state.

Fillmore would not or could not control his men. His men lost in the New York convention and in a disastrous split, they bolted from Weed's control. In the autumn elections, the Whig candidate for governor slipped through by a meager 262 votes; the state's Whig delegation in the House of Representatives dropped from thirty-two to seventeen. Over the country, the party lost support. In the Thirty-second Congress, the Democrats held a clear majority in both houses.

Weed's prediction was proving true. The biennial elections of 1850 marked the beginning of the end of the Whigs. Slowly in that year, and with increasing rapidity during the next four, the coalition Henry Clay had created broke up. Those first two years of decline were confusing. Both parties had been able to lay claim to the compromise, and in 1850, that claim by pro-compromise candidates provided the margin of victory in several areas. In the South, the Fillmore bloc made slight gains over the Democrats. But in the North, where anti-compromise feeling was strong, the party lost heavily, a casualty of its internal disputes and the temporary return of most Free Soilers to Democracy.

Basically, through all its life, the Whig party represented a minority of the population. Several of its more perceptive leaders, like Clay and Weed, had often been at cross-purposes, but they were constantly in search of the popular issue to bring their party into office. After 1850, Clay was an exhausted old man and Weed had abdicated everywhere but in New York. Many of the others had grown too old or were tired of disappointments. Placed under Millard Fillmore's safekeeping, Whiggery was left in the hands of a politician who lacked the necessary gift of unifying the inharmonious. Weed understood that the real strength of the party lay in the capitalism and antislavery of the North; Fillmore raised up the compromise as the "final settlement" of the slavery issue and lost his own section. So far as loyalties went, Clay and Fillmore were one; but in the test of leadership, the two were obviously cut from different cloth. Clay energized men, fascinated them by his personality, moved them as easily by his casuistries as by his logic; Fillmore had none of these qualities. His course in 1850 resulted in double defeat—by Weed in New York, by the Democrats across the country.

*   *   *

The remainder of the last Whig administration was similarly without inspiration. Brave words were said of the success of the compromise; but in New England, mobs prevented the return of captured fugitive slaves. Fillmore issued proclamations and messages appealing for adherence to the law. He told of his power to intervene with federal troops to suppress disorder, and then explained his doubts at the soundness of such methods. It was politics once again—the politician seeking to placate one section by brandishing a nerveless finger at the other.

Three times he was rebuffed by a hostile Congress in his request for an increased tariff. In the State Department, Webster engaged in a bit of sword rattling with Austria over American sentiment favoring a Hungarian revolt against the monarchy; but this was more an incident of boisterous Yankee diplomacy than a studied policy for war. In the main, the country relaxed from the great debate of 1850 and enjoyed

the stimulating thrill of California's gold filtering through its financial
arteries. A prosperity founded upon exploitation of the nation's abundant land and mineral resources and upon easy money distracted men
from the trivialities of politics.

Fillmore read all this to be a good omen. He wrote another letter
stating his reluctance to be a candidate to succeed himself. He reviewed
the "gratifying result" of a policy of "equal justice and impartiality,"
where "angry strife which for a time threatened to array State against
State, and brother against brother . . . has fortunately passed away."
He reiterated a preference for retirement, but submitted that he would
"cheerfully make any personal sacrifice" for the sake of his friends or
"the good of my country." The message was for the eyes of the chairman of the national Whig convention. That its intent was something
else is evident from the cover letter to the man to whom the renuncia-
tory document was entrusted.

That second addressee was Representative George Babcock of New
York, one of the President's leaders in the House. His instructions
were to exercise the utmost circumspection in releasing the contents of
the self-abnegative missive he bore. It seems likely that Fillmore felt
certain of the nomination, but wrote of his hesitancy to inaugurate a
draft if the delegates appeared to be veering toward another choice.
That the letter was never presented is more interesting than important.
Although Babcock can be charged with overextreme delicacy in withholding it, the more reasonable explanation perhaps comes from the
President's overestimation of his popularity within his own party. To
have publicized his written wishes probably would have been, by convention time, to have insured them.

For Fillmore's conciliation of the South and his war on Weed and
Seward had left smarting resentments among northerners. The Whigs
were forced to accept the compromise as an article of their faith; but
they were under no obligation to select Millard Fillmore. And led by
Seward, they repudiated him by naming General Winfield Scott, whose
military heroism in two wars well fitted the party formula for presidential candidates and whose Virginia birth mixed uncomfortably with antislavery principles. Whiggery's time, however, was running out. Northern men were finding it increasingly difficult to assimilate conservative
economics and radical antislavery within one party. Southerners increasingly refused to associate themselves with a party committed to an
expanding capitalism and not uncordial to slavery's more restrained
critics. With Scott's defeat, organized Whiggery disintegrated. The
timid and the compromisers of the North as well as the aroused of
the South found place in the proslavery Democracy of Pierce and Bu-

chanan. The angered, the irreconcilables and the ambitious regrouped to organize a party of sectional strength with national obectives, the party of Republicanism.

In 1856, Millard Fillmore tried again. While he was traveling in Europe, that political phenomenon of the middle of the decade, the Know Nothings, nominated him. Shortly afterward, a handful of southerners grimly hanging onto the compromise and calling themselves the "Whig Party" seconded the endorsement.

The society in which the candidate chose to place himself deserves attention. The "Whigs," of course, represented a forlorn hope. The Know Nothings, however, represented a third-party nova in American politics that flamed brightly, hoping to divert northern and southern thought—at grips with fundamentals—by an age-old nostrum. They denied the problem of slavery by saying the problem did not exist, and therefore required no discussion. Instead, they offered Catholics and immigrants as the cause for America's troubles; in some sections, they suggested that the enslaved Negro might also bear some of the responsibility. They had other generalities which softened the effect of these blunt preachments; and, as a result, offered a halfway house to those out of Whiggery but undecided between Republicanism and Democracy. But, in fine, the movement was bankrupt. Possibly, for this reason, it borrowed glory by naming itself the "American Party."

In fairness to Fillmore, it should be said that he felt embarrassed by the blatant nativism of some of his supporters and tried to divest himself of their cloying touch. But the presidential bug had infected him and blinded his discretion. He accepted the nomination and waged a serious campaign. That he did so in the face of certain defeat says much for his tenacity and his will for office; it speaks poorly for his judgment and his principles. One other accidental president would wage a third-party campaign for the coveted office. Yet, if in 1912 Theodore Roosevelt believed religiously that he and his followers stood "at Armageddon" while they "battled for the Lord," Millard Fillmore in 1856 chose to serve gods whose field was barren and whose toleration was limited. His was a far shabbier crusade.

*　　*　　*

Several years ago, the *New York Times,* in reporting on a survey that disclosed the unstartling intelligence that American students had a deficient knowledge of their country's history, spewed editorial heat and sorrow that Millard Fillmore was among the country's forgotten men. A closer reading of his career would have justified that oblivion.

V : IN THE WAKE OF A HERO

To FOLLOW immediately in the footsteps of one of his country's greatest figures is a not very enviable fate for any man. This was the trick history played on Andrew Johnson. Yet at the time of the event the trickery involved was not so apparent. Only five months before, 1,808,725 Americans had thought General George Brinton McClellan a better leader than Abraham Lincoln. Not a few others believed that the order of the standard-bearers on the victorious National Union ticket should have been reversed in the offices the candidates sought.

By April 1865 some would have modified their opinions in consequence of the surrender at Appomattox. Flushed with the triumph at arms, they would begin to perceive intimations of Lincoln's greatness. But it would be years before they admitted his full stature as a war president and created around him a legend that became the nation's most beloved epic. During his lifetime, he was the recipient of less adulation and confidence than was his last partner in politics, Andrew Johnson.

1. A TENNESSEE DEMOCRAT

"He was an immense worker and student, but always in the practicalities of life. His habits were marked by temperance, industry, courage, and unswerving perseverance; also by inveterate prejudices or preconceptions on certain points, and these no arguments could change. His faith in the judgment of the people was unlimited, and to their decision he was always ready to submit. One of the people by birth, he remained so by conviction. . . . He was eminently faithful to his word, and possessed a courage which took the form of angry resistance if urged to do or not to do anything which might clash with his convictions of duty."

So spoke Jefferson Davis in 1865 to the prison physician of Fortress Monroe, where the erstwhile president of the defunct Confederate States of America lay incarcerated awaiting the trial for treason that never came. The man he thus characterized was his sometime colleague in the United States Senate, Andrew Johnson of Tennessee. Of President Andrew Johnson, Davis knew only what he read in the papers, and was, therefore, unwilling to make a judgment. Others in that year, considered less satanic by northern public opinion than Davis and thus more free to practice statesmanship, could as easily have come to the same conclusion. Had they done so it is nevertheless probable that the broad panorama of the post-bellum era would have remained unchanged; but a clearer view of the consequences of Johnson's personality on the country would have been possible. And, unless the course of history is inflexibly predetermined, the turmoil and problems raised during his four years in the presidency might, at a minimum, have been softened or restricted in scope.

For Andrew Johnson was, of all the men and elements of national life churning in the wake of the Civil War, perhaps the most stolid, the most measurable. His rise had been one of few compromises and an open enunciation of beliefs. His efforts in his own behalf had been aided by no man so much as by himself. Having any less ambition, lacking only a fraction of that immense force that drove him headlong into, and through, the battles and crises of thirty-five years of public life, he could never have come within other than dreaming distance of the White House. That he arrived there as the result of an assassination was perhaps the only political accident of his life.

*   *   *

Born in Raleigh, North Carolina, the second son of a father who was a tavern porter, and incidentally a sexton and town constable, and of a mother who laundered and sewed to keep the family above the starvation line, he received little from his parents but his name. The poverty of the Johnsons was further deepened by the father's death when the boy was three years old. When, during Johnson's presidency, the townspeople of Raleigh erected a monument to the father as "an honest man" —certainly one of the very few such dedicatories given honesty as a sole human virtue or achievement—the hard pressures of Reconstruction rather than fond memories of a humble citizen were probably the instigating reasons. For in life Jacob Johnson and his family were, to the landed who ruled the state, the mudsills of society; Negro slaves were considered worthier specimens of usefulness. To young Andy, growing up, the town mainly offered the opportunity to run wild. Its only schools required tuition fees; his mother was working far too hard at scraping up a living to supervise him; and his older brother was already apprenticed to a tailor. At fourteen, therefore, to learn a trade and to lighten his mother's intolerable burdens, since made heavier by her marriage to an indolent waster, he too was apprenticed to the tailor.

Two years later he ran away, having learned his trade from his master and developed a thirst for education from the discussions and readings he had listened to in the shop. Two more years of wandering through the western part of the Carolinas and East Tennessee as an itinerant tailor gave him the ambition to own his own place. Meanwhile, the care of his worn-out mother and her prodigal second husband had fallen upon him. By law, he was still bound to his master and would be until he was twenty-one. There seemed no possibility of his getting started independently at home or, as a runaway apprentice, of finding employment in any North Carolina shop. Led by the eighteen-year-old head of the family, the Johnsons therefore left Raleigh and crossed the mountains for East Tennessee where, Andy was confident, he could make a living consistent with his responsibilities.

In September 1826 they straggled into Greeneville and stopped, not because this was their destination but because their meager funds were gone. Six months later, A. Johnson opened his own place and in May he married Eliza McCardle, a young seamstress who had befriended him on the day he arrived with his dusty, broken retinue. Both Eliza and Greeneville gave direction to the young tailor. On coming to Tennessee he could barely read; by tracing out printed words with his finger he could extract meanings from simple sentences. Writing and arithmetic were beyond him. But ambition overwhelmed the disadvantage of a belated start. During the next years, his more literate wife added her patient teaching to his own dogged perseverance. He devoured what newspapers and books he could find. Systematically improving his knowledge, he exhausted the modest libraries of the two small local colleges. Financially also, his situation improved; the shop expanded and Johnson began investing his slight surplus. Rising from poverty he sought the one safe thing on earth; and never having had property, he felt that no man was truly free until he owned a piece of ground. Thus, following the age-old aspiration of the landless, he took his spare cash and bought land, first the cheaper farmland and then city lots. To him, their ownership represented security and independence.

Besides Eliza and independence and the beginnings of an education, Greeneville meant something else to Johnson, something Raleigh could never mean to an underdog. It meant the place where his kind of man was given a chance and esteemed. Set in the mountains, its surrounding slopes were unsuitable to the plantation system which dominated North Carolina and was coming to absorb the central and western parts of Tennessee. Since slavery played a minor part in the local economy and the ownership of slaves counted comparatively little in the definitions of social caste, the small farmer, the merchant, and the workingman were recognized as East Tennessee's substantial men.

Few other sections of the South were so democratic. Fiercely proud of their plebeian status, acutely conscious of their differences, these people were forever at odds with the planters who tried to govern them. In the 1780's, years before Tennessee achieved statehood, they revolted against their North Carolinian government in an abortive effort to define their own destinies. Appropriately enough, they named their "state" after Benjamin Franklin. In the nineteenth century when the plantation system hemmed them in, while others established slavery in the lower hills and along the river bottoms to the west, the Eastern Tennesseans retained their individualism and their pride in themselves as common men. Here, they gave abolitionism its one strong foothold in the South. And, when the Civil War came, East Tennessee belonged in its sympathies as much to the Union as to the Confederacy. Ever since it has sent a consistent flow of Republican representatives to Washington and Nashville, a bastion of unorthodoxy in the South, in what otherwise is the most homogeneous section of the United States.

The Greeneville of 1829, however, was as yet unshaped to any kind of politics except an opposition to domination by an incipient aristocracy. It idolized Andrew Jackson as the spokesman of the common man while it applauded the hyperbolical frontier anecdotes Davy Crockett told in the interest of Whig conservatism. It was Jackson's egalitarianism that attracted Johnson and remained one of his cardinal principles. In it Johnson found reason to exalt his own simple beginnings and substantiation for his belief in the essential rightness of the people. It infected him with a suspicion of the rich, the aristocratic and the powerful. Throughout his career, he had no eye for their problems, no real interest in promoting what they desired. Thus, in the South, where the problems of the rich and aristocratic were slavery and the extension of the plantation system, he was not their ally. As Andrew Jackson had considered slavery the lesser matter, so did Andrew Johnson. Incidental to other matters, he might occasionally find himself on the side of the slaveholders; but just as incidentally, he would find himself in opposition to them. If, in later years, he sometimes took his stand against abolition and the other emancipation schemes that came out of the North, he also could be totally unperturbed at what his southern colleagues thought northern aggressions. The differences between his reasoning and theirs were too wide to be bridged by the accidental fact that he was a southerner by birth and residence.

Because Jackson was a Democrat, Andrew Johnson aligned himself with the same party. Until his death he gave lip service to the dogma of party regularity. But his was the Democracy of the Jacksonian ideal;

he detested the rigidity of creed and the implicit class-stratification Calhoun's wing of the party stood for as much as he despised some of the Whigs for their aristocracy and plunderous instincts. Though the party gradually lost its egalitarian drive during the 1840's and 1850's and fell into the control of those sympathetic to the South and those determined to extend slavery, Johnson continued to argue his case—that of benefiting the plebeian. On certain vital issues, as the annexation of Texas and the fugitive slave law of 1850, he could vote with the South; but more and more he found his allies in the North, sided with them and accepted their help. More and more he diverged from the other southern leaders until, by 1860, he was one of the few active Jacksonians left in his section. Being a Jacksonian above all else, he had identified himself with the common man in an era when the core of southern philosophy held that commonality and the plantation system were antithetical.

* * *

To Johnson, the artisans of Greeneville and the mountaineers of East Tennessee were the people. His occupation as a tailor, his ownership of a small farm—these made him feel he was one of them. These people helped to educate him; from them he believed he had received his values and his principles; they had made his first success possible. As the first audience he ever addressed they had cheered him, given him confidence in his abilities as a speaker, an accomplishment of which he was pardonably if greatly proud. In a region where stump oratory was a major sport, they had pronounced him the best around, warmed to his words, and by their response so roused him out of his normal reticence that he became a different man so long as he held the rostrum.

Then too, the local debating forums and the group of artisans that met in Johnson's shop had carried him into politics when he was but twenty years old. Three times they elected him a town alderman, and three times they made him the town's mayor. It is no wonder that these were the people to whom Johnson felt closest. Significantly, these were the only men, aside from President Abraham Lincoln, that Johnson ever fully trusted or spoke with easily. Toward all others he maintained some of his impenetrable reserve, partly out of distrust for their representing something other than what he represented, partly in fear of revealing some nuance that might point up the lowness of his origin and the informality of his education. For, though he readily admitted his hard struggle, he never quite overcame a sense that he might be inferior to those who had been better favored in birth and schooling.

This inferiority, however, was not manifested by his playing the sycophant, by seeking the endorsement of those who might scorn him for his social position. Johnson was quick to recognize the social gulf between the farmer and workingman on the one hand and the planter on the other. With occasional demagoguery he exploited the latent hostility between them, but he openly stood foursquare with the people from whom he had come and toward whom the Jacksonian ideal was directed. While in the state legislature at Nashville from 1835 to 1843, he fought the Jacksonian battle. As Jackson had concentrated his fire on the aristocratic and the privileged, so Johnson advocated a program designed to appeal to the common man. His suspicions were those of the small man, those the agrarian holds toward the methods of capitalism. A measure authorizing a bond issue to pay for a system of turnpikes came up. The roads were especially needed in the mountain country, like the district he represented, but he thought the plan of financing too wild and, though it temporarily cost him his seat, opposed it. He was vindicated in the crash of 1837.

A few years later he was fighting the state policy of hiring out convicts in competition with free labor. During his last term as a state legislator he fathered two measures aimed toward giving independence and power to the free laborer and the small farmer who did his own work. Drawing from Tennessee's past he called for a new state, again named Franklin, to be made up of the mountain sections of Tennessee, Virginia, North Carolina and Georgia. Here, the small farmer and the mechanic would be freed from the "tyranny of a social and industrial system [slavery] which held them fast"; manual labor would have its true dignity and chattel labor would have reduced importance.

Foreshadowing the agitation to come upon the South from the North, Johnson attacked the state constitutional provision by which slaves were counted for representation in the legislature to the amount of three-fifths of their total number. Borrowed from the Federal Constitution, this clause produced the same effect in Nashville that it did in Washington. Where in Congress citizens of the free states were underrepresented while citizens of the slave states were overrepresented, in the Tennessee state capitol, members from the western plantation counties sat in actual control over the eastern common folk. That the planters as a minority of the state's free population should hold a preponderance of power over the majority chafed at Johnson's democratic instincts. His proposed solution was as bold as any a northerner could suggest, short of abolition. He demanded that the old basis of representation be wiped out and replaced by a new plan under which only whites would be counted. Understandably, his scheme earned him the lasting enmity of local slavery politicians. Needless to say neither this nor the idea for the state of Franklin made headway.

In these years Whiggery was carrying off its bid for power, and Johnson, popular at home but in a hopeless minority at Nashville, decided to carry his fight to Congress. Once again, he stood as a laborer, and on his election through five terms remained a southern maverick. True, he voted to annex Texas; but he also agitated for the "reoccupation of Oregon" in contradistinction to most southern Representatives, Whig and Democrat alike. When Jefferson Davis attacked him for his unconventional stand on this and other matters, remarking disdainfully on his low birth and his mean trade, Johnson struck back with the full venom of a man long smouldering under abuse for his nonconformism and independent convictions. All the anger and frustration and pride in self of the ambitious mudsill were poured into the carefully chosen words he used in slashing at Davis, the personification of Mississippi's plantation civilization: "I know we have an illegitimate, swaggering, bastard, scrub aristocracy who presume to know a great deal, but who, when the flowing veil of pretension is torn off from it, is seen to possess neither talents nor information on which one can rear a useful superstructure. . . . Sir, I vindicate the mechanical profession."

But all in all, ten years of independent behavior in the face of southern criticisms, ten years of finding occasional allies among the northern antislavery men, produced an unimpressive legislative record and, on the whole, a not very rewarding series of orations on the issues before the country. Yet, Andrew Johnson had gone to Congress as the spokesman of the underprivileged, and to one important measure he gave his name and devotion. Remembering his own insecurity as a man with only his labor to sell, sympathetic with the plight of the landless who wished to farm but lacked the means to purchase, he took as his province the fostering of the dormant homestead legislation first proposed years before. That the landless would be rendered happy and prosperous if given their own land, he felt intuitively from his own experience. That there was land for all who wanted it in the western territories seemed to him obvious.

The existing policy had been generally to sell lands at $1.25 an acre; or, where the impecunious had simply gone west and appropriated the unsettled tracts to themselves, Congress would periodically heed their pleas and petitions by granting them their ownership rights in a series of pre-emption laws. To Johnson, the holding of the public lands for sale was merely a device for keeping from them those who needed them most, the poor. His thesis ran: the revenue derived from sales was negligible when compared to what could be obtained from the taxation of these same lands covered with prosperous farms. But the fiscal argument aside, "the life, the liberty and the happiness of the people" were contingent upon their owning land. The laborer bound by his lack of capital to stay in those large cities Johnson so distrusted, the small farmer ruined from competition with the large operator or going deeper into poverty as he clung to his exhausted farm in the East—these were the men who were the country's backbone and who must be saved. Give each man free and outright ownership to 160 acres of the western lands after he had farmed them for a certain length of time and the evils in the country would most certainly be mitigated.

As was to be expected the homestead bill met a diverse and well-prepared opposition. The southern aristocracy, which in legislative terms meant the great majority of the southern congressional delegations, saw in it the end to the spread of the plantation system. Land speculators mobilized to protect the opportunities for high and easy profits that such a law threatened. Within a few years railroad and mineral promoters were busy fighting to keep their rights-of-way and their government-granted concessions free of stubborn, pauper farmers. And, during the fifties, Know Nothings took the point of view that free land meant an inevitable influx of Catholic immigrants, first to overrun the face of the country and then its government and the Protestant religion.

When in 1846, Johnson first offered his bill to the House and saw it pass, his support, not unnaturally, came from northern Congressmen—those who were in a short time to join the fervid Free Soil crusade, the abolition and emancipation movements, and eventually the Republican Party. The South, even including its slaves, had by then slipped into a minority and no longer controlled the lower chamber of Congress. In the Senate, it still held power; and in concert with the conservative senators sent to protect the commercial interests of the Northeast, it regularly defeated this single proposal of Johnsonian democracy that had found its way into legislative expression.

After 1857, when Johnson sat in the Senate and the popular clamor for free land could no longer be summarily rejected, the homestead bill became inextricably tangled with the great debate on slavery. The Tennessean received his strongest assistance from the outspoken abolitionist Benjamin Franklin Wade of Ohio and the ambitious and slippery William H. Seward of New York. As formerly the chorus of condemnation was led by Senator Jefferson Davis of Mississippi. Mention of a homestead law was certain to evoke from the austere Mr. Davis a counter-proposal to purchase Cuba for the extension of the South's "pe-

culiar institution." The author of the homestead bill displayed his old
blindness to the connection. "Why lug slavery into the matter?" he
asked. A discussion on the Ten Commandments or the Lord's Prayer,
he continued in despair, would cause someone to "find a negro in them
somewhere."

In June of 1860, a modified version which set a price of twenty-five
cents an acre was finally agreed to by most of the dissidents, and the
bill passed the Senate by the wide margin of 44 to 8, Davis joining Johnson, Wade and Seward in the affirmative. President Buchanan was understood to be committed to signature. But the President discovered
evidences of European radicalism behind the intent of the measure and
returned it with a veto. Davis and his coterie blithely reversed themselves, upheld the veto, and once again killed Johnson's hopes. Two
years later, with his southern brethren gone from their seats in rebellion, a Republican Congress finally made the bill into law. Lincoln
signed it without hesitation. But it was too late. Many of the best lands
had been settled. Grants to promoters of western railroads had taken
more. And most significant of all, the rapid industrialization of the
North, induced by the war, was to kill forever the Jeffersonian dream of
an arcadia populated by small independent farmers.

* * *

In 1851, having been five times unable to defeat Johnson in the
mountainous First District of Tennessee, the Whigs attempted to secure their revenge by gerrymandering him out of his constituency. Successfully, they removed him from the House of Representatives but he
returned home to capture the governorship—in his victory taking the
measure of the man who had engineered the scheme. For two terms he
gave the state an administration consistent with the plebeian views he
had spoken for as a legislator. But the range of the governor's chair he
found too narrow. He had benefited the poor by forcing through an extensive public education and library program supported by broad taxation; out of sentiment, he had gotten the state to purchase the Hermit-
age. He had successfully challenged "easy money" speculators in bank
notes. In Washington, however, his homestead program was stalled. A
dissatisfied Governor, he therefore arranged that his legislature send
him to the Senate of the United States, and Andrew Johnson returned
to assume his role of spokesman for the nation's underprivileged.

By this time the Jacksonian debate had been superseded. The issues
were no longer egalitarianism versus privilege, or individualism against
monopoly. In the North, abolitionists said the issue was freedom or

slavery, agrarians denounced encroachments by industry and the city, the conservative business community on the one hand opposed abolitionism and on the other fought to master or contain the young behemoth of industrial capitalism. Between the sections, free soil contended with the ambitions of slavery. And in the South, the keynote was defense, the preservation of the foundations of southern society. Andrew Johnson, who had come for other purposes, was lost in matters that had always been secondary in his thinking. He floundered about, seeking to divorce homesteads and Jacksonian democracy from the central problems of the times. That he failed to do so was implicit in his faith. Where most southerners who faced that contradiction chose slavery and rejected Jacksonism, he held fast to what he thought would have been the way of Old Hickory. His decision was difficult; but slavery being of lesser importance, he could look at it without the moral indignation of an abolitionist or the fevered approbation of a planter.

Like all the statesmen and politicians of the ante-bellum period, Johnson swore his allegiance to the Constitution in every important speech. But unlike many of the rest he placed nothing above it. He recognized none of Seward's "higher law"; he wasted no words on the logic-chopping of Calhoun, Toombs and Davis whose involved doctrine admitted the Constitution might be the supreme law of the United States but declared that the desires of South Carolina, Georgia or Mississippi were superior to any federal compact. To the states as the guardians of simple democracy and as the agents of the beneficent individualism in which he believed, Johnson was willing to grant full power; but to the states as entities capable of disrupting the federal government he gave no recognition. The Constitution, he believed, by reason of its preamble belonged not to the states but to the people. The states had rights, but no sovereignty whatsoever; they had long since surrendered it to insure a perpetual Union. These two pillars of his faith—the Constitution and the Union—when added to the third of Jacksonian democracy, rendered him impervious to the southern exhortations that he behave like a southerner. But they could not save him from a devious course. So long as there was peace he vacillated between the demands of his section and the demands of his faith.

Thus, during the anxious period in which the people of the free states were refusing to abide by the provisions of the fugitive slave law, in which the men of slavery, abetted now in their ambitions by the Dred Scott decision, pressed for the extension of slavery into the territories, Johnson could argue against abolition and vote with his section. He could vote for the extreme position implicit in these resolutions presented by Jefferson Davis in February of 1860 to the effect that Congress must legislate slavery *into* the territories, that the federal government was duty-bound to provide the same protection to slaves "as to other species of property." In the campaign, he could give active support to the southern Democratic ticket of Breckinridge and Lane which adhered to the Davis resolutions and more than tacitly endorsed the Davis theory of secession.

Yet, there was always the fundamental difference between Johnson and the slavery men. He defended slavery simply because it existed, not because he considered it "a positive good." He accepted the Davis resolutions in trade for votes on the homestead bill; and he campaigned for Breckinridge on the unlikely assumption that this was the best road toward the preservation of the Union. When the southern statesmen demonstrated clearly that they believed the homestead proposition a dangerous northern plaything, and that slavery was antecedent to any ties of Union, Johnson needed no deep heartsearching to know where his first loyalties lay. His faith in the Union was his ready guide.

Lincoln's election had sent the statesmen of the lower South scurrying in the direction of secession and had left the Border States—North Carolina, Virginia, Maryland, Tennessee, Kentucky, Arkansas and Missouri—undecided between disunion and adherence to a United States granting new concessions to slavery. Johnson refused to be moved by the danger the secessionists said was now at hand. While South Carolinians in convention were leading the way by going through the formalities of declaring themselves independent of the United States, Johnson told his decision to the Senate, where many other southerners still hung on, awaiting word from their own states.

Both sides were wrong, he said, the North for enacting its "so-called liberty bills" which contravened the fugitive slave law and the Constitution, the South for arrogating to itself the wanton doctrine of secession. But this, he contended, was not the real point of issue. "It is this and only this, we are mad because Mr. Lincoln has been elected President and we have not got our man. If we had got our man we should not be for breaking up the Union, but as Mr. Lincoln was elected we are for breaking up the Union!" There was no doubt that while Johnson had failed to perceive the deeper causes for division, he had nailed down the surface impulse that had brought strife into the open.

The effect was sensational. To the southern mind Johnson's words seemed close to treason. Jefferson Davis, Wigfall of Texas and Lane of Oregon—a Senator from a northern state but himself a "doughface" of Virginian birth—were long and vitriolic in their replies and ridicule.

Only Judah P. Benjamin of Louisiana, soon destined for the Confederacy's cabinet, tried reasonable persuasion to coax the Tennessean into the otherwise solid southern ranks. To the awakening North, however, the speech provided an unexpected prop to the Union cause. It caught something of the fervor in which politicians, laboring men, small farmers and the press had espoused Republicanism. And it won Johnson both a heroic reputation among them and a position as the pre-eminent unionist of the South. For immediate purposes, the latter was the more important. Governor Harris, his successor, had been spurred by Lincoln's call for 75,000 men on April 15, 1861, to make extra-legal moves toward aligning Tennessee with the Confederacy. Johnson went home, at some peril to his life, to fight Harris; and though he lost the state to the secessionists, East Tennessee remained loyal, eventually supplying the Northern armies with 35,000 troops and innumerable guerillas.

*　　*　　*

In July, 1861, a special session of Congress met, called by Lincoln to take official cognizance of the insurrection and to ratify the actions already accomplished by the Executive. To these purposes, Johnson gave quick assent. Of more lasting importance to Lincoln and Johnson were the resolutions defining the aims of the war that the Tennessean laid before Congress. Because in the following years this statement was to become Lincoln's justification for his conduct of the war and Johnson's foundation argument for his own policies of the peace, it deserves extended quotation. "The present deplorable Civil war," ran the text, "has been forced upon the country by the dis-Unionists of the Southern States, now in revolt against the Constitutional government and in arms around the Capital; in this National emergency Congress, banishing all feeling of mere passion or resentment, will recollect on its duty to the whole country; this war is not prosecuted upon our part in any spirit of oppression, nor for any purpose of conquest or subjugation, nor for the purpose of over-throwing or interfering with the rights or established institutions of those states, but to defend and maintain the supremacy of the Constitution and all laws made in the pursuance thereof, and to preserve the Union, with all the dignity, equality and rights of the several states unimpaired, and as soon as these objects are accomplished the war ought to cease."

After some debate the resolutions passed. In the House, the same set was fostered by John J. Crittenden—grown venerable in political service and now upholding his nationalistic Whig beliefs by adhering to the

Union. But foretelling the rupture of the future were those old-line abolitionists—Senator Charles Sumner of Massachusetts and Representative Thaddeus Stevens of Pennsylvania—who refused to vote rather than sanction such limited objectives.

By February of the next year, the successes of General Grant in central Tennessee had not only given encouragement to an administration exasperated by McClellan's disinclination to make progress below the Potomac, but had also presented Lincoln with the problem of setting up a military government over the conquered region. Accordingly, on the President's nomination and with the Senate's confirmation on March 4th, Andrew Johnson became Military Governor of his home state with the rank of Brigadier General.

Arriving at Nashville about a week later, Johnson stepped into perhaps the most unenviable job of the war. Occupation governments are seldom popular, and his followed the general rule. The people of this part of the state were sympathetic to the Confederacy and would remain so long after it had collapsed. The indecisiveness of Northern arms kept them in constant hope that the invader might eventually be repulsed, and Johnson's government pulled down. Alternately, their hopes waxed and waned at the outcomes of the more than 700 separate military engagements and 100 battles proper that were fought on Tennessee soil. In the end what they got was a state thoroughly devastated with its people sent into destitution.

Over this scene Johnson ruled in a manner not calculated to win him local applause. As military governor he was at once the executive, the legislature, and the judiciary. He tried to be fair, but both the subjects and his unionists were in an unco-operative mood. Efforts he made to relieve civilian distress were constantly nullified by new battles. Attempts to reclaim the state's broken transportation system were upset by Union losses and the depredations of Confederate guerillas. The hostility of the population brought recurrent enforcements of strict martial law. Union military commanders were a continual source of irritation. Disagreements arose over jurisdictions, over interpretations, over objectives. Johnson, having been charged with the duty of not only contributing to victory but of leading his state back to peace and an acceptance of the Union, found perpetual conflict between the two obligations.

The problems of dealing with Forrest's and Morgan's raiders and of supplying the Northern forces made constant inroads on his time. Meanwhile, as long as the war lasted, he was obsessed by the thought that southern resistance was treason, and that "treason must be made odious." Secessionists found in him little that was forgiving. Especially against the wealthy and the planters, whom he believed to be the instigators and the leaders of rebellion, was his hatred directed. For all practical purposes, he excommunicated them; all others who gave aid, comfort or friendship to the Confederacy, he suspected. His instructions called for bringing Tennessee back into the Union, and Johnson was determined to bring her back only as a state cleansed and purged of her sins. Here, he collided with the ambitions of unionist politicians who had returned with him to Nashville but who looked ahead to peacetime when they might rule the state themselves, without Johnson and his federal bayonets. They courted the temporarily disfranchised in the hope that appeasement would give them popularity by contrast with the Military Governor. They took issue with him over his loyalty oaths and tried to secure open elections in which they might unseat him. War or no, politics was never in abeyance.

Through it all, Andrew Johnson fought his battle, living in danger of assassination or capture, working furiously toward winning the war, reclaiming Tennessee's loyalty. For three years he persevered oblivious to his future, scotching political conspiracies against him, devoted to his principle of preserving the Union. But while he labored outside forces were in motion—forces creating a different Union than the one he knew, forces to lift him from the turbulence of war and set him within the vortex of political faction.

2. LINCOLNIAN SUCCESSION

In the spring of 1864 General Dan Sickles came down to Nashville on a secret mission. From his title one would have suspected he came on military matters, and ostensibly he did; but, in reality, his task was to investigate for President Lincoln the record of Tennessee's Military Governor. If Andrew Johnson had not been too much a tyrant, Lincoln thought he might be an excellent running mate in the autumn presidential election.

Probably Sickles himself had no knowledge of the President's ulterior motive as he probed for information. Throughout that spring Lincoln was even more taciturn than usual. When anyone, by indirection or subtlety, tried to extract from him his favorite vice-presidential candidate, the answer was amiable but vague. Vice-President Hannibal Hamlin of Maine had been elected with Lincoln in 1860. There were those who supported him for renomination, though Hamlin openly expressed scant personal respect for the President—a viewpoint Lincoln apparently never held against any man—and disagreed with the administration's war policies as well as its methods of rehabilitating pacified areas. Yet the White House raised no strenuous disapprovals at suggestions that Hamlin succeed himself. Leonard Swett, who had once been the Chief Executive's law partner, was promoting the candidacy of Joseph Holt, a rabidly loyal Kentuckian. Holt, a Democrat, had been Postmaster General under Buchanan and, during the last weak days of Buchanan's term, a strong-willed but futilely energetic Secretary of War attempting to prevent southern aggressions from getting out of hand; now he was the Army's Judge Advocate General. That Swett was talking up Holt's name led to the presumption that Lincoln could not be averse to this candidacy.

Other rumors filled the air wherever men gossiped about politics. There were stories, originating with former War Secretary Simon Cameron and Major General Benjamin F. Butler, of how Lincoln had sent Cameron to offer Butler the nomination, and how Butler had refused the tender out of preference for the security of his army commission. Several felt Butler had his eye on a higher goal, that he wanted no association with an administration he thought was bound for defeat. Still others were to disclose, in after years, that they had received an explicit presidential blessing for Andrew Johnson; at least, they had overheard Seward pronounce for the Tennessean, and surely the Secretary of State would not differ from his chief over the matter of the potential successor to the presidency.

But well did Lincoln carefully refrain from giving any endorsements. Though he and his managers were confident of his own renomination, they were by no means certain of his re-election. At the beginning of the war popular opinion on both sides had insisted it would be over after a single decisive battle. Instead, it had dragged along for three years. The President had not been one of the optimists; but many forgot this fact in their own unwarranted confidences, and charged the protracted length of the struggle to his bungling. That spring General Grant's bloody grinding at Lee's forces in The Wilderness seemed to be producing nothing but horror. To the tired people of the North, the incessant calls for ever more men and always more money were becoming exasperatingly monotonous. The mistakes and inconsistencies that every fallible human leader and his more fallible subordinates commit when bending all efforts to one huge goal had created irritations and frictions. These were seized upon by opposition politicians and by "Copperheads" as arguments in condemning the war as a failure.

Within what was nominally his own party, a sizable group of extremists, dissatisfied with the President's methods of leading the nation in war and greatly perturbed at the indications of how he proposed to handle the peace, were plotting to overthrow his party leadership and put up Grant or one of their own number. Or failing that, they considered a third party movement, the result of which would split the Republican vote and give the election to the Democrats. In fact, that May, one such combination did nominate General John C. Frémont and only with the strongest reluctance and worst grace did he grudgingly withdraw to make room for the regular ticket. Obviously Lincoln played sound politics in avoiding the merest hint of dictating a vice-presidential selection on his party.

Still, there were plain facts to be considered by the delegates to the Republican convention when they picked their second-place nominee. Ultimately the party would stand or fall on the record of its first administration; and assuredly it could depend upon a certain quantity of votes from its regular adherents. But in a race likely to be exceedingly close, the gravitational pull of the vice-presidential candidate might determine the outcome. To make the façade of the party more attractive to the outside public and to render life happier for War Democrats like Gideon Welles and the Blairs who had come within its inner gates, the convention officially dropped the contentious name of Republican and adopted the soothing one of National Union. After such a recognition of the multifarious elements that the war had encompassed inside this one party, it seemed more fitting that Lincoln's partner should be a War Democrat and perhaps a champion of labor rather than an old-line Whig transmuted into a Republican. Since the party presumed to be national rather than sectional, a southerner from one of the Border States or from one of the reclaimed "wayward sisters" seemed preferable to an out-and-out northerner. And, to the President and those others who thought above the purely mundane computations of votes, a southerner on the ballot would demonstrate to a heretofore dubious Europe that the Confederacy was divided while the Union was strong.

Clearly, in these terms, Johnson was the most acceptable possibility and Hamlin, the incumbent, was among the least. Yet this by no means gave assurance that Johnson would be nominated. The exigencies of politics have been known to defeat the higher logic of things, unless sometimes aided by curiously illogical influences. Such was the case in the behind-the-scenes maneuvering of the Baltimore Republican convention. Only the essential moves and countermoves are set down here.

The central figure in the scheming that eventually put over Johnson was Senator Charles Sumner, the stiff-necked Massachusetts abolitionist who was avowed by some to be the premier among the New England statesmen of the day. Sumner, though he claimed to think only in terms of morals and never of personalities, had developed an abundant loathing for two men high in the administration councils. Toward Senator William Pitt Fessenden of Maine he thought black thoughts because that gentleman apparently gave forth the best of his considerable talents as a logician when riddling Sumner's carefully wrought theories. For Secretary of State Seward the unforgiving Sumner desired political extinction because, he was convinced, the New Yorker was the genius behind the soft policies and peace plans bearing the Lincolnian stamp.

A means of double vengeance withdrew Sumner from his higher thinking and cast him willingly into the arena of practical politics. Why not, he thought, work for the nomination of someone other than Hamlin, perhaps for a War Democrat from New York? It might appear superficially disloyal to work against the New England candidate; but still the nation would benefit. A vice-president from New York would free Hamlin to persuade the Maine legislature to give him Fessenden's senatorial seat when it came up for contest in 1865; and because it would be an impossible political situation for one state to hold both the vice-presidency and the State Department, Seward would be forced to step down. The man amenable to these arrangements was Daniel S. Dickinson, a New York Democrat with a fine record in support of the war, a personal enemy of the Secretary of State, and a man readily acceptable to those enemies of Seward and Weed who had eagerly seized upon the Sumner plot. Thus encouraged, the Massachusetts Senator began culling New England's delegations for Dickinson votes.

Word of these startling developments reached the imperiled Seward-Weed clique on the opening day of the convention. Controlling a majority of New York's delegation, the machine, on Weed's advice, quickly switched its support from Hamlin to Johnson. Thus, New York went into the balloting a divided state. The change proved the decisive one. It gave Johnson a plurality on the only roll-call vote taken, and pointed up Hamlin's poor New England showing for which Sumner had so carefully arranged. The tabulation gave Johnson 200, Hamlin 145, and Dickinson 113. In a preconcerted move Pennsylvania withdrew her complimentary fifty-two votes for the incumbent and gave them to the Tennessean. The stampede was on. When it ended, Andrew Johnson had received his nomination. The President was believed satisfied, and Charles Sumner was reported to have said he thought the ticket would be stronger if the nominations had been reversed. Thad Stevens, however, had sounded a sour note: "Can't you get a candidate for vice-president without going into a damned rebel province for one?"

*   *   *

With its leading candidate expending his energies in directing a war, and with its second man busy trying to pacify a recalcitrant state, the National Union party relied upon its lesser men and its press to pound its truths into the people. The task of all appeared overwhelming. The Union armies were apparently stalled; Grant lost men in his assaults faster than he gained ground; Sherman's troops were skirmishing indecisively in the Georgia and Tennessee mountains. Behind the lines, the administration's currency experiments had pushed prices into a cruel inflation. Wages and farm prices were good, and profits were high; but men were frightened at the economic specter. Paper money had driven gold into hiding; the dollar had fallen to half its prewar purchasing power. The party was divided, with its Lincoln wing discouraged and its extremist or Radical wing still pondering a bolt to independent action behind Frémont or Ben Butler. By the time Congress adjourned in July it looked as if it and the President had fallen out permanently over a bill of Senator Benjamin F. Wade and Representative Henry Winter Davis to take stronger action with the reconquered South than Lincoln contemplated.

The administration itself seemed on the point of collapse; for the irreconcilable cabinet members had long since refrained from giving the mildest pretense of politeness in the uncomplimentary opinions they entertained for one another. In June, Salmon P. Chase, Secretary of the Treasury, petulantly sent in his resignation only to be astonished when it was accepted; three months later Postmaster General Montgomery Blair departed, sacrificed to retain to the party the laggard support of his enemies. Clearly, the Lincoln ticket was not going to be elected if it depended merely upon the efforts of the party's politicians.

Yet, while the jealousies and disagreements continued unabated, the outlook changed. The Democratic candidate, General George McClellan, was having his own troubles. Proclaiming himself a warrior, he rode a peace-at-any-price horse and ineffectually tried to shake himself loose from the shameless endearments of the Copperheads. Despite the long war, the North was not yet prepared for such a drastic reversal of policy and leadership. More to its taste was the news that Grant was now sending his troops crashing through the Confederate lines on the road to Richmond. In the Shenandoah Valley, Sheridan's cavalry had permanently suppressed rebellion by the awful expedient of ruining the entire countryside. To the West, Sherman had finally cut his way out of the constrictions of the mountains, had taken Atlanta, and was now in pursuit of Joe Johnston's retreating force. Lincoln's generals were giving testimony to the strength and wisdom of his course. And with that lesson in mind, the deeper faith of the majority of northerners returned, and they went to the polls to elect the National Union ticket by 300,000 votes, 212 electoral votes to 21.

* * *

Between his election and inauguration day, Andrew Johnson remained at home, intent upon completing his work as governor so that his successor, W. G. Brownlow—a man who had proved his Union sympathies by going to jail rather than abide the Confederates—would have an easy time in bringing Tennessee back into the full exercise of her statehood. A carefully selected convention met at Knoxville in January 1865 to draw up amendments which would revise the state constitution to conform to a number of tenets implicit in the coming northern victory in arms. Slavery was to be abolished; loyalists who bore arms, not excluding Negro troops, were to be permitted the franchise. These having been accepted by the convention, the retiring governor felt his work near completion.

During February, however, disquieting word came from Washington. Sumner was refusing to permit recognition by Congress of the Lincoln-reconstructed state of Louisiana after she had ratified a new constitution that forbade slavery but denied Negro suffrage. To prevent a vote which, at this time, was certain to overrule him, the Senator had filibustered until the recommendation to approve had been withdrawn. Perhaps it was for the reason that Johnson's prestige as a trustworthy southern unionist might go a long way toward quelling new incipient anti-administration revolts in Congress that Lincoln desired his new Vice-President to be in Washington for the ceremonies of March 4th. Meanwhile, Johnson had been ill with typhoid. Pleading indisposition and the fatiguing journey, he asked to be excused. But the President was firm in his demand; too much was at stake to be lost by a man's illness or reluctance. Lincoln's will prevailed; the Tennessean came east.

Establishing himself comfortably at the Kirkland House he fell into the pre-inaugural social whirl. On the night of March 3rd, his admirers tendered him a party at which the animal spirits were lively and the liquid ones potent. The next morning the Vice-President-elect arose sober but rueful. Hamlin and Senator Doolittle attended him to the Capitol where, awaiting noon, when his hour would come, Johnson started to feel again the painful effects of the previous evening. Mistaking the cure of such symptoms, as certainly many others have since, he asked for some whiskey. Hamlin, a temperance man, virtuously informed him that liquor had, at his instance, been banned from the Senate restaurant, but sent out for a bottle. How much Johnson actually drank will never be known; for Hamlin told the story a number of times in the ensuing years, and with each telling, Johnson's thirst increased. But when the time for proprieties arrived, drink, a weakened physical condition, and an overheated Senate chamber had done their work on Andrew Johnson.

Washington's elite stirred slightly as it watched him step forward and begin to speak without notes. In his opening words, there was a slight belligerency in the insinuation that possibly someone, not named, had not wanted a plebeian in the office he was about to assume. In fact, as the speech progressed—if such can be the word—the plebeian note assumed a too obvious insistance. Senators, Supreme Court justices, Seward, Secretary Stanton, the Secretary of the Navy were admonished that they owed their places to the people. Then, in remorse at his plebeian ignorance of parliamentary law, he begged the indulgence of the body over which he was to preside. Again in defiance, Attorney General Speed was given to understand that Tennessee was as loyal as Kentucky, the assemblage as a whole sharply reminded that his home state was free, that it was in the Union and had never left it. Finally, with a mumbled oath of office and a grand flourish as he kissed the Bible, the spectacle was over.

The Republican senators were noted to have studied their desks. Sumner, in "exquisite" shame at the indignity of it all, had covered his face with his hands and buried his head. Lincoln had visibly drooped, and every cabinet member but Seward was plainly disturbed. Chief Justice Chase had sat like a rock. The diplomatic gallery had barely restrained itself. To those who heard both the Vice-Presidential harangue and the magnificent Second Inaugural Address the President delivered shortly afterward, the comparison left the first all the more invidious. Francis Preston Blair, the elder—a Kitchen Cabinet fixture under Jackson, unofficial adviser to the current prairie statesman, and wise and urbane after many years as an editor and politician—was among the few who chose to apply Lincoln's dictum of "charity to all" to the immediate case. Andy Johnson, he remarked, was "all right"; what had been said was not "bad sense, only bad taste." To the Blair estate at Silver Spring, Maryland, the repentant plebeian withdrew to recover his health and good name; the Senate adjourned a week later without having utilized his services. As Lincoln told his Secretary of the Treasury a few days later, Andy had "made a bad slip," but, said the President, he "ain't a drunkard."

* * *

On Good Friday, the 14th of April, Washington was still exuberant over Lee's surrender to Grant and the fall of Richmond. General Sherman was seeking Joe Johnston further south to arrange for surrender of the Confederacy's only remaining strong field force. That afternoon the Cabinet had engaged in a lively discussion over the reconstruction of the "Rebel States"; Secretary of War Stanton was detailed to revise his rough proposals into separate plans for Virginia and North Carolina. The Vice-President was in the city, back after his retreat to Silver Spring, kept in Washington from returning home to Greeneville by the surge of events. In the evening Mr. Lincoln attended a benefit performance of *Our American Cousin,* the indifferent play on the boards at Ford's Theatre; the actress Laura Keane and not her vehicle was probably the chief attraction. Mr. Johnson, once again a practicer of impeccable habits, had retired early to his rooms.

Then came the thunderclap. At the height of his greatness, Lincoln was murdered. For the first time, a President of the United States had been assassinated. Word of the tragedy spread. The city trembled in apprehension over what appeared to be a conspiracy of enormous magnitude—for Seward and his son Fred had also been attacked, how seriously none knew. The Vice-President, roused from his bed, found himself under a heavy guard of volunteers and of soldiers dispatched by Stanton. In anxiety over the news, he rushed to the house where the wounded President lay. It was too late for words; Abraham Lincoln never recovered consciousness.

The following morning Secretary of the Treasury McCulloch and Attorney General Speed carried the official tidings of Lincoln's death to Kirkland House; a letter from the Cabinet advised Johnson of his succession to the presidency. Chief Justice Chase stopped by to set the time for the swearing-in ceremonies. He was also requested to prepare a speech for the new President. Shortly afterward a somber inauguration took place in one of the hotel's parlors before a few distinguished witnesses. Chase resonantly read the oath and the Tennessean repeated it with strong feeling. When the congratulations had been given and received, Johnson responded with a short address. As the newspapers reported it he expressed grief at the circumstances that had raised him into office and humility in approaching his task. The direction his administration would take, he said, would indicate his policies. In his many previous years in public life would be found the guide to his principles. "Toil and honest advocacy of the great principles of free government have been my lot. The duties have been mine—the consequences God's.[1] This has been the foundation of my political creed."

Meanwhile, some of the members of the Cabinet, McCulloch in particular, were agitated over their own futures. Nevertheless, if Johnson had time to ponder the question of his advisory family, he must have realized that their numbers must remain intact, as he had inherited them. His predecessor, upon his first election, had clearly understood the agglomeration of minorities and factions that composed the successful Republican party. The selection of the original group had been made with that point primarily in mind. As many diversities as could be accommodated within the persons of seven individuals were ascertainable in its makeup. After four years of internecine warfare during which no one man was in the least degree appreciative of the talents of any of his six colleagues, only two of the first group remained. Still the balance of the component elements continued unchanged; the political creeds, economic faiths, geographic distributions, contending leaderships and conflicting personalities were as accurate a cross-section of the National Union party in 1865 as they had been of the Republican party in 1861.

William H. Seward—garrulous, informal, diplomatic, personally charming—the Secretary of State and one of the original Lincoln cabinet, satisfied New York, the Weed crowd, and the old-line Whigs, who constituted the bulk of the party. Ever a calculating man in his actions, he could never quite sort out what was to be done in the name of expediency and what under the dictates of principle. Much impressed with his own importance and never able to concede that Lincoln's nomination was something other than total accident, he could not quite recognize the leadership of his first chief—nor was he to assent wholly to the superiority of his second. Hugh McCulloch, Secretary of the Treasury, was new, having been in the office only a month. A banker, not a professional politician, from the key state of Indiana, he had served as comptroller of the currency before his appointment. His ap-

---

[1] The phrase was not original with Johnson. Four years before one of his Tennessee political lieutenants had used it in a letter condemning the irrevocable backwash of Buchanan's weaknesses. Coming out of the new President's mouth, however, the injunction upon the Almighty provoked a storm of criticism from the religiously sensitive. In the more turgid but never delivered message composed for him by Chase, there were far greater theological overtones, but the ways and responsibilities of the Lord were left unanalyzed.

peal, if any, lay in his essential conservatism and in his "sound money" views so important to the bankers and the new bondholding aristocracy.

Of the holdovers, the man to have unquestionably the gravest effect on Johnson's administration was Secretary of War Edwin McMaster Stanton of Pennsylvania. Contradictory is perhaps the mildest word that describes both his personality and career. A nervous, fear-ridden neurotic, he was nonetheless a highly competent official, capable of lightning and accurate decisions; a sickly man most of his life, he possessed a capacity for doing the hardest work over protracted periods of time; an abolitionist from childhood, he found no inner torments in espousing the proslavery Buchanan administration and serving it, at its end, as its Attorney General. A leading attorney and a confirmed Jacksonian, he consorted happily with and evidently suggested guidance to the Radical Republicans whose program was legally dubious and certainly revolutionary in respect to older doctrines of Union. Swearing loyalty to Buchanan's policy, he wrote detailed letters disclosing its methods and secrets to Seward, an oppositionist; then protesting his faith in Lincoln's actions, he wrote more than critically of them to Buchanan. Yet Stanton was necessary for his ability, his Democratic label, his Radical affinities, and his residence.

His counterpart in the Navy Department was Stanton's opposite in nearly every respect but the undoubted competence and sour temper they shared. Gideon Welles of Connecticut, and hence New England's member, was the other survivor from 1861. Despite his early adherence to the Republican party he still retained to himself the label and convictions of a Jacksonian Democrat. Utterly loyal to his chief and unshakable in his principles, he was in the privacy of his famous *Diary* and the more open cabinet meetings the outspoken critic of Seward and Stanton. Though prevented from securing many elective offices by his penchant for speaking his mind, his excellent judgment won him respect and not inconsiderable power among political leaders. His antislavery opinions had never verged on abolitionism; consequently, he was frequently assailed by the Radicals. He and a cabinet member of later times, Harold Ickes, held remarkably similar traits in common —complete honesty in their devotion to duty and the public service; a stubborn independence of opinion regardless of party; the quality to detect the bad and the weaknesses in the men with whom they had to work; the gift of pillorying a man with a phrase; a self-righteousness that approached belligerency when confronted with a contrary opinion. Both have left ample words and judgments on their respective eras;

a surprising number of Welles's are accurate; Ickes', of course, have still to be tested.

Border State representation in the cabinet fell to Attorney General James Speed of Kentucky. Holding his position by virtue of the 1864 shakeup, he had benefited from his brother Joshua's friendship with Lincoln and his own previous work as the Great Emancipator's adviser on affairs in the Bluegrass country, when it teetered precipitously between Union and secession. Having been an antislavery man where and when such sentiments were markedly repugnant, he was thought to be a worthy addition to a coalition government; with the end of the war his politics were moving closer and closer to Radical Republicanism. Before Speed's exit from Johnson's ministry, Charles Sumner would call him the "best of the Cabinet."

Postmaster General William Dennison had been Ohio's energetic if unpopular war governor, chairman of the 1864 convention, and beneficiary of Montgomery Blair's demise. His banking and railroad interests made him a genuine conservative in economic views; but his political and moral thoughts were wavering between conservatism and extremism. Interior Secretary Usher had previously submitted his resignation, and Johnson, giving evidence of the spirit in which he wished to carry on his predecessor's policies, appointed James Harlan of Iowa who had already been designated as Usher's replacement. This frontier lawyer and schoolteacher had been a long-time advocate of sectional legislation—homesteads, college land grants, railroad grants—and came with a strong record of participation in the Free Soil and Abolition movements. He would connote the West and its aspirations.

Thus, all in all, the ministry mirrored the National Union coalition and the incongruity of its elements. Whigs, Free Soilers, Democrats, Radicals, conservatives, moderates, reasonable men, fanatical men, men from each loyal section, compromising men, inflexible men—all were to be found in the personalities and records of the seven officers who headed the executive departments.

Congress was not to meet until December. By all standards, but those of the members of the legislature, this perhaps was a good thing. For by then, hostilities would definitely have ended; those congressional agents that had been Lincoln's constant irritants would have vanished. The most persistent of them, the Joint Committee on the Conduct of the War, would have lost its reason for existence. In 1861, Lincoln had gotten the jump on more experienced politicians and statesmen—who would have been only too happy to direct the nation's course—by the simple fact that Congress was not in session. Using his advantage, he had carried the supremacy of the Executive through his term. His successor had a longer period in which to establish control; and he had, as well, the lessons of the immediate past to guide him in his strategy. Through the next eight relatively unhampered months, Johnson would have his chance to promote a policy that Congress could set aside only at its own peril.

But when Congress did convene, its heavy Republican majority promised nothing so far as support of an administration program was concerned. While open rupture between the Radical and moderate wings had been averted—and barely averted at that—for the purposes of winning the election, the battle for dominance of the party was far from settled. Where the Radical Henry Winter Davis had been defeated by his Maryland constituency, and where the moderate Lincoln had won the country, the mandate handed down by the voters was certainly far more an endorsement of the happier turn the war had taken than of the reconstruction policy of the President. To the country as a whole reconstruction was still a debatable issue. Proof of this lay in the composition of the House. If Davis was gone, many Radicals, notably Thaddeus Stevens and George Julian, had been returned.

The same was true in the Senate, though, of course, only a third of its seats had come before the consideration of the state legislatures. Several essentially conservative men like Fessenden of Maine had strong influence when the question at hand called for logical reasoning; but these solons were erratic in their decisions if the sole issue lay in supporting or attacking policy created by the Executive branch. Their usefulness was limited by an extreme jealousy of the co-ordinate position of Congress in the framework of government and of the independent status of the upper house. Moderates of the stripe of John Sherman of Ohio, brother of the General, and Lyman Trumbull of Illinois had in the past been unstable in their partisan loyalties, swinging between three poles—administration policy, congressional criticisms and their own independence. The Radical coterie centering around Wade of Ohio, Chandler of Michigan and Wilson of Massachusetts would be wanting things its own way. The years of tilting at Lincoln and champing at his successful ripostes had left it, if anything, more determined on rule. The fact that the Radicals had not been headed—merely put off—had permitted them to retain and perhaps increase their strength.

One man, with slight leadership in Congress but strong influence with the old abolitionist societies, was certain to join them on most vital matters; Charles Sumner—holding himself aloof from all he thought mundane, icy toward all that smacked of emotionalism or sentimentality, warmed only by the implications of the many theories he had evolved and by his hatreds—would vote Radical. To whatever subject he turned his attention, he deemed that field his especial province; and, without question, it felt in turn the impact of his considerable intellect. A better man than his recent critics have portrayed him, he was nevertheless not nearly the hero his contemporaneous idolaters thought him. For the post-bellum period, he had decided to encompass as his own the extending of equal rights to the Negroes; on how closely any given party group or wing agreed with him would determine Sumner's power.[2]

Thus the Republican engine which Lincoln had driven for four years and which was to be Johnson's for four more was a makeshift affair. Many of its pieces bore small relationship to the others; in fact, some conflicted with others and impaired its efficiency. That it had taken one direction under the railsplitter President was no indication the same course could or would be followed by a driver who had succeeded him. Indeed, the possibility was that the engine would be stripped of some of its superfluous parts and the machine itself switched to a new track. The questions were, which parts were to go and which track was to be taken?

3. PRELUDE TO BATTLE

At his first meeting with the cabinet Johnson allayed McCulloch's fears on tenure by asking the entire ministry to remain in office. Again he repeated that his acts would disclose his policies, but this time he added that "in all essentials" these would follow Lincoln's. The second meeting, the next day, came closer to grips with problems. With Lee's force surrendered and word of Johnston's capitulation expected momentarily from Sherman, the war was, for practical purposes, over. Kirby Smith's roaming hordes in Texas would be pacified at the administration's convenience and ease, or would find their way over the Mexican border; they constituted no hazard to the peace. In any case, the government of the South could no longer be put off. And the

[2] Sumner's critics have made much of the fact that he advocated equal rights for Negroes wholly as a theoretical proposition, that socially he had not the slightest interest in mingling with the beneficiaries of his plans. The statement is undeniably true; but the implications are false. Sumner was a cold, ungregarious soul who unbent only in the Olympian company of Emerson and Whittier, of whom he was a close friend. A number of his critics, who are quite impassioned on his faults, in discussing this manifestation of Sumner's refusal to practice his own theories, appear suspiciously happy in the telling. In citing the contradiction and impaling Sumner on his inconsistency, there are overtones in their discussions that suggest they believe the theory rather than the practice to be the element of inconsistency.

President, after three years of experience in Tennessee, seemed eminently fitted for the task of shaping his section's new place in the Union.

The Radicals undoubtedly thought so. On Johnson's first evening in office, Sumner called to press the matter of Negro suffrage. The new President evidently listened quietly and without comment, for the Senator came away supposing he had a friend in the Executive. That same day a caucus of Radicals made plans for a total revision of the cabinet and the scotching of "Lincolnism." Coming to the President the following afternoon, they listened appreciatively to his remarks on the proper fate of traitors. "Johnson, we have faith in you," said Ben Wade, enthusiastically. "By the gods, there will be no trouble now in running the Government." Unfortunately, where agreement had been so easy, neither party thought of asking the other what he meant by "treason."

Within the bosom of the Executive branch, considerations were meanwhile turning toward setting the postwar Republican machine in motion. If the record of the railsplitter was to count, a fair start at reconstruction had already been made. As early as 1862, Andrew Johnson had begun his work in Tennessee; by the time of his ascendancy, he believed her ready for full recognition. A shadowy government had existed in Virginia, chiefly to give legality to the wartime separation of West Virginia from the Old Dominion. "Ten per cent" governments—based on Lincoln's plan of December 1863 to set up civil authority wherever that proportion of the legal voters had sworn their loyalty to the United States in a mild test-oath—were functioning in Louisiana and Arkansas. Moreover, at the cabinet meeting on that fateful April 14th, Stanton had been instructed to prepare schemes giving more substance to the Virginia adumbration and providing for the establishment of civil authority in North Carolina. That the majority of southerners had never had a word to say on any of the plans, that the plans had been handed to Congress as *faits accomplis,* never troubled Lincoln in a legal sense. His job, he felt, was to end the military phase as easily and speedily as possible, and to return the southern states to civil rule. His strictures were simple: they must renounce secession; they must swear loyalty to the United States; they must be done with slavery. Negro suffrage, in some degree, he rather wished for but did not require unconditionally; revenge or dire punishment he consistently opposed.

Johnson's first real problem, therefore, revolved around Virginia and North Carolina. Stanton's plan again came up at the second cabinet meeting. Its major features were that the Pierpont administration in Virginia be strengthened and the President initiate a provisional government in North Carolina. The latter step would supposedly establish the formula for the beginning of civil rule in the other six southern states. These cabinet deliberations were, of course, to remain secret until Johnson decided on the exact method he chose to use. His energetic Secretary of War, however, was consulting with Radical leaders, presumably informing them of the discussions, and working with them on the best means of including Negro suffrage in the plan. Meanwhile, Attorney General Speed was at work on an amnesty proclamation, the contents of which would guide the provisional governors in the appointments they made to office and in carrying out elections for delegates to the constitutional conventions that would have to draw up new codes of organic law for the returning states. Both the reconstruction and the amnesty proclamations were to be issued at about the same time, so as to present, in its entirety, the administration's program for the resumption of government in the South.

On May 9, by executive order, the Pierpont government was given full recognition. On the same day, there was an explosion in the cabinet. Stanton had presented his draft. Comprehended within it was a statement that state constitutional convention members were to be elected by "loyal citizens of the United States residing within the state." Welles gagged on this, and forced from the colleague he abhorred the admission that "blacks and whites" were intended in the coverage. A general debate followed over the legitimacy and advisability of federal "interference" in state affairs and on Negro suffrage in particular. In a poll of opinions the ministry split down the middle—Stanton, Dennison and Speed strongly favorable; Welles, McCulloch and Usher as strongly opposed;[3] Johnson expressed no opinion but decided to give his personal attention to the draft. Together with Preston King—an old Jacksonian, an abolitionist, now a New York ally of the Seward-Weed machine, and a man high in the presidential confidence—he shaped the North Carolina proclamation into final form. On May 24th, each cabinet member was specifically asked to state his feelings; each, including Stanton, registered his full endorsement of Johnson's reconstruction plan.

The 29th of May saw the announcement of the two proclamations. For North Carolina, the President appointed a provisional governor who was charged with the duty of convoking a constitutional conven-

---

[3] Seward was still absent, recovering from the assault made on him the night of Lincoln's assassination.

tion "at the earliest practicable period." The convention was to alter the existing (i.e., prewar) state constitution so that it conformed to republican principles of government. This done, the state could then expect to be restored in its "constitutional relations" with the rest of the Union. One limitation was set down: no one would be permitted to participate as a voter or delegate unless he took the amnesty oath and was qualified to exercise these privileges under the laws in force prior to the "so-called ordinance of secession."

For the South as a whole, the President set down an oath under which repentant southerners, with certain exceptions, could return to political grace. Some were specifically banned from participation—generally speaking, high government or military officers of the Confederacy, all who left certain important civil posts to go over to the South, officers who quit military or naval service with the United States, men who left the North to join the slavery cause. These were required to make direct application to the President for pardon. One proscribed class, those rebels with over $20,000 in property, reflected, by their enumeration on the list, Johnson's lasting contempt for the "scrub aristocracy." In effect, under the amnesty terms, the leaders were to be punished, the rank and file let off with an apology and a promise of future good behavior.

In all, between May 29th and July 13th, seven presidential rescripts were announced inaugurating civil government in those pacified states left unprovided for at Lincoln's death. This done, Johnson considered the next step—the establishing of republican forms of government and restoration in the Union—up to the states themselves. Mutterings, however, were beginning to fall from Radical lips; Radical pens commenced to scratching busily. As might be expected, the first attack came from Boston abolitionism at the hands of Sumner and Wendell Phillips. From there, it spread toward the Middle West. In Lancaster, Pennsylvania, Thad Stevens saw the chances for the strong policy he advocated growing dimmer; to Sumner, he wrote suggesting an alliance, a movement of mutual self-protection before Johnson was "crowned king." To the President, he wrote with unaccustomed conciliation, respectfully pleading with him to hold off "and await the action of Congress."

From the South, too, came unpleasant tidings. Ostensibly on a mission gathering information for the President, Major General Carl Schurz was supplementing his military income by sending regular dispatches on his findings to northern Radical newspapers. That Schurz was normally a man of integrity made these press reports particularly damaging to Johnson's program. They had the additional quality of telling the Radicals what they wanted to believe; for, in this instance, the investigator had arrived at his conclusions before he ever left the North and was selectively picking his evidence—finding what he wanted to find, closing his eyes to those facts that disagreed with or negated his prepossessions. Chief Justice Chase, also on tour, was addressing southern Negro mass meetings on the high ground of racial equality, but with the lower purpose of building votes for the presidential candidacy he fondly expected in 1868.

Yet, dispersed over the country, the congressional Radicals and their associates were in no position to levy a concerted attack upon the "restoration" program. Most northerners, possibly remembering Lincoln's offers of easy terms, quietly approved the Johnsonian policy. Northern Democrats, who a few months previously had termed the tailor "worse than Lincoln" and compared him unfavorably to Caligula's horse, suddenly were ready to embrace him as one of their own. Their motives, however, lacked an essential purity; for as one of them told Montgomery Blair, the price of their avowed adoption of the President and his program was a cabinet revision, a conformity to their other policies, and control of the patronage.

On the whole, the South, recalling Johnson's fearsome days in Tennessee, was agreeably surprised. And spurning not the olive branch, it set to making constitutions with vigor. One after another, through the late summer and autumn of 1865, conventions met to efface the mistakes that had led to war. But here, the portents of peace faded. Some men opposed repudiating the Confederate war debt; others asked compensation for the property loss they sustained from the abolition of slavery. Most of the conventions granted the emancipated Negroes a number of civil rights, but none of them displayed the mildest inclination for permitting that limited suffrage which both Lincoln and Johnson favored. Furthermore, in each assemblage, a minoriy of latter-day "fire-eaters" noisily opposed repudiation, abolition, abrogating secession, and the slightest consideration for the Negro. Though this group was invariably voted down by the more subdued majority, their statements, published widely in the northern press, gave the Radical reader all the justification he needed for his belief that the entire South was taking its defeat in something less than proper humility.

By keeping the telegraph wires warm Johnson brought pressure on his provisional governors to push the minimum program—annulment of secession, abolition and repudiation—through the conventions. When it came to the state elections, he had less power. He probably hoped that southerners who had been loyal to the Union throughout the war would receive the confidence of the people. In this, he was disappointed. The popularly elected governors were, in the main, men who had in 1860 and 1861 clung to the United States as long as possible before going over to secession. But in the analysis of the North they too were ultimately rebels, and some had held fairly important offices during the days of the Confederates. Further still, some required a special pardon before they could assume the duties of their new offices. Again, the new state legislatures elected by the people seemed to be composed predominantly of men who all too recently sympathized with the southern cause. To make the picture even more dubious, the greater number of the senators and congressmen elected by the South in the hope that they would soon be seated in Washington were unable to qualify under Johnson's amnesty proclamation.

Disappointed as the President must have been in these selections, he received from Mississippi his worst setback thus far. Her constitutional convention had been the first to meet, and its course therefore was followed with special interest. Repudiation went through easily, but secession died hard. Among the contentions of the debate was the proposition that secession should not be renounced for fear of offending the memory of the disunionist gentlemen of 1861. The state's elected governor, the first so chosen in the South under the new order, was an "unpardoned rebel," unable to exercise his office until reprieved by the President. A special legislative commission had meanwhile been assigned to draw up statutes defining Negro rights and to provide a plan for their place in a revamped southern society. The commission unfortunately devoted less effort to rights and more to laying down a code restricting the Negro's newly won freedom.

Without doubt, chaotic conditions required some definition of how the two races were to live together; also, there was the immediate need for a labor supply and the wish to get on with the beginnings of recovery. But whether the Mississippi legislature or the federally operated Freedman's Bureau should have the power to govern the Negro was a germane question. That the Bureau was already working on the ground provided a powerful argument to northern minds that its operations continue. It was equally obvious that the state code pronounced the Negro legislatively inferior almost in the moment of his freedom. Mississippians could argue that the "Black Code"—as it and similar enactments came to be called—was drawn from northern apprenticeship and vagrancy laws.

Yet the point had less strength than its proponents claimed. The

North indeed had such laws, but they applied to a minute percentage of the population; in Mississippi, one half of the population was arbitrarily placing the other half under undeniable restrictions without giving it a voice in the determination of its fate. Nor could the northern critics find reasonableness in the attitude under which the laws were drawn. In the preamble to its recommendations, the special commission had referred to those who disagreed with it as "sickly modern reformers" and invited others who found its code too hard to "flee and take sweet refuge" elsewhere. Clearly, Johnson's position was not helped by this incredible southern blindness to the conclusions being drawn by the northern conquerors. When finally the Mississippi legislature pointedly refused to ratify the Thirteenth Amendment on December 4th—the date the first postwar Congress met—the Radicals were near having their case proven for them.

❦ VI : THE PRESIDENCY DISINTEGRATES

JOHNSON in December 1865 appeared to have the support of the country. It being before the day of scientific public opinion polls, there could be no accurate measure of the extent of his popularity. Nevertheless, if the groups favoring his policies are set off against those opposing them, there is no question where the majority lay. Old Jacksonians, old-line Whigs, the rank-and-file Unionist Democrats, conservative and moderate Republicans, the great generals, veterans, a portion of the laboring class, part of the financial community—all adhered to the President and his policy. And, though their opinion would be considered valueless in any test of strength, so did most southerners. The Radicals could count in their numbers only the abolitionists, some discomfited Republicans, a group of secondary generals, and parts of the laboring class and the business community.

Yet, if Johnson had the numbers, his forces lacked what even current polls cannot fully ascertain—intensity of belief. This quality the Radicals had in abundance. Where a persistent barrage of presidential propaganda would be unseemly, propriety imposed no such damper on the opposition. Johnson had to limit himself to addresses to visiting delegations or depend upon newspaper reports; he had to leave the influencing of the great public to his lieutenants and their subordinates. And the explanations these presented were much too broad or unsatisfactory, so divergent were their reasons for supporting him. On the other hand, the Radicals had no such trouble. For one, negative criticism better permits an alliance of forces than does positive policy. For another, the extremist ranks were well united and capably generalled. Finally, Sumner, Stevens, Wade *et al.* had their forums, their organizations, their press, and their freedom to speak out as often and in whatever terms as they chose.

In a country but eight months removed from its worst war, in a country where the past fifteen years had wrought change after change without apparent pattern, in a country where most of the elements of living and thinking had seemed uprooted for four years, confusion reigned. Somehow the times would have to find direction. The postwar years were the testing-ground.

1. MORALITIES AT WAR

The era of which the Civil War was the center has rightly been considered an age of revolution in the United States. Its meaning immeasurably transcends the lexicon of defeats and victories. Different men were in revolt for diverse purposes. Certainly abolitionism was one thread of the revolution; certainly industrial capitalism was another; again, landless workingmen and small farmers added their voices and hope; and, after the fighting, there were the strivings of the newly freed Negroes. When the revolution started and when it ended are matters of points of view, of an individual's choice of the decisive factor.

After seventy or eighty years it is a relatively simple matter to determine the revolution's course. It is possible to assess the important leads, to weigh the impact of one contender against the other, to find out the contributions of all. But during the revolutionary years, when policies and traditions were still being shaped, the outcome might be anticipated in a number of ways but not assured. As the revolution ground on, many people and not a few of the leaders fitted the facts of the present into the concepts of the past. The conflict continued.

The major difficulty was that Americans were not in agreement—neither in politics nor in economic outlook nor in social relations nor ethical *desiderata*. The Jeffersonian and Jacksonian impulses still had considerable hold on many minds. To others, Hamilton's conservatism and Henry Clay's Whiggery remained guiding doctrine. The names of course were unimportant, but the liveliness of these older unsettled beliefs seemed unimpaired. Individual liberty, coonskin democracy, humanitarian ideals tilted with absolute guarantees for property, rule by an elite, individual initiative. Agrarianism, maintaining a full vitality in the West, faced its ancient enemies of privileged property and capitalism in the East. A fascinating individualism, triumphant in the ante-bellum years, ran head on into an ever rising demand for more government assistance to trade and commerce. One had expressed itself in small independent farm units, workmen who owned their tools and shops, and calls for free homesteads; the other in protection for industry, huge land grants, easier incorporation laws, and better guarantees to vested interests.

Superimposed on these older conflicting ideals had been the doctrine of states' rights, amplified from a *modus vivendi* of democracy in Jefferson's time to a near religion by the 1850's. Its strongest hold was on the South; and, for that reason, after the war it could not call its full number to its support. Still, a good number of northerners were fervent in its defense. In fact, so powerful was its appeal that states' rights had become, to its believers, the very core of that other veneration, constitutionalism. That a number of Lincoln's expedients had done violence to the word of the Constitution—as he had more than once admitted—states' righters refused to concede as being anything other than wartime necessity. The return of peace would, they felt, reestablish the sanctity of the written document in its past interpretations. And thus, in the Johnson years, they insisted upon an older framework inside which all political acts must be reconciled. It is perhaps a tribute to the power of the states' rights logic and the depth of constitutional feeling that the revolutionists were ultimately to enact their measures in the form of amendments to the organic law.

One other major prewar faith had left its mark on the country. Slavery had been ended by the war, but the abolition spirit remained. The driving hatreds could not be put off by proclamations of emancipation or the victory of antislavery. That freedom had been obtained for the Negroes only by force suggested to some that the conquered needed additional punishment. At least, the South would have to show itself repentant for its wrongs. The forms of self-abasement abolitionists wished in Dixie varied; but the minimal Johnsonian requirements were far from sufficient. For abolitionism, the war had been a crusade; and the battle having been sacred, so in its aftermath the worth of victory had to be realized. For some, fulfillment would come with the granting of economic and political equality to the Negro; for others, social equality was a final condition; for the extremists, the revolution would end only with the partitioning of the old estates among the new freedmen.

The great majority of white southerners, of course, had no such notions of submission. To them, it had also been a holy war. The end, however, had come not because of any conversion to Yankee ideas but from total exhaustion and military defeat. In their view, the President's peace was just but not soft. None had been convinced that the Negro was any the less inferior; defeat had merely demonstrated that he could not be held as private property. He had been freed, it was true, but the white mind refused to accept him as an equal. It doubted his capacity to own property or to move about the country on his own volition; it balked at his presence on the witness stand or in the jury box; it absolutely refused to countenance the intimation that he had rights in a polling place. His freedom it chose to consider a technical condition, to be circumscribed as much as possible without violation of the letter of the law. It was still a white man's country; it would continue one. If the war had proved anything, it had been simply that se-cession was an impossible method of saving southern supremacy. This the South would have to accept. It would even dismiss the hope of southern domination over the Federal Union. But, in matters local to the region, like the question of the Negro's status, it neither sought nor wanted the advice or rules submitted by the North. After the war, as before, the South still considered the abolitionist its greatest enemy.

*   *   *

A major source of confusion lay in the fact that, in the North, agree-ment on war aims had never been reached. To be sure, Lincoln had repeated time and time again that the object of the war was the preser-vation of the Union, that secession was illegal, and that one sworn to defend the Constitution could not, under it, permit the disintegration of the states it governed. Even emancipation had come as a war meas-ure, as an assault upon the property resources of the South. As a hu-manitarian action, however desirable as an end in itself, emancipation had no place in the legal definition of the Lincolnian position. Never-theless, abolitionism could never agree to these announced purposes. It preferred to regard slavery rather than secession as the evil. It went to war against slavery and it came out determined that the Negro would receive justice.

Here, apart from any false ideas the South might hold, was ground for dispute. Victory had come for both Union and Abolition; in the name of each, men had given of their lives and substance. But Un-ion, though a moral conception in men's minds, was old; it no longer possessed the fire it had when Andrew Jackson answered the South Carolinians. Furthermore, it was interlarded with ante-bellum burdens —a certain degree of local rights, agrarianism, a laboring class con-sisting of independent mechanics, a mercantile capitalism, a static or at best slow-moving attitude toward the Constitution. On the other hand, Abolition was an emotional response. Its ingredients were not only a passion for Negro freedom and a sharp rejection of traditional constitutional doctrine. They were, as well, the establishment in per-petual supremacy of those groups and institutions the sacred war had raised to power. The North must never lose its dominance; the party of abolitionism, the Republican party, must never surrender owner-ship of the government.

Yet, because abolitionists had never been in the majority in the North, they needed allies if their postwar program was to have a chance of success. These too would be products of the revolution, interests elevated and made supreme in the course of the war. For the revolution had not alone been one of politics, of social institutions and of ethics. In its wake had come a new economic order. The merchant and small banker had capitulated to the industrialist and the financier; coal and the machine had overpowered wood and the tool; iron had replaced gold as the metal the world lived by. The free market place was enshrouded by a protective tariff wall; the handicraft shop buckled before the industrial giant; huge aggregations of capital in a few hands precluded competition in manufacturing; fabulous land grants stimulated monopolies in transportation, minerals and lumber. Small farmers, no longer bent in subservience to southern cotton, had discovered the profits in wheat, cattle and corn. Sold in the industrial cities and shipped to Europe, the produce brought in more cash than ever before. And with new riches, farmers were converted to faith in industrial capitalism. As mercantile capitalism had bowed to industrialization, so the Jeffersonian dream of arcadia gave way to commercialization.

Over all lived the new elite created out of the financing of the war. As Johnson was to observe later, a propertied aristocracy based on slave labor was destroyed only to erect a new aristocracy based on government bonds. But in 1865, the distinction was not so plain. Bondholders held the national debt, and the debt, having been incurred in a crusade, was itself thereby imbued with sanctity.

* * *

No amount of argument could change these facts. Nor were the propertied and the abolitionists interested that the facts be changed. Having benefited from the revolution, they resolved to preserve and extend their benefits. On the other hand, there were the others who would not recognize the facts. Holding stubbornly to their belief that the wounds of war could best be healed by conciliation, they looked on abolitionism as foolishly sentimental and wildly fanatic. Convinced that the United States was—except perhaps for slavery and secession—a better place in the 1850's than the 1860's, they wanted to return it to its old ways and principles. Thinking in habitual patterns, they did not understand that the past is recaptured in memory but not in the reality of existence.

And because the past was not merely an old world but a casualty of war, the two views were irreconcilable. Each side spoke about rather than to the other. There was no common meeting ground. Each wanted its own will to prevail. Neither attempted to adjust to the other. There was no strong effort at harmonizing differences; the cleavage was fundamental. It is not surprising, then, that each believed itself to be absolutely right and the opposition absolutely wrong. It buttressed its arguments by drawing from every resource—from religion, ethics, economic theory, political creed, law, and from pragmatic experience. Although both spoke the same language and often the same words, there was no exchange of comprehension.

Out of the division emerged the basic issues. Industrialists and bondholders sought the advancement of the new capitalism that had made them rich and powerful. Anti-monopolists, agrarians and extreme conservatives with fortunes founded on shipping or foreign trade and on farm lands opposed them. In a somewhat different category were the "easy money" advocates who warred against the bondholders. Ethically, the North became bisected on the question of racial equality, with the abolitionists leading the favorables and abetted in numbers by those who were unconcerned for the Negro's future but strongly interested in enlisting Abolition's fervor behind capitalistic projects. Marching in the van of the unfavorables were those who often said publicly that they agreed to the equality principle, who often said privately that they thought the Negro unready for full citizenship. Their major debating point was the doctrine that citizenship was a function of statehood, not the federal government. In effect, therefore, they stood against principle. Among their allies, of course, were men who made no pretense of believing the Negro had equal capacity—presently, eventually or ever—to the white man.

These disparities in outlook naturally carried into the sphere of government. Capitalism's needs and Abolition's demands for racial equality dictated that the North remain supreme. Here there was collision with those who had been pro-southern, those believing in a soft peace, those adhering to the older type of Federal Union with its imperious states and sections in counterbalance. Here too, there was conflict within the Republican ranks between those who saw the organization as the party of Union and those—the Radicals—who saw it as the party of revolution. Since revolution is necessarily sanguine of the future and seeks to tear out old moralities and implant its own new code, the Radicals saw nothing wrong in aspiring for the everlasting power of their own brand of Republicanism.

2. POLITICIANS AT WAR

That Andrew Johnson had been running his own show to the detriment of the country and the people—that is, the North and Republican party—was obvious to the Radical mind by December, 1865. It was equally clear that he had not the slightest idea of changing his ways. Sumner and Stevens had attempted to persuade him and failed. Among the horde of advice-givers who had called at the White House during the summer and autumn were delegations asking a hard peace. They had been received, listened to respectfully by the President, and allowed to depart without rancor. Their words, however, had carried no tangible effect. Having once determined his own opinion and set the direction of his policy, the Tennessean was confident of his strength. He had control of the patronage, and the offices were filled with local Johnson and Lincoln appointees. In his methodically kept files and scrapbooks were many letters and clippings he had received in praise of his plans for reuniting the country. He was certain the majority approved; he saw no necessity to "compromise"—that ever odious word —in order that one disaffected wing of the party might be appeased.

For the Radicals, it was plainly an uphill fight. As their Congressmen arrived in Washington for the opening session of the Thirty-ninth Congress, they were embittered but hardly discouraged. To 279 South B Street, near the Capitol, where were the rooms of Thaddeus Stevens, they came to take counsel and rage at Johnson. For the old man, long wise in the strategy of forcing a bold minority program on a complacent mass, had evolved his course of action. The Radical cohorts knew why they wanted power, what they wanted for the South; some of them also had certain ideas they wished to apply in reconstructing the North. With the use of presidential power denied them, their engine logically became Congress, the co-ordinate branch of the government equal to or, according to the old Whig ethic, even superior to both the Executive and the Courts by virtue of its direct responsibility to the people. How were the Radicals to control a Congress where they had less than half the vote? Stevens had the answer.

Most Republicans, because of the old Whig creed and the past fights, and because of the lingering tradition against strong executive power, had at bottom a greater faith in the legislature. Most Congressmen, by sympathy of occupation, inevitably took the same view. Keeping this notion in the foreground, the Radicals would use Congress to undo Johnson's work and substitute their own program. Since no one could deny the Republican majority its right to enact a legislative program, it was incumbent upon the Radicals to secure control of the party and invoke a rigorous discipline that bound all elements—whether extremist or moderate or conservative—to party regularity. According to Stevens, this goal could be achieved if the Radicals acted as a unit in the party caucus.

The first hurdle was crossed easily, without incident. Two days before the opening of the session, the party caucus met. Stevens arrived with his faction briefed and a disarming resolution in his pocket. Having come with a positive program well thought out, he had an immediate advantage over the slower moving and slower thinking moderates and conservatives. The resolution he proposed to the caucus said that *all* Republicans in Congress would vote to admit no Southern members until both Houses agreed to send the credentials of Southerners as well as all other questions concerning the status of the South to a joint congressional committee. No debate or action would precede such reference; all such matters would be handled automatically; no action was to be taken by either house until the committee had reported its findings and recommendations.

To most men present, the resolution was but a reassertion of Congress' constitutional right to pass on its own membership. Henry J. Raymond, a Seward-Weed henchman and the leader of the administration forces on the House floor, failed to grasp its significance. As chairman of the party's National Committee and as editor of the *New York Times,* he had been backing Johnson; yet he gave no argument to the Stevens resolution. In the caucus, Old Thad had insisted that unless things were done his way, he would split the party. The complacent majority, without a ready alternative to the Pennsylvanian's scheme, assented in order to keep internal peace. The deeper implications of the plan had escaped them.

Outside the caucus, awaiting the opening of Congress, were would-be senators and representatives sent from all the late members of the Confederacy except Texas. Most of them had held office under the defeated government. But despite the fact that this prevented their claiming purification under the presidential Amnesty Proclamation of May 29th, few expected to be refused their seats. For among their numbers was Horace Maynard, Congressman-at-large from Tennessee. His would be the test of the Stevens plan for exclusion; and Johnson himself was mistakenly certain that Maynard's presence would cause the entire Radical plot to be "knocked in the head." The basis for this opinion was that his fellow Tennessean's loyalty was incontrovertible. A congressman at the time Tennessee had allied herself to the South, Maynard had stayed in his seat, working for the Union. The House, therefore, for all its power to determine the fitness of its members, could not question this man's faith or purpose. With Maynard's admission, Johnson apparently believed would come the entrance of a good share of the Southern members; and with their presence, the defeat of the Radicals would be insured.

But when Congress did convene, the administration and the southerners found they had underestimated Thad Stevens' capacity for generalship. The House admissions roll was in the hands of a clerk who owed his position to Stevens. The list he read from contained no southern names. Maynard and the Democrats stormed at the omissions, but their objections were ruthlessly pushed aside until "the proper time." Under a suspension of the rules, Stevens introduced his resolution. The party having been tied to it in advance, it passed with little debate. In the Senate, meanwhile, Sumner had moved an identical measure, but Fessenden, his tormentor, spoke cogently against the doubtful constitutionality of one house allowing the other a voice in the seating of its membership.[1] The point stood, and as passed, the resolution set up a joint committee to deal with southern reconstruction. The matter of credentials was reserved to the independent judgment of each body.

Nevertheless, Stevens had gained much that he wanted. The southern members had been already barred from the House; the Senate had done the same. And more to the point, the committee's fifteen members contained twelve Republicans, of whom eight were consistent Radicals. Although Fessenden, as a senator, was its titular chairman, Stevens, heading the nine representatives, could acknowledge himself the guiding spirit. Furthermore, his chairmanship of the powerful House Appropriations Committee gave him more authority than any other member of Congress, Raymond included. Adding his place as director of the Radicals, the old man held the position he needed to match Johnson in the contest for power. In his multiple role, Thaddeus Stevens, representative from Pennsylvania, was virtual, if unofficial, prime minister of the United States. If the supremacy of Congress were once established, the inherent possibilities of the position would indeed become a reality.

* * *

Caught off balance by the first Radical joust, the administration made no countermove. The President's Annual Message to Congress

---

[1] Technically, the separate introduction in each house made the proposal a *concurrent* rather than *joint* resolution. For the purposes of strategy, this was highly important. A joint resolution is subject to presidential approval; a concurrent resolution states what the policy of Congress shall be without reference to executive action. Being on its face a mere revision of the legislature's ground rules, the Stevens resolution offered Johnson no chance to register his official condemnation.

was an able state paper, compounded as it was of the historian George Bancroft's literary felicities and Johnson's thoughts and eclectic gleanings from the best writings on popular government. It developed again the reasoning behind the theory of a limited central authority and the reserved powers of the states; it reiterated a conviction in the indestructability of the Union. It narrated once more the steps taken under presidential reconstruction to bring the southern states back to their full participation in the life and affairs of the country; it took a hopeful attitude toward the solution of the Negro problem within the confines of state action and urged a "dispassionate treatment" of the subject of Negro suffrage. It declared that monopolies and class legislation were inimical to the national welfare. It reported the activities of the Executive Departments; and it closed with a paean for free, popular, constitutional government. No one overtly disagreed with the actual words. While praise flowed from conservative and moderate Republicans and even Democrats, the Radicals took a most effective stand: they ignored the document. Presidential messages are, in any case, seldom popular fare for reading; issued at comparatively infrequent intervals, they can never begin to refute, in themselves, a daily flow of vituperative editorials and speeches.

Here was one weakness of the Johnsonian forces. Sound as they thought their logic to be, their side was receiving but sporadic presentation. Part of the press supported the President; but he had no organs which he could directly "inspire" with his own views. Worse still, it was becoming apparent that the patronage machine nominally under his command had no serious loyalty to him; in the absence of a tight rein, appointees were proving amenable to Radical blandishments. When a few experiments in the removal of disaffected or lukewarm officeholders were tried, conservatives became outraged and moved closer to the Radicals. New appointments proved similarly unlucky; for without any test of worthiness but the confused ones of party label and the recommendation of a politician, men given commissions of office were as likely to be extremists as Johnsonians. At the top of the patronage pyramid, the President refused to carry out the expedient of wholesale dismissals, fearful that the outcry and consequences would totally isolate him. So Johnson did nothing, and one of the administration's most powerful political arms rapidly atrophied.

In Congress, the Radicals were consolidating their position. Having won their first sortie—the establishment of the Joint Committee—without a real skirmish, they settled on their new line, sniping at the administration and awaiting its mistakes. December saw both the Johnson forces and the fates playing into their hands. In Stevens' timetable the first months of the session called for "delay, delay, delay." Meanwhile, wavering Republicans were to be stiffened with the extremist ramrod into voting consistently Radical, and the public was to be "educated" through the party press. The chief catalyst in the process of stiffening and "educating" was a constant denunciation of the continued "rebellious" attitude of the South. For the dual purpose of noising the allegations over the North and provoking the President and his followers into unwise words and deeds, a long and tedious discussion of the southern problem occupied the oratorical energies of both houses and forestalled legislative activity.

On December 18th, the Senate wrung from Johnson the report made by Carl Schurz on the state of the South. That his views were well known from the newspaper articles written concurrently with the tour, and that Schurz need not have left the North for all the alteration the trip made in his conclusions, has been suggested already. Several years later the investigator was to repudiate his own findings; but in 1865, his massive compilations of incendiary occurrences, recorded with supposed eyewitness veracity and backed up by his reputation for integrity, served the Radicals well. Johnson was helpless to resist the senatorial demand; he doubted the correctness of the statements set forth—for he had directly contradictory reports from other equally reliable men—but he had nothing to match Schurz's weight of detail. Consequently, he sent along a rather extended letter by General Grant. But where Schurz set down presumable fact after fact, Grant merely was able to offer his opinion that "the mass of thinking men of the South accept the present situation in good faith" and were anxious to do what was required of them so that they could return to self-government. In the comparison, the Schurz document won praise, the Grant effort was condemned as a "whitewash."

In the House, at the same time, Stevens laid down his Carthaginian terms for the South. Raymond, as the administration's floor leader, was scheduled to answer; but before he could do so, a notorious Ohio Copperhead delivered his own peculiar justification for Johnson's policies. The defense was more damaging than the Radical attack. Raymond was forced to strike first at the Democrats and next at the Radicals; his fire was thereby too dispersed for effect. As though these were insufficient blows, Preston King, port collector at New York when he had not been advising the President, had a month previous silently jumped into the Hudson River, a suicide. The gossipy innuendoes did slight damage; for the future, however, the administration had lost an able lieutenant. The slipping Seward-Weed machine, on which Johnson necessarily placed reliance, was deprived of a field general perhaps second in capability only to the aging Thurlow himself.

For all these outside losses, the most serious injuries to the administration were being sustained internally. Johnson's cabinet members, not quite so mutually incompatible as the first strange collection gotten together by Lincoln, were nevertheless at political loggerheads. Gideon Welles continued to level his suspicions at everything Seward and Stanton did, and entered in his diary tart thoughts on the abilities and doctrinal weaknesses of the others. If possible, his constitutionalism and his opposition to compromise were more toughly ingrained than his chief's. If Johnson showed signs of giving way Welles was at hand to reinforce the President's old confidence in his faith and righteousness. Often the agreement of the Wellesian argument with the Johnsonian logic was all that was necessary to cast the Chief Executive's thought into an inflexible mold.

But Seward, their less exacting colleague, was running a different course. While in the last analysis, he too would side with Johnson, the widening chasm between the Radicals and the administration appalled his strong feeling for party. Having smaller influence in party circles than had been his under Lincoln but having lost none of his desire to lead, the urbane New Yorker pleaded for conciliation. Since he was a man without conviction but a man who nonetheless enjoyed the center of the stage, one is driven to seek motive behind his pleas. Perhaps a partial reason for Seward's placatory argument arose from his knowledge that his talents for accomplishment were always hampered where men stood on principle. When they forced the fighting by placing one another in positions from which they could not retreat, he found it impossible to step between them. His influence thereby suffered. But furthermore, ever in his calculations was the possibility for arranging the fulfillment of his thwarted wish—the attainment of the presidency for himself.

Treasury Secretary McCulloch, in meetings of the official family, was steadily in agreement with Johnson; but banker that he was, his major concern was with the currency difficulties left by the war. Where reconstruction matters touched his Department, he was willing to submit to a division of patronage with the Radicals and not inquire too closely into the fraud and depredations carried on by both sets of appointees. His major hope was to get some of his monetary program well stabilized. Of the lesser ministers, Dennison was uncertain, but generally with the President. Speed and Harlan, however, were drawing ever more closely to the enemy and Welles received rumors that Harlan was also entertaining presidential notions. With them, it was only a matter of time until their resignations would be presented.

The swollen War Department had become the center of a most curious ambiguity. Secretary Stanton had never been distinguished for his engaging personality; yet he was being lionized by the Radicals. Where the President was backhandedly applauded or sharply criticized, his own War minister was accorded resolutions of commendation. In all his disgust for the Executive cabal, Sumner had nothing but praise for this one of its key men. Yet, in the cabinet, Stanton had strongly reprehended the Senator's statements and ideas. As Welles commented, "Of course, some one is cheated." With the Army, the Freedman's Bureau and the military governments under his direction, Stanton was working with characteristic efficiency, and still had time enough left over to receive personally the reports of his corps of spies and detectives.

Precisely how wide was his net or to what end he sought to use his power will probably never be known. Certainly, he played his game carefully. Johnson was unable to prove what seemed the obvious source from which secret decisions of the Executive branch came immediately to the knowledge of the Radical high command. Though Welles believed him another presidential aspirant, Stanton had never held elective office, and indeed desired a Supreme Court seat before all else the country could offer. That he might have wanted power for its own sake seems equally unlikely; for this strange man was almost abjectly servile before both those Radicals and Johnsonians he wished to please. So much the courtier was he that he could not have attained leadership over others; a shrewd counselor in conspiracy, his best hope was mere partnership. For eighty years, Stanton's twisted character has been debated without final conclusion; he remains a fascinating riddle. But in his days as Secretary of War, he was, to his chief and to the doctrine of presidential reconstruction, an unquestionable menace.

*   *   *

While the War Department followed its mysterious course, the Joint Committee of Fifteen was slowly accumulating testimony to the effect that Yankee and Negro lives were unsafe in the South. In a manner not dissimilar to congressional hearings of more recent date, the committee, by and large, chose to hear only that evidence favorable to the majority's point of view. Its witnesses said or, by suggestive questioning, were led to say what best satisfied the convictions of those hostile to the President's methods. When the time was right, there would be another bale of "proof" for use against Johnson and the unregenerate rebels he pampered.

The play passed temporarily to the Senate Judiciary Committee where Lyman Trumbull, its chairman, had presented two bills. The first would have enlarged the scope of the Freedman's Bureau by charging it with the responsibility for protecting the civil rights of the Negro. Instead of trusting to the courts, the measure proposed granting local agents of the bureau judicial authority to hear cases and render final judgments which might include fines and prison sentences. In effect, civilians would be tried by a military tribunal from which there was no appeal to the civil courts. Trumbull's second bill, foreshadowing the amendment being slowly formulated by the Joint Committee, departed from tradition and possibly the contemporary interpretation of the Constitution. Stating that all persons born in the country were citizens of the United States, it declared them entitled to equal rights and treatment. Stringent provisions for prosecuting any who sought to infringe those rights of citizenship were included.

Beyond the clauses of the two measures lay a vital consideration to Johnson. The bills represented the compromise position of the moderate Republicans on southern reconstruction. Though Stevens and his Radicals had since discarded all pretense of co-operation with the President, Trumbull and Fessenden, as representatives of the less violent majority of the party, were seeking methods of working with the strong-willed Tennessean. In exchange for upholding the Johnsonian governments which were slowly rebuilding southern life, the moderates asked White House recognition of their own pledges of guaranteeing the Negro's future political and economic equality. To sweeten this admittedly bitter pill Congress was preparing to readmit Tennessee's delegates to its halls as soon as the bills were signed.

The Freedman's Bureau bill emerged in early February, the first major piece of legislation produced by the Thirty-ninth Congress. Immediately, gratuitous advice to sign and to veto flooded the White House. On the 19th, Johnson showed his message of disapproval to the cabinet. It was calm in tone, but its arguments emphasized the gulf between the Congress and the President. The courts-martial feaure he found particularly objectionable. He questioned the propriety, as well as the validity, of legislating for a section of the country while it went unrepresented and unspoken for. He doubted the advisability and necessity of providing relief and educational programs for the freedmen at federal expense. The reception of the veto by his "constitutional advisers" was as one might expect. Stanton, Speed and Harlan showed disappointment but acceded without debate; the others approved.

On its release the next day, the message excited the nation to joyous shouts and furious rantings. In revenge, the Joint Committee pigeon-holed the Tennessee offer. The House, under Stevens' promptings, passed a resolution declaring that no state was entitled to representa-tion until Congress specifically approved its claim. In the Senate, the veto was narrowly sustained by Democratic votes; all but a handful of Republicans had sided with the Radicals. Yet, if Johnson appeared out of step with his party in Congress, his action brought forth an out-pouring of popular congratulation from northern cities and the Border States. Washington's Birthday, 1866, provided an occasion for rallies and bonfires more in celebration of the presidential negative than in memory of the Father of his country. That evening in the Capital City, where pro-southern sentiment was readily aroused, a deliriously happy crowd called at the White House for a speech. Johnson had been coun-seled by a number of his intimates to refrain from giving way to his weakness for delivering extemporaneous remarks, and he had agreed to the soundness of their advice. But the cheers given in his name and the demands for his appearance were too powerful a call for an old stump orator.

Though he delivered no harangue but spoke, for the most part, quietly and pointedly, his address was interpreted as a clear declaration of war. As he warmed to his topic, the declaiming Chief Executive equated his enemies with the leaders of the recent rebellion. The crowd interrupted, calling for names. The speaker obliged them. Thaddeus Stevens, Wendell Phillips, and Charles Sumner, he expostulated, were "opposed to the fundamental principles of this government" and were "laboring to destroy them." The remainder of the speech was an avowal, in the purple oratorical style of the times, that he would re-main true to Lincoln's memory, his "honest conviction," and the Constitution.

The responses were not long in coming. Thurlow Weed thought the address "glorious" and capable of driving the oppositionists into hiding. Orville H. Browning, once Lincoln's friend and adviser, called the next day to press for Stanton's removal in favor of that elder Whig statesman, old Thomas Ewing of Ohio. Weed, however, had underesti-mated the resiliency of the Radicals. Far from running for cover, they made capital of the denunciation leveled at themselves and their cause. That the President had pandered to the voices of the mob was excellent demagoguery; but it was also a loose usage of the dignity of his office.

To the many who read of the speech in the press but had not heard of the generally placid manner in which it was delivered, Johnson was initially guilty of a breach of etiquette. That some in the throng were drunken was also duly reported.

From these two points, it was a short step for the Radical press to recall Andy Johnson's previous unrehearsed effort, on March 4th last. Liquor, the cause of that indiscretion, became the explanation of the latest one. Despite the fact that Johnson had been the soul of temperance since his unhappy inaugural, rumors, sometimes supplemented by "eye-witness" accounts, now flew on the depraved tailor's drunkenness. Robert Johnson, the President's favorite son, had unfortunately permitted his own chronic alcoholism to go on unrestrained during his father's White House tenancy. It was simplicity itself to impute, in the reverse of the proverbial order, the sins of the son upon the father.

The furor over Johnson's excoriation of the Radicals had hardly died when Congress presented Trumbull's second measure, the Civil Rights Act. One of its features most provocative to pro-southern circles was the section dealing with enforcement. This had been drawn from the old and dead fugitive-slave law, once so repugnant to northern antislavery men. One significant amendment was added by the House—a statement that the bill was not to be understood as contravening the suffrage laws of any state.[2]

This time, those urging presidential signature were stronger. They argued that expediency was the better part of policy. As consistent an administration supporter as Ohio's Governor Cox wrote that Middle Western sentiment demanded that the war gains be preserved and that the President would do well to concede to that sentiment where principle was not involved. Cunningly, Cox suggested that southern legislatures could pull the teeth of Trumbull's measure at their leisure. Johnson, however, chose to stand on principle. Although only Welles fully seconded his reasoning and conclusions, he sent back a veto on constitutional grounds. In the bill's definitions of what constituted rights and in its provisions to use the federal courts and Executive departments as enforcement arms, the measure, Johnson said, invaded

[2] At the time, only six northern states permitted the Negro to vote. Connecticut, Wisconsin and Minnesota had rejected the proposition when it was submitted to their electorates in 1865; other non-slaveholding states were to follow their example in the next few years. So far as the bill went, it would on passage apply to northern and southern states alike. The House amendment was therefore accepted by the Radicals. Honest as some of them were in their desire for the Negro's political equality with whites, to have forced the bill through without this qualification would have meant their certain defeat in the next congressional elections.

the legitimate authority and jurisdiction of the states. For those left cold by legalistic arguments, he implied it would unjustifiably overturn the reconstructed social and economic orders of the South by giving the freedman more status before the law than his former masters enjoyed. Whether or not he was correct in either his law or his sociological opinions would here be a fruitless discussion; but as a determinant in the course of his presidency and the government of the country, the veto shattered the Tennessean's few remaining claims to leadership over the party that had selected him.

Congress had prepared for the veto. In the House, there was no difficulty in repassing the bill. On a doubtful technicality, Senate Republicans had, in the interval, combined to unseat a Democratic senator from New Jersey. Delays on the vote gave the Radicals time to badger undecided moderates. When the vital day arrived, they had secured the two-thirds majority necessary to overriding. The constitutional revolution was on in earnest. And for the logbook of history, Congress had, for the first time, repudiated a president's use of the veto power for reasons of unconstitutionality. Where Johnson's first dissent had produced uncertain victory, his second had left him in outright defeat. He had lost the moderate and conservative Republicans to the extremists; his initial advantage had been overtaken and his position had become wholly defensive. Congress was in the saddle.

*   *   *

Its power to work its will now underwritten, Radicalism prepared to undo presidential reconstruction. From the tedious hearings and the reams of evidence issued the Joint Committee's labor of five months— an amendment to the Constitution which, if ratified, would provide a most sweeping revision of the nation's organic law. Though the philosophy behind the creation of this, the "great" Fourteenth Amendment, has already been discussed elsewhere, and though its enormous consequences cannot be explored here, a number of circumstances surrounding its passage should be noted as germane to the political war.

That its intention should have been given to the nation in the form of an addition to the Constitution instead of as a mere statute reflected a twofold determination of the Radicals: first, that their creed be given extraordinary sanction; second, that their program be rendered safe from the judgments of the Supreme Court and later Congresses. To this end, the rights of citizens of the United States laid down in the Civil Rights Law were included. But on the clauses, compromises had to be made. The Sumner abolitionists and their wishes for immediate Ne-

gro suffrage were ignored to attract moderates and to influence toward
ratification those many northern states that barred their own colored
men from the polls.

On the other side of the question lay the matter of the South; once
its delegations were re-admitted to Congress, they would have an increased voice over the ante-bellum years because Negroes in their full
numbers would be counted among the population. The subdued in-
surrectionary states, coming out of the war, would be in a stronger
political position than when they had left. Yet, to prevent this by aban-
doning Negro citizenship and Negro suffrage would be to drive the
abolitionists into enraged opposition. It was clearly a devil's choice.
And seeing no forthright way out of their dilemma, the politicians
shifted the decision on the South. As the voting clause was finally written a state that discriminated against any part of its citizenry would
have its representation in the House reduced in the proportion to which
it denied the franchise. Presumably, thought the creators of this clause,
the South would be more avid for congressional seats than averse to
Negro voters. But, as northern ardor cooled, the South found methods
of subverting the law and maintaining its congressional bloc undimin-
ished.

Still another Radical dream had to be jettisoned. Stevens entertained hopes of proscribing all who had given "aid and comfort" to the
rebellion. The less vindictive members of the Joint Committee, however, limited the term of penitence until July 4, 1870. The old Pennsylvanian ungraciously acceded to conservative pressure. Far from being
too hard a punishment, he told the House, it was "too lenient for my
hard heart." "Not only to 1870, but to 18070, every rebel who shed the
blood of loyal men should be prevented from exercising any power in
this Government." The Senate was even more magnanimous than the
House. It cut down the list of the guilty to those who had broken an
oath of loyalty to the Constitution by deserting federal posts. These too,
would be forgiven if they applied to Congress for special pardon, and
if a two-thirds majority of that body chose to overlook their transgres-
sions. Old Thad received the last change disapprovingly, but permitted the House to accept the final conservative judgment. He wanted,
he said, to hasten the adoption of the amendment as a whole, and he
offered no objection because "I dread delay."

So far as strategy went, his new-found fear of further dilatory tactics
had sound basis. However much the amendment's specifications varied from the Radical blueprint, its passage by Congress announced to
the people that Andrew Johnson's reconstruction policy was dead, that

thereafter the national legislature would set the country's policy. To Stevens this was perhaps a more important matter at the time than the actual provisions of the bill. For, in his heart, he doubted that the southern state legislatures would accept it. And without their ratifications it could not become law. Thus to this veteran political manager, the Fourteenth Amendment was not to be an imposition of terms on the South. That would come later. It would be a document for the Radicals to use in the autumn congressional campaigns. The shrewdness of Stevens' thinking can be gauged by the fact that, prior to the elections, only one of the rebellious sisters, Tennessee—her Brownlow government working in perfect complaisance with the Radicals—accepted the amendment.

*   *   *

To the President, the amendment was a challenge he could refuse only by surrendering to Congress. Since, by the Constitution, he had no direct association with its passage, he decided to lay his administration's opposition to the measure before the people. On May 1st, the entire range of congressional reconstruction occupied the cabinet discussions. Seward, McCulloch and Welles registered their unalterable antipathy to the Radicals' work. Dennison generally disapproved, as well, but was uncertain on what should be done. The entire value of the protracted conversations rested, of course, in what the enigmatic Stanton would say. Should he condemn the Radical program in the sharp terms of Seward, the revenge of his congressional friends would make his political future a cloudy one indeed. Trapped as he was, the Secretary equivocated in a loud voice, protesting at great length on how he approved Johnson's actions from the beginning. This gratified no one; and the uncomfortable probing of Stanton's opinions continued. Once more came the long asseverations of loyalty to his chief, but with them came the damaging admission that he felt the Committee's propositions could be "essentially improved." As a final desperate soporific, Stanton uttered the unrealistic hope that an attempt might be made to reconcile the President and Congress on a single course of action.

A detailed account of this singleness of opinion in the cabinet was published the next day in the press by Johnson. The Radicals were caught unprepared by the words attributed to the "great War Secretary" they had eulogized. One regular tack of their propaganda line had been that Stanton was on their side, that the administration was divided against itself. Now, Stanton's penchant for duplicity was being considered in other quarters.

Nevertheless, meeting the congressional offensive called for better methods. In the spring of 1866, conservative Republicans under the leadership of A. W. Randall, the first assistant postmaster general, and War Democrats headed by Montgomery Blair, had formed National Union clubs to provide the administration with organized support. In June, the two groups consolidated, and with Johnson's approval, issued a call for a convention to meet at Philadelphia in August. Written by the Republican Senator Doolittle and the aged Democrat Frank Blair, the call heartily endorsed presidential reconstruction. To Gideon Welles's discomfiture, it dissembled on the proposed amendment; and he filled pages of his diary with his disgust. Suspiciously, he saw the hand of Seward in the deed and, therefore, doubted the honest intentions of one entire faction of conservative Republicans. But whatever the influence of the genial Secretary of State on Johnson and Randall, the call successfully enlisted Henry J. Raymond and a number of old-line Seward Whigs into what might otherwise have been a purely Democratic affair.

With the aim of weeding out the unfit, the committee in charge of the convention issued semi-public invitations to each cabinet member. Decorum demanded an answer. And if the reply stated antagonism to the principles under which the assembly had been called, the resignation of the writer from his place in the administration was an obvious necessity. Nearly three weeks passed before the reluctant dissidents could be cleared from their posts. But eventually, Dennison, Speed and Harlan—the last had to be requested to resign by Johnson—left the cabinet. All three were, by then, Radicals, although with an unwonted charitableness, Welles ascribed Dennison's defection to the ambitions of his wife and party pressures in Ohio. Stanton, however—the chief target of the invitation letters—played a more adroit if graceless game. With a characteristic disregard for the niceties of etiquette, he refused to answer the communication. In his papers left to posterity in the Library of Congress is a response he drafted but never sent. It contains a burning defense of the Fourteenth Amendment and of the "Constitutional authority of Congress" along with a stinging rebuke to his correspondents. Their principal adherents, he proposed to tell them, were "those who carried on the war against the government" and "those in the Northern States who sympathized" with insurrection. Had this response gone to the committee, instead of into Stanton's files, he too would have been forced to quit. But second thought led him to keep silence, and he remained to practice his devious ways.

The convention itself was a harmonious gathering with delegates from Massachusetts and South Carolina embracing one another in mutual forgiveness. Resolutions, endorsed unanimously, sung hosannas to the constitutional basis of the war, the constitutional right of the states to representation, the constitutional abolition of slavery and the submission to that fact by the South, and the constitutional devotion of Andrew Johnson. Unfortunately, while Republicans like Randall, Doolittle and Raymond held the offices, Democrats made up the rank and file. And in their numbers were several whose loyalties to the Federal Union had been not unswerving during the war years. Only with difficulty were the notorious Copperheads Clement L. Vallandigham of Ohio and Fernando Wood of New York prevailed upon to give up their seats. Yet on the whole, the gathering made a strong popular impression. And the Radicals, for all the invective and ridicule their press mustered in reporting the event, decided to answer one convention with another—this to meet on September 3rd.

That month saw two more meetings, one in Cincinnati by war veterans and generals who lauded the President and demanded Stanton's scalp, the other in Pittsburgh by veterans and generals of different minds who lavished praise on the Secretary of War and called for Johnson's head. Though the first of the gatherings had come together for organizing a new species of political party or, at least, recementing the National Union alliance, it was the fourth which had lasting results. To the alarm of the taxpayers and the pleasure of Republican politicians, from it grew the Grand Army of the Republic. In future years, its policy of "pensions and the 'bloody shirt'" was to mean raids on the national Treasury and the near fulfillment of Thad Stevens' aim—"the perpetual ascendancy of the party of the Union."

Meanwhile, apart from the tumultuous conventions, the issue was probably already settled in the public mind. Race riots in Memphis, late in April, and in New Orleans, at the end of July, as reported to the North, did Johnson's cause irreparable harm. That there was dereliction in the conduct of both parties to the riots has been incontestably proved by historical research. That Stanton deliberately withheld from Johnson information which might have averted the New Orleans massacre has also been established. But whatever the provocations, there remains doubt whether southerners were ethically justified in leaving forty Negro dead on Chickasaw Bluffs and two hundred dead on the Crescent City's streets. At least, the northerners who would soon vote thought so. The Radical press contributed its share to the molding of public opinion by pronouncing its adversary in the White House personally responsible for New Orleans. James Russell Lowell, having before him a catalogue of other similar deeds by which southern whites sought to escape what they termed "Africanization," assured his readers that the "American people are resolved, by God's name, to Americanize" the recalcitrant South.

After the National Union Convention, Johnson decided on a grand tour of the principal northern cities. With misplaced confidence, he believed his direct words to the people would counteract the Radical tide. Flanked by the redoubtable personages of Grant, Farragut, Seward and Welles, he embarked on his "swing around the circle." In the beginning he was well received. But as he spoke on and on, it became obvious he was delivering the same address at each point on the itinerary. His antagonists were thus able to telegraph his words ahead. Given full publicity, together with full answers, in the Radical press, their possible influence was negated in advance. In Cleveland, hecklers were in the crowd, and the peregrinating orator paused in the exposition of his theme to exchange words with them.

By St. Louis, and across Indiana, Ohio and Pennsylvania, on the way back, the interruptions became more and more studied until he was fairly shouted down by the mob. Johnson, therefore, was prevented from reaching some of that part of the population he had hoped to sway. For the rest, the Radical newspapers willfully misrepresented and misquoted his statements. The Cleveland and St. Louis incidents were reported as drunken spectacles. Fabulous stories were manufactured to conjure in susceptible minds a picture of the excursion as one long alcoholic and sexual orgy.[3] Johnson's choice of vocabulary added fuel to the Radical blaze. A tendency to speak of his administration in the first person singular found itself mimicked by unfriendly sources as "My Policy." Recitations of his rise from inferiority offered possibilities for a wealth of caricature. In fine, the tour lost more than it won. One example of the huge store of ammunition it provided—as well as the quality of the shot—will suffice.

In Lancaster, Pennsylvania, Thaddeus Stevens edified his constituents: "There was a serial account from day to day of a very remarkable circus that travelled through the country. . . . I expected great wit from the celebrated character of its clowns. . . . I shall not describe to you how sometimes they cut outside the circle, and entered into street brawls with common blackguards; how they fought at Cleveland and

---

[3] As later testimony made clear, only Grant did any serious drinking. Johnson abstained completely. But Grant, then a prized hero in the popular eye, had not yet suffered the blemishes to his name which were to come later; his conduct went unprobed and unmentioned.

Indianapolis. But coming round, they told you, or one of them did, that he had been everything but one. He had been a tailor—I think he did not say a drunken tailor. He had been a constable. He had been a city alderman. He had been in the legislature. God help that legislature! He had been in Congress; now he was President. He had been everything but one—he had never been a hangman, and he asked leave to hang Thad Stevens."

By mid-September the electoral result was ordained. As if the race riots and Johnson's stumping were too slight an onus for presidential reconstruction to bear, the voters were, in most districts, faced with a choice of the extremes. The Republicans were Radicals who, for all their fanaticism on abolition or congressional prerogative, had supported the war and the Union; the Democrats, had selected candidates with lukewarm war sentiments or records of downright disloyalty. Further ineptitudes like the sending of Fernando Wood into the canvass in abolitionist Maine illustrated the myopia of the Democratic chieftains to issues and popular feelings. When the returns came in, the middle-of-the-roaders over the country seemed to have come to a uniform decision. Radical majorities were not high but they were regular. The House of Representatives would see 143 Republicans and a mere 49 Democrats. The state legislatures would send 42 Republicans and 11 Democrats to the next Senate. Andrew Johnson's veto, contending with these overwhelming majorities, would be an unavailing instrument.

The Radicals had totally conquered their rivals; they now marshalled their forces to destroy them.

3. JOHNSON'S MARTYRDOM

When the Radicals of the Thirty-ninth Congress reconvened for the "lame-duck" session, they assumed that revolution had been endorsed by the voters. What had gone before were the preliminaries to revolution. What followed would be the revolution itself. In its broadest outlines, the program for the future was relatively simple. The victors had three major objectives. They proposed to enfranchise the Negro, particularly in the South. They intended to entrench industrial capitalism, guarantee its dominance and provide for its growth. They sought to nail down their achievements by insuring the continuance of their party in power. All three were interrelated.

A determination for success transcended all thought for an observance of form. Radicalism meant to engraft itself upon the nation with or without the sanction of the Constitution. Or, in other words, the interferences of the Constitution were to be brushed aside both by amendment and, where that was impossible, by practices that were patently contrary to existing law but demanded by the spirit of the revolution. At some later date, the legality of the practices would be worked out and incorporated within the organic law; in theory, what was done would be rendered proper by sweeping constitutional reinterpretations.

Those opposing Radicalism could submit quietly and allow it to take its course while they rearranged their lives and consciences accordingly. But if one would not submit, it was a certainty that he would feel the fury of the victors. All but two of the Supreme Court justices tried to swim with the onrushing tide. As surety, Congress passed an act that removed Reconstruction from the area of judicial review. To make certain that more independent men did not come to the high bench, it cut down the number of judges as members left the Court, so that Johnson would be unable to appoint men sympathetic to his cause. Of those who survived, Chief Justice Chase's silence is the most interesting. A strong man who loved power, he nevertheless permitted the judicial prerogatives of his branch to be cut away. His motive lay in his never-stilled ambition for the presidency; he hoped that the Radicals would turn to him in 1868 as the ablest man which he believed himself to be.

Johnson too could have made his peace with the Radicals if he accepted the terms of the revolution. But he was persuaded that Radicalism was the subversion of the American creed. In so far as he believed the creed included a profound reverence for the Constitution and for states' rights, he was correct. Yet, in clinging tenaciously to his older faith, he became, because of his position, the prime enemy of the congressional leaders. They moved in every way to circumvent his power. They attempted to pare it down to nothingness so that their program would not be impeded. On his side, Johnson chose to fight after the people had repudiated his administration. He used his veto unremittingly, applying it to every important measure the Radical Republican Congress sent to the White House for signature. Just as certainly, and with but one exception, a two-thirds majority overrode his negative. But, sworn to administer the laws, Johnson accepted the verdict, once it was engraved in the statutes, and executed the edicts sent him. He looked for relief from the courts. He hoped that the legislation he considered misbegotten would fall before ringing judicial pronouncements for the Constitution and the old traditions of the law. He was disappointed. So far as the high tribunal was concerned, justice had pulled down its sword and scales, and was watching the contest between the Executive and the Legislature as a spectator.

Only the broadest aspects of Congressional Reconstruction need be set down here. The story is well known; it has been told often and from innumerable points of view. Presidential Reconstruction was destroyed. The governments of the southern states were overturned and replaced by military commands. A southern Republican party, based on Negro voters and officeholders, for ten years was a reality. Excesses were committed; but much constructive work was done. There was conspicuous jobbery and there was conspicuous honesty and high purpose. Overdue reforms were instituted in land and taxation, and in the extension of democratic principles; gross frauds were perpetrated, and corruption was the order of the day. By the standards of no one, except those who made personal fortunes in the process, was the reconstruction of the South a success. Republican state governments ratified the Fourteenth and Fifteenth Amendments, but fell from power when Union arms were withdrawn.

The humanitarian aims of the amendments were nullified. Furthermore, Stevens' plan for confiscating southern lands and wealth to aid the Negro and pay off the federal debt never passed into legislation. The southern white governments and people that have made the South Solid found that the constitutions written by Yankees, carpetbaggers, scalawags and Negroes were adequate; but they never forgot the ordeal of Reconstruction nor attempted to preserve its blessings while sorting out its faults. To them, it had no blessings. Northern abolitionists were disappointed. Theirs became a lost cause as age debilitated their crusade and time thinned their numbers. The other Radicals, who proved more radical in the dictionary sense of the term than in the political, deserted the crusade without regret. Their first intention had been a reconstruction of the North. The South had been a lever they used in going about their task. When their mission was completed they dropped the tool. Of all the parties interested in molding the postwar era, they did their job most thoroughly; industrial capitalism was firmly established in the United States. That accomplished, they joined the Democrats, the old Johnsonians, the dubious northerners and the white southerners in scuttling Reconstruction.

It was in the earliest stages of Congress' government of the South that President Andrew Johnson was a force with which the Radicals had to reckon. His Annual Message in December 1866 was temperate but without the barest hint of surrender. His subsequent vetoes demonstrated the stiffness of his backbone. With Congress writing any laws it wished and with Johnson honestly administering them, albeit with as much leniency as he and his Attorney General could read into the hard terms, there seemed every likelihood that the general ideas of Thaddeus Stevens would be the law of the land.

Yet Radicalism was bound to overlook no contingencies. The Army, and hence Stanton's War Department, was the major arm for enforcing the legislative will. The President was deemed capable of changing from extremely negative co-operation to positive obstruction. If Johnson decided that vetoing bills was not enough and was tempted to follow the wild advice that he suppress the "rump" Congress or the even wilder advice that he accept the volunteered military services of ex-Confederates and non-Radicals to drive his foes from Washington, the entire revolution could conceivably be overthrown.

Congress moved to minimize danger from the Executive. It passed a Tenure-of-Office bill that denied the President the right to discharge a man from office without the advice and consent of the Senate. After much seesawing and argument, cabinet members were placed in a special category. It was set forth that they would be protected in their posts "for and during the term of the President by whom they may have been appointed, and for one month thereafter." During that period they lived under the protection of the Senate. A reading of the debates on the measure indicates the upper house apparently accepted the proposition that ministers lasting beyond the "one month thereafter" were exempted from the aegis of the bill. At least, the President's defenders made this point specifically in relation to Stanton, Seward and Welles—all Lincoln appointees—and no Radical arose to challenge the interpretation. Johnson, of course, protested the entire piece of legislation when it came to the White House. Of his official family, the Secretary of War was the most emphatic in his denunciations. "No man of proper sense of honor would remain in the Cabinet when invited to resign," he said. But when asked to write the veto message, he begged to be excused because of "rheumatism in the arm." Finally he agreed to assist Seward in the composition. Both made an able historical and legal presentation of the arguments favoring Executive control over appointments and discharges. Needless to say, Congress ignored the arguments.

The second truly important arrow in the congressional bow was the determination to get rid of Johnson. Certainly, a portion of those prepared to impeach the Tennessean first settled upon his guilt before they knew of what he was to be found guilty. There can be no question that ignorance and bigotry joined with hysteria in provoking the demand. There is no doubt that Johnson's steadfast assertions—but only assertions—of the powers and rights of the presidency assumed meaning as "evidences of treason" when interpreted by inflamed minds. Yet, calmer heads like Thad Stevens, who knew what they were doing, also wanted impeachment, but they wanted to "make it stick." Their problem was one of finding suitable grounds. Limited by the Constitution to "Treason, Bribery, or other high Crimes and Misdemeanors," the legally cognizant were unsure of themselves.

Stevens took the view that impeachment was not necessarily an odious step or a criminal prosecution. Rather, he believed it the proper and reasonable way out of the constitutional dilemma wherein a president can remain in office after the people have indicated their lack of confidence in his policies by electing another party to congressional power. In short, Stevens assumed the impeachment process to be a valid political act, wholly divorced from punitive application of the law and wholly necessary to further the policies approved and directed by the majority of the electorate. A number of his responsible colleagues, however, disagreed with him, upholding the forms of the law; others thought him right but doubted that the Senate, sitting as a court, would adopt such an attitude.

Stevens, therefore, did nothing to assist the lunatic fringe that attempted to impeach the President in January, 1867. He stood by idly while the House Judiciary Committee spent the better part of a year desperately raking over Johnson's public career and private life in its search for a useful flaw. Unfruitful as the quest proved, five of nine committee members nevertheless recommended indictment. Stevens refused to bail them out; from the start, he had been openly contemptuous of the circus they were conducting. In silence, he allowed the lower chamber to reject their findings. Meanwhile, he directed the supplementary reconstruction measures that refined and clarified the first ones. He did not waver from his intention to depose Johnson; he waited for congressional sentiment to espouse his idea or for the President to commit a culpable act. The old man's vigil was eventually rewarded.

Even before the National Union convention in August, 1866, Johnson's supporters and intimate advisers had been telling him to demand Stanton's resignation. But the normally iron-willed Tennessean could not nerve himself for the act and could not muster proof to substantiate the tales of his minister's perfidy. Since then, historians and men who reminisce for publication have detailed the "great War Secretary's" concurrent services to the Radicals; but in life, Stanton covered his tracks well.

In late July of 1867, Johnson discovered that the author of the Supplementary Reconstruction Act was Edwin M. Stanton. Putting an end to vacillation, he curtly requested the ambidextrous gentleman to step out of office. While this note was in transmission and under consideration by the addressee, the President learned that two years before, when he was considering the death sentence imposed on Mary Surratt for complicity in Lincoln's assassination, the War Department had withheld from him the court-martial's recommendation for clemency.

Johnson now hungered for an acceptance of his invitation by Stanton. Instead, the Secretary of War showed a certain obtuseness toward that "proper sense of honor" he had once spoken of. "Public considerations of a high character, which alone had induced me to continue at the head of this department," he told the President, "constrain me not to resign. . . ."

With his will now hardened, the Chief Executive suspended the officeholder who esteemed his position for such noble reasons, and appointed Grant to act as Secretary of War *ad interim*. The General was, by this time, becoming increasingly fascinated by Radical talk of his availability as Johnson's successor; but he took the job with the understanding that his tenure was temporary. There matters rested until Congress resumed its sessions. Dutifully, the President reported the suspension to Congress, and for a month the Radicals let the report slumber. Stanton was out of Washington; Grant administered the office; Johnson worried over executing the reconstruction laws. In January, while the President made plans to dismiss Stanton permanently— as he assumed to be his right under the Constitution—the Senate decided to reinstate the fallen Secretary—as it assumed to be its right under the Tenure-of-Office Law. Grant knew Johnson was determined to resist, and did not enjoy the picture of himself as the instrument the White House might use in defying Congress. In fear, he saw his presidential chances fade and himself an unfrocked general, fined and imprisoned for having violated the Tenure Law. After promising to return the keys of office to the President so that any successor Johnson selected might have at least physical claims to the post, the hero of Appomattox saw that they came into Stanton's hands. In this way, the Radicals were spared the need of employing a locksmith to ensconce Stanton in his place once more. He moved in, complete with a battalion of GAR veterans and congressmen to guard his inviolability.

Thoroughly aroused, Johnson declined to concede to the authority of numbers and possession. Selecting the nearest available replacement, a general with a positive talent for buffoonery, he tried to do one of two things—supplant Stanton or force the case into the courts. For a brief time, he almost had his second alternative. The new appointee went to see Stanton in his self-imposed state of siege, demanded the office, was refused, and left the War Department to boast around Washington how he planned to "meet force with force" and break down doors that were barred. Shortly afterward, the general was arrested, but quickly released. A quiet drinking party with Stanton in the Secretary's office patched up ill feeling. Prosecution was dropped. The Radicals still feared the Supreme Court might grow independent if forced to deliberate on a case that required clear-cut decision. Moving swiftly, they jammed impeachment through the House under Stevens' sharp lash, and informed the Senate before specifications were prepared. Then, an eleven-count indictment was drawn up. The first nine surrounded the President's alleged violation of the Tenure-of-Office Act; a tenth (the personal work and favorite of Benjamin F. Butler, now a Massachusetts Representative) charged the Chief Executive with disrespect for Congress in three speeches during his "swing around the circle" in the 1866 campaign; the eleventh, by Thad Stevens, rehearsed the accusations of the first nine in an effort to strengthen a feeble complaint.

Johnson himself was not brought to the bar for his trial. His case was left to his five attorneys who included the incomparable William Evarts, Benjamin R. Curtis, a brilliant legal mind and former Supreme Court justice, and Henry Stanbery, who resigned as Attorney General to participate in the defense. The prosecution was somewhat hampered by the illness of Stevens who, though in constant attendance, was near death. This left the case for impeachment principally to Butler—of whose career a dispassionate study is yet to be written—and John Bingham of Ohio, a Radical whose chief interest in the possibilities of Reconstruction lay for the area north of the Mason-Dixon line. At best, the House "managers," as the prosecutors called themselves, had a weak case in law. Bingham toiled at making legal points that were not in existence; Butler chose to harangue and presented so violent an argument that Stevens' point of impeachment as a political process was probably damaged. It required no great store of knowledge and skill for Curtis and Evarts to demolish the charges. As the law was drawn in reference to cabinet officers, Johnson had not overstepped his authority in dismissing Stanton. And this totally ignores the question of whether the law was constitutional; in a calm atmosphere, the Supreme Court would probably have nullified it.

The trial, if such it was, set something of a record for the unjudicial tempers of the judges. Prior to the hearing, the Senate had officially condemned the removal of Stanton. Before the first speech was made or the first testimony taken, it was known that eleven Democrats were solidly for acquittal and thirty-one Republicans inflexible for conviction. Eleven Republicans were doubtful. A sidelight of the trial was the presence among the judges of Ben Wade, president *pro tem* of the Senate and President of the United States if Johnson were found guilty. On each important vote, including the final ones of guilt or innocence, Wade stood with the Radicals. In the end, seven Republicans joined the Democrats and saved Johnson by a single vote. They resisted the pressures of their colleagues, their constituents, the press, the churches and General Grant who appeared on the floor soliciting ballots for conviction.

After the trial, the President remained in office for the ten months necessary to complete his term. He was vindicated in law, but no more popular than he had been before his narrow victory. The Radicals still thundered, but awaited the advent of Grant. The Democrats, enmeshed in fratricidal politics, dropped Johnson, evaded Chase, and settled on Horatio Seymour, a competent governor of New York but one who had been outspokenly critical of both the Lincoln administration's war policies and the Radicals. He was beaten. On March 4th, 1869, Andrew Johnson refused to attend the inauguration of his successor. Six years later, he returned to Washington, the duly elected Senator from Tennessee. He lived to make a scathing attack on President Grant. On July 31, 1875, he died.

*   *   *

The tragedy of Andrew Johnson is not without its overtones of Greek drama. He was a better than average man. He was an honest man. He held powerful convictions and was firm in defending them. He was obviously courageous. For most of his life, he fought the battle of the common man. Yet, in his character, there was the tragic flaw. His faith was too narrow. He stood by the common man but he would not admit the freed Negro into that fraternity. Negroes in government he took to be a sign of black domination, "worse than military despotism." While it may be doubted that Johnson, aside from his southern feelings on race relations—feelings that were restrained for a man from his section—wanted to re-establish slavery under another name or to reconstitute the ante-bellum South except for the secession doctrine, his policies were outside the stream of northern intentions. His rigid adherence to the states' rights creed and the old constitutionalism set him apart from the masses of the North. He thought that the race problem and the reconstruction problem could best be handled within the scope of local rights. The northern majority did not agree with him. But Johnson did not appear to understand how fundamental was this disagreement. Nor, for that matter, did his close advisers, except to think of their opponents as "tyrants" and dishonorable men.

Although neither side had a monopoly on virtue, the Radicals had men like Stevens and Sumner who honestly preached the widest possible extension of democracy. These men had the additional pragmatic advantage of guiding and gauging the temper of the victorious North. Oppressive, unjust and perhaps vindictive as some of their policies were, extra-legal as some of their acts were, they had the bulk of their section's opinion behind them. Still, it must be remembered that they dominated the nation when emotional tension was at a peak. At such times, appeals to higher law in justification of harsh measures and methods seem tenable. But if one assesses their work in light of the broader sweep of American history, when peaks are averaged out, and excesses are discarded from the nation's policies and brought to rest uncomfortably on its conscience, it appears that the Radicals did much that was wrong. In proposing to revolutionize a region of which most of them had only the sketchiest knowledge and extensive misinformation, they were, in the long run, destined to fail.

On the other hand, Johnson, in refusing to analyze the consequences of his creed, was correct only if discrimination and vested privilege are just in a society that strives for democracy. Otherwise, he was an indubitably honest man defending a dishonest cause. Granted that he was a man behind his times. Granted also that he was hardier in his desire to uphold the Constitution than in opposing Negro equality in economic and political life. He nevertheless became so enmeshed in his own dogma that he was reduced to ineffectiveness in his office and possibly made justice for the South more difficult to obtain. As a Jacksonian, he missed, until too late, the significance of the industrial revolution in the North. Only in his last message did he seek to make an issue of the huge reward the bondholders were receiving from the people of the United States. This new aristocracy, having purchased its certificates in depreciated wartime paper, was being paid high interest rates in gold and benefiting further from a more stable monetary system and a growing economy. Johnson made his point after Radicals who would have supported him were out of power. Stevens was dead, Butler and Wade without influence.

Yet, reckoned by any standards of conventional morality, Andrew Johnson, the self-made man of strong moral fiber, received less than fair treatment by his personal enemies and political opponents. He was far more a victim of his times than a villain. It is true personal failings contributed to his fall. But this is the essence of tragedy.

IN STRIKING similarity the years between the Civil War and the beginning of the twentieth century approximate the first years of manhood in the American success story. If the period of the Federalist and Jeffersonian lines be taken as childhood, and if the period of Jacksonian democracy, Whig capitalism and the slavery debate be considered the adolescence of the nation, the Civil War and the Johnson era become the time when those confusions in youth—the dragging ties of the past, the hopes, the sentimentalities, the ambitions and inchoate ideals—are sorted out and unscrambled. It becomes the time when one, no longer an adolescent but not yet an adult, fiercely questions and searches and flounders, and finally decides on the dedication of his lifetime. He has indisputably reached manhood as soon as he starts his career.

The post-bellum period is the start and the early years of that career. Like so many young American men the career their country embarked on was one of business. The United States was past the odd-job and pocket-money stage of mercantile capitalism; it had come of age and was out on its own. Its job, its profession was industrial capitalism, the career it had selected out of the turmoil of military, political, social and economic warfare.

Once the choice was made the nation began building a business civilization. America concentrated on this, its primary task. It guided itself to a single purpose: that capitalism must grow. A high tariff wall insulated capitalism against foreign competition, and an easy immigration policy supplied it the necessary cheap labor. Natural resources and huge tracts of land were transferred from public to private hands, to speed the progress toward industrialization. Although much the greater proportion of the people were still farmers, although homesteaders still went West, agriculture was no longer dominant. It was being sucked into the vortex of industrialization; it had become commercialized to supply industry's cities and to purchase industry's products. Far from ruling, it had become industry's adjunct.

The entire process was a magnificent one to watch, an even more splendid one in which to participate. Wide horizons opened; enormous returns were promised. Energy had but to be expended. And America, in her manhood, had energy in abundance, in the natural endowments of her land and the virility of her population. Out of the riches, the driving force, the imagination and the ambition grew railroad webs, factories and mills, more and larger cities, the giant power of steam and the colossal strength of the machine.

But the job of making capitalism work and prosper shoved to the background those considerations that might be thought of as ancillary. Thus the age belonged to those charged with the foremost leadership in a business civilization—to the Rockefellers, Goulds, Vanderbilts, Carnegies, Armours, Huntingtons and Stanfords and Morgans. Satirists of the social order like Mark Twain, critics like Henry George; dissatisfactions which manifested themselves in agrarianism and greenbackism and the Knights of Labor represented occasional twinges of conscience and divergences in attention from the main interest of young manhood, a career in economic expansion.

That politics and government, therefore, occupied a lesser place in shaping the country than they had before was a sociological consequence. Professionals continued to enter the field and sway the people. There was a continuing excitement within the arena in which politics operated. But the whole estate of the occupation had fallen. It was no longer watched as a determinant in national life; its place had changed. It had been converted into a diversion; its course was followed much as men follow baseball pennant races and the standings of prizefighters. Fascination, relaxation, the joy of partisanship, vicarious pleasure— these were the compulsions that drew the public into giving the political game its attention. Only among the professionals and their business managers was there a deadly seriousness.

Only the relationship between the politicians and the managers seemed to bring the game within the orbit of the era. That politics and business were related parts of the same whole is, of course, true. But there is no gainsaying that the captains of industry and finance far outshone the captains of government. In a later day, Chester Arthur, James Blaine, James Garfield, Roscoe Conkling, Don Cameron and Judge William Robertson are relatively obscure, as are "Pop" Anson, Roger Bresnahan, Alexander Cartwright, Ed Delehanty, "Ban" Johnson, and "King" Kelly. Yet, the first group manned the battlements of the Republican party fifteen years after the Civil War; the second are "honor men" in baseball's Hall of Fame. All of them were transitory heroes.

1. LIFE AMONG THE REPUBLICANS

Ever since 1860, when the Republican victory started the hardening of American political parties into their still existent channels, New

York and Ohio have contributed a larger share of both the presidents elected and the seekers nominated to the throne than has the rest of the country. In twenty-two campaigns, major candidacies have represented the two states *twenty-seven* times[1] against eighteen for the less favored majority. If it is thought that the four efforts of Franklin Roosevelt and the three of Grover Cleveland may somewhat overweight the figure, a compilation of the individual men named by the parties shows an even greater dominance—nineteen from the two states to eleven from the remainder. Explanation of this constant reappearance of New Yorkers and Ohioans for high place rests not so much with the quality of the men as with the nature of their states. For in both cases, the states are and have been so heavily populated as to make their electoral votes highly desirable acquisitions, votes that might determine—and have—a close election. Again, through their delicate internal balances of agriculture and industry, city and country, racial and religious strains, competing political machines and strong partisan traditions, the two states have long been classified as politically "doubtful." And, it being part of the folklore of politics that a certain number of the local voters will be influenced by the "honor" given their home province, doubt plus electoral potency have joined to raise Empire and Buckeye aspirants to national prominence.

Inevitably too, whether in lean years when these states have been unable to produce magisterial timber or in fat ones when they may have grown a plethora, their politicians and statesmen of the second class have thus possessed a perpetually strong voice in the party councils and a power capable of destroying the ambitions of men so unfortunate as to lack the favor of a New York boss or reside in a less populous, less doubtful, more homogeneous state. In part, that had accounted for Thurlow Weed's denial of Daniel Webster. In part, as well, that explained the difficulties of James G. Blaine and the fierce and spectacular maneuverings in the Democratic and Republican ranks after the Grant years when the parties had developed an abundance of leaders but no national suzerains.

But there was another of the fated irrevocabilities that lay in the strategic position of the two states. The very size of the power a local boss, machine or controlling faction could exercise in national affairs was a persistent attraction to those at home who were underneath and unendowed. New York bosses and machines were perpetually afflicted with drives from below. Though Tammany was always able to protect itself, this was nevertheless true with other portions of the Democratic

[1] This figure includes the Progressive candidacy of Theodore Roosevelt in 1912.

party. It was particularly true of the Republican party where possession of the state organization gave the holders not only national strength but a first call on the federal patronage handed out by the string of Republican administrations in Washington.

In 1880, power in New York State was almost, but not quite, synonymous with Senator Roscoe Conkling. After the downfall of Weed and Seward he had rebuilt the party in the state along his own plan of architecture. Through an alliance with the Camerons, father and son, of Pennsylvania and John Logan, the political general who ruled GOP fortunes in Illinois and the Grand Army of the Republic, he had established the most compact, most powerful single faction in the party. Its façade was the blemished but still mighty reputation of General Grant. But inside New York, which the Senator presumed to be his private pasture, there had grown two ineradicable species of tares. One, the less dangerous, was in New York City, at the unfertile edge of the pasture, where Tammany and other aspects of the Democracy tended to stunt the growth of any sort of Republicanism. This was the group centering around the intellectual efforts of George William Curtis and his *Harper's Weekly,* E. L. Godkin's *Nation,* Carl Schurz, and relatively independent papers like the *Times* and the *Post.* Their quarrel was not with the capitalism Conkling so ably represented, but with those practices of its political arm that were variously known as "Grantism" and the spoils system. For these objectionable doings, they would have substituted honesty in government—the government was still to remain conservative—and a standardized set of rules covering the appointments, competence and dismissals of public servants.

Out in the verdant stretches of the pasture, however, flourished a second group, more dangerous than the reformers because it traded not in intellect but in jobs, because it sought not honesty in politics but power. Its leader in local matters was Judge William Robertson of Westchester County, a pale man indeed when compared to Roscoe Conkling but one who could rally those politicians who dissented from rule by the regulars. For backing, it mustered the monetary and economic strength of such men and institutions as Chauncey Depew and the New York Central Railroad, and the press power of Whitelaw Reid's *Tribune.* But these were, after all, inconsiderable local resources when totted up and set alongside those of Conkling. By 1880 he had long since gathered to himself much of what emanated from Albany and a goodly share of the homage paid by New York's privileged and wealthy. He was only awaiting another term of Grant or a president cast in the image of the hero of Appomattox to regrasp the reins of fed-

eral power that had been cut away from him by President Rutherford
B. Hayes and Secretary of the Treasury John Sherman. Such a prospect
displeased the disputants to the Senator's right over the New York
dominion. And without a suitable presidential nominee among themselves, they clustered around James Blaine of Maine, the most popular
and the strongest of Conkling's opponents in the national arena.

They could have selected a less tainted standard-bearer, but it would
have been difficult to find one so implacably set against Conkling, and
one with so attractive a personality. For Blaine of Maine—with name
and place of residence a convenient rhyme for doggerel jingles and
campaign songs—was easily the most winning and most "magnetic"
of the Republican leaders, and an excellent orator. He was perhaps not
Conkling's equal at the epigram and he could not soar quite as high
on the wings of rhetoric. But he had given the country's cartoonists a
picture of the New York boss's "grandiloquent swell, his majestic, su-
per-eminent, overpowering, turkey-gobbler strut"; and this the cartoonists never forgot and Conkling never forgave.

If words could kill, the two would have annihilated each other years
before. Yet, Blaine had a weakness fully as open to criticism as his rival's hauteur and political associations; he enjoyed living at a pace that
was plainly faster than could be afforded by a Speaker of the House or
Senator with his salary as the only apparent font of his wealth. When
questions were asked and written evidence produced to indicate that
the railroads were favoring his luxurious whims, he made dramatic
denials that temporarily washed away the doubts of his hearers. But in
calm afterthought, it was seen that his answers were unsatisfactory; it
was suspected that James G. Blaine, however charming a man, was less
than honest in his public dealings.

While New York's Republicanism felt tremors threatening to un-
dermine the monolithic structure that was Conkling's bossism, and
while Conkling and Blaine each contested to heap greater damnation
and ruin on the other, Ohio was struggling to make the most of her
patrimony. Here too was a dominion of numbers and of political doubt.
But here was a dominion seemingly incapable of profiting on the in-
dubitable value of her position.

No single boss stood on high to direct the traffic in patronage; no
statesman outlined a definite party policy. Rather, Ohio was a home to
faction. Her well-separated cities and her rural areas were split in their
outlook according to their proximity to Lake Erie, the railroads or the
river. They were divided off by many differences in a heritage that was
Yankee and Virginian along with generous infiltrations from the mid-

dle states and Europe. Traditionally Republican counties sat adjacent to old Democratic strongholds in a pattern that speckled a map and made unification of either party under state-wide leadership almost unattainable. Politicians toiled at constructing formidable coalitions with only occasional success. There were too many groups to hold them all together for long; there were too few plums for so many hungry mouths.

In 1880, Rutherford B. Hayes, an Ohio Republican, resided in the White House. But he was committed to one term, and had, in any case, alienated both the Conkling and Blaine wings of the national party. He had not even won the unqualified support of the small reformist element. The state did have its perpetual aspirant, John Sherman; but he was not one to arouse enthusiasm. He was a regular, but he was dull; competent but uninspiring. He had been unable to raise even a solid bloc of convention votes within his own state; and although he had a majority of the delegation, he suffered because a number of managers from outside had come into Ohio and pledged strays for Blaine and less likely contenders.

Only Sherman believed he could win in the national gathering at Chicago. He had worked hard to promote himself. Not the least of his efforts was the securing of James Abram Garfield to manage his candidacy on the convention floor. It was admittedly a good choice in many respects, for Garfield had served Ohio during nine terms in Congress, was an expert parliamentarian and was one of the party's leading orators. That Garfield had also been mentioned as a possible "dark horse" for the nomination had made him a threat in Sherman's home state; but his acceptance of the managerial post seemed automatically to remove him from consideration.

Mere good nature alone had not led him to surrender his chances so obligingly. John Sherman had likewise parted with a cherished love. In the *quid pro quo,* Garfield had received a seat in the United States Senate where the tenure of office is three times that of the House. This arrangement, however, was hardly a case of outright bargaining. Though Sherman was, in his forty years of national politics, nearly a permanent fixture in one of Ohio's senatorial seats, he was at the time Secretary of the Treasury. The seat in question belonged to a Democrat whom the state legislature would not return. Sherman's contribution was to forswear his own wishes for the office and press other Republicans to withdraw their claims in favor of Garfield. Originally, Garfield's repayment was to have been an endorsement of Sherman for the presidency. But in this he procrastinated, and finally gave it only to be asked to become the Secretary's floor manager. Once more he wavered, and then agreed, not from any confidence in Sherman's candidacy but in the hope of uniting with the Blaine forces to stop Roscoe Conkling's drive to rule the party.

*   *   *

Thus the Republicans came out to Chicago. By that time their major wings had received informal labels to make identification easier. Originating out of the divisions in New York, the Conklingites characterized themselves as "Stalwarts," firm in their old-guard approach to party domination and their refusal to compromise with any who would revise the balance. Contemptuously, they referred to the Blaine-Robertson faction as "Half-Breeds," a definition the latter neither accepted nor repelled. Instead, by popularizing the obstructive and dictatorial qualities of "stalwartism," the Half-Breeds gave national significance to both terms.

The two groups agreed generally on anything that could be considered an economic or social issue, but they faced each other in bitter antagonism over the coarse question of who should devour the loaves and fishes. Conkling came determined that General Grant should have a third term. The well-oiled machines, Cameron's from Pennsylvania and Logan's from Illinois, were with him. Three hundred and seventy-eight votes were necessary for the nomination and the three bosses were certain of an immediate 300 to 350. The "Blaine Legion's" strength was dispersed through the delegations to the extent of 225 to 285 votes. John Sherman's ninety backers and seventy-five others were scattered around to be bargained out of their preferences. On appearances, Grant or Blaine managers had only to do some efficient work among the partisans of the hopeless candidates and one or the other would receive the nomination.

But appearances neglected deeper considerations—the doggedness and arrogance of Grant's promoters; the unrelenting will of their combined adversaries to prevent his endorsement; an abiding distrust of Blaine; Sherman's obstinacy at suggestions that he release his delegates to either major contender. It was the arrogance of the machines and the anti-Grant feeling that ultimately set the convention moving in ways inimical to Conkling's ambitions. Uniting under Garfield's leadership, the anti-Grant forces secured the chairmanship of the assembly—always a vital post in a close contest—and rejected the Conkling unit rule doctrine that would have forced a unanimous casting of a state's vote for the candidate who had a majority of its delegation. The importance of the first victory became clear during the nominations; the meaning of the second victory was immediately apparent. Before the balloting started, Grant lost fifty votes among the Half-Breed minorities in the Illinois, New York and Pennsylvania delegations.

Nominating speeches were perhaps of little influence in persuading delegates to jump over the tightly drawn lines. The effort in Blaine's behalf was incredibly bad;[2] Conkling's exaltation of Grant ranks in the annals of convention oratory as carefully prepared, well delivered and nicely worded, but so sarcastic in its references to others as to cement the alliance against his man. Garfield spoke ably for Sherman, advising that calm and moderation were better criteria in selecting a nominee than was passion. He succeeded in calling more approbation to himself than to his candidate.

The roll calls followed. Through thirty-three counts, the managers held their forces together without substantial defections but without gaining any advantages. On the next vote Wisconsin switched to Garfield. He jumped from his seat to protest, but meekly returned to it when Chairman George Hoar, employing his gavel against the Stalwarts, ruled him out of order. A movement had begun. Blaine and Sherman men hysterically went over to the new favorite. On the thirty-sixth ballot, while he hid his tearful emotions within the cover of the Ohio delegation, they nominated him. But, ominously, 306 Stalwarts held out for Grant until the end.

The Half-Breeds stopped to review the events that had brought them a candidate. The selection of Garfield had not been entirely accidental. Some had worked for him and kept his name before the convention by throwing a vote or two his way during the deadlock. He had been employed as Sherman's manager with the understanding that delegates pledged to the Secretary might be called upon to change to Garfield's standard if a possibility developed. Throughout the session, a paid claque in the gallery had regularly given him the best ovations that money could buy. On one such occasion, Conkling had acutely sensed the influences in the background, and had sent him a tart note: "I congratulate you on being the dark horse." Now, that the remark had become a reality, the New Yorker did not bother to hide his rage.

---

[2] Incomprehensibly, the speaker was almost apologetic in presenting his candidate's name, and got wrong Blaine's middle initial and the facts of his career. A memorable contrast was the oration of Robert Ingersoll four years before, when his portrayal of the politician from Maine as a "Plumed Knight" riding against the dark foes of Republicanism sent the delegates into delirious celebration. So neat was the phrase that Blaine men adopted it as a permanent sobriquet in describing their hero—not without, however, having to still his disquietude that it might carry also implications of the white feather.

And, as he went, so would go the other bosses and the Stalwart 306.

Men from Ohio caucused. Realizing that November promised defeat unless Conkling's ruffled feathers were smoothed and preened, they approached the New York delegation bearing a gift—the vice-presidency. First, they sought Levi P. Morton, a wealthy and respectable Stalwart lieutenant who could give funds and dignity to the campaign. Morton was willing, but his chief was discouraging about Garfield's chances of winning; and Morton wistfully turned down the offer. Still pursuing unity, the Ohioans moved on to Chester Alan Arthur, the courteous and affable second-in-command of Conkling's machine. In him, they found not only a willing man, but one brave enough to endure the Senator's displeasure. Very simply, Arthur believed that even a "barren nomination would be a great honor." He was not put off merely because Roscoe Conkling snarled, "If you wish for my favor and my respect you will contemptuously decline it."

Thus, the pact was sealed. New York nominated Arthur, and Ohio seconded him. Amid the hisses of reformers and adamant Half-Breeds, the practical politicians confirmed the bargain on a single roll call.

*   *   *

Meanwhile, the Democrats, on the scent of their first win at the national polls since the Civil War, had stolen a Republican tactic and nominated General Winfield Scott Hancock—like his namesake a military hero. Having been narrowly beaten in 1876 under what today would generally be considered a fraudulent election, they had, for the intervening four years, held control of one or both houses of Congress and now expected to wrest the elusive Executive branch from their rival party. Apparently, they did not see how they could lose. For in a wild disregard for caution, they quickly fired off their most potent charges— Garfield's unsavory connection with the Crédit Mobilier scandals and Arthur's associations with the naked use of the spoils of office. Worse yet, they first permitted Hancock to espouse a "tariff for revenue" when industrial America obviously approved of some degree of protection, and then declare the whole question a "local issue." Finally, they circulated a patently forged letter imputing that Garfield favored free immigration of Chinese to the western states. In its proper place, the letter may have done its intended work; but Democratic timing of its release was so bad that the falseness of the statement was easily proved before election day, and even the press sympathetic to the party condemned the infamous device.

Encouraging as were these mistakes, Republican quarters were gloomy. On his nomination Garfield retired to his farm at Mentor, Ohio, to receive the pilgrims and take personal direction over as much of the campaign as he could control in his own hands. He was unhappy that the prestige of the presidential office forbade candidates from diving deep into the political issues involved. But he indulged his redoubtable eloquence on non-controversial subjects as often as his advisers recommended that he speak. Otherwise, he kept a worried eye on the reports and itineraries of his Half-Breed and reformist supporters who toured the country trying to explain why Garfield and Arthur, with their reputations, and the Republican party, with its record, deserved election. Of course, the Democracy was still castigated as the "party of rebellion," the "bloody shirt" waved and old Union soldiers urged to vote as they shot. Not content with the enemy's political and ethical failings, Robert Ingersoll found it guilty of conspiring with nature. "The Democratic party," he edified his hearers, "is a party of famine; it is a good friend of the early frost; it believes in the Colorado beetle and the weevil."

But the gloom was not easily dispelled. If Blaine and Schurz devotedly led their followers into battle, the New York men were conducting a campaign of silence and indifference. Arthur had refused to come to Mentor for a conference. Garfield had selected Stephen W. Dorsey to handle the details of the canvass. Dorsey, an ex-senator and carpetbagger from Arkansas, where the people had turned him out as soon as they no longer feared reprisals from the North, was a Stalwart; but Conkling continued to sulk. The candidate's letter of acceptance had practically repudiated the civil service reform plank in the party platform by promising he would consult on appointments those "whose knowledge of the communities in which the duties are to be performed best qualifies them to aid in making the wisest choice." Other Stalwarts accepted the statement in glee. But not Roscoe Conkling. He wanted direct assurance that his rule would go on, abetted but unsupervised by Washington. Until he received what he wanted, he and Chet Arthur spent their vacations together, fishing.

This intolerable state of affairs was exceedingly painful to Dorsey and other politicians of the party. It reduced their strength and it shut off large sources of funds in Wall Street. Finally they prevailed upon Garfield to make a triumphal tour through New York State, winding up with a peace conference at the Fifth Avenue Hotel, headquarters of the Senator's machine. There, meetings were held—with Morton, Chauncey Depew and Jay Gould to settle money matters; with Blaine, Logan, Sherman, even old Thurlow Weed, and lesser celebrities to patch

up a unity; with Arthur, Governor Cornell and Tom Platt to secure the
co-operation of the state organization. Only "my Lord Roscoe," as the
uncomfortable presidential candidate called him, was conspicuously
absent, but his henchmen represented him well. The New Yorkers set
to work at home and Conkling and Grant went into Ohio and Indiana
to stump for the party. Though they barely mentioned the nominee,
it was satisfying to see all members of the Republican team pulling in
approximately the same direction. Dorsey too began to smile as banking and industry delivered its financial subsidies and as John D. Rockefeller turned his Standard Oil organization in Indiana into an append-
age of the party so that another doubtful state might be hauled bodily
into the Republican column.

Exactly what were the terms of the "Treaty of Fifth Avenue" has
never been agreed upon. Garfield said, and perhaps thought, he had
made no promises to leave Conkling an absolute monarch in the New
York domain. His biographers tend to take this view. On the other
hand, Tom Platt, who affluently employed a press agent to write his
"Autobiography," and several more adherents of the Conkling wing
said flatly, years later, that Garfield surrendered all control over the
state's share in federal patronage in exchange for the New Yorkers'
promise of a vigorous effort to deliver the vote.

Probably, the truth is closer to Platt's version. For Garfield, despite
a usually clear mind, was capable of self-hypnosis when he entered into
his occasional deals of doubtful morality. Perhaps, while he spoke to
Conkling's lieutenants, his mental reservations were more ambiguous
than his words. Certainly, the Stalwarts knew their trade, and were not
given to arduous labors in a cause where the rewards, in their understanding, would be a matter of speculation. To them the candidate's
speeches must have sounded like an acceptance of a contract. And, because in politics such things are better left unwritten and unsigned,
they probably reasoned that Garfield's statements, qualified and sharp-
ened from two days of negotiation, were his bond. In the peculiar ethics
of their profession that would have been sufficient. That Garfield had
another interpretation, however, would soon be demonstrated.

In the meantime, Stalwarts and Half-Breeds caught up on the time
they had lost. In Blaine's Maine, the party met defeat in September; but
the Indiana expenditures proved more fruitful in October. Gradually
the initial advantages of the Democrats were overcome. Hancock's ineptitude and the forged letter tilted the scales. Because of the protesting
Greenback vote, neither candidate received a popular majority. In the
closest general election in American history, Garfield's plurality was

fewer than 10,000 votes, or .08 per cent more of the total than Hancock received. The electoral vote of the states was more decisive, 214 to 155.

2. A TARNISHED SOUL

Chester Arthur's nomination may have appealed to practical politicians as the way out of their dilemma. It awoke scant approval in other quarters. John Sherman accepted the blow to his hope of the presidency by "heartily" endorsing Garfield as soon as he heard the convention's accolade had gone to his fellow Ohioan. But of the vice-presidential selection he was critical and suspicious: "The nomination of Arthur is a ridiculous burlesque and I am afraid was inspired by a desire to beat the ticket." A few days later, he had reconciled himself to the fact that in voting for Garfield, he would also have to vote for his New York running mate. But he thought it "rather a scandalous proceeding." To independent Republicans, E. L. Godkin wrote consolingly in the *Nation's* editorial columns. They would do well to accept the slate, he said, because the vice-presidency would serve the double purpose of removing Arthur from the sphere of New York politics while tethering him in an office where "his powers of mischief" would be small. The possibility that Garfield might die was "too unlikely a contingency to be worth making [any] extraordinary provision for."

This lack of appreciation for the candidate was echoed in private conversations and capitalized upon in the Democratic press. Because Arthur had no party standing outside his own state, it was generally believed that Roscoe Conkling had exacted the nomination as the price of Stalwart peace. Very few were aware of the Senator's strident disapproval of the arrangement when it was first put before him; the most that all knew of was his unhidden outrage at Grant's defeat. Therefore, they took Chester Arthur on what superficially was his record, and sensitive Republicans cast their ballots for him with averted nostrils. That he had never held an elective office before the 1880 campaign accounted for some of the questions raised about his abilities. That he had been a henchman in Conkling's machine for thirteen years, however, was more responsible for the doubts.

Yet, a closer reading of his past would have served to clear a number of the misconceptions surrounding him. For Arthur was something more than a caricature of a machine politician. Personally, he was an upright man and a capable attorney. His interest in politics aside, he demonstrated every quality required of a gentleman in his day. He was polite and dignified. His culture was the culture of good taste and literary discrimination. In an amateur way, he was an expert in Robert

Burns's poetry. He read and reread Scott and Thackeray, two of the classical favorites of Victorian America. At dinner, his conversation was polished; in the drawing room, his manner perfect; in the office, his attitude deliberate and confident. His elegance of dress, tailored to meet a fastidiousness that stopped just short of foppery, belied his Vermont birth and a boyhood spent in following his father, a Baptist minister, from one upstate New York church to another.

His family background gave Chester Arthur many things—a feeling for books and study, the abolitionist's creed, and conservative instincts. But neither his father's religion nor the small town could satisfy him. New York City opened visions of a career in law, and the law career led him into club life and politics. The city thrust aside the conventionalities of the hinterlands and educated him to good wines and epicurean meals. It introduced him to society and to the girl from a fine Virginia family who became his wife. Not surprisingly he threw off the Baptist faith and returned to the Episcopalian church of his English forefathers.

Originally, he had gone into politics to enhance his future as a lawyer in much the same manner many young lawyers take a swing in the game, hoping not so much for public office as for the connections that will bring them in a few clients. In time, the clients came and Arthur's practice grew. By then politics was in his blood or, more accurately, in his brain, for Chester Arthur was too imperturbable a man to become inflamed by partisanship. He continued in the law, but his best work was done in the field of negotiation rather than in trial work or the writing of briefs. This was suggestive, too, of his approach to politics. National issues, public issues in general, were outside his interests; platform writing and public speeches were the necessary chores he left to others. What fascinated him about the game was its susceptibility to manipulation, the chances it offered for directing men and controlling situations. Being an intelligent man he recognized readily that political power was capable of diverse uses, that it could bend a single given situation in a number of directions according to what application might be chosen. But Arthur seldom concerned himself with the *what* quality of his fascination; the *how* quality consumed too much of his attention. As a politician, he bore the same relationship to a statesman as a mechanic does to a scientist or a printer to a poet.

This attitude, in a large measure, explains the peculiar nature of Arthur's career—his single elective office, his few appointive offices, his years of devotion to the restricted work of keeping the New York Republican machine in power. Essentially, he was a private citizen steadily pursuing a hobby. That politics took much of his time, that he became an expert practitioner of its arts on the level he chose for himself, in no way changed its status as the hobby in his life. Though he demonstrated an unusual proficiency for an amateur—indeed a skill beyond that of most professionals—he was ultimately controlled by the masters of the craft like Conkling. His primary occupation remained the law. Only with his strange inclusion on the Garfield ticket did he renounce his amateur standing and set himself up as a master in his own right. In doing so he permitted ambition to supersede sophisticated interest, he allowed a lust for office to overcome his more dispassionate study of the workings of political methods.

But this was a picture of Chester Arthur generally unknown to the public. Even politicians who had not met him or those who were barely acquainted with him tended to think of him in stereotyped terms. Newspaper and magazine cartoonists caught his six-foot height, the elegance of his apparel and the care he took of his impressive side-whiskers and moustache; but their jobs were to portray him conveniently, not correctly. They saw him as Conkling's lieutenant, and because their organs opposed the Senator, they pilloried Arthur whenever his doings were sufficiently newsworthy to merit the attention of the press. Since Arthur's legal practice was seldom significant enough for editorial comment, he was given to the public in the unlovely trappings of his avocation, as a chief mechanic who worked to keep a wayward political machine in running order.

If, however, this emphasis improperly portrayed the true intentions of the man, if it implied that his deeds and thoughts were darker than was actually so, it nevertheless placed him in the correct category of the political stream of his time. As the public knew him, so it reacted to him. Because Arthur rarely bothered to defend himself against the flood of journalistic criticism, it came to be more or less assumed that he was what the press said he was. This, in turn, was reflected in the attitude that the "clubhouse boys" held toward him. Though his personal honesty and dignity set him apart from them, his geniality and his persistent concern for the party's success gave them a wrong impression. Behind his back, they called him "Chet," a nickname he did not like. They thought of him as one of them, perhaps a trifle removed by his culture and expensive tastes, but a regular organization man. That he was a serious student of their profession probably did not occur to them. As a result, Arthur allowed himself to be categorized in such a way that he became identified inseparably with Conkling's Republicanism.

In the beginning of his career this had not been true. Before the Civil War, his abolitionist upbringing had naturally led him into the young Republican party. His capable work in the precincts of New York City had won him the friendship and gratitude of Edwin D. Morgan, who in 1860 was elected the Seward-Weed governor of the state. Young Arthur's first reward at Morgan's hands was a staff appointment as engineer-in-chief of the state militia, a decorative post of no significance. But the coming of the war rapidly expanded the opportunities for young politicians; and Arthur was soon, with Morgan's blessing, quartermaster general in charge of equipping New York's troops before they went to the front. One of the concomitants of the post was its military title; but its basic political nature is clear from the fact that, in 1863, there was a change of administrations and "General" Arthur was retired to private life despite his excellent record in the position, and without reference to the incidental fact that the war was still being fought with no apparent sign of its rapid termination.

Back he went to his practice and his hobby. Being a conservative, he generally supported the national administration, especially against the Radical Republicans. In later years, he claimed to have been one of those who swung the state delegation to the 1864 convention over to Andrew Johnson. At any rate, he sided with Seward and Weed in their fight to retain control of the party in New York in the days when Johnson's course was making it increasingly difficult for a man to be pro-administration and loyally Republican at the same time. In the defeat of 1866, Arthur went down with the rest; but being more curious of device than of principle he was quickly on the road to recovery. By aligning himself with the more moderate, and ultimately successful, Conkling faction that was one of three battling for control of the party within the state, he was able to save himself from the obscurity that engulfed so many others who had stood behind the stubborn Tennessean. Contributing calm judgment, administrative ability and his faculty for efficient organization, Arthur helped the Senator consolidate his power and create his machine. Gradually he moved up the pyramid of the party structure from committee to committee, until in 1871, President Grant paid one of his many tributes to Roscoe Conkling's services by appointing Chester Arthur to the Collectorship of the Port of New York.

The New York Customs House was the cornerstone of the state Republican machine. Here there were jobs with which to reward loyal workers; here there were salaries of political appointees that could be taxed to keep the party war-chest filled. Its balance sheet showed operations worth $900,000,000 annually and out of this certain employees and probably some collectors profited past their legal emoluments. Almost automatically the head of the Customs House was endowed with a strong voice in the direction of local affairs. Chester Arthur, therefore, became the acknowledged boss of the Republican party within the city. On the whole he used his power benignly but always toward the end of keeping the machine intact. In President Grant's Washington, Roscoe Conkling, at the apogee of his influence, was pleased. A single blemish, however, brought on disagreeable consequences.

The collector's income from the office was, at the time of Arthur's appointment, derived from a percentage of the fines he collected. By this system Arthur was able to average about $40,000 a year. In 1872, he received information that one of the city's largest and richest importing firms had, by the process of undervaluing its goods that passed through the Customs House, rendered itself liable for $1,750,000 in forfeitures and fines. Rather than subject itself to a long court suit and the attendant unfavorable publicity, the company quietly agreed to a compromise payment of about $270,000. But, after paying, it discovered that its undervaluations had deprived the government of exactly $1,664.68 in duties, while the larger sum had already been divided, according to the law, between the higher officers of the port and Conkling and some others who had provided legal advice. Naturally a cry was raised, and naturally the cry culminated in a congressional investigation. The result was an end to the system of moieties and its replacement by a fixed annual salary of $12,000 for the collector.

Yet the incident cast no more than a temporary shadow. In 1875, Grant reappointed Arthur for another term. Meanwhile, the machine rolled smoothly. A few more men than were absolutely necessary to efficient operations drew pay from the Customs House largess; here and there, a political enemy was removed from his sinecure; the regular assessments for party purposes continued without grave discomfort to the jobholders; the revenue laws were fairly interpreted and judiciously inforced.

Then, in 1877, President Rutherford B. Hayes took a genuine interest in reforming the customs service, and John Sherman, his Secretary of the Treasury, saw an opportunity to appear the reformer without actually having to become one. A special commission was appointed to investigate Arthur's domain, discovered the conditions outlined above as well as a number of minor defalcations among the subordinates, and imparted its unfriendly biases to a report highly critical of the collector's administration. Probably, the real faults lay more in the statutes, as they were drawn, than in the men enforcing them; but Hayes was convinced of the alleged derelictions of the port's officers and his Treasury minister did nothing to disabuse him. The President was intent upon separating politics from the Customs House; Sherman, who had not been above sending officeseekers to Arthur for placement while the investigation was going on, wanted to create a personal machine in New York's patronage keystone so that he might use its potent leverage to secure the Republican presidential nomination in 1880. Under the existing circumstances this meant lining up with the Curtis-Godkin reformist element against the threatened Conkling faction, and depending upon them to capture the state's delegation.

In October Hayes nominated Theodore Roosevelt, Sr., a respectable businessman, to head a slate of appointees replacing Arthur and his organization. In the Senate Conkling invoked the hoary doctrine of senatorial courtesy and blocked confirmation. There the struggle rested until July of 1878, when the President suspended the incumbent sinners in the Customs House and substituted for them a group who were, Sherman assured him, his friends. Meanwhile Roosevelt had inconveniently died, and Edwin A. Merritt had been elevated to the collectorship. That winter the fight went back to the Senate. This time Conkling was weaker; Sherman had lobbied among his Republican friends in the upper house who were joined by twenty-five Democrats prepared to believe the worst about New York spoils politicians. Banding together, they upheld the President. Exultantly, John Sherman set out to break the "anti-Administration ring" in the Empire State.

Sherman, however, had engaged a resourceful enemy without making certain of his own front-line generals. Collector Merritt was indisposed to use his new office for the benefit of John Sherman or anyone else. Instead, he worked to clear the Customs House of political connections, and thereby left Chester Arthur in control of the district and city committees of the Republican party. The total political effect of almost two years of assault on the Stalwart machine had been to remove the port patronage from its control. Thus the Conkling faction had been somewhat weakened in comparison to the others in the state. But it still retained enough strength to dominate local conventions and nominate its own candidates. Sherman had gained practically nothing except a reputation for friendliness to reform. Even this latter disappeared a few months later when, to give the appearance of party unity, he was forced to come into New York on Arthur's invitation to speak approvingly of the Conkling slate in the state elections.

* * *

James Abram Garfield shared with Chester Arthur a number of common characteristics—intellectual curiosity, a God-fearing family background, a genial manner, a frame well-built and tall. He too could thank the Civil War for the impetus it gave his political career. Before the conflict he had first dallied briefly with the ministry and then had turned to education and become president of a small Ohio college. In joining the local prestige of his academic name with his speaking abilities, he had entered Ohio politics as a conservative antislaveryite. With the outbreak of war, he secured a commission from Governor Dennison and, in a short time, was commanding a brigade in the campaigns in western Tennessee. But though it was only 1862, Garfield's expansive soul was already feeling hemmed in by the stringencies of military discipline; he wanted to escape the Army, but he wanted to leave it for a higher political post than the one in the Ohio legislature that he had when he donned the uniform. Meanwhile, his friends back home were keeping careful watch over his civilian future. After assiduous preparation and skillful use of his military record, they secured him the Republican nomination for Congress from Ohio's nineteenth district. This was tantamount to election. The district, lying in the Western Reserve, was New England in its background and outlook, Yankee in everything but geography; for twenty years, it had regularly returned the thick-and-thin abolitionist Joshua R. Giddings to Washington. Its rockbound Republicanism would do the same for Garfield until 1880.

On his election Garfield could immediately have retired from the Army, but chose to stay on until Congress met in December, 1863. Conflicting with his distaste for the military regimen and subordination to the will of a superior was his genuine belief that he should fight for his abolitionist principles. Moreover, as yet, his war career was indistinguishable from that of thousands of other soldiers, and less distinguished than that of many. On the one hand was his selfless readiness to help the Union cause; on the other was his understanding of the political value of heroism. Securing an extended leave from his brigade and combat service Garfield went to Washington, hoping to persuade an independent command from the War Department, one that would provide the opportunity of associating his name and leadership with a significant victory—so certain was he of his military genius. Or, if his experience in generalling troops was thought too limited, he wanted something unspectacular but noteworthy, like an amphibious expedition against undefended Florida.

Garfield's wish was unavailing. Secretary of War Stanton was having his own difficulties in fitting the plethora of politicians in uniform into posts where they might do some good, or a minimum of damage. In the competition, Garfield, whose political rank was still comparatively minor, lost out. Finally, after months of importuning, he compromised and accepted an assignment as chief-of-staff to General Rosecrans of the Army of the Tennessee. His job was primarily administrative—work which he performed adequately—but it could not hold him; after a few months, his dissatisfactions mounted at his superior's caution in refusing to smash a hard blow at the entrenched Confederates. Surreptitiously Garfield wrote to Secretary Chase, who had helped him secure the job, on Rosecrans' slowness; indiscreetly, he commented to journalists about what he considered were his commander's failings. Then Rosecrans lost his caution in a bold ill-conceived thrust that resulted in the Union disaster at Chickamauga.

The remarks of his chief-of-staff and others produced their desired effect in Washington; the General was removed from his command. In the defeat Garfield had played a minor heroic role that was quickly blown into proportions far larger than either its daring or its contribution to mitigating the defeat. But it won him major general's stars for his part in a battle that had disgraced his leader. The promotion ended his military days; the time had come for his return to Washington for congressional session. Without regret he exchanged the uniform for the tail-coat; but he never forgot the title he had been given. During his next seventeen years those stars were worth many times their weight in the votes GAR veterans poured into the ballot boxes to keep him in office.

From the start Garfield's war rank, his intellect and his skill in declamation made him something of a leader in the House. In his first few terms, on the issues of Lincoln's conduct of the war and Reconstruction, he tended to side with the Radicals, but never in the same bitter spirit that men like Henry Winter Davis and Thaddeus Stevens displayed. After Stevens' death, when Radical Republicanism disintegrated, Garfield was generally to be found on the conservative side of most questions. If he could not find the conservative side he found the safe one. On the whole he tried to fit in with the majority of his party; and thus, in a period when Congress was doing little that was striking, his name did not appear on any piece of important legislation.

Probably his most important work was done on the conservative side of the monetary battles that marked the post-bellum era—in fighting for a continuance of the gold payments to bondholders, and later, in holding out against the periodic cries for "cheap money," greenbacks and free silver. Coming from an agricultural district, he was, at first, unenthusiastic about high tariffs; but as industrialization came to Ohio, his opinions became more protectionist. The salient factors of his rise, therefore, cannot be said to have come from his contributions to government; they came, rather, from his efforts as a party chieftain.

Gradually he inherited the Republican leadership of the House. In part he owed this to his long tenure and his persistent presence while others passed on—Thaddeus Stevens to death, Schuyler Colfax to the vice-presidency, James Blaine to the Senate. But Garfield also possessed a certain likeableness and warmth of personality that safely carried him through several scandals in which he appeared to be either the accomplice or the dupe of undoubted corruptionists (the verdict, undecided in contemporary investigations or in history, depends upon the personal sympathies of the judge). Furthermore, in keeping himself clear of the Blaine and Conkling factions while maintaining his party regularity intact, he was able to stand between them, mediate matters that affected the party in the House, and retain some of the confidence of each side. After 1875, when the Democrats were in control of the House for three consecutive Congresses, his seniority and experience made him the recognized leader of the Republican minority. His work was difficult. The Hayes administration had to contend with not only the hostile Democratic majority but with its unpopularity among members of its own party. Garfield, as its spokesman in Congress, had the prodigious task of holding in check the wild horses of Republican factionalism. That he did so with considerable skill ultimately made possible his presidential nomination. That his leadership seemed trustworthy cemented the Republican unity necessary to elect him President.

Once elected, however, his chances for success rested upon the preservation of that unity. The interpretation of the "Treaty of Fifth Avenue" became uppermost in setting the note his administration would sound. It soon leaked out that the payment for Blaine's support was to be the State Department. Appreciating realities, the New York Stalwarts were disposed to accept the appointment without protest. For their campaign labors they had understood that their reward would be a counterbalance to the cabinet prestige of the State Department and a post of greater power—in short, the Treasury. They had already handpicked Levi Morton for the position. Two complications blocked Garfield's way: the West, even western Stalwarts were demanding the office; and Morton, being a Wall Street banker as well as an easterner, was therefore doubly unacceptable. In terms of principle, the New York point was obscure; but from the standpoint of his slipping power, Conkling needed control of the office, and somehow felt that the symbol of his power required the first man he named be selected. It did not matter to him that other Stalwart chieftains were satisfied when their men received lesser posts, or that Morton was offered the Navy portfolio. In the end, of course, the decision lay with Garfield who, after months of irresolution, finally gave the office to William Windom, an independent from Minnesota. New York was represented but hardly mollified by the inclusion of Thomas L. James, an honest Stalwart, in the Post Office.

The strain of cabinet-making had its effect on Garfield. On his second night in the White House, he recorded in his *Journal:* "I love to deal with doctrines and events. The contests of men about men I greatly dislike." Nevertheless, that he was fated to deal with men became quickly apparent. From the outside, after the selection of the ministry, it looked as though Blaine would be the prime minister of the administration and the President his figurehead. How true this was, in fact, is open to speculation. But Garfield, in the beginning, evidently struggled against domination by the brilliant personality of his Secretary of State. He still sought to occupy the central ground of the mediator. To soothe the irate Conkling he nominated a number of machine regulars for federal posts. For three days after this peace offering, the Senator felt himself secure. On the fourth, the peace was abruptly shattered. The Senate received from the White House another nomination—for Collector of the Port of New York, William H. Robertson, regional head of the "Blaine Legion" and fugleman of the opposition to Roscoe Conkling's rule.

The strategy was obvious; though the nomination was made in Garfield's name, the quicksilvery figure of James G. Blaine was readily perceived in the background. At the Customs House, Merritt's term had two years to run; while he had done the Stalwarts no good, he had also done them no harm. Robertson's appointment was thus a clear bid to break the Conkling machine and supplant it with a new one. Highly placed callers descended upon the White House to plead with the President to change his mind—Postmaster General James, Vice-President Arthur, Republican senators, many of whom detested their colleague from New York but foresaw future troubles to themselves if the Secretary of State won a patronage victory. Senator Thomas C. Platt was particularly active. A Stalwart, he nevertheless owed his position to a bargain he had made with the Half-Breeds; in exchange for their votes in the New York State legislature he had solemnly promised to abide Robertson in *any* office. Now he was caught in the trap he himself had baited.

Meanwhile the President's will was being strengthened by praises of Blaine men and the promise of John Sherman, once again back in the Senate, to lead the administration's battle. On May 5, 1881, Garfield played his trump. Without warning, he withdrew the Conkling slate from the Senate's consideration, leaving the Robertson appointment to be acted upon. Eleven days later the senior Senator from New York shook the chambers of the upper house and blasted the Washington air by resigning his office in a righteous fury. Platt, who had conceived the tactic, echoed, "Me too." Together, they went back to Albany, expecting quick vindication by the state legislature, a rapid re-election, and a triumphant return to the Capital.

Then, something went wrong. Governor Cornell raised no hand in their behalf; Stalwart legislators slipped from under the grasp of the boss who had ruled them for ten years. Conkling lost his arrogance and was reduced to the status of one politician wheedling other politicians for support. Chester Arthur surrendered his dignity by buttonholing state legislators in lobbies. James Blaine of Maine did the same down in New York City, using his magnetic charm and Secretarial majesty to offset the cultured blandishments of the Vice-President. One night in late June, Tom Platt was caught in his hotel bedroom with a lady whose virtue was frequently easy. Victorian America or no, the story was too good to be left to back-room gossip; it made the anti-Stalwart newspapers. The publicity over the incident—wholly unmentioned by Platt in his *"Autobiography"*—forced him to step out; he relinquished his claims in favor of Conkling.

But the proceedings at Albany had dragged on too long. On July 2, Garfield was leaving on a trip through New England. Blaine was going with him. The two were in animated conversation on the Secretary's pan-American diplomacy while they went to take the train. As they walked through Pennsylvania station, an insane man, who thought himself a "lawyer, a theologian and a politician" but was none of these, stepped out of the crowd and fired two shots at point-blank range. As the President fell, the assassin shouted words that could not be recalled exactly because of the excitement, but were recalled well enough to make their general tenor and meaning clear: "I am a Stalwart and Arthur is President now!"

The Vice-President received the news in Albany, where he had gone on another lobbying junket to assist his beleaguered friend Conkling. Immediately, he left for New York and seclusion. The implications of the assassin's cry were damaging in the extreme. Politically, Conkling was ruined; the legislature counted him out of public office, never to return.

Garfield fought for life for eleven weeks. Only fifty years old, in possession of a vigorous body, he bravely looked forward to getting well and creating a signal administration. He and the country were cheered by the optimistic bulletins the doctors issued. In reality, his strength was keeping him alive. When that gave out his life ebbed away.

3. THE TARNISHED SOUL PERFORMS GOOD WORKS

If recent events were not enough to raise doubts of the new President's worthiness for the office he had inherited, his lack of experience and his political friendships were easily recalled. None questioned his knowledge of machine politics, but many doubted that it was applicable to the presidency. The opposition was forced, by the grandeur of his office, to treat Arthur a trifle more deferentially than it had in the past. Nevertheless it continued vigilant. Among his own followers, there was a similar questioning, not to mention astonishment, at the sudden twist of fortune's wheel. One of them, whose name is unfortunately lost to history, summed it up with: "Chet Arthur, President of the United States! Good God!"

Arthur himself moved cautiously, acting with the deliberate slowness of a man not quite certain of what his next step should be but realizing that he must take it in some direction. Cabinet replacements were an inevitability; yet, while they went on steadily, Blaine was among the last to go. It took seven months before the official family was reshaped; and withal, the Chief Executive accepted the resignations of Attorney General McVeagh and Postmaster General James only with genuine regret. Contrary to predictions Roscoe Conkling was not called upon to act as an official or unofficial adviser. At one point, the President offered his old chieftain a seat on the Supreme Court only to be refused. It was Arthur's last show of friendliness. The Albany episode, with its embarrassments to Arthur, had started a permanent estrangement between the two men.

Other Stalwarts, naturally, received first consideration in appointments. Irredentist Half-Breeds and Sherman partisans were carefully sorted out and starved. Still, there were no wholesale turnovers—Robertson, for example, was allowed to remain. Arthur hesitantly worked to bring better men into federal jobs. Stalwartism plus competence became the criteria of office. Among the sufferers under the new dispensation were some surprised members of the old machine.

The test of Arthur's sincerity began from the moment he assumed the presidency. In Garfield's legacy was an item of a corruption ring that had systematically mulcted the Post Office Department of millions of dollars through fraudulent mail contracts. Of itself, this might have been a routine case for government attorneys if two important Stalwarts had not been instrumental in making the conspiracy workable. But one defendant was Stephen W. Dorsey, the manager of the 1880 campaign and a friend of the Chief Executive;[3] another was Thomas J. Brady, Second Assistant Postmaster General and a Stalwart who had taxed the Department's employees for Garfield's political benefit a short year before. These complications the President set aside in his determination to prosecute "with the full vigor of the law." Evidently, however, the law was not vigorous enough. Defense attorneys secured delays and technical advantages; witnesses for the state recanted their confessions; one "hung" jury forced a second trial; the second jury was probably bribed. Finally, the accused were freed without punishment. The Attorney General and his lawyers tried hard; the law defeated them. Those outraged at the miscarriage of justice did not stop to weigh the causes; Arthur's administration was blamed.

The real evidences of Arthur's conversion arose in his dealings with Congress. The Forty-seventh, which met him at the beginning of his term, was the first in six years to have a Republican majority in both houses. From it Arthur hoped to obtain a number of enactments that might draw some credit to himself, help the country, and improve conditions in those peripheral areas where the government made its impact upon the people. In those years of peace, economic expansion and small government, he had no thought of presenting a correlated legislative program. The President, in his conservatism, would not have asked for one; probably the United States did not need one. His desires were simple. He asked for tariff revision (not, it will be noted, sweeping reduction), for an improved presidential succession law, for power

---

[3] In February 1881, Arthur, as Vice-President-elect, had attended a testimonial dinner in honor of Dorsey and his contribution to the victory. Speakers had extolled Dorsey's services and many toasts had been drunk when Arthur arose to give his remarks. As reported by the newspapers the next day, what he said was loose and slightly enigmatical; but the inference drawn was that Indiana had been literally purchased for the Republican column in 1880 and the speaker was prepared to wink at the method in view of the accomplishment. That these words would be remembered on his accession was another of the sins he was forced to live down.

to use United States troops in dealing with the "cowboy wars" in the western territories, for funds to renovate a Navy that had fallen into disrepair and obsolescence after the Civil War, for measures to create a modern merchant marine, for a reduction of excise taxes, and for a civil service law. It was a moderate program. It contained nothing that congressmen, spawned in a tradition of subjugating Presidents Johnson, Grant and Hayes, could construe to be infringements upon their power. Yet the legislature granted him little.

Despite the fact that Garfield's death was directly traceable to the patronage wars, the congressional majority preferred to think of the popular agitation for a merit system in government appointments as "snivel service reform." Despite the surplus coming into the Treasury there was a marked reluctance to reduce taxes or tariff duties. Although many industries were protected to the point where they showed bloated profit statements, few legislators were ready to allow protection to work both ways and give relief to the American consumer. Instead, Arthur's recommendations were either forgotten or ridiculed while Senators and Representatives passed a host of private pension and relief bills and traded votes on a huge pork barrel entitled "An act making appropriations for the construction, repair, and preservation of certain works on rivers and harbors, and for other purposes." The good and evil in it were mixed; the "other purposes" predominated. Arthur courageously vetoed it, only to watch the Republican majority override and denounce his reasonably worded message.

What was necessary was strong public pressure. That came in the mid-term elections, with disastrous results to the Republican party, as will be seen shortly. Only in its "lame-duck" session of 1882-1883 did the Forty-seventh Congress take up the Presidential requests. While Democrats jeered, the GOP suddenly discovered virtue in Senator George Pendleton's civil service bill. More to freeze Republican appointees in office under the measure's tenure provisions than in a genuine spirit of reform, they made it into law. Showing a somewhat keener sense of honor, Arthur selected three competent commissioners to administer the act and draw up regulations. During the rest of his term, he encouraged them in their work while they took employees of the Post Office and Treasury under their jurisdiction and away from the politicians.

His revenue proposals had a harder time. Tax reduction is always popular and the elections had returned such a mandate. This, the House had no difficulty in meeting; but to the problem of government finance became inextricably bound the question of tariff revision. Theoretically, tariffs for revenue are appropriate subjects for consideration in the wider areas of financing the government's budget. The existing philosophy, however, was undoubtedly the product of a desire for protection rather than income; it was the preference of protectionists that rates should be set so high that no foreign goods could compete with domestic goods in the American market; if no foreign goods entered, so much the better—there would be no duties collected to provide the Treasury with surpluses; if no surpluses existed, agitators would be deprived of an argument for tariff reduction.

In 1881, Congress had authorized the President to appoint a tariff commission which would give expert advice on a "scientific" readjustment of the rates. In late 1882, its report was ready, including a draft for a bill that would generally cut rates between twenty and twenty-five per cent, simplify schedules on certain commodities, add several items to the "free list," and bring the protectionist system into closer relationship with the recent developments in the nation's rapidly growing economy. Consumers were to be helped by lower duties on necessities, conservative manufacturers benefited by reductions on imported raw materials.

Congress accepted the report and shelved it. The House set to work on its own, creating a bill that had no connection with the commission's suggestions. The Senate began constructing another, attaching it as an amendment to the tax reduction law—by which method the upper house, though constitutionally denied the power to originate revenue measures, circumvented an explicit prohibition.

Now that there were three tariff laws proposed, none could secure the required passage by both houses. By sharp parliamentary practice, the Senate amendment was referred to a joint committee packed with protectionists. Their method of resolving the difficulty was interesting: wherever there was disagreement, they simply raised the duty on the commodity under dispute to a level above any of the three proposed revisions. In twenty-four hours they rewrote the entire tariff law. Appended to the revenue bill, it was enacted. If John Sherman is to be believed, every lobby, but that of the wool growers he represented, got what it wanted. With misgivings President Arthur signed the bill. Personally he had favored the Tariff Commission's plan, but the extent of his pressure on Congress constituted bare recommendation. Thus what he received he could not veto without killing those excise tax reductions he had also asked for.

*　　*　　*

The new tariff law passed Congress with frenzied speed on March 3, 1883. On the next day the Democrats took control of the House in accordance with the recent dictation of popular opinion. From that moment upper and lower houses glared at one another and ripped into each other's programs. Neither paid much heed to the wishes of the Executive. On the last day of his term, he was permitted to approve part of the naval program he had asked for so hopefully three and a half years before. The few reciprocity trade treaties he submitted to the Senate were cut to ribbons by Republicans who moved in response to the anti-administration criticisms of James G. Blaine. Most of the time both parties girded for 1884, the Democrats by investigating Republican peccabilities, the Republicans by retorting to the charges.

4. THE PENITENT SPURNED

The melodramatic utterance of Garfield's murderer had blackened a name already recently besmirched by the Dorsey dinner and the electioneering at Albany. Adding these to what they knew of Arthur's record in New York, Washington gossips were amply prepared with conclusions. Any new evidence that presented itself they automatically set down to conform with what had already been decided about him. His naturally florid complexion was adduced to mean that he drank excessively. His friendship for one of the daughters of his Secretary of State was blown up into an infatuation or worse. He was observed to set flowers daily before the picture of an attractive woman; semi-officially, it became necessary to circulate the intelligence that the picture was of his dead wife. There were endless rumors of his impending marriage, the prospective brides ranging from several ladies of the city's corps of rich widows to Frances Willard, the temperance advocate.

What these tales did to Arthur's reputation can only be imagined. His experiences in politics during his presidency are more easily measurable. The Half-Breeds were opposed to him from the beginning. The reformers partially revised their opinions on the President's unexpected dignity in office and his urgings for civil service legislation; but they remained wary to the end. Stalwarts were not only disaffected by the leanness of the patronage; they were tired of the old Conkling dictatorship. In New York they began clustering around Governor Cornell and Collector Robertson; outside, the allied machines made peace with the Blaine faction, a unity blessed by talk of a Blaine-Logan ticket in 1884. Indications of the respect given the Chief Executive's intentions are to be found in the mail fraud trials where the defendants were unblushingly represented by Robert Ingersoll, the veteran popularizer of Blaine, and by Roscoe Conkling, the unregenerate Stalwart. Nor was Arthur aided when the fallen Senator's references to "His Accidency" passed into common conversation.

A real test of presidential appeal could have been the mid-term elections. The deeds of the Forty-seventh Congress precluded that. In its mulish disregard for the President's recommendations, it illustrated how weak was his leadership; but in doing so, it even more highlighted its own refusal to answer the popular demands for legislative progress. In November the people revenged their dissatisfactions by giving the Democrats almost two-thirds of the House. Through control of a few key state legislatures the Republicans narrowly preserved their majority in the Senate. Of itself the result hardly reflected well on the administration's strength. Still, Arthur might have escaped the implied censure directed so greatly at Congress and the Republican party were it not for his misadventures in his home state.

In New York the unedifying senatorial struggle at Albany during the previous year remained a living memory. Out of the wreckage of Conkling's machine had grown the alliance of strength between Cornell and Robertson; in 1882, it was still feeling the warm comfort of its victory and demanding permanent recognition. On the other hand, in Chester Arthur were stirring the rampant ambitions he had suppressed for so many years; in the presidency by chance, he wanted the office by popular mandate. For this he would need control of his own state, though the raw materials he had to work with were unprepossessing. His supremacy could be insured only by designating a governor who represented the Arthur Stalwarts, and the most likely man was Secretary of the Treasury Folger.

Partly concealed attempts were begun to win state delegates for Folger's nomination. The President visited New York City "on vacation"; departmental patronage was dispensed to facilitate the immediate end in view. But sitting athwart the plan was Cornell's resolution for another term. In the very close division of the party, secrecy on the President's moves was lost. Folger received the state convention's endorsement by the slightest margin amid a fraudulent use of proxies by his managers in organizing the assemblage. The nature of the Secretary's exalted backing became well known and even exaggerated. In addition to the Republican record in Congress, "Presidential bossism" became a major issue in the local campaign. The voters heeded the cry and overwhelmingly elected Folger's opponent, Grover Cleveland, the relatively obscure mayor of Buffalo. For Arthur, it was a disastrous rout; in his first real venture as an independent leader, the seriousness of his loss was magnified by the distance and prominence from which he sought to impose his will.

In the national sphere, meanwhile, James G. Blaine soon emerged as the President's leading antagonist. As Secretary of State he had pursued a rather reckless jingoist course toward Europe—England in particular—and an expansionist one toward the rest of the world. Arthur's accidental succession numbered Blaine's days in office; on his withdrawal his policies were completely reversed by his replacement, Frederick T. Frelinghuysen. Being a conservative like his chief, the new Foreign Secretary gave the Department an unexciting administration; what he did was, for the most part, to pull in America's diplomatic antennae and return American foreign relations to the unimaginative ways of the pre-Blaine years. This became the first stick the Maine politician used in belaboring the new government. Out of office, he was addressing himself to writing impartial history in his two-volume *Twenty Years of Congress*. Sold at private subscription the work gave him a larger income than any public salary but the presidency's. In his book the author managed to restrict autobiographical references to a modest minimum, though he was not quite able to rein in his Republican prejudices.

But every so often he turned away from his literary efforts. From Augusta, where his house stood on the active political path across the street from the State Capitol, or from other parts of the country, where he might be touring for other than authorial reasons, came criticisms and denunciations of Chester Arthur and the contemporary conduct of national affairs. Besides foreign policy, Blaine had his own program for the revenue surplus. The President wanted to apply it toward reducing the Civil War debt and replacing the naval antiquaries with new ships of the line; Blaine advocated a variation on an old Henry Clay theme: distribution of the excess tax receipts among the states. Meanwhile he conferred with regular organization politicians over the 1884 nomination. Logan, as has been indicated, was promised the vice-presidency; out of the convolutions of New York factionalism Tom Platt reappeared from under his cloud waving the "Plumed Knight's" banner.

Coming into the convention Arthur stood for nomination on his record of conservatism and moderation. He owned the venal southern delegations, still counted some old Stalwart retainers and had fair support among Republican businessmen. But he also had enemies. Grant had grown embittered when the New Yorker showed independence of the General's advice and an unwillingness to favor the General's jaded office-seeking friends. Wayne McVeagh had helped drive off Independent Republicans with a public letter which said, with obvious innuendo, that "Guiteau [Garfield's assassin] was the original Arthur man." The reform element was behind Senator George Edmunds of Vermont. Its leader was George Hoar of Massachusetts, who had been offended by a non-political appointment to the collectorship of the Boston port and who became an active foe when Arthur vetoed the rivers and harbors bill. Hoar was assisted by George William Curtis and a noisy, high-voiced, wild-eyed young man who threw his arms around while he stood on his chair and orated—Theodore Roosevelt, Jr. of New York, son of the man who had once been named to supersede Chester Arthur at the head of the Customs House. The totality of this opposition forced Arthur's drive back onto the defensive before it was well under way.

In the preliminary roll calls an anti-Blaine majority won the organization of the meeting. On the first ballot Arthur was second to Blaine by virtue of his southern adherents. But he was not the candidate to unite the party. During three more ballots his support fell away and Blaine was nominated while reformers and old-line Salwarts raged. The President cheerfully acquiesced in the decision, congratulated his rival and promised his "hearty support."

The campaign that followed was probably the dirtiest in American history. Republicans uncovered the fact that Grover Cleveland, the Democratic nominee, had sired an illegitimate child in his younger days of roistering. A new sheaf of letters, signed by Blaine, appeared and once again demonstrated the writer's penchant for allowing his office, name and influence to secure him commissions and payments from ambitious promoters. In one damaging piece Blaine sent his best regards to his correspondent's wife, after which he requested, "Burn this letter." It was to the candidate's misfortune that the injunction was not followed by the addressee. His exact phrases were turned into song by the Democrats and chanted through the streets. Other dubious procedures included his attendance at a gaudy millionaire's dinner—to be publicized as "Belshazzar's Feast"—and his negligence in failing to renounce, until too late, a clergyman's benediction that characterized the Democratic party in a burdensome alliteration of "Rum, Romanism, and Rebellion." Lukewarm Stalwarts were but another of many factors to contend with in the Empire State. In sum there were too many liabilities. Blaine lost New York by 1,000 votes; as in 1844 and 1848, that result was crucial. It tipped the election to the Democrats.

The defeat was a hard disappointment for the "Plumed Knight" to take, but he took it in silence. His backers showed poorer manners. That the party had lost the presidency for the first time since the Civil War, had lost with its most popular leader heading the ticket, was too much for them. Reasoning that might have discovered to them their mistakes in New York was abandoned in favor of excuses, and excuse searched for a scapegoat. One was found by looking toward the White House. Chester Arthur, so the chairman of the Republican National Committee charged, had withheld "loyal support," would not consult on strategy and had contributed no money; his cabinet members had likewise given nothing tangible, except for one speech by the Secretary of the Treasury to a Wall Street meeting. The dignity of his office had caused Arthur to refrain from electioneering as it now prevented his answering the accusations. Actually it could have been pointed out that his New York friends had been exceedingly devoted to the party ticket during the canvassing, and that egregious errors had cost the Half-Breeds their prize.

But, as is frequently the case in beating at scapegoats, there was ulterior design in the attack. Arthur's partisans had quietly been working for his election to the Senate after he should retire from the presidency. Their hope was to consolidate all factions around him by persuading other candidates to withdraw. The attack on him was made to forestall their efforts. Its fury, and the credence given its allegations by Half-Breeds, accomplished the desired results. Arthur refused to permit his name to be presented. The political factionalism upon which he had thrived as an amateur had made him its victim in his professional days. At the end of his term he went back to the law and died less than two years later. One does not know his last conclusions on the proper fate of the spoils politician who is converted to honesty when he reaches his ultimate power. In his urbanity he probably would have been amused that Tom Platt, his Stalwart subordinate who never reformed, overcame the near-fatality of the hotel bedroom incident, and went on to build a new Republican machine and sit once more in the United States Senate.

NEITHER the rise nor the fall of Chester Arthur and James G. Blaine raised questions. Victorian America, aside from its Jeremiahs, saw nothing truly evil in their type. Rather, it honored them. And the local politicians—the Conklings, the Platts—it munificently tolerated.

Nor did the society think itself sick; on the contrary, it felt certain of its health and viability. Steel, coal and oil; shoes, clothing and homes; railroads, factories and mills—all were enriching the country. Industrial capitalism had triumphed. Its commodities proved its wisdom. Its growth and its power demonstrated its promise of the future. Its leaders were confident; its believers satisfied. Its acceptance amounted to a national faith.

But the prickings of dissent made their inroads before all thought became as standardized as ingots. Populism raged in the West, and believed industry's supremacy a bondage rather than a blessing. In diluted form it captured the Democratic party with William Jennings Bryan for its spokesman. Under the onslaught conservatism lost its self-assurance. Some advocated repression, others conciliation; still others perceived weaknesses in the old creed and looked for new doctrines.

Significantly, an era was ending. The clarity of the old times vanished before the confusions of the new. J. P. Morgan, the financier, was more revolutionary than he thought when he bought out industrialists like Carnegie and placed business enterprise under the hegemony of the banks. Labor leaders like Gompers and Debs were creating lasting monuments where the work of their predecessors had been ephemeral. Self-assessment increased, self-criticism went deeper. The continent had been conquered; ambitions broadened. The American spirit now interested itself in lands overseas—in Hawaii, in China, in Cuba, in South America. On the threshold of world power the United States discovered its humanitarianism intertwined with nationalism, its missionary zeal allied with the profit motive. The totality of their expression was war.

1. A "SCHOLARLY COWBOY"

On May 29, 1898, a portion of the citizenry of San Antonio and the military authorities at Fort Sam Houston breathed a collective sigh of relief. The First Volunteer Cavalry—or as the newspapermen had christened it, the Rough Riders—had left for Tampa to take the boat for Cuba and the war with Spain. Somehow, in the period of less than a month that this highly publicized regiment had been quartered at the city's fair grounds—to keep its men separated from the regular army men of the city's garrison—local enthusiasm for its fabulous heroes had almost died. True, its expert horsemen had been drawn from the western ranges and from the polo fields in the East, and a few of them had made reputations in outdistancing sheriffs' posses. Yet together, they obviously were below standard as a military unit. They might be first-rate shots, but they drilled poorly and they lacked discipline. Worse, so far as their recent hosts were concerned, they had an unquenchable thirst for beer and whiskey, and took a boyish delight in discharging firearms in public places. Colonel Leonard Wood, their commander, had small appreciation for these traits that individualized his organization from the rest of the Army; but only the War Department knew him as its tactical leader. To the public, and to the men themselves, the outfit belonged to its second-in-command, Lieutenant Colonel Theodore Roosevelt, recently the vociferous Assistant Secretary of the Navy, and before that a Police Commissioner of New York City with instincts for nocturnal prowling, as well as a United States Civil Service Commissioner with a talent for baiting congressmen and cabinet officers. A well-read few knew him also as the author of a number of biographies and historical works and of some highly personal books on life in the Great West.

Nevertheless, whatever the shortcomings of the Rough Riders as a precisely trained combat force, their *esprit* was excellent. They were proud of their regiment and they adored their cocky Colonel Roosevelt. They were keen for a fight and they knew of his efforts to promote one. That the responsibility for war rested primarily upon publishers like William Randolph Hearst and Joseph Pulitzer was undeniable; still, the Colonel had been in the van calling for preparedness and the salvation of Cuba; in the final result, his words had merely carried less influence and had smaller circulation than those of the *Journal* and the *World*. His intention had been their equal. When Spain was forced to give battle rather than abjectly surrender her honor without a salvo, he fretted that the Navy would smother all opposition before his cavalrymen could leave the Florida beaches. He would have held back the war, if he could, to preserve a few Spanish targets for his own pistol and sword. This eagerness for the field he communicated to the men.

To their undisciplined habits he was a perfect counterpart. Having little military training himself, he had taken on few of the rigidities of conduct and attitude with which the Army seeks to set officers apart from enlisted men. Thus, his expansive, gregarious and even personal manner toward anyone in his command of volunteers won affection where, in regulars—stiffened from years of observance of the caste tradition—it would perhaps have returned scorn. Not that the westerners, at heart, ever wholly accepted him as one of them. Like the cowhands at the time of his earlier ranching experiments his soldiers were loyal to him and liked him, but they thought him a curio.

In his place, the Colonel held for his men a warm feeling. His admiration for daring and animal courage was lavished on a command that so fully exhibited these virtues. Its men were, ever after, to enjoy a distinct advantage from this affection. Later on, as Governor and as President, if he had the power or if action had to be pushed to the limit of discretion, a Rough Rider received favor or assistance. It was of no consequence that Santiago was an insignificant fray indeed beside Gettysburg, Shiloh or the Wilderness battles that had gone before. Santiago he regarded as his test and the test of those who were with him; the experience of the Rough Riders was for him, the great event of life. As such, it rendered its participants peculiarly worthy to enter claims and receive them.

*   *   *

The impetuous nature of Roosevelt's short military career—consuming fewer than four months—was but one facet of a personality in which reason, apologia, outright impulse, and astute calculation perpetually conflicted for the ultimate direction of his deeds. Henry Adams, who had been his teacher, remembered the younger man, even when President, as a virtual embodiment of "pure act"—surely an ironical conclusion, as Adams certainly must have recognized, to draw of one subjected for four years to the influences of the Harvard Yard. And in the popular mind, the boisterous quality of Roosevelt's outbursts gave an appearance of sheer energy turned loose without benefit of sober thought. The vitality first evoked attention. Then it became infused into a public moved to applause by the pyrotechnics of the display.

Yet, violent energy, showered exuberantly on all within range, was a manifestation of the force of the man rather than an explanation of the force itself. To be sure, with a wife and five children at home, opinion made no demands that he go to war. With his job in the Navy Department, he could—and actually did before he resigned—contribute more to victory by staying in Washington. On the face of it, and in the opinion of his friends, his decision to take the field seemed foolish, a childish reaction to the stimulant of beating drums. But if Roosevelt had rejected what seemed the practical way, he knew why he chose the other. His works, his thoughts, his impulses, his emotions were of constant fascination to him. He dug at himself, and when he had searched, he found his answer. That his anticipations of battle and his performance as a warrior verged perhaps on adolescence in the friendly eyes of his contemporaries could not have deterred him. For Roosevelt felt that having been an instrument in provoking war, he was obligated to fight.

If others had doubts of his actual motives, he had none. Motive was the one basis for his actions that he seldom examined. He presumed himself to be a just man; and what followed in his acts was therefore inevitably righteous. His side was the right side; not because he was on it, but because he could not, he believed, have been so guilty or so remiss as to pick the wrong one. Right—a word which, together with its derivatives, he was wont to use almost excessively—was more than a defense; it was a guiding sun. If this appears inconsequential today, it was not so for a goodly portion of those who dominated the political and economic jungle in the years between the Civil War and Roosevelt's presidency. For their calculations were all too frequently restrained only by—to use Boss Tom Platt's phrase—"the Ten Commandments and the Penal Code"; and occasionally loopholes were discovered in even those catalogues of proscribed activities.

The amoral atmosphere in which the public business was transacted, and in which private enterprise worked out its destiny, repelled him. He conceived himself to be fundamentally honest, and he looked for the same trait in others. Absence of principle in others he could tolerate, so long as it remained a personal eccentricity; but where dishonesty made its impact upon society, Roosevelt objected with all his vast store of vitality. Whether outrage or reasonable dissent or practical necessity forced him on a given course, the strength of the eruption gave him his audience. But his vigor flowed from the conviction of Right and would not dissipate itself after the first bold stroke. Once embarked on a crusade against evil, he continued hammering blows long after his admirers tired of the novelty, or suddenly found themselves threatened with inconvenience should the plague spot be fully eradicated.

Such an attitude would undoubtedly have left Roosevelt's political ship permanently beached were it not for his other qualities. Certainly, such self-confidence bordered on rank egotism and would have made him a pariah in his circle of highly accomplished and extremely influential men. But the Colonel had his eminently human phases as well; and these delighted his associates and the public. He loved stories, and he thoroughly enjoyed humor, including those barbs that found in him so admirable a target. He was an intensely social creature, avid for hours of "good talk" and, in his turn, anxious to fascinate his listeners.

Unlike many men with fixed notions, his range of knowledge was horizontal rather than vertical. This proved at once a liability and an asset. Though he was almost jealously proud of his work as a historian, as a naturalist, and as a soldier, his contributions to each field are more tangential than positive. Much of his scholarship was spotty, many of his conclusions warped by the strong biases he deemed righteousness. His method was one of selecting materials to prove a thesis instead of weighing the evidence to reach a conclusion. In natural history his major gifts are a number of stuffed carcasses scattered through museum galleries. His military reputation never impressed Army men; and his most perceptive biographer, Henry F. Pringle, gives an unforgettable picture of a tactician who gauged the success of the battle by the length of the casualty lists.

But the same superficiality permitted him a wide circle of friends. Cowboys, wardheelers, prizefighters, polished diplomats like Sir Cecil Spring-Rice and Baron Speck von Sternberg, wise men like Henry Adams, found themselves equally at home in his company. He had something for each of them. His political associates and those who served under him—when he trusted them—were made to glow under his compliments and were sure of his loyalty. In a very real sense, this breadth of interests kept him familiar with the public's feelings and its prejudices; a deeper concentration in any one subject may well have cost him this amazing touch.

The intricacies of economic theory never troubled him; and thus he gave little thought to the tariff or the banking system. That economists had worked out laws and theories ostensibly independent of individual whims he ignored; the basis for his own economic thinking was founded in the morality of righteousness. This may have caused both financiers and scholars to tear their hair, but the grander faith made him the more popular with the masses. Most important, this lack of depth enabled him to be a politician and to participate in the compromises a politician must inevitably make to hold his position. If, to others, deference to principle was notable for its absence in some of his dealings, Roosevelt failed to see the impropriety. A pact with a political boss like Tom Platt or an announcement in support of some particularly odious Republican form of boodle called down on his head the especially embittered venom of the critics not under his spell. He, however, could not in these instances discern the error. It was not exactly that the highly moral ends were justified by immoral means; rather, the acts were done on some greater moral level that comprehended everything which led to the realization of the Right.

For one with so much pride in his personal achievements and such confidence in the rectitude of his decisions, it is to his credit that Roosevelt often admitted he possessed only an ordinary mind. His acknowledged physical prowess, his accomplishments as a conversationalist, his excursions into so many diverse realms were all, he freely stated, the product of diligent application; of superior endowments, he said he had none. This kind of unexpected humility undoubtedly brought him friendships and supporters. No matter how far wrong he might go, and despite his refusals to concede errors, this unusual honesty of self-appraisal prevented desertions.

Yet there were always the foes his personality could not convert and his arguments could not down. To them, the crackling epithets and pithy sentences were infuriating. His famous teeth and the drooping moustache—useful in producing a wide grin or an expression of ferocious anger—were hostilely thought the mask of a poseur. The furious gestures merely emphasized an absence of constructive thinking and the man's incredible narrowmindedness. And Roosevelt's part in the creation of these hatreds was considerable. His opponents were never to be conciliated; they were to be damned. Implacably he went after them; a mistaken opinion became an arrant sin; a criticism or a rejection a personal affront. In "malefactors of great wealth," in "muckrakers," in "reformers," and in "anarchists" he found little to commend. Their disagreement with him or with his methods, he answered with all the picturesqueness of his vocabulary.

It could hardly have been otherwise. The unwavering faith in the morality of his causes recognized no other pretensions. The confidence in self as the instrument of righteousness automatically interpreted contrary views to be irrevocably tainted. It is perhaps the fate of the Roosevelts to arouse violent emotions among their proponents and detractors. At any rate, the Colonel, in his lifetime, busily defended himself in an enormous body of writings on his deeds and his principles. What he made of his life and how he affected his world will be considered later. For the moment, however, the nature of his thought deserves examination. In it are discernable the mainsprings of his policies and methods, the reasons for the partisanship that marked the public's reaction to him.

As has been said, his course was founded in a conviction of personal righteousness and honesty. Premises lodged in his brain became moral dicta. They were unshakable. In his intense curiosity about himself, he explained them to his own mind and then set out toward proselytizing the public to his beliefs. The correction of abuses coming out of the aggrandizement of the individual or the privileged at the expense of the whole community he made a first article of his creed. At the same time, he rejected communism or socialism as solutions—though some in moneyed circles here doubted his sincerity—in favor of private property and capitalistic enterprise. By 1900, however, he had concluded that free competition was an impossible ideal, that large-scale industrial organization had rendered it impossible, and, in any event, was more efficient. Yet, he approved this conclusion with mixed feelings. Efficiency, as a word, had, to him, almost religious significance. Thus, efficient economic organization was to be encouraged. But somewhere in the process of growth he found that efficiency became secondary to power, that industrial giants used their strength to rule the community, to dictate conditions, instead of producing for the benefit of all. This was the point at which Roosevelt's delight for capitalism and the capitalist ceased. Where trusts changed from instruments of good to machines of plunder, the public welfare demanded their control.

Roosevelt never doubted such control was possible. In a legal sense, he always advocated obedience to the law; but, at heart, he was ever impatient with "legalism." Restrictions on the scope of the government, as long as it acted in the public interest, he could not see. Both the Constitution and the law under it were, in his interpretation, boundlessly elastic; they put only small restraints upon a government charting its course for the good of the people. Inevitably then, he saw public control of private industry as an incontestable necessity, since industry seemed incapable of going its own free way without engaging in piracy.

In the larger public policy, the role of government was similarly great. Since Theodore Roosevelt was a devotee of strength, it was natural for him to believe in strong government. His passion for efficiency dictated that the government be central, that its powers be sufficient to overcome the hindrances of localism or private interests. As constitutional theory, this, of course, placed Roosevelt in the camp of the old Hamiltonians. His thinking, however, went beyond ideas of mere Federal Union. To him the United States was a Nation; its government was National. So much the nationalist was he that the very word became a symbol, to be capitalized as if to give it profounder truth. And through his nationalism he developed a faith in the compelling destiny of his country. Her course, he was convinced, was purer than that of any other in the world. Her future was brighter and must be realized. Where other politicians might say these things as platitudes and empty pomposities, Roosevelt believed them implicitly. Those who denied them were "utterly and hopelessly wrong." If he became a jingo in the process of advancing America in her mission, or if he sounded a trifle ridiculous when he warned against our becoming "effete," he was unconscious of fault. His brand of Americanism was part of his morality; it represented truth beyond question. Whether pursuing domestic or foreign policy, he tried to equate the action with the shining objective. When circumstances forced him in a given direction—during the coal strike of 1902, for example—his personal justification lay in harmonizing the event with the goal.

His presence in the Republican party was explained—to himself, at least—in just such terms. It was not enough that his aristocratic birth and family lineage made him a Republican by inheritance, or that a member of his social stratum drifted normally into that party's ranks. Roosevelt, once again, explored *his* reasons for joining in the drift. Thus, he uncritically accepted the party's reputation for having sustained the cause of Union and justice during the Civil War. Probably more to the point, however, was the party tradition advocating a strong central government—a doctrine it held to with astonishing consistency against the counteradvocacy of Democratic localism until the advent of the second Roosevelt gave Republicans a sudden enthusiasm for states' rights. That Republicanism placed power in the Congress, and not the presidency, apparently, bothered the Colonel little. He was fond of recalling the dominance of Lincoln as the ultimate example of Executive strength in the GOP. The cases of the weaker men whose careers separated his from the Great Emancipator's he conveniently ignored. Nevertheless, once a Republican, he covered his chosen political side with the same high morality in which he blanketed all his other fundamental precepts. The party, he felt, was the destined guide to the United States in her mission. Its aberrations, therefore, were minor when compared to those of the Democrats; its candidates, no matter how poor, had an initial superiority in their label that no man of the opposition could meet. In 1912, when Roosevelt was to upset party regularity by running as a Progressive, his reason—to be differentiated from the obvious fact that he wanted a third term—was simply that the older party had ceased to be a guide, and had fallen on the wrong side of grace. By 1916, he was again prepared to believe in its purity.

Obviously, a man of energy equipped with these bed-rock faiths—a moral purpose, strong government in the public interest, efficiency, ardent nationalism, a dominant Executive, unflinching Republicanism—was bound to cause more than a ripple, if given the opportunity. In those times America was easy and complacent. Set against this norm, a man of action stood out, his importance magnified by the absence of intensity in those around him. Provided he did not stray too far from convention his strength of purpose won approval and his leadership won recognition.

Until the country found Woodrow Wilson, Theodore Roosevelt inevitably assumed the stature of a colossus in national life such as had not been seen since 1865. Recent students—historians and biographers—have had few greater delights than in cutting him down to a more normal size. Discrepancies between the faith and the works have been laid bare. A more skeptical generation has found even the faith, as explained by its apostle, a bit tawdry. From study of his voluminous writings, there has emerged the conclusion that the first Roosevelt was neither logical nor philosophical in enunciating his creed. Words he piled on words to justify each article of the dogma, but in total, they fail to persuade the questioning reader. In the sum there is no unitary whole; in the parts there are contradictions which cannot be sustained on pragmatic grounds. Thus the scholars have made of him less than the towering figure the people esteemed him to be, and perhaps a smaller man that he thought himself.

Some of the explanation for the evanescence of the fame of Theodore Roosevelt is, of course, in his weaknesses. No man can be righteous without calling upon himself a certain amount of criticism. But the Colonel had several other characteristics which are maddening to any who are not confirmed idolaters. His capacity for self-hypnosis led him to claim credits to himself which he did not deserve. His penchant for overdramatization took him into interpretations which were palpably false, and which, in other men, would be thought downright dishonest. Thus, in the restless years after he had left the White House, he pictured the course of the foreign relations of his administration in a way that blotted out the substantial work of John Hay. Moreover, in his concern for creating a carefully drawn portrait of himself before the public, those incidents of his life which might not appear harmonious to the picture were forgotten.

Reasonable men are willing to forgive inconsistencies in politicians' records if the contradictions are not too blatant. For politicians, if they wish to retain their leadership, must shift their ground in accordance with what they believe public opinion will want or accept. Roosevelt, however, was less than frank about his mistakes and his reversals. His *Autobiography,* written when ambition was still hot—though he had in fact passed the height of his appeal—is more striking for its omissions than its candor. Part of it is charming, much of it is interesting; but that which does violence to the preconceived pattern of Justice and Right is left unsaid. The fact that he married twice, or indeed mention of the existence of a first wife; the financial losses he sustained from his incursions into ranching and book publishing; the well-publicized imbroglios with other public figures while he was a Civil Service Commissioner and a Police Commissioner; the hard sluggings he and Taft dealt each other when Roosevelt found his heir apparent straying from the righteous path—these are parts of his public and private life he preferred to pass over in silence.

But for all his faults, or possibly because of them, Theodore Roosevelt was not merely the outstanding personality of his time—one traveler considered him co-equal with Niagara Falls among the natural wonders of the United States. He was one of the six or seven Chief Magistrates who gave genuine stature to the office. His rise was, despite his birth to the purple, a struggle against adversity. Though his obstacles were not of the same kind as confronted Lincoln and Andrew Johnson, they were nonetheless genuine. The temper of the political era of the late nineteenth century was certainly against him. The rigidity of his thinking was hardly an advantage. Yet, in the main, he turned the handicaps to his use, and at the age of forty-three became the youngest of American presidents.

2. NEW STYLES IN POLITICIANS

The noisy young politician of the 1884 Republican convention firmly believed his public life was finished. His short career had been spectacular, but apparently it was over; his experiment in politics had seemingly failed. Four years earlier he had been restless. His law studies as a postgraduate student at Columbia were tedious; business did not appeal to him. Then, to the horror of some in his circle and the amusement of others, he decided to go into politics. Why young Roosevelt should have selected that hazardous profession is a question which cannot perhaps be answered rationally. From his father he had inherited a respectable fortune—not large for even the standards of that day, but enough to relieve him of the necessities of working during the rest of his life. It had, of course, freed him from the pressures of studying law seriously; but it also took from him the *raison d'être* of most contemporaneous politicians—the income to be derived from a none too careful accounting of the public funds, and from the payments by business for services rendered.

There is little question he had accepted from his father's ethics and his schooling the vague generalization that the "better people" should participate in civic affairs. And to those who looked dimly at his understanding of the maxim, he replied he wanted to be one of the "governing classes." Yet, at twenty-two, he had little or nothing of a coherent program that might incite a well-bred young man to political action. If he possessed any ideas for implementing man's rule of himself, they were the unrealistic ones drawn from the sheltered influences of an aristocratic home, supervised foreign travel, and a customary Harvard education.

How and to what ends the "better people" engaged in public affairs has been suggested in a previous chapter. In 1880, such activity was obviously denied Roosevelt because of his age and his lack of equity. Political life, for one of his years, was available only in the party club of his district. On this level the "better element" was conspicuously absent; it paid its dues, gave its campaign contributions, and avoided meetings and responsibility. The moving spirits were the ward politicians, the importuners for petty office, the saloonkeepers, and a few sharp lawyers of uncertain scruple. Here were the "governing classes" to which the budding politician aspired.

Fortunately for his chosen career, New York's Twenty-first Assembly District was a Republican oasis in a city well subdued under the paw of Tammany. Luck was also his when, in the echelons far above, Chester Arthur unaccountably renounced spoils politics. In the factional battles within the state, Jake Hess, the district leader, had been a Conkling man. The reversal of form by the immaculate President caused strange reverberations in the local domain. Federal jobs were now refused his loyal workers, but Hess failed to recognize the stirrings of discontent in the faithful. In 1881 he demanded the renomination to the State Assembly of one Richard J. Trimble, a pliant nonentity of the Hess school of thought. Joe Murray, a lieutenant to the local leader but with ambitions of his own, read the auguries more cleverly and labored underground for the nomination of Theodore Roosevelt. By the time of the district convention, Murray had won his point, and his superior capitulated. So far as feelings went, Hess had no reason to like the nominee, for two of the youthful aristocrat's gaucheries in the clubrooms had been an advocacy of civil service reform and a resolution for nonpartisan administration in the street-cleaning department. Nevertheless, he stilled his emotions concerning dudes and neophytes, and Roosevelt went to the New York State Assembly, a Republican from a Republican district by a more than normal Republican majority.

The new assemblyman provoked considerable attention in the legislative chambers and hotel lobbies at Albany. His sartorial elegance and his cultured accent immediately set him apart from his fellow legislators. His reputation for independence won plaudits from the reformers he was soon to denounce. Others derided him both among themselves and in the press. In all likelihood they would have forced him out of the profession, were it not for the benisons that seemed to fall his way.

Heretofore, his eccentricities would have been intolerable in a minor public figure. But the war between Stalwarts and Half-Breeds permitted individual anomalies like Roosevelt to spring up unnoticed before either giant faction could be diverted to disciplining them or stamping them out. Secondly, the uninspiring quality of those who were presumed leaders magnified the energy and impulsiveness with which the young man went at his "civic duties." Surrounding himself with a few mavericks who eschewed Stalwart or Half-Breed Republicanism or Tammany Democracy, he was able to lead several forays against the seamiest aspects of groaning machine rule. Their effect was more annoying than permanent. The alliance between business and politics was appalled when the little group demanded an investigation of the stratagems by which Jay Gould, Russell Sage and others secured receivership of the Manhattan Elevated Railroad, and of the details whereby an eminent judge volunteered to "go to the very verge of judicial discretion" to assist them. But the squabbling factions temporarily united to exonerate the accused. In 1884 Roosevelt fathered a bill prohibiting cigar manufacture in tenements. Within a short while, the courts found it invalid—a violation of the sanctity of the home and its pleasant associations, said the judge.

On the whole Assemblyman Roosevelt gave New York State few lasting good works. During his first two years, with the Republicans in a minority, he became something of a floor leader and received good committee posts. In his third and last year, when they had a majority, he wanted and deserved the speakership. The party caucus, however, coldly turned elsewhere to a man of its own kind. It was not that Roosevelt had been the complete renegade and showed sympathy toward labor's demands for better pay, shorter hours and improved conditions. On the contrary, he had voted regularly with what he deemed his class interests—even the tenement bill had been conceived as a public health measure. His were the sins of having demonstrated certain nonpartisan tendencies—a fault he soon squelched—and of having been naive in his attacks upon the alliance.

The year 1884 was a bad one. The speakership defeat was the least of his sorrows. In February, the joy that should have been his from the birth of his first child was destroyed with the deaths of his wife and mother on the same day. The shock was terrible and he tried to escape his loss in close attention to his profession. April and May found him diligently fostering the candidacy of Senator George F. Edmunds for the presidential nomination. The effort won New York's delegation to the National Convention. With Henry Cabot Lodge of Massachusetts he went to Chicago to fight Blaine's surging drive. Their disgust with the old corruption, personified in the "Plumed Knight's" candidacy, was evident; their independence in putting forward Edmunds, who if less distinguished a man was also less notorious, made them the hope of the reformers. But the party machinery was well oiled and the "intellectual" coterie lost. Blaine was nominated and, in anger, Roosevelt left Chicago for the peace of the Dakota prairies and hills.

But while reformers in the East revolted, the young politician's wrath subsided. Days in the saddle produced practical thoughts, or at least coincided with them. By mid-July he was back East to join Lodge in supporting and campaigning for the orthodox ticket. At best, it was an unhappy compromise. At twenty-six, politics and private life had disappointed him. He had lost interest in the Assembly, and decided to retire from its futile precincts. He had lost the confidence of the reformers and was being assailed. He sorrowed for his dead wife. Blaine's defeat in November sent him back to Dakota discouraged. To Lodge, he wrote, "The Statesman (?) of the past has been merged, alas, I fear for good, into the cowboy of the present."

* * *

Ranching disappointed him. It provided the "strenuous life" and the material for a number of books for easterners who preferred to get their adventure vicariously. It could not satisfy ambitions for a public career. So in 1886 Roosevelt came back to New York to re-enter the political game. Circumstances appeared propitious. Restive working men had persuaded Henry George to seek the city's mayoralty as a labor candidate. Tammany Hall had cleverly countered by naming Abram S. Hewitt, an exceedingly wealthy Democrat of unimpeachable honesty and a conservative's answer to the single tax. The Republican machine under Tom Platt thought it saw an opportunity to squeeze in between the divided opposition vote. The "better" men of the party approached their own respectable conservative who had lately returned east in search of more interesting employment. He accepted "with the most genuine reluctance." When he had disavowed certain free trade utterances he had made in 1883—though it is difficult to understand what connection these might have had with municipal administration—he was acclaimed as the party's choice. In reality his nomination was an empty honor. Conservative men were determined to elect experience as well as security. They united behind Hewitt; Roosevelt finished third in the three-cornered race. The loss did not enhance his party standing; it added to a growing list of defeats. The advantages he had gained from his running start as an assemblyman had now been overcome by the hedges built around him. His independence rendered him suspect to Republicans; his party affiliations had cost him independent votes.

The stalemate continued until May of 1889. Literary labors consumed most of his time, although he was able to dash off imprecations against the Mugwumps as proof of his continued fidelity. The campaign of 1888 found him again certain of the Republican mission. Cleveland was a spoilsman; his very moderate requests for a downward tariff revision were dangerous; the Treasury surplus, which had caused the request, should, according to the author of *The Naval War of 1812,* go into the construction of battleships. In contrast to the last presidential election, the party had taken Blaine at his word—that he wanted a unanimous nomination or nothing—and had given the "Plumed Knight" nothing, by-passing him for Benjamin Harrison, grandson of the old general. With him, it eked out a victory. And, in Washington, Cabot Lodge began impressing on the new President the aid given his campaign by Roosevelt. Blaine and Speaker Thomas B. Reed also submitted encomiums on the deserving young man. Harrison finally found a place in the innocuous Civil Service Commission and tendered the position. Something should have warned him at the dispatch with which Roosevelt snapped up the offer.

Since its organization in 1883 the Commission had barely maintained itself, starved as it was for funds and all but unable to resist the depredations of politicians. Garfield's death may have forced the passage of the Pendleton Act. It utterly failed to convince the politicians of the law's implicit philosophy. That certain enumerated offices should be filled under the merit system they knew was a ridiculous notion. The mere presence of the law on the statute books was sop enough to the reformers. They should be content. The real criteria of merit were, according to unvisionary party men, a man's political loyalties and his obedience to discipline.

Roosevelt's essential belief in civil service reform immediately overrode all such thinking. His energy galvanized the Commission to action. The pallid subject of public administration began to appear regularly on the front pages of the newspapers. For the new Commissioner would not keep to his office and spend his days writing regulations. Nor would he blandly overlook the feverish haste in which patronage-hungry Republicans sacked Democrats from office.

President Harrison was a personally honorable gentleman, thoroughly at ease in the mundane politics of his time. Reform he believed a pretty but impossible thing; a change of administration made rotation in office a consequence. He must, therefore, have grown increasingly uncomfortable while he watched his ebullient commissioner enforce the law at the expense of the party and to the humiliation of important Republicans. John Wanamaker, the department store magnate, had been rewarded for his generous disbursements of cash, given to promote the partisan cause, by an appointment as Postmaster General. His attitude toward the merit system may be gauged by the circumstances of his selection. And his procedures in the lush realm of the Post Office Department mirrored his attitude. That Wanamaker's practices should have offended Roosevelt, who was already illustrating his ability to use the potential powers of every office he held, was preordained. The ensuing conflict lasted long enough for a Democratic House Civil Service Committee to throw its report condemning the merchant-politician into the 1892 campaign. Harrison suffered more than Wanamaker from the revelations. During the same years, unenlightened congressmen who made the pained cabinet minister's cause their own were routed ignominiously. They lacked the force, the information, and the argumentative power to set the upstart commissioner in his place.

Roosevelt's tenure continued into the second of Cleveland's divided terms in the presidency. But, if Cleveland understood and approved the lesson given the spoilsmen, his Secretary of the Treasury, John G. Carlisle, did not. Republicans in that department began to receive dismissal slips, in spite of the protection of the law. Roosevelt took his complaints to the White House where they were upheld. Carlisle, the veteran of decades of political warfare, was defeated by the tyro. By 1895, therefore, civil service reform had gained considerable prestige as a result of the victories of its ardent champion. He, in his place, was becoming tired of the old battle. Besides, a more important job had been offered by New York's new reform mayor, William L. Strong.

The city's police department had long been ripe for the sword of re-form. Its unseeing eye had not prevented its itching palm from par-ticipating in the profits of vice, gambling and the illegal sale of liquor on Sunday. Its higher officials had grown wealthy and its patrolmen corpulent. In short, it provided just the chance for a man fresh from other tilts with corruption and inefficiency to add to his laurels. For the moment, it seemed to Roosevelt the best possible place for his talents. Thus, when he received his appointment to the board of commissioners, he immediately applied his energy to the task of utilizing all the granted and implied powers of the position. On the first day he had himself elected president of the board; thereafter the other three members faded from view. Station houses were summarily inspected, patrolmen accosted in their bemused wanderings or unofficial conversations with prostitutes and bartenders, new physical standards instituted, and the Sunday blue law enforced. Personnel were rotated to break unhallowed connections. And behind all this energetic reform was the restless fig-ure of the new president.

The initial public reaction was favorable; Roosevelt's ferocious teeth became standard in the cartoons approvingly drawn to illustrate his fearsome crusade. Then came complications. Beer drinkers discovered thirst to be more compelling than reform and demonstrated for their "liberty." The other commissioners, obscured by the one-sided publicity, charged their president with using his office as a stepping-stone to polit-ical advancement and began to block his program. Commercialized vice assumed new forms of protective coloration. The reform adminis-tration at City Hall was beginning to lose its popularity. By 1897, Roose-velt had been hamstrung, and had given his resignation to the harrassed Mayor Strong. The police department was ready to sink back once more into the slough from which it had been so rudely extracted. In the final reckoning, the ambitious board president had been a failure. Yet, many others of more disinterested intention have met the same fate in a large number of American cities. For him, however, there was no dis-couragement; Lodge had secured him another post.

* * *

Meanwhile, the state of Ohio had witnessed the development of the most successful political partnership in American history. Often enough, there have been instances where one man has helped a second rise only to find himself eventually outdistanced by the prominence achieved by the other. The aid given Theodore Roosevelt by such di-verse personalities as Joe Murray and Henry Cabot Lodge is an adequate example. Frequently too, a man of marked ability has identified his career with that of another, but in a manner so as to leave no doubt as to which of the two was the leader. The relationship between Andrew Jackson and Martin Van Buren, or—in a more recent day—Franklin Roosevelt and Harry Hopkins or Henry Wallace, are three of many similar cases. Seldom, however, have the public careers of two men intertwined with the result that each is inseparable from the other; that both united perfectly toward a single end; and that, lacking the one, the other would have been relatively unimportant. Such was the lifetime association of William Seward and Thurlow Weed. Its closest approximation was the duality of William McKinley and Marcus Alonzo Hanna.

The parallels are interesting. Seward, the public figure, was the lawyer; Weed, the backstage manipulator, was the businessman. McKinley, the Canton attorney, was a perennial officeholder; Hanna, the owner of iron mills, steamship lines, coal mines, accomplished his most memorable political deeds as a Republican committeeman. Weed adored Seward; Hanna meekly worshipped McKinley. Weed poured money and skill into Seward's presidential aspirations; Hanna raised huge sums and applied his managerial wizardry to put McKinley into the White House. Neither good fairy asked for repayment; both received back the best Seward and McKinley could return. Strangely, Seward was almost killed in the conspiracy that took Lincoln's life; McKinley was assassinated. And, in their last years, Weed and Hanna each watched his power in the Republican party disappear.

There were, of course, differences. Hanna and McKinley achieved their goal—the presidency—where Weed and Seward failed. Hanna eventually made politics his sole profession; Weed continuously increased his business holdings. The Ohioans had certain fixed principles; the New Yorkers generally acted in defiance of any consistent morality. The Auburn-Albany axis enjoyed daring maneuver and brilliant strategy; the Canton-Cleveland combine much preferred plodding along established paths, ever seeking the safest way of organizing for victory. On the other hand, in their economic thinking—even in a relative sense—the earlier duality was the more conservative. Again, Seward and Weed were cultured men, while Hanna was rough and colloquial and McKinley limited his interests to the tools of his trade.

The traditional pictures of William McKinley as a nullity and Mark Hanna as an omnivorous robber baron are both unfair. The one was not a mere creature of a rich benefactor; the other was not an irresponsible boor. Both had qualities which were important to their mutual success. Unlike Seward and Weed these two had come together when both were developing national reputations. McKinley was recognized as the premier exponent of the high tariff. If such a theology can be rationally organized, he had done the job. Moreover, as a member of the House of Representatives, he had, in 1890, written the unpopular act that bore his name.

Hanna had made millions in his various enterprises, and, at the same time, earned the reproaches of eastern industrialists by recognizing the right of his workingmen to bargain collectively through unions of their own choice. He had come to political action through a sense of personal responsibility. In his city Hanna had seen the alliance between business and the Republican party consummated. But unlike most of his associates Hanna believed the troth demanded participation in government by his class beyond a writing of checks and a scooping up of profits. The interests of business and the entire community he considered identical; patriotism, therefore, required businessmen to work actively in politics. For Hanna, this could be only the advancing of the Republican party and its worthy candidates. And, apprenticing himself to ward politics, he started attaching Cleveland's stake in capitalism to the partisan banner. Having no preceptor, he made numerous mistakes; but by 1891 he was one of several leaders within his state.

In that year he recognized in McKinley a potential president. Though the two had known each other for a long while—had, in fact, been on opposite sides of a labor case fifteen years before—the Canton lawyer's gubernatorial canvass caught the rugged Clevelander's fancy. In 1890 the Congressman had lost his seat in the Democratic landslide. That the ruthlessly high schedules of his own tariff law had been a major factor in the disgrace that came to him and his party was undeniable. Yet, the next year he had been able to swing Ohio back to Republicanism—her normal status, thought Hanna—and by a small plurality got himself installed in the Governor's Mansion. What had been friendship on Hanna's part now ripened into something that resembled love. The factions dividing the party in the state were placatingly unified behind the new governor, and Hanna took his place as foreman over the organizational machinery. A slight boom for the 1892 presidential nomination was permitted, but suppressed before it grew disconcertingly large. Whether Republicans liked him or not, they would have to renominate Benjamin Harrison or admit the disastrous nature of his term to the voters and to themselves. In any case, after 1890, and with depression creeping toward the industrial East from the agricultural plains and prairies, it was doubtful if any human could have saved the Grand Old Party.

After a dull campaign the luckless Harrison took his fated licking— the worst to a major contender in twenty years—and Grover Cleveland's conservative Democracy returned to the White House. Ohio Republicanism, however, was far from gloomy. Its new governor was popular. In 1893 he got himself re-elected by a nicely improved majority, and Mark Hanna commenced president-making in earnest. All who might be delegates or influence delegates from the central states in 1896 were catechized in the word, and the word was McKinley. In the fall of 1894 Hanna quit forever his business associations and announced his retirement to Georgia. The upshot was the pocketing of the Southern delegations—those so-called "rotten boroughs" of the Republican party which carry no electoral votes but determine the selection of a nominee. By convention time, the candidacy of William McKinley was assured. The constructive work by Hanna had been stolid and perhaps unimaginative; it had been done without promises to the eastern bosses or the western silverites; it had been conceived out of arithmetic and cash. But it was architecturally sound. Only one ballot was necessary to demonstrate the strength of the party's new hierarchy.

3. THE OHIO METHOD

If Daniel Webster, in form, voice and the affection of his followers, was denominated "godlike," William McKinley likewise deserved sublime comparison. In every respect he cultivated the appearance of perfection. His face was always well groomed, his hair brushed meticulously. His countenance could register sternness, tolerance, forgiveness, and the kind of appreciation that never verged on subservience. His slightly obese body was immaculately covered by neatly tailored frock coats, trousers, and double-breasted vests, set off by impeccable linen. Personal habits were unexceptionable; and, more than that, personal relationships were conducted to impress even the stray acquaintance with the man's gentleness, forbearance and keen interest. Toward his neurotic, epileptic wife, whose tragedy was heightened by the early death of their children, he had only tenderness and devotion. Inwardly there waxed a fervent religious sense; the thought of God was never far from his mind. That all this was mere acting was, of course, the constant accusation of his detractors. Nevertheless so sharp a prober as William Allen White was unable to penetrate the façade the man presented to the world. To the Emporia journalist, the McKinley destiny appeared to be a "statue in the park." So appropriate is this generalization that it suggests the essence of McKinley, the politician, as well as of McKinley, the demi-god.

McKinley was active in the political game throughout the thirty years after the Civil War. Discharged from the Union army as a young major, he had been able to depend upon the Grand Army of the Republic for endorsement. His antislavery views had led him directly to the Republican party. With industrialization supplanting agriculture in Ohio's economy, the young lawyer staked his entire faith in the rising economic order. To insure its supremacy at home and over the world he studied and expounded the doctrine which was his party's greatest pride—the protective tariff. The arguments of those who wanted free trade or tariff reduction appear not to have troubled him. A wall of taxation against any goods of foreign manufacture that might conceivably compete with American goods was the McKinley answer. He compiled statistics of the national progress made under the high Republican tariffs; he adapted his figures to illustrate how prosperity was a condition of protection. Until shortly before his death it is doubtful if he ever examined the premises on which he based his reasoning.

And, just as McKinley's protectionism was orthodox, his ways as a politician were of the mold of regularity. He had run with the long line of Ohio leaders—John Sherman, Rutherford Hayes, James Garfield, Joseph Foraker. He had echoed their platitudes without developing any of his own. Even his prodigious work on tariffs was mere building on the work of others. Yet, there was a profound difference. McKinley's concern for the Eternal led him to review the consequences of his faith. As he watched the growing capitalist giant he tried earnestly to understand its place in life, its relationship to government. He became obsessed with the idea of peace between individuals, between competitors, between capital and labor, between nations. He hoped for, rather than evolved, a plan for the end of conflict. He wished for all men the inner peace he was sure he had achieved.

For him, a clear conscience was the only way of existence. Name-calling and enmities were below him. Compromises with principle were intolerable. Instead, he hoped that his soft insistences would bring over those who disagreed with him; but, if not, he refused to be a party to their sin. Nevertheless, the peace dream kept him from vigorous fundamentalism. He knew the faults of his associates and he forgave them. The sinner could go his own way, undenounced. But McKinley could not permit his name to be linked with scandal or taint or innuendo. That his reputation for personal integrity be forever unmarred became a fetish. Though it almost meant complete bankruptcy he once assumed the default on another man's note simply because he had countersigned it. Only the generosity of Hanna and other wealthy friends saved him from the consequences. In 1896, an alliance with the notorious Quay-Penrose machine of Pennsylvania would have removed the last problem to his candidacy. He refused—in fact, forbade—any bargains. To his credit, he probably prized honor more than office. In these respects McKinley was something more than a mere nineteenth century politician. His unoriginal mind, his pious declarations, his orthodoxy were characteristic of his political type. But because his words represented convictions instead of expedients, and because his personal honesty was rockbound, he was the highest distillation of the breed.

* * *

The genius and the money that Mark Hanna had used to secure McKinley's nomination carried on into the campaign. A dramatic explosion had occurred in the convention over the question of gold versus bimetallism, and a number of western leaders had bolted. When the dust had settled, Hanna's compromise—the gold standard to eastern capitalism in return for his hero's middle-western candidacy—had left the Republican party in an equivocal position. The Ohioans had expected the debate to be waged on the old reliable issue of the tariff, but western farmers and miners in the throes of a depression had raised the money issue to prominence. Unfortunately, McKinley had half-played the silverite in a public speech, and was now being forced to explain what he had meant. Then too, the unpredictable Democrats had made a direct play for the poor and the mortgaged by repudiating the Cleveland administration and raising up the young spellbinder, William Jennings Bryan of Nebraska. And Bryan had married himself to the silverites and the "radical" Populists.

In reality, there was probably no need to worry over the result. Bryan's oratorical blasts at the gold standard could not alone have swayed the heavy vote of the East. Yet Hanna had planned too long to trust to chance. He whipped the press into a scurrilous abuse of the opposition; he plagued wealthy Republicans for funds and then blatantly distributed the money where it could best correct heresy. While Bryan roared through the country, McKinley smilingly received admiring delegations on his front porch in Canton. He did not understand the anger of the silver crowd and the terror in the hearts of those who clung to gold. That the discontent was symptomatic of a basic popular unrest he could not, according to his ideal of peace, recognize. He continued to throw out provocative statements on the tariff only to find Bryan still cursing gold.

Fear infected the Republican camp. It applied Gresham's law of money to political truth. Free silver seemed to be driving the tariff out of the market place of ideas. Hanna collected and spent more money. In Roosevelt's words, McKinley was being advertised "as if he were a patent medicine." The shouting grew louder. The hysteria mounted. Hanna became gruffer, more impatient as the weeks passed. Only the candidate kept his imperturbability. He was correct in his outward confidence; his victory margin was a comfortable one.

The same calm demeanor marked the presidential office for the next four and a half years. Outwardly, McKinley was behaving as had his Republican predecessors. A general business improvement became identified with his accession. In 1890 the McKinley tariff law had been unhappily described as the "advance agent of prosperity"; now, its author appeared to be confounding the cynics. After 1897 conservatives pointed to the phenomenon of a Republican prosperity as a warning against future flirtations with monetary panaceas. The anti-trust laws lay somnolent while industrial combinations were capitalized at hundreds of millions of dollars. Then the elder J. P. Morgan announced the creation of the United States Steel Corporation, the first billion-dollar organization. If—to anticipate a later Chief Executive—the "business of the United States is business," the *fin de siècle* was witnessing an administration bent upon proving the maxim true. Though Hanna abruptly dismissed fanciful schemers and their notions for despoiling the country of the remnants of its public domain, he and his chief were convinced that the solider interests were fulfilling the American dream. True, the piteous cry of the outlander at the exorbitant freight rates went unheard, but to illustrate where the Republican party stood, Congress took a page from the President's book and passed the highest tariff on record. Exportable agricultural produce was included in the protection. Business, McKinley contentedly believed, was on the broad highway to industrial peace.

In the political sphere, matters went along in the same outward spirit. Inwardly, a subtle change was occurring. The major cabinet posts went to westerners; a scant two—Navy and Interior—were filled by Republicans from east of the Alleghenies. Old John Sherman's reward for four decades in the front ranks of Ohio's sons was the State Department. The appointment created a vacancy—some said a purposeful one —in the Senate. Gossips expressed false shock when Mark Hanna joined the "millionaires' club." Not that the great manager didn't deserve something; but McKinley should have permitted him to play with the Post Office. That was the usual practice.

They did not know it, but the offer had been made; Hanna had refused. For Hanna, the self-made man of Cleveland, was justly suspicious of the manner Wall Street chose in dividing the take with the provinces. In the Senate he felt he could better harmonize the divergent economic interests of the country, seeing to it that each got its fair share. Never the speaker, and unfamiliar with the legal tangles and parliamentary niceties of the legislative mill, he was to labor valiantly in the cloak rooms to hold his colleagues back, to prevent them from embarrassing the administration and destroying his work. They might be thinking of tomorrow's dividends; he was remembering that Bryan would be back in 1900.

Yet while Uncle Mark ruled his senators, imperceptibly the pressure came from another direction. His messianic cohort at the other end of the Avenue was displaying signs of remarkable individualism. Republicans no longer remembered that Lincoln had fought his own party where the congressional program differed from his own. The supremacy of the Legislative branch had long since become an acknowledged doctrine. And McKinley, in his regularity, respected it. But he was coming to understand also the need for executive leadership. He would not back up stubbornly nor would he bluster. Instead, he used the devastating approach of pacification. Senators and Representatives, visiting the White House for a conference, found themselves taken in by his courtesy and tact. Their prerogatives were admitted, and the President's ideas were outlined fully. Did they agree? They did. Could they support him? They could. They left entranced, not realizing they had surrendered to his angelic simplicity. Only a bitter man like Speaker Thomas B. Reed could hate him, and Reed believed himself swindled out of the presidency by Hanna's organizing genius. Still, even Reed dared not oppose the new leadership. Thus, by divine light or by necessity, the Executive was regaining its co-ordinate position. A harmony was being created in the government.

* * *

The broadest quest for peace, however, lay in the world at large. And here the tide against it was running strong. Cuba had been a gleam in the slaveholder's eye half a century before. Its proximity now invited the gaze of robust expansionists. Spain's stupid colonial policy gave them their excuse. The Americas must be cleared of European dominion; the time had come to demonstrate America's right to full partnership in the leadership of the globe.

McKinley and Hanna found the sounding bugles vulgar. War was not their way. That Spain was being hopelessly foolish, that the United States was entitled to recognition as a first-class power, they agreed. But as men of peace they proposed to mitigate international wrongs through arbitration. As the demands for battle and glory multiplied, they resisted. Their efforts, however, were finding unfertile ground within the administration itself.

Constant petitioning by Lodge had got for Theodore Roosevelt the Assistant Secretaryship in the Navy Department where John D. Long of Massachusetts was enjoying the fruits of a long life in Republican politics. Tom Platt—the referee as to which New Yorkers were to receive the benefits of federal patronage—had approved the plan upon realization that the noisy young man would do the State Republican machine less harm in the nation's capital than at home. On the truly positive side of the selection, Roosevelt's researches on the War of 1812 had given him a name for expertism in naval affairs. Thus, Lodge, Platt and scholarship outweighed the natural objection of Roosevelt's jingoism; and McKinley granted the boon on assurances that the administration's policy would be adhered to in silence by the appointee.

Obviously such promises were impossible to keep. Within a scant two months Roosevelt was eloquently praising the "war spirit" and demanding a strong navy, "not merely for defense," but "to protect" those who looked upon the United States as their savior. "Diplomacy," he said, "is utterly useless where there is no force behind it; the diplomat is the servant, not the master of the soldier."

McKinley remained uninfluenced. He applied the reverse of Roosevelt's assumption on the conduct of foreign relations and continued negotiating with Spain. As the year 1897 dragged on without war, the jingo developed increasing restiveness at his superior's pacifism. The shillyshallying after the sinking of the *Maine* left the suppressed warrior contemptuous. The President, he privately informed his correspondents, had "no more backbone than a chocolate eclair."

Finally, on February 25, 1898, the deficiencies of American policy were somewhat remedied. Secretary Long had taken the afternoon off, leaving his strong-willed assistant to handle routine matters. Roosevelt, however, had his own ideas of where routine ended and policy began. In a few hours, Admiral George Dewey, commanding the Asiatic Squadron, received orders to begin "defensive operations" in Philippine waters and to be prepared to deal with the Spanish fleet "in the event of declaration of war." The act was unauthorized, perhaps insubordinate; but it did provide an insurmountable tactical advantage which culminated in the famous victory at Manila Bay.

By April the war crisis could no longer be denied. With troubled consciences, the men of peace within the administration joined in officially pronouncing Spain an enemy. If the moral dilemma had its compensation, it was that young Roosevelt decided to substitute a cavalry mount for a desk, and resigned from the Navy Department.

The war was too short to damage Republican popularity. Government orders kept the market rising on its prosperity curve. The public made no sacrifices. Nationalistic thirsts, therefore, were unquenched. After another bout with his conscience, McKinley catered to them and accepted the Philippines as a conquest of war. Judge William Howard Taft was called out of Ohio to govern the islands and placate the natives who believed their portion of victory was to have been independence. In the Caribbean, Cuba was being prepared for a hothouse form of liberty. Under Senator Orville Platt's auspices the United States allowed the island self-government, but it reserved the right to interfere any time it felt the Cubans had embarked on political or economic heresy. All told, it was the launching of a hopeful career in world empire. For the handling of military detail, the pathetic War Secretary Alger, who had badly bungled his part of the recent "glorious adventure," was replaced by Elihu Root, the capable New Yorker.

But more important than empire was the undoubted fact that the United States had become a world power. The placid man in the White House recognized the fact. Yet the spectacle of Germany, Britain, France and Russia competing with one another for territories and trade was not to his liking. The United States had somehow to assume new relations with them, but McKinley wanted no long series of international crises. Here too, he wanted prosperity and he wanted peace. Through their good offices, he was convinced, a brilliant new era of triumphant capitalism would appear on earth. Accordingly, John Hay was called home from the London embassy to exercise his urbanity and knowledge as head of the State Department. Together he and the President drew up their program of peace through conciliation. Their logic was elementary: the world had to accommodate all kinds; it could do so more easily if the parties arbitrated quietly rather than fought; why not, then, fix a set of conditions, by diplomatic notes and treaties, on how nations shall get along with one another? Chief Executive and Foreign Secretary slowly put forward their rare plan. They were well started on drawing Great Britain into the orbit of *status quo ad infinitum* when an anarchist shot McKinley.

4. THE COWBOY IN THE WHITE HOUSE

In the midst of these ambitious plans to temper human folly the quadrennial election intruded itself. That McKinley would be re-elected was almost certain. Whether Bryan and the Democrats decided to fight on the old issues of free silver and the tariff, or the new one of imperialism, the country had no desire for change. There were no problems of platform since the administration would stand on its popular record of the past four years. There was, however, the matter of the vice-presidency, left vacant by the death of Garret Hobart. A number of wheelhorses were available and even desired the ornamental position. Although the President repeatedly denied his intention of forcing any choice on the party convention, he was inclined to favor his Navy minister, John D. Long. Hanna preferred New York's Cornelius Bliss after he had shown competence as Secretary of the Interior and as national treasurer of the party. Others like Senators Elkins of West Virginia and Fairbanks of Indiana were prepared to accept the nomination and bask in the reflected glory of the saintly President.

Complicating the entire matter was Theodore Roosevelt of New York. The short, happy war had made him a national hero. In 1898, no sooner had he debarked at Montauk, Long Island, than he became a candidate for governor. Independents were ready to forget his harsh epithets and his castigations of Cleveland and Bryan if he would carry their banner. More practical were the thoughts of Boss Tom Platt. His current governor was a good machine man. But millions of dollars had disappeared in a canal project and the public was indignant. Another candidate was necessary. The Colonel of Rough Riders appeared ideal. Platt, therefore, offered the regular Republican nomination and Roosevelt accepted. The election was close, but the hero won.

Then followed two years of sorrow for the old state chieftain. His governor disagreed on the apportionment of offices. Under Roosevelt's guidance the state legislature soundly rapped the knuckles of the New York City traction interests. Platt realized that a new governor would have to sit in Albany after 1900 if the Republican machine was to remain intact. He had not determined whether to use sly maneuver or a brutal frontal assault when providential voices arose in the western states talking up Theodore Roosevelt for the vice-presidency. Pleased, the boss urged the "advancement" on the governor. Platt's joy cooled rapidly. Roosevelt wanted another term, for two more years as head of the country's most populous state automatically put him in line to succeed McKinley. From Washington, Hanna too was advising his continued residence in Albany—not, however, with any intimations of future progress.

The threatened Colonel uneasily assessed his future. He could not see himself presiding over the Senate and keeping his opinions to himself. Despite Hay's sensible advice that no vice-president had ever been elected by violence, he feared that Platt might manipulate a convention draft. Another fear gnawed: if Platt let the convention alone, but dictated his own candidate for the governorship, Roosevelt's elective career was over. Positions he might still secure, but the presidency was not an appointive office. In the West, his name was still on delegates' tongues. Disclaimers for a berth on the McKinley ticket became less sharp.

Meanwhile, unknown to Roosevelt and Hanna, several bosses were evolving a *modus operandi*. At an earlier date, Matthew Quay of Pennsylvania and the gruff Ohioan had discovered a mutual dislike. In 1899, the state legislature had refused to elect Quay to the Senate, but he had wrested the appointment from an obedient governor. The ethics involved provided Hanna an excuse. In one of his few open appearances of leadership, he prevented Quay's seating in the upper house. By the next year, the Pennsylvanian, who combined a memory of wrongs done him with a sense of humor, had selected his method of revenge.

Knowing Platt's situation *vis-à-vis* Roosevelt, he offered the New Yorker a prescription for relief. Pennsylvania would help remove the obstreperous governor to Washington if New York would support Quay's motion that the size of future state delegations to the national convention be based on the actual vote cast for the party in the previous election rather than on the state's electoral vote. Platt had no animus for Hanna, but necessity outweighed personal consideration. He consented; and the conspirators awaited the convention.

There, Quay submitted his motion. If it passed Hanna's southern delegations would be cut to nothing. And in 1904, when the rule would first be applied, the selection of a successor to McKinley would be out of his hands. It is uncertain if Hanna saw himself as the next president; but he did enjoy kingmaking. When apprised of the Roosevelt alternative the Senatorial boss exploded. Remembrance of that one February afternoon's activities in the Navy Department and of other Rooseveltiana flooded over him. "Don't any of you realize that there is only one life between that mad man and the Presidency? Platt and Quay are no better than idiots! What harm can he do as Governor of New York compared to the damage he will do as President if McKinley should die?"

Clearly, Mark Hanna was upset, but he acceded finally. The convention shouted itself hoarse for the Rough Rider. In the ensuing campaign, Republicans flocked to hear him rage at Bryan and the "doctrines of anarchy." In contrast, his running mate issued sedate, if occasional, bulletins from the White House or Canton, Ohio.

November 6, 1900, showed that the country wanted Bryan even less than it had in 1896. The following March 4th produced little that was sensational unless it was the fact that McKinley's inauguration was comparatively shadowed by the publicity that centered on the new Vice-President. To the newspapers and the politicians it seemed not too soon to begin discussions of Roosevelt's chances in 1904. The object of their solicitude was, meanwhile, contemplating a series of tours designed to keep his name and exuberant personality before the country. In his more despondent moments, he considered studying law so that he might have a profession should the bubble burst. As an alternative, he dallied with the idea of teaching history in some college adjacent to Washington, the better to pass the hours when the Senate was not in tedious session.

There was no time to test either thought. On September 6th, McKinley received his fatal wound while speaking at Buffalo; eight days later he died. In epitome of his life and work, the calm man expired while reciting a graceful acceptance of his fate. Sorrowful listeners heard the gentle voice falter over the words of "Nearer my God to Thee." And then it was over. . . .

*   *   *

Roosevelt was sobered by the tragedy. It had not been his wish, regardless of how much he wanted the presidency, to take office under a cloud. At forty-three, he had come to the top suddenly. William Allen White, in his *Autobiography,* recalls that this youngest of Chief Executives was ready to fight Hanna to stay there in 1904, but that he was also worried at what would happen to him after 1909 when he would have to retire, barely fifty-one years old.

The problem of age took on other complications. Heretofore, he had been a source of amusement, an adolescent with grandiose dreams, a joke, a brash youngster to the governing heads of the party and the administration. Men like John Hay and Elihu Root called him "Teddy" and "Theodore," and tolerantly watched his capers. John D. Long still held the naval portfolio; Lyman J. Gage, an unsentimental Chicago banker, ruled the Treasury for industrial capitalism's sake. They had all been over him; now he was their superior. They tried to forget the disparity. Mark Hanna thrust back his old suspicions and, adopting fatherliness and respect, offered his valuable advice. Newspaper gossip to the contrary, he and the "cowboy" were trying to resolve their differences. The suggestion of the older man that the President "go slow," hear everyone but decide at leisure, was gratefully received and acknowledged. Other old heads, Senator Nelson Aldrich—conservative boss of the upper house—Senator Fairbanks, Senator Foraker, were invited to present and discuss their views.

Perhaps it should be recalled that, thus far, Roosevelt had evidenced a mere handful of the progressive tendencies that were beginning to stir the provinces after the collapse of Populism. Civil service reform and a dislike for overt corruption were old hat. Juster taxation of traction interests was meager leftism indeed when compared to the programs calling for regulation of trusts, tariff revision, a fair standard of railroad rates, a graduated income tax, protection of the dwindling national resources from economic brigandage, the direct election of senators, the recognition of the right of labor to bargain collectively. Yet conservatives were fearful of anything less than McKinleyism.

By courting the senators, by listening to Hanna, by retaining the cabinet, Roosevelt allayed their excitement. His first message to Congress was a long document that faced Janus-like on any subject capable of provoking argument. Control over business, he advanced, was desirable, but its exercise should be careful in order to prevent discouragement and decline. Tariffs might be lowered, but business must not suffer. Organized labor was entitled to rights but must be wary of abusing them. Reciprocal trade with foreign nations was a commendable goal, but its practice must be fitted to the tariff laws.

Responsibility had apparently conferred wisdom on the young President. A rough draft of the message had been sent to Hanna, and in deference to that statesman's opinion, certain allusions to trusts and their overcapitalization had been excised. What had finally been expressed was a differentiation between "good" trusts and "bad" trusts, between "good men" and "evil men." In addition, several unradical Rooseveltian dogmas were expounded—a stronger Navy, subsidies to the Merchant Marine, the soundness of the Monroe Doctrine as a guide to foreign policy, the need for conservation of natural resources, the desirability of reclaiming desert areas and worn-out lands. That work should be begun on an interoceanic canal was suggested, but no location was specified. Two points set forth aroused remembrance of the man's irrepressible nature: the railroads' practice of granting rebates to favorite customers should cease, and a Department of Commerce and Labor, its secretary to have cabinet rank, should be created to compile information on corporations and defend the rights of labor.

On the whole, conservatives felt relieved. Evidently the wilder rumors about the Chief Executive's determination to take up in Washington where he had left off at Albany were exaggerated. As for rebates, some conservatives who went unblessed by that beneficence found them intolerable; even the railroads opposed them as inroads on profit. It was a minor reform. The new department was more dangerous; but unless the standpat majority in Congress approved it, none could be set up. Seven and a half more years of McKinleyism were in prospect. Corporations would go on merging; businessmen would go on stockpiling wealth. Private enterprise was safe; the tariff was safe; taxes were safe; money was safe. The public at large would be diverted from questioning a do-nothing executive policy by Roosevelt's captivating personality and anecdotes concerning the "strenuous life" in the White House.

WHAT sound conservatives neglected to appreciate about Theodore Roosevelt was his vigor. For him, the first few months in office were a quiescent period. The grist for the publicity mill—the strenuous athletics, the exhausting social schedule, the amusing epigrams—was only normal activity. Meanwhile, he was feeling out the area of mobility which the Constitution and the Republican party permitted the President.

Of previous Chief Executives, he had found stimulating the examples of Lincoln and Jackson—two men whose usage of the executive prerogatives had gone unfettered, if loudly challenged, by Congress. Washington's deference to the Hamiltonian theory of strong central government he had studied approvingly. These three men, he believed, were worth emulating. As for Jefferson, that gentleman's belief in the people and the commendable expansion of the country by the Louisiana purchase could never atone for his having formulated the doctrine of local rights or pandering to the national legislature. Worship of the founder of the Democratic party, he later said, constituted "a discredit to my country."

But more fascinating than history was the fabric of executive power. Of its latent strength he had no doubts. In his view its sole limitations were those specifically imposed by the Constitution and the "legitimate" acts of Congress. Customs that had walled in the office but were not clearly and openly set down in the fundamental law were not restrictions but weaknesses that other presidents had shown. To admit otherwise was to promote inefficiency in government. There was nothing innately wrong with a concentration of power in a single person's hands provided he used it courageously, honestly and to the benefit of the "plain people." Congress had no authorization to consider the President its office boy. In reality, he was "a steward of the people," responsible directly to them and bound to expend the last iota of his enormous power in their behalf.

Had the gentlemen of Wall Street or the Senate or the Republican National Committee known these thoughts lived in Roosevelt's mind, their new confidence in his leadership would have been shaken. That he pledged himself "to continue absolutely unbroken the policies of

President McKinley" was perhaps a source of their delusion. For, aside
from Hay's diplomatic formula, there existed no real charted path.
Though the Ohioan had labored in the domestic sphere to harmonize
all interests, his way had been a purely personal one. Conciliation, arbitration and negotiation, associated with his innate tranquility,
smothered tensions. If the result was increased trustification, bigger
capitalism and unabashed materialism, it was because he presumed
these the true ends to be sought. His contribution was to help these
forces rule themselves. Thus, only insofar as his own character produced the environment in which the public business was conducted
could the martyred president be said to have a policy. More precisely,
he had substituted negativism for chaos.

The disparate personality of his successor made the McKinley
method impossible. A penchant for excitement and a will to affirmative
action precluded gentleness. A predisposition that government must
show its strength inevitably banished business—as a single interest—to
a secondary position. Since the meaning of righteousness differs in accordance with who has the power of definition, Roosevelt's understanding of the word replaced McKinley's. In its new phase, after September,
1901, it meant free play to a dominant nationalism, unprecedented intervention by the Executive in domestic matters, and his undisputed
leadership in the Republican Party. In the practical terms of politics it
meant that an accidental president was seeking hegemony over his
party, his country and his world. Strangely, indications of success came
in the reverse of what might have been the expected order.

1. TAKING OVER THE WORLD

John Hay was Roosevelt's senior by twenty years. The distinguished
Secretary of State had first known his energetic chief as a sickly boy of
twelve. By that time Hay had already made his mark in public life as
an able private secretary to Abraham Lincoln. During the ensuing forty
years he flitted in and out of public affairs showing deeper acumen than
a dilettante but less managerial skill, where his own rise was concerned,
than the average politician. After he grew wealthy he contributed liber-
ally to the war chest of the Republican party. Yet the political brethren
preferred his money to his talent. Basically, the dislike arose from his
high standard of honesty. For, though Hay embraced conservatism
wholeheartedly, his doctrine was moral, not expedient. Worse still, he
tended to let his opinion of public figures be outspoken. As a result his
career was entirely appointive; and the offices he received dealt with

foreign relations in an era when the United States concentrated all but its meagerest attentions on domestic matters.

Still, by 1901, on his record, Hay appeared abler than Roosevelt. If both had demonstrated a genius for antagonizing important political personages, the Secretary's true accomplishments outshone those of the President. As a literatteur he had produced several volumes of creditable verse, a best-selling novel, and a host of editorials for the *New York Tribune*. Of more lasting value was a monumental biography of Lincoln, written in collaboration with John G. Nicolay, and still the most complete single published work on the Great Emancipator. Under McKinley he had finally achieved the recognition he deserved. Called home to handle the State Department after the war with Spain he bent to the task of reshaping America's foreign policy in accordance with the Ohio method. Himself a peaceful and conservative man, Hay found no difficulty in working for a preservation of McKinley's *status quo*. The "open door" notes on China represented such a policy. If they failed in their stated purpose the cause rested with the other world powers who never accorded them much credence, and with the people of the United States who were uninterested in the defense of the Far Eastern balance. Nevertheless, his diplomatic work with Britain gave a new tone to Anglo-American relations.

Perhaps Hay's contribution stemmed from his lifelong reluctance to subscribe to the American game of twisting the British lion's tail. As a man of culture, as a traveler, as a semi-professional Anglo-Saxon, he entertained a large sympathy for England. He could understand her motives, and he could talk easily with her gentlemen. It was well; for American heads were once again mulling over the desirability of an Isthmian canal. The battleship *Oregon's* long journey around Cape Horn from the Pacific to the Caribbean had, during the late war, shown the difficulties of joining the fleets of either ocean. Addition of the Philippines to America's imperial chain pointed up the necessity of more efficient naval operations. Furthermore, the expectation of more commerce with the Orient demanded a shorter route for shipping from the east coast. But the Clayton-Bulwer treaty remained to block ambitions in Central America.

Fortunately, European circumstances were on Hay's side. Britain was friendless in Europe, and the exigencies of that situation prompted her to revise her old attitude toward the United States. Suddenly she assumed a new one of friendship. To evidence her good intentions she sent as her ambassador the amiable Lord Julian Pauncefote. To the

American Secretary it was a happy selection. Together, the cultured diplomatists leisurely discussed conditions for a new treaty which would permit the United States to act unilaterally on the Isthmus. The talks matured into an agreement that gave America free rein in the actual building of a canal but prohibited its militarization. Hay was satisfied; the Senate was not, and rejected it. Once again the conversations began. And, under the spell of the persuasive Secretary, the British minister consented to forgo the offensive militarization clause. By the time the second treaty was ready for the Senate, McKinley was dead. A louder note was being trumpeted across the earth.

*　　　*　　　*

That Hay, at sixty-three, should have felt anxiety on Roosevelt's accession was to be expected. Their long acquaintanceship had never blossomed into mutual cordiality. Age had regarded youth and its idiosyncrasies with superior indulgence, if not distant amusement. Occasionally it played the annoyed instructor. Thus, when the first Hay-Pauncefote treaty was under consideration Governor Roosevelt enlarged the sphere of his constitutional duties by publicly denouncing the pact and offering his own solution. In replying, the Secretary addressed his letter to *"Et tu."* "Cannot you leave a few things to the President and the Senate, who are charged with them by the Constitution? As to 'Sea Power' and the Monroe Doctrine, we do not act without consulting the best living authorities on those subjects." Needless to say neither swayed the other's opinion.

But after September, 1901, it was incumbent upon the older man to accommodate or resign. Being averse to making the decision that would upset the pattern of his remaining years, he stayed on with mixed feelings and mixed results. His insistence on protocol was to save Roosevelt from some of the pitfalls of strong-arm diplomacy. In most instances, however, Hay was forced to join his chief on the improprietous path. That the major leads of foreign policy had been set by the time Roosevelt entered the White House did not prevent their being stamped with the Roosevelt imprint. What their form had been under the McKinley-Hay guidance became almost unrecognizable. For example, President McKinley had, before his death, perceived the impossibility in the economics of maintaining a steep tariff against all imports after the United States began to export larger quantities of goods and services than came in from abroad. He had, therefore, ordered his Secretary of State to negotiate bilateral reciprocity treaties, and had taken a personal interest in their ratification by the Senate. On the other hand, President Roosevelt cared little for the reciprocity principle. He placed the burden on his foreign minister's shoulders and left it there. That gentleman, whose relations with the politicians has already been described, found the going hard. Several embittered though penetrating remarks expressed when the Senate refused to sanction his first agreement with Pauncefote had further estranged members of its Foreign Relations Committee. Consequently some reciprocity treaties passed while others did not.

Where remaking the world took on a more dramatic hue, the Chief Executive gave a closer view to the doings of his Secretary of State. Venezuela provided a first test to Rooseveltian diplomacy. Cipriano Castro, her president, had secured his office by means not yet outmoded in Latin America. He had also borrowed heavily from European and American investors, and had then insouciantly disregarded their requests that he meet his country's financial obligations. From July of 1901 on, Germany had been urging arbitration of the debts by the Hague Tribunal on Castro with no noticeable effect. In December her ambassador was sounding out Hay on American reactions to a possible naval blockade of the recalcitrant country. The Berlin foreign office, conscious of American reverence for the Monroe Doctrine, was denying intentions of territorial aggrandizement in the western hemisphere. Hay's answer was a referral to the apparently explicit language of Roosevelt's first annual message. "This doctrine has nothing to do with the commercial relations of any American Power. . . . We do not guarantee any State against punishment if it misconducts itself, provided that punishment does not take the form of the acquisition of territory by any non-American power."

Meanwhile Britain supported her aggrieved bondholders by delivering stern notes to Castro. At the same time she was tempting the Wilhelmstrasse with adventure. A joint naval expedition against the Venezuelan gunboats and customs houses, it was hinted, would settle the matter with dispatch. The Kaiser, who admired Roosevelt enough to have presented him with a medal a few months before, preferred to wait in the hope of cultivating American amity. Thus a full year elapsed before the indignant European powers presented their final ultimata on December 7, 1902. Five ports were blockaded and four gunboats captured. On December 13th, a naval force consisting mainly of English ships retaliated an alleged insult to the British flag by bombarding Puerto Cabello. Castro's lack of concern over the debts vanished; he begged the Yankee President to enter the case as arbitrator, and save Venezuela. The State Department in Washington merely forwarded the request "without comment" to the belligerents, who accepted it. Because American claims were also involved, and because he wanted to build the power of the Hague Tribunal, John Hay diverted the arbitration role from Roosevelt to where it belonged.

Clearly Great Britain had been the aggressor and Germany the unaccustomed follower. Equally clear was the absence of a strong official stand by the United States before the shooting began. In private it is safe to assume that Roosevelt was disapproving with von Holleben, the Kaiser's ambassador, prior to actual operations. In public, arbitration was not formally recommended until after the European powers had already agreed to it. Yet Roosevelt turned the event to his advantage. In spite of Kaiser Wilhelm's efforts Germany's popularity with the American public had been waning. Her heavy-handed tactics in China during the days of the "open door" notes and her evident commercial designs on South America had aroused disfavor in this country. Roosevelt and Hay shared the feeling. Von Holleben not only failed to appreciate this fact, but consistently misinformed his government about American sympathies. His mistakes were compounded when he uttered some undiplomatic words about Lord Pauncefote, whose gentle attitude was softening the traditional American suspicions of England.

Criticism of the German envoy grew. Coincidentally, therefore, he was recalled by Wilhelm and replaced by Speck von Sternberg, the President's friend, shortly after the Venezuelan crisis. To outsiders, it appeared that the Rough Rider had been busy laying down terms to the Kaiser, and that Britain was blameless. Probably, Roosevelt and his Secretary, in their prejudices, also inclined to the second half of this view.[1] In any case, European powers were showing a greater desire to conciliate the United States; from the view of American foreign policy, their retreat from the Latin American coastline to the Hague meant a tacit recognition of the principles of the Monroe Doctrine.

*   *   *

Rooseveltian diplomacy took on clearer outlines in the case of a long standing boundary dispute with Canada. The seed of the trouble went back to an Anglo-Russian treaty in 1825, vaguely defining the borders

---

[1] Thirteen years after the fact, Roosevelt imaginatively expanded his part in the affair. He had threatened Germany with a choice of arbitration or the guns of Admiral Dewey's Caribbean squadron; he had been requested *by Wilhelm* to arbitrate; he had forced von Holleben's withdrawal. More disinterested scholars have since proved him mistaken.

of the Alaskan panhandle. It continued dormant when Seward arranged his famous purchase in 1867. Where the line actually lay had aroused little interest, and, until the discovery of gold in the Klondike in 1896, American claims were generally recognized. But when fortune hunters rushed to the new Eldorado, Canadian officials took the opportunity for advancing a dubious pretension to most of the territory in question. Their hope was not the land but the trading off of its title for greater advantages in the Newfoundland fisheries. American diplomacy would hear nothing of arbitration, however, for Hay feared that any third party to whom the case might be submitted would simply split the difference. And there the matter stood, with the United States in possession.

In the interval the Canadian public had become convinced of its country's rights and their government was feeling the need to end the problem it had created for itself by overzealousness. Too, Downing Street's new courtship of Uncle Sam had led the British cabinet and its Washington ambassador to admit tacitly that Canada's claim possessed faint validity. Facing these pressures Dominion spokesmen looked for a face-saving device. They discovered one in accepting Hay's formula for adjudicating the dispute—a commission of "six impartial jurists of repute," three representing the United States, three the Empire. A treaty was drawn up, and, after the Senate had deleted all references to "arbitration," was ratified.

The President's first thoughts on the subject had been to "let sleeping dogs lie." But talk of settlement set him on the demonstrative course. Additional troops were sent to Alaska. Dreams of reprimanding Canadian "truculence" filled his mind. He accepted the treaty and selected three American commissioners whose naming was, to say the least, surprising. One, Secretary of War Elihu Root was, it was true, an excellent lawyer, but also a cabinet member of the Administration. The other two, Senators Henry Cabot Lodge and George Turner were neither "impartial" nor "jurists of repute." The qualifications they brought to the Commission were a preconceived opinion and an abiding hatred of England. But along with two Canadian lawyers Britain chose its Chief Justice, Lord Alverstone. On hearing the evidence he was to side with the Americans in declaring against the Empire. Before this decision was reached, diplomatic channels saw two unofficial letters. Roosevelt's, declaring the intention of the United States to disregard an unfavorable verdict, was destined for the eyes of Colonial Secretary Chamberlain. Hay's, couched more delicately but intimating the same thing, edified Lord Balfour. Alverstone, aware of their contents, was the one judge who decided the case on its merits. Consequently, in his country, he attracted condemnation; in the United States, Roosevelt was credited with a personal triumph. The autumn elections of 1903 went Republican.

*   *   *

The dream of an Isthmian canal overlay all other considerations of foreign policy during Roosevelt's first term. For years he had desired an inter-oceanic link, all-American in construction and operation. With the ratification of the second Hay-Pauncefote treaty in early 1902, prospects were bright. Two routes were possible. The first, through the Colombian province of Panama, would cost less to build; but the bankrupt French Panama Canal Company still held a concession and was asking $109,000,000 for assets which were worthless unless digging was resumed at American expense. This substantial sum would have to be added to the cost proper of building a canal. The second, through Nicaragua, though more expensive, had no stockholders to be satisfied. Its total price would, therefore, be lower. Moreover, aside from these details, in the spirited bidding for American cash, the Nicaraguan government asked a smaller down-payment and annual rental than did Colombia. It seemed she would get the highway. Public sentiment and a House majority favored that route.

At this juncture Roosevelt was indifferent to location so long as something was dug. Hay favored Nicaragua. Suddenly, the French directors reduced their price to $40,000,000. Panama gained in attraction. The company's New York attorney and lobbyist, William Nelson Cromwell, increased his efforts on behalf of his clients. A gallant French gentleman, Phillippe Bunau-Varilla, arrived in the United States to contribute his undeniable talents toward revising national— and, failing that—senatorial opinion. Mark Hanna held forth on the Senate floor. In all the propaganda spread by the three, a few basic points stood out: total costs for either route were now approximately the same; Nicaragua was volcanic and therefore more dangerous. Obligingly, while debate in the upper house approached its close, Mont Monotombo erupted to prove the latter contention. M. Bunau-Varilla underscored the event by sending each senator a Nicaraguan postage stamp. On it was a smoking volcano; written below was the republic's inscription—"An official witness of the volcanic activity of Nicaragua." The Senate gave preference to Panama, the House concurred, and Roosevelt signed the bill. Hay was set to work drafting a treaty with

General Concha, Colombia's minister. Cromwell scurried between them to forestall any possible breakdowns.

Through the summer of 1902, the discussions went on. In September, a revolutionary outbreak occurred in Panama—a type of volcanic activity unmentioned by the French company's Washington lobby—and the United States, without consulting Colombia, landed marines to keep the railroad across the isthmus open. Concha considered this an affront to his country's dignity, broke off negotiations and departed for home. Dr. Herran, the chargé, took up where his insulted superior had balked. In January he and Hay signed a treaty; in March the Senate ratified it.

Difficulties arose immediately. President Marroquin of Colombia, whose methods resembled those of his neighbor Castro, felt the popular pulse and determined to oppose the agreement. The $10,000,000 down-payment and $250,000 annuity arrived at by Hay and Herran were too slight a compensation for so fair a prize. Since the French company's concession was worthless, except for the American dollars soon to be paid, he believed his country entitled to a share of the $40,-000,000. Furthermore, he had discovered that the treaty gave insufficient guarantees of Colombian sovereignty in Panama City and Colón, where ownership of the railroad would turn the cities over to American control. Consequently he acceded in his Congress' refusal to accept the Hay-Herran concert and blandly ignored Bunau-Varilla's prophecies, by telegram, of dire things to come.

The spring and summer of 1903 saw Roosevelt and Hay in futile rage. They comforted each other by coining epithets to describe Marroquin and his assembly. "Greedy little anthropoids" was the Secretary of State's characterization. To which the President countered with "foolish and homicidal corruptionists," "jack rabbits," and "inefficient bandits"—in the last remark, a doubt existing as to which moral failing was the greater. Hay's delicate suggestion that the Nicaraguan route was still available the Rough Rider refused to consider. The thought of waiting until after 1904, when the French company's rights in Panama would expire, was likewise repugnant. Perhaps he held ideas of seizing the isthmus without any justification but the righteousness of America's mission. Luckily he was saved that trouble.

Cromwell, Bunau-Varilla and assorted patriots rescued the Chief Executive from his dilemma by promoting Panamanian "independence" through insurrection. The uprising they staged is a prototype of comic-opera revolution—with its bribery of Colombian officers, amicable arrests, United States warships off Colón, and shouts of "Viva Presidente Roosevelt!" The vulgar haste of the United States to grant recognition to Panama and to conclude a canal treaty covered the transaction, in the Latin American view, with less humorous overtones. It fertilized the firmly rooted weed of distrust for Yankeedom. At home, it shocked anti-imperialists and the more timid believers in manifest destiny. Their protests were unavailing; the administration had committed itself beyond recall.

Impatient to "make the dirt fly," the jubilant President perceived nothing untoward in his part of the drama.

"I simply lifted my foot," he said.

Attorney General Philander Knox, whose ability to turn the perfect phrase made him one of his chief's favorites, replied, "Oh, Mr. President, do not let so great an achievement suffer from any taint of legality."

*   *   *

As the campaign of 1904 approached, Latin America remained a problem to Roosevelt. The Hague Tribunal had given a verdict in the Venezuelan case that the coercing powers deserved preference in repayment on the debt. This enhanced the utility of violence. In the same breath, it provided future excuses to powers that might wish to sidestep the Monroe Doctrine. To one who saw the Doctrine as the lever for removing Europe from the Americas South, danger was incarnate in the decision. Roosevelt, therefore, rushed to add an expression of the responsibilities of the United States for its self-denoted sphere of influence. Magazine articles, inspired by the State Department and embodying the new conception, began to appear. Administration spokesmen pressed home the argument. In a letter that received widespread comment, the President wrote that nations that knew "how to act with decency in industrial and political matters" need not fear American interference. "Brutal wrong-doing, or an impotence which results in a general loosening of the ties of civilized society"—such as the refusal by a Latin American nation to recognize the financial obligations a succession of dictators might impose on a helpless country—"may finally require intervention by some civilized nation, and in the Western Hemisphere the United States cannot ignore this duty."

In substance, this is the Roosevelt Corollary to the Monroe Doctrine. In practice it assumed the form of taking over the customs-houses of Santo Domingo in January, 1905 to satisfy that unhappy republic's American and European creditors. But that incident and the peaceful aspects of Rooseveltian diplomacy in ending the Russo-Japanese war and participating in the Algeciras Conference are outside the range of this work. The energetic President had already been pronounced a success by his re-election.

It is, however, worth noting that he considered "taking Panama," "settling" Santo Domingo's affairs, and the earth-circling voyage of the Navy his greatest triumphs in foreign relations. His receipt of the Nobel Peace Prize for his work in stopping a war was, to him, of less significance. Perhaps he was correct. The matters in which he took pride established precedents, however egregious; on the other hand, conditions of war and peace still alternate uncertainly in man's precarious existence on earth.

2. TAKING OVER A COUNTRY

Much has been made of Theodore Roosevelt's radicalism from time to time. His "trust-busting," his cordiality toward organized labor, the reactionary nature of his enemies, his fight for a more enlightened use of the nation's resources—these, together with his independent presidential campaign in 1912, have created the legend. In fact, Roosevelt clung fairly close to the middle of the road. His extremism was displayed only in such things as his frequently inaccurate judgments of men, his advocacy of simplified spelling, and the exhausting pace at which he drove himself. Consummate politician that he was, he went only so far as he could lead the public and his grudging party. No politician who hopes for office and influence can do more.

Exactly when he took cognizance of the progressivism that was boiling beneath the McKinley prosperity is difficult to determine. Before his ascent to the White House he had displayed leanings toward reform and the correction of some of capitalism's grosser abuses; but he had always been pulled back to the Republican line when party leaders waxed less enthusiastic than did he. The presidency, however, had made him leader of his party. Where a young assemblyman could be forced to subside and an unruly governor shelved in the vice-presidency, a Chief Executive could not be fought by his nominal backers with impunity. Party disaster is too often the result.

It was inconceivable that Roosevelt should merely copy his predecessor's ways. His energy, his driving need for self-expression dictated otherwise. At Buffalo McKinley had intimated that the new commercial position of the country might necessitate tariff reductions; but this portion of the inheritance the successor pigeon-holed. Protectionist congressmen filled the seats in both houses. At best, such a policy would divide the party; at worst, it could ruin the untested new President. Besides, the drawing of tariff schedules was the work of Congress; little credit redounded to the administration. And Roosevelt was interested in building the power of the Executive. The first humility toward elder statesmen—more apparent than real—abruptly halted as the New Year began. His first annual message, it seemed, had been no perfunctory statement to Congress; it became a declaration of intentions. Ambiguity disappeared when he commenced squeezing the last ounce of meaning that could be wrung from its phraseology.

Lingering on the statute books was the Sherman Anti-Trust Act, passed in 1890 during the hapless Harrison's administration. Never very diligently enforced since its inception, the law's effectiveness had been still further whittled away by the Supreme Court in 1895. In a decision that came close to the narrowest of hair-splitting the justices said that the manufacturing process did not constitute interstate commerce, that ownership of the majority of an industry's capacity did not necessarily, in the meaning of the act, constitute a trust. The implicit suggestion was that a holding-company, owning the stock of the manufacturing plants of the industry, was not engaged in commerce and, therefore, was not a trust. Subsequent decisions against outright price-fixing agreements had somewhat softened the blow. But the holding-company device reigned unquestioned as a method of consolidating former competitors under one board of directors. Thus, in November, 1901, J. P. Morgan had the Northern Securities Company incorporated for the purpose of ending competition between the Burlington, Northern Pacific and Great Northern railroads.

Looking over the land for a field to conquer—preferably the corporate one—Roosevelt and Knox espied Mr. Morgan's latest handiwork. The President asked his Attorney General for an opinion and was told the scheme was illegal. No one else had been consulted when it was announced that the government would prosecute. The suddenness of it all unnerved financial circles and Morgan came down to Washington to negotiate with his "big rival operator." His mission was a failure; suit was filed in St. Paul on March 10, 1902.

The objective of Roosevelt's action was only secondarily the breakup of the monopoly. Primarily he was searching for sources of power to bring corporations under federal control. That he had found what he sought was obvious from the outcry. The conservative press accused him of showing disrespect for the Supreme Court; it pilloried Knox as an "unknown country lawyer from Pennsylvania." Unwittingly it also aroused the President to battle. The White House became a resting place between speaking tours during which he took his case to the people. As he ranged south, north and west, millions heard his words and joined his crusade. He emphasized he was not opposed to corporations; he simply denied that they were superior to government. He told the country he was seeking a formula to enforce the law, to use the government's power. Over and over, he underlined his distinction between good and bad companies, between beneficent and evil men—this being before the discovery of that more quotable phrase "malefactors of great wealth."

The spectacle of a president stumping the country pulled out the crowds. Common men came to cheer the colorful orator's assertions. The men under challenge covered their confusion by inviting him to address his unwelcome criticism to the criticized. In November, the Philadelphia Union League steeled itself as it heard, "Time may be needed for making the solution perfect; but it is idle to tell this people that we have not the power to solve such a problem as that of exercising adequate supervision over the great industrial combinations of today. We have the power and we shall find out the way."

Yet, conservatives uninfected by the hysteria engulfing their newspapers comprehended that this was neither a dreaded anarchism nor an all-pervasive assault on big business. After the first furies died it was to be noted that no more suits were filed—and would not be until Roosevelt was "President in his own right." Meanwhile, company and government attorneys nursed the case through the maze of legal arguments and slow-moving tribunals. On March 14, 1904, it finally emerged from the Supreme Court. Four justices felt the law had been drawn to forbid all combinations in restraint of trade, whether "reasonable or unreasonable," and ordered the Northern Securities Company dissolved. One justice said that only unreasonable combinations were forbidden, but ruled against the Morgan concern. Justice Holmes, surprising many by associating himself with the dissenting minority, was sarcastic on the reasoning of four-fifths of the majority opinions. He defended the right of merger and ridiculed the "interpretation of law which . . . would make eternal the *bellum omnium contra omnes* and disintegrate society so far as it could into individual atoms." According to the wits of the day, the administration had gained a 4¾ to 4¼ victory; but the President was satisfied. He had vindicated his executive power. He was justly proud of his part in turning the direction of the law; it was "one of the great achievements" of his first term.

James J. Hill, builder and head of the Great Northern Railroad, sadly recorded his bitterness. "It seems hard that we should be compelled to fight for our lives against the political adventurers who have never done anything but pose and draw a salary." More than a court verdict accounted for his feeling.

While the courts were still deciding the fate of the Northern Securities Company, Mr. Hill's poseur was giving Congress and another section of big business a demonstration of leadership qualities. That Roosevelt had asked for a Department of Commerce and Labor in his first message the Senate knew and then conveniently did nothing about. In his message of December, 1902, the President repeated his request. Once again Congress was disposed to overlook it. It was not that anyone resented an agency that would harmlessly compile statistics and issue neatly printed reports. The basis for the covert hostility lay in the demand for a Bureau of Corporations, with investigatory powers, as a *sine qua non* of the projected Department. Adding this to the Northern Securities suit industrialists had drawn the proper alarming conclusions and counseled their pliant representatives in both houses to inaction. But in January and February of 1903, John Archbold, a vice-president of the Standard Oil Company, went past the unprovable spoken word and sent a number of telegrams to strengthen congressional resistance. The Colonel in the White House, learning of the move, put this intelligence to its best service. Calling in the newspapermen he informed them of the messages, changing the signatory from Archbold to John D. Rockefeller, whose name raised far greater inflammation in the public mind. Spread over the nation's press the story produced its desired stimulus. Within four days House and Senate members experienced a change of heart and generously gave Roosevelt his Department, complete with the detested bureau.

Under Secretary George B. Cortelyou the Department started slowly. Its corporations commissioner, James R. Garfield, gathered his facts on tobacco, oil and meat packing. Temporarily they were filed away. The Chief Magistrate was eyeing the 1904 assizes and remembering where campaign contributions originated. In 1905, with corporate payments made to the political war chest and the administration approved by the people, Garfield's compilations came into use. During the succeeding three years a record for anti-trust prosecutions was inscribed on the administration's slate of good works. The record was soon to be shattered under Taft's presidency; but far more important than either number of suits begun or convictions obtained was the impetus given the federal government in voluntarily rising to the defense of the public against unrestrained privilege. Roosevelt rightly pointed out: "the most powerful men in this country were held to accountability before the law."

* * *

If capital was discovering strange things about a Republican president organized labor was meanwhile being treated to the first White House occupant hospitable to its cause since Andrew Johnson. While the lawyers drew out elaborate contentions at St. Paul, while the conservative press and the President belabored each other over the merits and sins of corporations, the nation was finding its attention diverted to—as periodically happens—the anthracite coal fields of Pennsylvania. There, low wages, long hours, irregular employment, company-owned towns and dangerous working conditions were among the more blatant factors that made the miners restless. During the summer of the election year of 1900 their union—the United Mine Workers—had called a strike. To the Republicans, who were preaching sermons of good times and the full dinner pail, the act seemed to belie the professions. Mark Hanna therefore hurried to the operators and forced from them a ten per cent wage increase. The walkout was averted; rank-and-file faith in the party gospel—that Republicanism was the true benefactor of free labor—remained undisturbed. For the miners it was the first pay raise in twenty years.

By 1902, however, the mine owners were cutting the heart out of the agreement. Heavier poundages were being required at the weighing of a ton of coal and wages were dropping accordingly. The president of the union, John Mitchell, had attempted, without success, to draw the companies into a series of conferences that would adjust the grievances. He had failed because the operators refused to concede that such a thing as a union could exist. They were willing "to receive and consider every application" of the men; but it was "unbusinesslike" to confer with "persons who are not interested in anthracite mining"— that is, with officials of the miners' union. Another strike loomed as a certainty.

Hanna worked valiantly to avert it. But this time, neither the fear of electoral defeat nor the perils of Bryanism were available to him as points for use in countering the unrelenting attitude of the railroad and coal companies that owned the mines. Their previous surrender had been bred of compliance with political ends; now, they felt, the party owed them a measure of *rapprochement*—that of staying out of the privacy of the coal business in a non-presidential year.

The National Civic Federation—listing among its members not only Hanna but John D. Rockefeller, Jr., Grover Cleveland, Samuel Gompers of the American Federation of Labor, Charles Schwab of Bethlehem Steel, as well as a number of distinguished churchmen— offered its services to arbitrate the dispute. Mitchell promptly agreed, and suggested as an alternate—if the Civic Federation's offices were not acceptable to the employers—a committee of religious leaders. George F. Baer, the leader of the operators, was equally prompt in his refusal to discuss the proposal. "Anthracite mining," he said, "is a business and not a religious, sentimental, or academic proposition." Management of the businesses was imposed by law on the president and directors of each company; Baer could not and would not delegate it to outsiders. As for the churchmen, he was unable to "call to [his] aid as experts in the mixed problem of business and philanthropy the eminent prelates you have named."

Such a thesis won Baer small applause outside the ring of his own associates; instead, it brought on the strike. On May 12th, 140,000 miners left the pits. They were peaceful, and ready to stay out a long time. They knew public opinion favored them. On the other side, the mine owners showed no signs of budging. In late June when the public's exhortations began coming into Washington, Roosevelt asked Knox whether the coal companies could be sued under the Sherman Act. The Attorney General, with one case already pending, expressed his doubt.

In July the last vestige of sympathy for the operators disappeared. Baer had received a letter telling him that his religious duty demanded he settle with the striking workingmen. Without pausing to inquire whether he was being led into a trap, he wrote one of his infuriating replies. "The rights and interests of the laboring man will be protected and cared for—not by the labor agitators, but by the Christian men to whom God in His infinite wisdom has given the control of the property interests of the country, and upon the successful Management of which so much depends. . . . Pray earnestly that right may triumph, always remembering that the Lord God Omnipotent still reigns and that His reign is one of Law and Order, and not of violence and crime." Widely reprinted, this document called down on Baer and his colleagues the wrath of the church and press. "Extraordinary" was the mildest editorial reaction. On the whole, comment ranged more generally toward "blasphemy" and "the divine right of plutocrats."

August witnessed a dwindling of coal stocks and unconscionable profiteering on the part of those who owned them. While the operators still refused to discuss terms the country had long since tired of their

stand. The high cost of what little fuel there was for sale, and the prospect of a heatless autumn and winter bulked larger in the public mind
than any possible impairment to property rights that might come from
raising wages. The alert politicians, ever responsive to the voice of the
voter, added their protests. The President fidgeted. "The rise in the
price of coal," wrote Lodge from Massachusetts, "we cannot argue
with." Unless the mines were reopened by November, when the by-
elections would indicate the feeling of the people for the exciting new
administration, the Senator predicted a "political disaster." The President, implied Lodge, must give at least the appearance of acting on the
problem.

Scanning the Constitution, and the precedents of law, Roosevelt
could have discovered no explicit authority for taking a hand in settling
the dispute. Nevertheless he evolved alternative plans. On October 3rd
the first of the two was inaugurated. Standing on the prestige of his
office—and very little else—he summoned operators and union leaders
to a meeting. Knowing he could not drive them to settlement, he appealed to their patriotism. Mitchell responded and offered to abide by
the decision of any commission the President might appoint. Baer,
speaking for the companies, was only too aware of the weakness of
Roosevelt's position. That he angered the Chief Executive is unquestionable, for he coldly denied Mitchell's right to participate in any discussions and answered the presidential plea with undisguised contempt.
His expressed opinion after the conference was a summation of his
argument: "We object to being called here to meet a criminal, even by
the President of the United States."

In the wake of his failure to solve matters by conciliation, Roosevelt
turned to his second plan. It was characteristically daring; it was without precedent. By a strict reading of the law he was bound not to interfere unless violence occurred. Even then he could enter only by sending in troops to preserve order, provided the state authorities either
requested his assistance or could not control the local situation themselves. But there was peace in the coal fields. There were no riots, no
fights; the miners simply refused to go to work until assured a hearing.

These circumstances of restraint Roosevelt could not countenance.
Since the country needed coal he decided to by-pass contending parties
and the prerogatives of private property by reopening the mines under
national auspices. He told rather than consulted Knox and Elihu Root
about his plan. He would send in the Army to "dispossess the operators
and run the mines as a receiver." He would assume full responsibility

for the action, thereby freeing everyone but himself from the recrimina-
tions that must soon follow. Then Senator Quay was called in and
asked to have the governor of Pennsylvania call on the federal government for troops to quell a disorder. Since this was the only part of the
story given the wily old politician, he doubtless presumed that the President was about to embark on a deft new form of strikebreaking and
readily agreed. The final person informed was Major General John M.
Schofield, the man selected to command the army on its industrial mission. To him the Commander-in-Chief was more open. The old warrior listened attentively and announced himself prepared to run the
mines regardless of strikers, operators or the courts.

Meanwhile, Secretary of War Elihu Root was discouraged at the
close similarity between the seizure idea and socialism. Moreover, he
was disgusted with the mine owners and believed his friend "Theodore"
needed help. Consequently, he put the connections of his years as a corporation lawyer to work. Securing Roosevelt's permission, he drew up
a tentative set of compromise terms with J. P. Morgan. In turn the financier was to cajole the operators into accepting them. Basically, the
dispute would be submitted to arbitration, but the sensibilities of the
employers would be saved by not requiring them to recognize the union. Morgan talked with Baer and compromised once again. Arbitration would be approved, posited the coal baron, only if the board con-
sisted of men of five enumerated occupations—a federal judge from
Pennsylvania, a mining engineer, an army engineer, a man familiar
with the mining business, and an "eminent sociologist." None but Baer
could have considered this an impartial panel. The absence of labor
members, or anyone who could be deemed friendly to the workingman,
was patent. Mitchell objected, and Roosevelt, recognizing the fairness
of the complaint, unhappily agreed with him.

Once again, Morgan attorneys came to Washington to see the President. In the ensuing all-night session he tried to apply reason but
found the attempt fruitless. In desperation, he applied ingenuity. The
five classifications were to be adhered to; but in the Rooseveltian definition, the "eminent sociologist" became E. E. Clark, grand chief of the
Order of Railway Conductors. To his dawning understanding of
the mental gyrations by which an unpalatable "tweedledum" became
an appetizing "tweedledee," he watched the lawyers fall over themselves to seize this opportunity for peace. Long-distance telephone calls
revealed the mine operators to be of the same receptive mind; they
cared not so much that Clark was a union leader as that his official status on the board would be recognized as something else. Roosevelt now

felt his power. By way of emphasizing his victory he added two more members to balance the commission more fairly—Carroll D. Wright, United States Commissioner of Labor, and Bishop John L. Spaulding, one of the churchmen originally proposed by Mitchell.

A satisfied nation went to the polls three weeks later, voting Republican in deference to the Presidential wisdom. In March 1903, the commission ordered a ten per cent wage increase and the adjustment of certain grievances; recognition of the United Mine Workers was withheld.

Forty-four years later President Harry Truman used the Rooseveltian precedent of executive concern in the labor relations of the country with curious results. Stepping in as mediator between General Motors and the United Automobile Workers he offered the federal government's judgment of what was an equitable solution to the disagreement. More politely than George F. Baer, but far more successfully, management rejected his conditions of settlement, allowing a long strike to follow. Viewed in the light of this incident Theodore Roosevelt's achievement comes into clearer focus. The true victor was the public. The operators lost no more than their conduct and attitude warranted; the union's gains were hardly damaging to the institution of private property; and certainly the individual miners benefited.

And the longer-lived value of his intervention lay in its legacy to the nation of a conception of labor relations heretofore unexpressed in the practice of the federal government. For all the boldness of his plan and whatever his motives he took the ideas of his times and implemented them. In so doing he struck a blow against older ones that can most charitably be described as belonging to the nineteenth century. Far better than Baer and others who would have preserved the alliance of business and politics to rule the nation, he appreciated the nature of the changes that were coming to the country. He understood the inequality of bargaining power between the individual laborer and the corporation. He therefore regarded unionization as a necessity. He saw it as the only method by which a workingman could obtain his "rights"—"to a living wage, to reasonable hours of labor, to decent working and living conditions, to freedom of thought and speech and industrial representation—in short, a measure of industrial democracy and, in return for his arduous toil, to a worthy and decent life according to American standards." Almost as if to make his general view relevant decades afterward he added the qualifying remark: "No man and no group of men may so exercise their rights as to deprive the nation of the things which are necessary and vital to the common life.

A strike which ties up the coal supplies of a whole nation is a strike invested with the public interest."

*   *   *

Far less amenable to vivification before his countrymen were the prosaic subjects of conservation, reclamation and irrigation. Yet Roosevelt was able to inject into them the life they needed to become popular issues. That the national resources were being squandered had been recognized prior to his enthronement in power. That little had been done to correct the abuses was equally plain.

His annual messages, his public speeches and his writings hammered out the truths of conservation. His broad usage of executive power gave color to the words. Committees of experts and men of prominence were appointed, without pay, to survey aspects of the problem. Their systematic work made them particularly valuable to the President and galling to those who wished ruthless exploitation, without thought of the future, to go on as of old.

The General Revision Act of 1891 offered ample opportunity for a man to whom conservation was an undebatable good. Under its provisions, the president was permitted to withdraw timber lands in the public domain from sale and retain them under the management of the government. Safe chief executives like Harrison, Cleveland and McKinley had set aside a total of some 45,000,000 acres. Roosevelt, knowing an instrument of power when he saw one, added 235,000,000 more; it took a typical congressional device—a rider to an appropriations bill (and therefore difficult to veto)—to stop him from further withdrawals.

By that time prodigal spending of the nation's natural resources had been put under some controls. Excellent bureaus managed the national forests; government attorneys were closing in on the poachers—some of whom operated on a very large scale indeed. To the process of saving what was left had been joined a program for reclaiming dry areas for cultivation. In 1902, when Senator Newlands, a Democrat from Nevada, presented a bill designed to provide irrigation facilities at federal expense to the arid western lands, Roosevelt overlooked the unregenerative character of Newlands' politics to lobby personally for the measure. Its passage opened the way to later reclamation projects over the entire country.

That the country benefited from the work is beyond doubt. Most of its present timber and mineral reserves can be credited to his farsightedness. That he convinced the nation of the necessity of preserving

what remained of its once magnificent stretches of forest and grazing
land is more doubtful. Periodically, efforts are made to hamstring the
administrative agencies charged with their care; bills are introduced to
give a little more of the public wealth into private hands for a short-
sighted profit. If Roosevelt put forward a proper attitude of reason in
man's use of his natural heritage the prejudices of individual selfishness have yet to appreciate the soundness of his approach.

Of all the controversy surrounding the accomplishments and intentions of Theodore Roosevelt his conservation program has received
the least criticism and his sincerity about it has seldom been questioned.
The Colonel himself believed it an important part of his policy. His rival, the elder LaFollette—anti-imperialist that he was—thought it his
greatest work. Until the congressional revolt at the end of the second
term few dared to oppose it overtly.

3. TAKING OVER A PARTY

That he had the favor of the electorate by no means insured Roosevelt an iron grip on his party. Not only did he understand that the
forces which had caused his nomination in 1900 gave him little personal
strength, but he knew that the four men who had previously taken his
road to the presidency—Tyler, Fillmore, Johnson and Arthur—had
been sidetracked before their terms expired. As one who had spent
half his life playing the politician, he knew how the "system" of political advancement worked. He had almost been its victim; he might yet
be. The assassin's bullet may only have been a reprieve.

Yet Roosevelt was habitually overnervous about his political future.
The first uncertainties in party minds were quashed when he retained
the McKinley cabinet. The respectables were pleased to see John Hay
remain in the State Department, and the conservatives relaxed when
Root, Knox, Long and Gage stayed on in their posts. Toward reactionaries like Senators Aldrich and Hale and Speaker Cannon, he went
more than half-way in seeking their co-operation. And these men, ha-
bituated only to thinking of policy in the whiteness of their own
thoughts or the blackness of Mr. Bryan's, were thrown off guard by the
humor and vitality and the balancing of pros and cons that were inherent in Roosevelt's exposition of a subject. With them and with other
political leaders he effected an unavowed patronage pact. For the good
appointments he submitted they granted confirmation; reciprocally he
permitted a certain number of the bad ones they asked for under the
mantle of senatorial courtesy. That this concord was of political design
rather than mutual pleasure became evident when, late in his second

term, Roosevelt had to employ all his strength in holding what he had accomplished. Righteousness had gone too far along the progressive road for conservative tastes; congressional Republicans rebelled and were whetting the axe to begin chopping at executive power. But before that day arrived he had so manipulated the patronage, so built his popularity and prestige with the public, that the party politicians, for all their dislike, would only have endangered themselves to oppose him. In fact only one man was ever a real threat to Roosevelt's domination.

Over the other problems of the cabinet, the Congress, and patronage loomed that of the Republican National Chairman, Mark Hanna. His hostility to Roosevelt was too well known to be let alone by the rumor-mongers. One story had it that, on McKinley's death, the Cleveland industrialist had mixed grief with rage. "I told William McKinley it was a mistake to nominate that wild man at Philadelphia. I asked him if he realized what would happen if he should die. Now look, that damned cowboy is President of the United States."

Thus, in 1901, neither saw the other as a likely candidate to lead his party in the next presidential assize. But circumstances forced them to work together—in the coal strike, on conservation, on Panama—and they discovered that they could be compatible. Each with his sense of humor, each with his unmistakable abilities, each with his strong personality found the same traits in the other, and admired them. Yet there were always latent suspicions. If Hanna never forgot that Roosevelt was "impetuous" and "altruistic," the latter continued to regard the gruff Ohioan as a species of jolly pirate. Moreover, that Hanna still controlled the bloc of delegates from the South and the Middle West, and could turn them in the direction he chose, worried the young President. A sense of caution therefore intervened to prevent complete trust between the two.

This was capitalized upon by senior Senator Joseph Benson Foraker of Ohio, whose ambitions and opportunism were frowned upon by Hanna. Under McKinley, Foraker had been fed a starvation diet in the patronage distribution. With the New Yorker in the White House this solon decided the time was appropriate for striking a deft blow at his enemy and beginning preparations for succession to the throne in 1908. Aware of the President's desire for constant reassurance, Foraker, in May of 1903, announced his faith in the administration and the Rough Rider's candidacy for the next year. He recommended that the Ohio state convention, to meet in June, do the same.

Hanna should probably have let the statement pass without comment; or, in choosing to speak, should have said something equivocal.

He did neither. He made the mistake of publicly opposing the suggestion, saying that other potential nominees would, by such a resolution, be unjustly criticized for entertaining ambitions. Of course, included in the comment was a denial of personal aspiration; but, in the final analysis, Hanna was Roosevelt's only potential rival.

The President, meanwhile, was on a speaking tour in the West. As with most of his other excursions this one had the double purpose of popularizing his policies and his candidacy. Hanna quickly sought to cover his blunder by wiring the contents of the interview before it was publicized, and adding, "When you know of the facts"—that is, Foraker's machinations—"I am sure you will approve my course." But the prime aspirant either lacked the facts or overlooked them. His answer clearly made endorsement a test of loyalty. There was no escape; and Hanna announced he would not oppose the Foraker accolade.

In effect the last obstacle for the popular Teddy was now removed. Intriguers continued attempting to set President and Senator into opposition—evidently with some proficiency, for Hanna was again to deny ambitions, and remark testily that he was tired "of going to the White House every day, of putting his hand on his heart and being sworn in." But the real drive to eliminate Roosevelt was over. In February of 1904 the plots ended permanently with Hanna's death. Because his machine had been a personal erection there was no successor to his peculiar place in the domination of the party. By default the leadership fell to Roosevelt.

George Cortelyou became national chairman on Roosevelt's appointment. State conventions dutifully indicated their support of the administration. Delegates to the Chicago convention expected an uneventful meeting. They were not pleasantly disappointed. Elihu Root keynoted the great deeds of the past four years—with the surprising omission of the coal strike settlement. Roosevelt, of course, was unanimously nominated. The party platform, hewn under Lodge's supervision, did the usual pointing with pride at the Republican record, and viewing with alarm the Democratic. As is traditional in American politics, it refused to hint that political opponents might possibly have done something worth-while in the course of their party history.

Under the delusion that a conservative candidate would attract the bankers of Wall Street, the Democrats selected Judge Alton B. Parker to lead them away from Bryanism and to entice a reaction from Rooseveltism. In both objectives they failed. Typical of capitalism's attitude was the endorsement of its organ, the *New York Sun*: "Theodore, with all thy faults—" Facing such handicaps, the judge lacked either the funds or the enthusiasms they can generate to make the election close. His opponent unwontedly stood on the decorum of the presidential office and refrained from conducting a formal campaign. A few statements from the White House effectively rebutted whatever telling points Parker was considered to have made. Electoral and popular majorities of record proportions were recorded on Election Day. In the landslide even Missouri entered the Republican column as a "welcome stranger"—the first breach in the Solid South since the return of free elections after 1876.

Roosevelt was elated. He renounced all desires for another term—to his dismay eight years hence. In the recent disturbances occasioned by Judge Parker's accusations about the corporate sources of Republican campaign funds, he showed no interest. That Standard Oil gave $125,000, J. P. Morgan $150,000, the New York Life Insurance Company $48,000, the New Haven Railroad $50,000; that Edward H. Harriman raised $125,000, were the facts of ancient history. If these handsome outlays, and others like them, were for the purpose of underwriting security during the next four years, they proved remarkably poor investments. As had the residents of San Antonio years before, the capitalists sighed relief on March 4, 1909, when William Howard Taft brought slowness, predictability and conservatism back to the presidency.

AMERICA'S balance sheet, beginning to show a profit in the days of McKinley and Roosevelt, suddenly took on a most optimistic appearance in the second decade of the twentieth century. A Europe at war discovered itself unable to attend to all the intricacies in the business of killing men on a large scale. Some of the ingredients imperative to continuing the enterprise had to be sought outside the combative circle. Europe turned, therefore, to the Yankee colossus, petitioning it to supply those industrial and commercial artifacts which a continent, occupied in soldiering, lacked the means to produce. And American capitalism, of course, answered the plea—but in the Yankee way. It sent what was wanted, but it named a price. It received from its customers their gold and their securities, and when they had no more assets that were negotiable, it arranged that the purchases be made on credit.

On and on came the demands, on and on went the shipments; credits piled on credits. Times were so good that any man who wanted a job could have one, and usually he got high wages with it. Meanwhile the United States had entered the struggle in a crusading spirit. Before that spirit was exhausted it celebrated the victory and accepted the task of reconstructing the world of peace. It gagged at the political rehabilitation of Europe, but unhesitatingly dispensed its economic resources. It failed to understand how antithetical were these two points of view.

Two continents now asked for so much that the hard-working machine could not produce all that was demanded. A price rise began, with Americans bidding against one another, and, in effect, against the Europeans to whom goods were graciously being sold on mere promises to pay. The balance sheet glowed with prosperity; the ledger joyfully reported record income, record dividends. America was no longer "the rich," it was "the richest" and becoming richer. Viewed as a business concern it fairly exuded confidence. Profits were boundless; the future was golden without end. The balance sheet said so. Or rather, men thought it did.

They forgot they already had all the gold, that the customers had none. They forgot that, in giving credit, one allows the customers an opportunity for repaying their borrowings, that one tempers the poor risks with good ones, that one does not develop huge expansions and enormous sales programs on a speculative theory of binding the customer to take the merchandise and hoping that perhaps in some good distant day he will pay for it. Certainly, they forgot—or never knew—that if one had to expand and, in thus expanding, gave credits, one nurtured the customers, permitted them to sell some of their own wares to regain a little of their substance; that one persevered in helping them find stability so that their debts gradually diminished and their purchases for cash gradually increased. Or one wiped out the debt and considered his expenditure a contribution, thinking of his return as a nonmonetary profit of liberty, security and peace.

Otherwise, one forced the customers into bankruptcy; and with their credit ratings worthless, realized they bought nothing. In that event, "accounts receivable" on the balance sheet shrunk into "bad debts," never to be reinstated. The pretty figure believed to be "surplus" was replaced by an ominous "deficit." Worse still, the industrial plant which had been erected and the laboring force which had been employed on the assumption that the customers would buy eternally became idle as soon as no one took the products, either for cash or credit. But this is anticipating the story of the Coolidge and Hoover eras. It is too soon to tell whether there exists equal application in the years of Truman and/or his successor.

More closely apposite to the chronological beginnings of the postwar era was a recasting of American thinking. The sun of liberalism, having held the sky for twenty years, was setting. Over Theodore Roosevelt it had shone brightly, though crossed by an occasional uncertain cloud. Taft had been broiled by its torrid—and, so he considered, unfriendly—heat. Woodrow Wilson had found its rays of the early afternoon stimulating and productive, and had persuaded a majority to worship with him. But as the liberal sun's intensity lessened while Wilson's afternoon wore on, the druids became enamored of other creeds. Once more, clouds obscured its rays. The task of winning a war relegated other portions of the ritual to a lesser place in the broad scheme of things; the dogmas of Patriotism and Hate-of-the-Hun overshadowed the original vision of his New Freedom doctrine.

New prophets arose to declare liberalism's truths false and Wilson, the high priest, a charlatan. Conservatism relapsed to reaction, and, finding the tired people ripe for the message, advocated the profit motive unrestrained by government and the right to work unhampered by labor unions. The fluid lines of toleration between liberal and conservative tightened into unrelenting prejudice. In the postwar period, during the price inflation and accumulation of profits, wages and working conditions moved too slowly along the upward curve of progress. Disparities increased. Prosperity assumed a sectarian look; and, in answer, those who believed themselves excluded took up the strike as their weapon. But now, there were no McKinleys to conciliate, no Hannas and Roosevelts to crack the hard shells of the "haves." Wilson, the discredited, first fought his battle for the peace treaties and then lay invalided in the White House. The men of capital were winning overwhelmingly—and, so it was to be proved, dangerously.

In different, less creditable causes, others were also winning. For the moment, a fanatically righteous prohibitionism succeeded in equating the moderate beer drinker and the chronic alcoholic as moral degenerates. New definitions of villainy were fabricated and old ones resurrected. The alien and the foreign-born citizen, the Negro, the Jew, the Catholic, the non-conformist and the eccentric—all had their Americanism opened to question by examiners who arrogated unto themselves the right to set forth the proper criteria of the ideal. Needless to say the inquirers discovered precisely what they sought to find—the suspected lacked certain of the attributes that in sum added up to the full one hundred per cent American.

Perhaps the most useful discovery was derived from the Russian Revolution. Infamy was no longer to be colored in somber black but in flaming Red. The workingman asking higher wages or shorter hours was Red; the educator asking a free expression of truth or recognition of the advances in social thinking was Red; the writer daring to criticize was Red; the person who displayed the flag improperly was Red. A few bombs called forth thousands of arrests and raids that destroyed Red office equipment, Red presses, Red posters, Red organizations. From it all, the bomb manufacturers went undetected, the communist ranks held firm, and Soviet Russia survived to grow stronger. In the main, dissenters were indiscriminately daubed, the more timid cudgeled into silence under threat of character assassination or outright persecution.

It is the faculty of Americans to hate more deeply those they consider an internal enemy than those whom they think constitute an external menace. Britain, Germany, Russia and Japan have aroused powerful enmities in the American mind from time to time. Yet, the emotional energies spent upon relatively weak minorities, the persistance of the frictions surrounding their presence in this country, the fantasy in ascribing motives to them, outweigh those acid hatreds directed across the water. As after the Civil War, so after World War I, the United States reached one of these emotional peaks. Liberalism and progressivism were exhausted from twenty years of aspiration and effort; they crumbled before the onslaught of reaction and bigotry.

To say that the pendulum had merely swung back to the nineteenth century is a mistake. Rather, the mood of the people had rejected Wilson's dream of world peace, Jeffersonian democracy, and genuine free competition. In a desire for change—whatever its relationship to progress—the people had espied the gospel of a sheer materialism without any attached responsibility. If they believed that the material ideal could be achieved through methods once before repudiated—monopoly capitalism, the tariff, credit booms, small government, weak unions and the rest—few honestly announced that divinity was inherent in their cause. They simply pursued selfishness on a personal, national and international scale, hoping but not much worried that out of it all order would somehow emerge. Finding it pleasurable, they set a pattern. That the Old Guard Republicans once more ascended to leadership while such was the temper of the mass was natural. They had waited long for the scepter.

1. FROM THE GREEN HILLS

Vermont's extraordinary attachment to the Republican party is proverbial. Twice, when presidential candidates in the low ebb of the GOP's fortunes have pulled but two states into their electoral columns, Vermont has been one of them. Never since 1856 have the Democrats been a worry. Its political individuality clearly established before the nation, the state continuously demonstrates its independent character by producing a rare breed of native, easily distinguishable in his habits and thought from his fellow Americans. Since the day Ethan Allen thundered: "The gods of the valleys are not the gods of the hills," and then withdrew to his green fastness before his New York hearers could recover from their bewilderment, Vermont has preserved an isolated type of Yankee, frequently incomprehensible to outsiders, impossible of survival outside its borders.

Except for the adjustments he necessarily made to life in Massachusetts and Washington, Calvin Coolidge was an authentic representative of the species. Where other Vermonters in history had left the state to merge with the culture of their adopted homes—Stephen Douglas with the Illinois frontier, Thad Stevens with Pennsylvania's capitalism, Chester Arthur with New York's cosmopolitan society and its easy virtue in politics—Coolidge remained an anomaly even when transplanted into a neighboring New England province. He was too well steeped in the lore of the hill gods to escape their call and directions.

Like John Tyler he was far more a product of his ancestry, local geography, and a rigid adherence to inherited ideals than are most men.

The Coolidge name had been carried to the New World in the early days of the Massachusetts Bay Colony, and there it had stayed until one Revolutionary War captain had penetrated the Vermont forest and settled in Plymouth township. The most adventurous of the family, he hewed a farm out of the wilderness and scraped a living from the serrated, stony land. Five generations later, on the same soil, Calvin Coolidge was born. The intervening generations had stayed on in that pocket of the Green Mountains, farming, storekeeping, doing their civic duties as constables, justices of the peace, and occasional town representatives in the state legislature. If their existences had been frugal, they had also been self-contained. No Coolidges had starved; none had become wealthy. Hard work was their portion, and they accepted it without second thought; their leading position among the families of the neighborhood stemmed from diligence in the field and in the store, and a capacity for leadership in local politics. Rather than from money, they drew their security from the land and the family name. Like other Vermonters they lived on a landlocked island, given little to adopting the changes of the years, transmitting language and ideas from one generation to the next.

Vermont's first settlers had been rural New Englanders, coming out of Massachusetts or pushing up the Connecticut and Housatonic River valleys. They had carried with them an unbending Puritanism and its Old Testament God; they had organized themselves in the traditional township governments; they had brought along the simple techniques of rustic life and the simple ideals of the eighteenth century. A few towns developed to support a handicraft industry based upon wool, lumber, limestone, slate and maple products. But the revolution of steam and coal that came to the states surrounding Vermont by-passed her hills and her people. The towns remained adjuncts to a rural culture, uninfected by metropolitan volatility or the complexities of industrialization. While urban New England evolved the Brahmin civilization and an aristocracy founded on mills and factories, Vermont, insulated in her green slopes, felt no change. It preserved its Puritan faith, perpetuated its horse-swapping Yankee, retained its eighteenth century values. Its one revolution was an espousal of Republicanism, but that had sprung from abolition rather than economics, from morality rather than a desire to expedite prosperity. And once engrafted on the Vermont mind, Republicanism became as ingrained as belief in the Puritan virtues.

By 1872, the year of Calvin Coolidge's birth, the state's population growth had already ceased to be significant. Thirty years before, it had begun to level off; prior to the annexation of Texas or the settling of the Great West, Vermont society was approaching rigidity. In the century that followed, that static condition helped make it an anthropological laboratory for the study of an earlier American civilization. Its sons of the Collidgean stripe grew up to be scrutinized more as specimens than as men, as relics of another world.

* * *

That Calvin Coolidge ascended to the White House after mounting each rung of the Massachusetts political ladder in no way diminished his Vermont nativity. In the Bay State he was as much the atypical politician of his era as his family back home differed from the average American. When he moved to Northampton after having finished school, he had been fully molded by his heritage. At Amherst College, he had picked up a philosophical justification for the virtues of thrift, simplicity, personal honesty, sedulous application, and individualistic effort. For the civic responsibility he had seen in the exemplars of his father and grandfather, he found an ethical rule—the "law of service under which men are not so solicitous about what they shall get as they are about what they shall give." Yet, the virtues and the "law" were already inculcated as normal standards of conduct before he ever heard their truths arrived at by logical processes in a college classroom.

So too, as councilman, town solicitor and mayor in Northampton and as assemblyman, state senator, lieutenant governor and governor in Boston, he accumulated knowledge and experience. But these merely reinforced a character and mind already set in the home at Plymouth. Moreover, during his vice-presidency and presidency, Coolidge gave few signs of having acquired additional depth. So thoroughly self-sufficient was the Vermont education that it explained all he thought necessary to understand. Had it been otherwise, Coolidge would have had to tear out the imbedded values and learn others more attuned to the problems he faced. Barring that, he would have had to retreat into psychotic repression or flee back to the farm.

Of course, he did neither. With an unbounded faith in his preparation, he applied his native ways to the world. He used Vermont's rasping dialect with its nasal drawl regardless of its effect on his listeners. Though florid oratory still prevailed—especially among the lower ranks of the politicians—Coolidge limited his expression to simple words and choppy sentences. Though the two- and three-hour harangue had by no means disappeared, his speeches were models of brevity. What they contained were ideas reduced to the lowest denominator. The complicated thought was filtered out until it became a convenient aphorism or an elemental tenet. At times the process carried so far that, to sophisticated minds, the result was banality. To rural Vermont, however, each maxim was a workable truth.

His humor was as pure as his talk. Chipped down to an understatement of some larger idea as one would fashion a flint from a native rock, it took the form of a gem self-contained and polished. Like his mottoes, it seemed the product of hours of labor with a mental burin. Dropped out suddenly in the course of serious talk and set into the middle of an unamusing sentence, it frequently startled the unsuspecting listener. Often delivered without a change of facial expression or softening of tone, unexplained and unaccompanied by further comic remark, the isolated wisecrack was left to arouse the hearer's mirth or incomprehending wonder. Coolidge liked to watch for its effect and appreciated laughter when it came. Perhaps this was the reason humor seldom made an appearance in his writing. He would not have been able to observe the reaction of his audience.

The pattern he consciously followed in his life, business and political, was endemic to rural New England. When he worked, he went at it hard, trying to do the job thoroughly. In his small law practice he tried to give his clients complete satisfaction; in his committee work in the state legislature he set an unusual standard by attempting to understand the hidden and overt implications of each bill; in his political canvasses for office—when it was possible—he sought to reach personally every voter. From every dollar earned, he tried to save a bit for the future. Thus, in the expensive task of being President, he thriftily set aside about two-thirds of his pay. For every political good deed given he accumulated a reservoir of good will and obligation toward himself. He entered each labor with the view that while its completion guaranteed no advancement, it might nevertheless develop such a chance. Cautiously, he watched for the appearance of the chance, and as cautiously, he inched forward to meet it. He made no headlong dashes; if the opportunity did not appear, he was not disappointed. But he never doubted that, in some one field, he would succeed. For the basic article in his creed of performance promised the individual his reward if only his efforts were persistent enough and his patience long-lived. If political rise were blocked, Coolidge would have thrown himself into the law; if the law failed him, he could turn to the farm or to storekeeping.

In tackling each job he believed entirely in concentrating on the issue at hand, in the Old Testament inference that a man was not his brother's keeper. In each office he restricted his sights to the area of its operation; he campaigned for himself and against his Democratic opponent. As Republican mayor of Northampton he did not suggest policies for the State House in Boston; as Republican governor of Massachusetts he did not presume to advise the President of the United States. Before he took action the problem had to seek him out; he precipitated none and met none halfway. He was a man who farmed his own fields without attention to what happened in his neighbor's.

Such an attitude appealed to the ordinary folk as "common sense" and made him, despite his oratorical weaknesses, a good vote-getter. It permitted him to sympathize honestly with the underprivileged who wanted better working conditions, more wages, poor-relief, improved educational facilities. These were, after all, human aspirations. But his individualistic approach led inevitably toward a stand against the realization of these dreams through an integrated social program, collectively adopted. It upheld the principle of clean government insofar as officeholders were to be strictly honorable in spending the public funds. But it added that government's place was minor, that the individual could pretty much rule himself. Antecedent to any consideration of government's sphere was its cost; the role of the state as tax-collector received attention prior to the role of the state as mediator in the divergent currents of life. Industrial society was viewed in its fragments—a factory equalled a field, a corporation equalled a farmer. That the whole system was interrelated, that one piece was bound to and affected by the other was unapprehended.

These were the well-springs of Coolidge's philosophy, the conditioners of his acts and outlook. Naturally, he felt comfortable with conservatives, and, in Republican circles, naturally he joined with the anti-Rooseveltian wing whenever possible.

Wealth he regarded as the fruit of virtuous work; the wealthy he admired for having reaped the harvest and erected a personal monument from its proceeds. Because he saw only the final pyramid and not the contributions of the others who helped build it, he gave full credit to the owner. Apparently he was indifferent to the process of construction. Certainly it never occurred to him to inquire about it. Thus when the builders protested that they were not receiving a fair share for their labors, Coolidge utterly lacked the equipment to assay the justice of their claim. The premises of their argument were outside his ken. He sat, disbelieving that their message could be addressed to him.

If others thought this a negative attitude, Calvin Coolidge intuitively felt it essentially positive. Given his view of the private nature of things, the range of public policy was necessarily slight. The public servant was obligated to recognize the limitations of his office and to perform his duties ably within these boundaries. He had no place in reconciling private conflicts. That the conflicts might be of public concern entered Coolidge's mind only rarely.

*   *   *

The details by which the Plymouth farmboy became governor of the Old Bay State are without excitement. Party regularity, buttressed by a clean, uninspired record won him designations for office by Republican leaders and election by the voters. His impeccable conservatism helped in rallying business toward supporting him. Yet the financial contributions of the wealthy were neither inordinately large nor binding upon him to surrender his independence. They did not have to be. Coolidge's public character was stainless; his philosophy allied him to capitalism without reference to regular cash payments from the masters.

A few circumstances militated in his favor. Hegemony over the state party was fairly evenly divided between Senator Henry Cabot Lodge and former Senator Murray Crane. The two men felt a thinly veiled dislike for each other but arranged a practical working agreement, Lodge receiving Boston and the eastern part of Massachusetts, Crane the remainder. Coolidge fell geographically into Crane's bailiwick, thereby enjoying a certain advantage. For Boston's habit of returning huge Democratic majorities always placed Lodge in an inferior bargaining position where state politics were the issue. For some reason, Coolidge's close-mouthed ways and hard-working habits in the state senate attracted him to Crane, and set him apart from the mill-run of Republican legislators in the State House.

In 1913, fortune beckoned. That year the party had lost the state's executive offices and the lower house of the legislature in the annual elections. Ancient districting provisions, however, rendered the state senate Republican; and, though their majority was reduced, Republicans continued their hold on one corner of the government. Murray Crane now dealt the choicest reward in his possession—the presidency of the upper house. The recipient was the senator from the Northampton district. In that famine year the selection technically made Coolidge the highest ranking member of his party within the state. He responded to the elevation by delivering an address calculated to swell conservative breasts and check radical foibles. It abounded in Cool-

idgean nuggets: "Men do not make laws. They do but discover them."
"The people cannot look to legislation generally for success. . . . The
normal must care for themselves. Self-government means self-support."
"Ultimately, property rights and personal rights are the same thing."
"Do a day's work. . . . Expect to be called a stand-patter, but don't be
a stand-patter. Expect to be called a demagogue, but don't be a demagogue. Don't hesitate to be as revolutionary as science. Don't hesitate to
be as reactionary as the multiplication table. . . . Don't hurry to legislate."

These chips from Puritan philosophy awoke a moderate applause
among conservatives. Seven years afterward, when the artisan was a
national hero, his simplifications would sweep the country under the
title *Have Faith in Massachusetts*.

Meanwhile Coolidge and his speech generated ideas in the mind of
a Boston merchant, Frank W. Stearns. A well-intentioned conservative
himself and frightened at Wilsonian democracy, he was suddenly possessed of a desire to promote this state senator. That Coolidge was a
total obscurity outside Massachusetts, as well as a secondary light within
it, could not dissuade him. Stearns had no knowledge of politics and
was therefore unaware of political obstacles. An Amherst man also, he
liked to believe that fair Harvard's domination of place and position in
the affairs of the Bay State could be overcome by one who was neither
a radical nor an Irish Democrat. By process of elimination this denominated the savior an Amherst alumnus. And Coolidge was most logical
among the few possibilities.

Stearns turned the talents of business and advertising to furthering
his man's career. He envisioned him as lieutenant governor, governor
and, at last, president. He would have dispensed with the intermediate
steps were it feasible. Thus, in 1916, Stearns more than casually suggested Coolidge's availability to lead Republicanism against Woodrow
Wilson—to the raucous enjoyment of Senator Lodge. State senators,
the businessman deduced from this experience, were not presidential
timber.

Gradually, Stearns learned perspective and a few rules of thumb on
how presidents are made. He talked up his hero for state offices, and
discovered, in delight, that Murray Crane agreed with him. In 1918,
aided by Wilson's blunder in calling for a Democratic Congress, the
two guided Coolidge through a successful gubernatorial campaign. To
the credit of the candidate, he showed a grasp of the technique of persuading voters that probably exceeded that of his backers. Yet he was
only one of forty-eight governors. Outside Massachusetts he was known

slightly for conservatism and a pronounced aversion to cluttering the books with laws.

* * *

However roseate the dreams of Frank Stearns, Coolidge thought he had achieved his highest place. His father, in Vermont, now saw the justification for having spent money on Calvin's college education and for his son's leaving the farm. Up in Plymouth the people were lastingly proud of their fellow townsman, his family of its most noted member. A "western" Coolidge had set a mark of "service" that the "eastern" Coolidges, the wealthy and cultivated Brahmins, had never approximated. Now, he was prepared, after two or three terms, to return to the law.

In 1919 fortune again beckoned. Its offer emanated unhealthily from the low wages and dissatisfactions of the Boston police. While prices skyrocketed to 225 per cent of their pre-war level, the wages of these guardians of the law had belatedly been increased by something less than twenty per cent. Moreover, what surplus and unreported income they had previously received from saloonkeepers vanished when the city decided to enforce the new prohibition laws vigorously. Unable to get further increases or secure relief in their additional grievance at over-crowding in the station houses, they organized a union among themselves and obtained a charter from the AF of L. In so doing they probably violated the department's regulations.

At any rate, the Commissioner of Police, Edwin U. Curtis, thought they did, and demanded that the union be dissolved. It quickly became obvious that Curtis knew the rules better than he knew his public servants. Collective action appeared to them more likely to give redress than individual protest. They refused. Curtis answered by summoning, trying and condemning nineteen policemen for insubordination, and promised to dismiss them from the force. In return the union promised a strike unless he reinstated the officers. The commissioner, a stiff-willed manufacturer who had his own opinions about labor unions, whether inside or outside the public service, accepted the gauntlet.

By curious workings of the law, Boston's Police Commissioner was appointed by the governor and removable by him. The city's mayor had little real control over him except that, under another statute, should an emergency arise, he held powers of suspension and the authority to call out the State Guard located within the city. But the mayor, a reform Democrat, wanted no emergency. He appointed an impartial committee of citizens to recommend a solution. In an atmosphere thick with rumors of a general strike by all union labor, the committee gave out its recommendations: the AF of L union to be replaced by an independent union to bargain for the patrolmen, the victims of Curtis' purge to be reinstated "without prejudice." Mayor Peters pressed Curtis to accept the compromise; but the commissioner was sure of his rights, his independence, and his principle. He stonily rejected the proposal. Fatuously, he believed his loyal if underpaid Irishmen would hold to their jobs. Peters was better informed. He appealed to Coolidge to effect the compromise, and found the governor averse to acting as his brother's keeper. With a walkout imminent, the mayor asked Coolidge for troops. The governor spurned the request, accepting instead Curtis's statement that the situation could be handled without additional forces.

On Tuesday evening, September 9, the strike began with most of the men refusing to report for duty. Sedate Boston slowly felt out the freedoms of living unrestrained by law and order. Crap games on the Common flouted the old puritanism; fist fights in streets were ended only by the exhaustion of the participants; windows were broken; plundering began. The strike became national news overnight with not only Boston but the country watching the distraught mayor, the stubborn commissioner and the unemotional governor. Peters suspended Curtis and called out the State reservists untrained in the techniques of law enforcement. In South Boston a cavalry charge into a crowd killed two citizens. Still, the man in the State House did nothing.

During the weeks of negotiation before the walkout, he had ostentatiously toured Massachusetts towns, addressed meetings, and visited institutions—done whatever he could to avoid the burden of involvement and decision, and, on appearances, to prevent his identification before the public with either disputing side. He had expressed commiseration for the unhappy lot of the policemen, but his dealings with Mayor Peters and his repudiation of the committee's suggestions had clearly favored Commissioner Curtis. Whether Coolidge was awaiting the crystallization of public opinion for or against the strikers; whether he had decided to instruct Bostonians and the country in a practical lesson on the meaning of law and order; whether he intended to do nothing without the word of Murray Crane, who was being besieged by hysterical conservatives to activate his immobile protégé; whether the governor was holding off for the ripe political moment to contribute the denouement—all have been advanced as theories in explanation of his delay in acting. Each has certain evidence to support its pretensions; possibly each was of influence.

Thursday found the city in peace. Violence had ended and plundering had ceased. Peters controlled the situation. But the newspapers in Boston and over the United States were reporting the bloodshed and disorder of the previous day. It was then Coolidge moved. The entire State Guard was mobilized and Peters relieved of his command over the remnants of the Boston police not on strike. Curtis was set back in his ducal chair by gubernatorial ukase; his decision on the dismissals was upheld. Plans were evolved to replace the disaffected patrolmen by recruiting a new force. The police strike was broken.

All day Friday the praise flowed in. Editorial writers for the conservative press enshrined a new national hero, the dour Vermonter in the Massachusetts State House. Animated by fears of Trotsky and Lenin they extolled Calvin Coolidge, the white knight, and his principle that government employees were outside the grasping hand of Red unionism. On Sunday the governor nailed down his fame and doctrine. To Samuel Gompers's request that the strikers be restored to duty, and their complaints arbitrated, he replied with a succinct motto that renewed the cheers: "There is no right to strike against the public safety by anyone, anywhere, any time."

On the face of it this dictum settled the affair. Its philosophy became the issue of the fall campaign. And in a mounting conservatism, with a near-pathological terror that took the strike's remote resemblances to communism and credited them to Soviet designs, the people re-elected Calvin Coolidge governor. That Peters had done the work of re-establishing peace in Boston was somehow overlooked; Coolidge had provided the popular phrases. *Have Faith in Massachusetts* was published in book form, along with other speeches and papers. Frank Stearns saw to it that a copy reached every Republican who by name, influence, significance of office or occupation might have a word in party councils. In late 1919 and early 1920 they were talking about sending Calvin Coolidge to the White House. This time Senator Henry Cabot Lodge did not laugh.

2. SATURNALIA

Chicago's Coliseum baked delegates to the 1920 Republican National Convention. The meeting hall's heavy stone walls could not repel the fetid June heat that seems always to grip the lake city when politicians, attracted by its central location and its North Clark Street and South State Street haunts, periodically converge on it for one of their quadrennial deliberations. That the building had formerly been a prison accounted in part for the sufferings of the delegates; its thick walls had been designed for other purposes than the comfort of those within. Yet architectural defects were no great consideration to those in attendance. All were sure it was a Republican year. But, by the evening of June 10th, the convention had seen more division than unity. For three days foreign policy statements had been fought over and discarded as offensive to one or another of the wings of the party. Finally, a meaningless plank was patched up so that the voter could believe whatever he chose, and find it in the Republican platform. Under that dispensation the United States would join some kind of a League of Nations or no kind; it would co-operate in European recovery and at the same time withdraw completely from the continent's troubles.

The selection of a candidate had produced even greater schism. Eleven contenders—some serious in their ambitions, some merely receiving honorary mention as favorite sons—had split the three ballots taken. Presumably Theodore Roosevelt would have won the nomination hands down had he lived; but his death had thrown the race open to all. Several of the candidates were logical choices as his successor— General Leonard Wood of Rough Rider fame, and, more recently, martyred by President Woodrow Wilson;[1] Senator Hiram Johnson of California, one of the Progressive leaders back in grace after the 1912 revolt and a strong vote-getter in the 1920 primaries; Nicholas Murray Butler, friend to the now deified Theodore and a man of intellect. Others were knocking for recognition—Governor Frank Lowden of Illinois, with a strong Middle Western following, and Governor Calvin Coolidge of Massachusetts, with a scattering of delegates. A few entrants were regarded as jokes; among these was Senator Warren Gamaliel Harding of Ohio. The galleries were shouting for Herbert Hoover, but very few on the floor wanted him. If there existed any unanimity it lay in a hatred of Woodrow Wilson by all present.

Wood and Lowden had suffered when a Senate investigation disclosed their quests for the nomination had cost, respectively, $1,770,000 and $414,000, before the convention met. With Johnson, they led in the voting; but the nature of their deadlock made it clear that none of the three could win the required majority of delegates.

It was then the true rulers of the party decided to end the masquerade. Years of dominance over Republican presidents and the House of Representatives had placed party leadership in the Senate. And the senators, fresh from their defeat of Wilson's peace plans, were pulling the strings of the obedient substratum of leaders out on the floor of the Coliseum. For those first three roll calls the delegates had

---

[1] Wood had been refused an overseas command despite his excellent record in preparing Cuba for self-government.

been allowed to frolic. Suddenly, when they were beginning to enjoy the tension of the stalemate, and demanding that the voting go on, Chairman Henry Cabot Lodge autocratically adjourned the session. He and his confreres needed time to select their man.

The senatorial line-up in the Republican high command is suggestive. Lodge was at the height of his power in consequence of his successful assault on Wilson. Senator Boies Penrose of Pennsylvania, boss of the internal councils of the party, lay in Philadelphia, supposedly dying; nevertheless, he had a direct wire to advise or to affirm or to veto the judgments being deliberated in Chicago. His colleague Philander Knox, the days long past since he had flirted with progressivism, was also absent, a potential nominee. But on the scene were others of the "Soviet"—as the senatorial command was irreverently dubbed—who responded to the Penrose edicts or could, where he was unable to exert his power, themselves administer the party. All were senators; none stood to the left of conservatism. Penrose did not have to be there; his spirit was one with that of those present. Reed Smoot of Utah, Medill McCormick of Illinois (allied by name with newspapers and farm machinery, through marriage with the Hanna heirs), Charles Curtis of Kansas, Brandagee of Connecticut, Wadsworth and Calder of New York—these rounded out the directorate. They wore, in addition to their senatorial togas, the elegant trappings of finance, coal, the railroads, the food industries, steel, textiles, wool, and oil—oil seemed, to more than one observer, particularly in style.

Corruption was not what bound them to the interests; their's was a stronger set of ties—sympathy for capitalist domination, faith in the superior rule of the rich, a confidence in American industry and finance. Thus, their task was easier; they believed in their right to power. They proceeded to use it. Ruthlessly they discarded the popular aspirants—Wood, Lowden, Johnson and Hoover—as too liberal or too independent. First-rate men were thought unimportant in the strategy of selection; what they sought was one who would sign the bills of the Senate, and send in none of his own for passage. In conning the list of hopefuls, one after another came under senatorial examination and was dropped. Eventually they reached Senator Harding. None spoke highly for him, but no one spoke against him. He was duly designated. The following day, word of the decision having been given the marionettes on the floor, a "boom" developed gradually, and Ohio, "the mother of Presidents"—though, this time, gestation really occurred in a room of Chicago's Blackstone Hotel—had another son headed toward the White House.

By way of afterthought the "Soviet" had picked Senator Irvine Lenroot of Wisconsin for the vice-presidency. With Harding named the delegates lost interest and started to shuffle out of the searing heat of the auditorium while Senator McCormick nominated the chosen candidate. Snatchers at glory followed with seconding speeches. In the hubbub raised by the departing members, the unstinting praises being lavished on Lenroot, who had no wish for the office, went unheard. The atmosphere was anticlimactic and even McCormick was leaving the hall when a large voice boomed out over the noise. Judge Wallace McCamant of Oregon was nominating Calvin Coolidge.[2] The overindulgent substitute chairman could not stop him in time. The lingering delegates caught the fever of revolt. As the Republican party had risen adamant over "too much President," so its rank and file suddenly rose against "too much Senate." One roll call confirmed the sentiment; Coolidge won overwhelmingly in the convention's single popular decision.

*   *   *

That Harding and Coolidge should have been joined on the same electoral ticket represented not incongruity but the handiwork of political convenience. In common they shared records of regular Republicanism, records which illuminated neither as a party leader or statesman of the first rank. Yet these records accounted for their desirability to chieftains of a party whose folklore esteemed weak chief executives. Otherwise the two men were opposites—another device generally thought salutary where the attraction of votes is a primary index of success.

Warren Harding had done his best and happiest work as the owner and editor of the Marion, Ohio *Star,* a newspaper he had bought for its debts and watched prosper, through no great show of ability on his part, while the town grew to give it circulation and higher advertising rates. His secondary career in the public service had been a sort of hobby. In the hurlyburly and factionalism of Ohio's politics he had been a lesser man in the Foraker crowd. This meant Republicanism in the style of Blaine rather than McKinley or Roosevelt; and a tradition, probably untrue, has it that the young Harding was thrown out of Mark Hanna's office when he approached the rugged Clevelander with an unsavory deal. During those early days a politician from Columbus,

---

[2] In 1926, the vindictive senators evened the score. McCamant, appointed to a federal judgeship by Coolidge, was rejected by the upper house.

Ohio, one Harry M. Daugherty, saw the Marion editor in a local canvass, and noticed in him a physical similarity to the presidential type. Since Daugherty lacked the quality of pulling votes to himself, he remodeled his ambitions toward advising behind thrones instead of sitting on them. In alliance with Mrs. Harding, he molded the small-town editor into what looked like a statesman. The tall, handsome physique was set off by well-tailored clothes; at some discomfort to the subject Mrs. Harding tried to impose a ban on chewing tobacco. By 1914 the two promoters had worked the willing Harding into the Senate.

Once in the clubhouse Harding was satisfied. He had come farther than he had expected; he enjoyed the poker games, the drinking parties, the impressive Washington society and the dignity of his office. Senatorial labors could be arduous or untaxing; Harding chose the latter way. His attendance at the sessions was sporadic; the golf course held keener attractions than the debates. In his five years he did not introduce a single important bill; his work on committees was equally undistinguished. When he voted, Harding lined up with his party. Before the war his record was one of obstruction; during the fighting, he stood for most of the Wilsonian measures requested to expedite victory; but, after the war ended, he went back into opposition. In summation his politics were anti-labor, imperialistic, isolationist, pro-business.

In general he did as little as possible, taking those positions forced upon him and selecting the side best calculated to secure his re-election. A man who loved his whiskey, he fought prohibition all the way, and then voted for the Eighteenth Amendment. Similarly with women's suffrage, he persistently refused to announce a stand on one side or the other. Finally favoring it when it was approved, he intimated that he had been one of its staunchest advocates and wished repayment from the feminine portion of the electorate.

The character of his public service was less Harding's fault than his backers'. Pushed when he would have vegetated contentedly, he amiably permitted the ambitions of others to take him into the deep waters. Once there he lacked the strength to swim back to safety. Instead he disported himself on the surface, unconscious of the currents and dangers that plucked from underneath. Uninformed on the problems before the country, poorly educated and uninterested in self-improvement, having ordinary mental ability and a deep and unquestioning faith in standpattism, he did not belong in the Senate.

In Ohio politics he had earned a reputation for conciliating factions and for rousing oratory. In the Senate he failed to influence deliberations by either technique. Agreement in national issues, he sorrowfully learned, was unattainable through mere comradely banter at a bar or over a card table. On the floor his speeches were ponderous empty flights, confused in their thought, turgid in their verbosity and boring to his listeners. Leadership he left to Penrose, Smoot and Lodge, and implicitly followed their direction. But, though he commanded no respect, his affability gained him a certain popularity. Other second-raters and he mixed easily and lived the life of pleasure and prestige. "W.G." Harding might not be a legislator but he was a darn nice fellow. He was welcome in the clubhouse.

Plainly, the Senate "Soviet" knew the man it had selected. He measured all too perfectly to the specifications; there was little chance he would demonstrate independence. Without qualms the candidate watched himself painted as a second McKinley. Obligingly, for "W.G." was always obliging, he sat on his front porch in Marion and received his callers. His speeches were pointedly indefinite, except where he attacked the Democratic administration. On the explosive international question he pronounced vaguely for an "association of nations." This would hold the international-minded Republicans like Elihu Root, Herbert Hoover and Charles Evans Hughes; it would also gain those who had grown to hate Woodrow Wilson, whether for his person or his policies. Sometimes Harding betrayed the shallowness of his thinking by stumbling through extemporaneous remarks on the elementary concepts which had been written into his talks by his publicity staff. At other times he became needlessly entangled in the English language. Thus, he gave the country, if not the dictionary, infelicitous words like "normalcy." Still, few seemed to care or to worry.

His running mate, who was to have stumped the country as had Theodore Roosevelt, was tried out at Minneapolis. But the Yankee twang and the clipped terse sentences fell cold on midwestern ears as yet unused to any oratory but the passion and flamboyance of the school typified by Harding. His managers rapidly dispatched Coolidge to the Solid South for the rest of the campaign.

There was but little real enthusiasm for the nominees. Little was necessary. Though the Democrats had named two abler men, Governor Cox of Ohio and the popular young Assistant Secretary of the Navy, Franklin D. Roosevelt, the country was not interested. It was tired of Wilson and energetic presidents. It wanted to escape from war, from regulation, from responsibility. Harding was the "average man" and his thoughts were average thoughts. He was the antithesis of Wilson and that was enough for the people. Though fewer than half of the eligible voters found the inclination to cast ballots, they elected the jovial Senator by a record majority of 7,000,000.

* * *

What the senatorial cabal did not know about Harding was his weakness for pleasure, no matter how derived, and his fidelity to his friends.

The poker games, for high stakes, went on as before. Gambling took on other forms as well. That central fascination of the Average Man of the Twenties—the stock market—also tempted the occupant of the White House. Without skill, he plunged unwisely, as did those he personified. At his death Harding was behind by some $180,000.

While the nation engaged in the "noble experiment" of prohibition, liquor flowed in the White House. That new professional, the bootlegger, was making his appearance and beginning to saturate Main Street with dubious brands "right off the boat." But the President here differed from less fortunate average men; Harding insisted on serving only the best. His whiskey was amber in color and properly aged. His gin was the product of the distillery, not the bathtub. In time, unconfirmed rumors circulated about his sins of the flesh.[3]

Most of these festive doings, however, went unpublicized and, of course, unacknowledged. Only after his death did the public know the fuller truths from the printed word. Nevertheless, from the beginning, the official acts of his administration were sufficiently disquieting during his lifetime.

The appointments were startlingly inconsistent. Because everyone expected a conservative regency, none was surprised when Charles Evans Hughes, Herbert Hoover, and the fabulous plutocrat Andrew Mellon entered the cabinet. But the presence of Harry Daugherty in the Attorney General's post and "Puddler Jim" Davis as Labor Secretary brought the critics on guard. Daugherty, a lawyer who had been more lobbyist than courtroom pleader, had only mediocre status before the bar. Davis, though he held a union card, was a banker of no apparent social outlook; the probabilities were against his exerting himself

[3] Four years after his death, when evidence of the crimes against the government committed by his appointees had so mounted as to make Republicans wish they had never heard of Warren Gamaliel Harding, the nation enjoyed a lurid saga of his personal life. Nan Britton published *The President's Daughter,* an account of Harding's extramarital relations with her from 1916 to 1923. The details, including the birth of a child about a year before he was elected to the presidency, were devoured by the reading public. In all its tawdriness, the picture was too accurately that of "W.G." to stand denial.

in behalf of the workingman. Yet Davis was to hold the place for three consecutive administrations, working efficiently and remaining unobtrusive. Daugherty, however, became an immediate liability despite his skill in manipulating men. He showed reluctance in prosecuting war frauds; he spent a large proportion of his time denouncing "Reds"; his associates, collected mainly from Ohio, prospered visibly without indication of any legitimate source of income; his intercessions for obviously guilty men kept the sword of justice clamped in its scabbard. In a short while, the nation was to have its explanations. It was also to learn that other cabinet officers, upright gentlemen when they were chosen, possessed unsuspected qualities—incredible stupidity in the case of Secretary of the Navy Denby and a blunted moral sense in the case of Interior minister Albert Fall.

But the secrets of the cabinet had to await Harding's death before Senate investigators brought them to light. Meanwhile the promised days of "normalcy" failed to come off to the satisfaction of all. The vexing League of Nations was swiftly repudiated while idealists wailed in futility. Separate peace treaties were signed with the erstwhile Central Powers. One of Harding's campaign promises was that he would consult "the best minds" in solving the international problems. Senator Lodge saw to it that the Best Minds did their own work without reference to the President's wishes. After the torpedoing of the League, Harding attempted to keep a small degree of faith by advocating American membership in the World Court; the senatorial clique snubbed him. Talk of an "association of nations" was heard no more. American backs turned on Europe, except for the periodic harangues of the isolationists who rubbed salt into that continent's wounds by asking for repayment of the borrowings made during the war.[4]

But international affairs worried few of the President's countrymen during these years. At home the flush of prosperity supposed to be ushered in by the return of Republicanism was slow in coming. Although prices had declined from their peak in 1919, the slump had sent wages

[4] In foreign relations, the pride of the Harding Administration was the Naval Disarmament Conference held in Washington during 1921-1922. Though Senator Borah had been the man to initiate the call, and though Secretary of State Hughes and Elihu Root did the hard work of persuading British and Japanese diplomats to accept the 5:5:3 ratio on capital ships, Harding received the increments of acclaim handed out by the American and European press. As the discussions proceeded, agreements of various sorts were reached. However warming were the deeds at Washington to hearts that desired peace, few of the provisions on arms reduction were observed for the length of the treaties. Hailed as a signal achievement in its day, the Conference proved better in its intentions than its accomplishments. Today, in the United Nations, one hears some of the familiar words; their meaning is yet to be implemented.

even lower. Strikes in 1922 called out 1,600,000 workers. Daugherty helped neither his own nor his chief's popularity with organized labor by securing against the railroad men an injunction, the stringency of which has not been seen before or since.

Among the legacies of the Wilson administration was an agricultural depression brought on by surplus production and inflated land prices, and accentuated by the declining world demand for American food. The new administration's answer was a fund whereby private banks loaned money to the farmers until the day when prices rose. Meanwhile a tariff was levied on foreign produce—a quixotic solution in view of the fact that American agriculture was suffering from low prices and an absence of markets, not from the competition of incoming crops of foreign nations. Desperately farmers increased their mortgages, trying to hang on until agriculture was again profitable. Now a minority in an industrialized country, they turned to government for salvation. In Congress their spokesmen organized the Farm Bloc, but were unable to make headway against the dominant conservatives. Symptomatic of the poor health of the national economy, farmers went bankrupt at an increasing rate, helped along that road by the credit the government invited them to take. Prices stayed low; there was no chance they would rise. And the administration, elected to help industry, stood pat in its offer of tariff and private loans. Out of such statesmanship the agricultural depression sped on unmitigated.

To businessmen, however, the future appeared pleasant. Harding signed an increased tariff law. Secretary of the Treasury Mellon—"the greatest since Alexander Hamilton," said some—advised Congress to reduce income surtax rates. His philosophy is instructive in understanding the ratiocinations of the Best Minds. Reduced income taxes, thought the aluminum king, would provide more funds for investment, thus increasing manufacturing facilities, thus providing more employment, thus stimulating greater buying, thus bringing more prosperity —and on and on, the cycle would go, without interruption. The lower tax brackets he would not touch; whatever was lost through his scheme of reductions for the upper categories, he suggested, could be made up from higher excise taxes and a consumers' sales tax. This bald program was not enacted because the Farm Bloc and the Democrats were in no mood to grant indulgences to the rich. When surtaxes were reduced, however, Mellon's prediction of where the money would go was in sad error. Speculation promised larger and faster returns than did industrial investment. "Normalcy" never arrived.

*   *   *

Fundamental to Harding's difficulties were the divisions within his administration and the factionalism in Congress. His Secretary of Agriculture, Henry C. Wallace, was a good golf and card partner, and told a fine story; but he was at odds, at one time or another, with Fall, Hoover and Mellon. Hughes and Hoover, the intellectual respectables of the lot, were personalities rather than politicians, and unable therefore to carry influence with Congress for the more praiseworthy intentions of the President's program. Mellon grew wrathful when Harding elevated a hometown friend to the Federal Reserve Board. In the Senate, where party leadership inhered according to the Chicago arrangements, the cabal had weakened. Penrose had died and Lodge was aging. Western Republicans tended to follow the Farm Bloc leadership on domestic questions. Progressives and Democrats carped at and obstructed the conservative policies; being a minority, they had no responsibility for developing a coherent program of their own.

The circumstances called loudly for a leader. A Roosevelt or a Wilson would have responded. But Harding waited for the Best Minds to point his direction. When his pet projects—the World Court, a shipping subsidies bill, a Department of Welfare—were rejected, he remained quiescent. While he shied from work the country grew uneasy. In the bi-elections of 1922, the voters threw a temporary fright into party ranks by cutting down the Republican majorities in both houses of Congress.

It was a warning. Unfortunately, it was already too late. The year 1923, for all the returning prosperity, was a bad one for the President. His trusted friend and Administrator of the Veterans Bureau, Charlie Forbes, was found to be conducting nefarious operations for purposes of self-enrichment. Incidentally, about $200,000,000 in goods and money could not be accounted for. The suicides of two presidential henchmen touched off more gossip and speculation around the capital city. Congress was doing less than before, except that Senator Walsh of Montana and Senator LaFollette of Wisconsin had become interested in some oil reserves transferred by presidential order from the Navy to the Interior Department.

That May Harding began a tour that was to take him across the continent and up to Alaska on a "voyage of understanding." His plan was to explain his policies and mend his political fences for the renomination boom Daugherty had started in March. At times the President was gay and charming, as he had been before entering the White House. When he reached the Pacific coast his confidence was gone. His patient efforts to convince Judge Elbert Gary and the Iron and Steel Institute that their laborers deserved better than a twelve-hour day seemed unavailing. Those industrialists wanted no gratuitous advice, even from one of their own sympathies. But the major source of the Chief Executive's grief appeared to come from the code messages he received from Washington. Enigmatically, he repeatedly asked Secretary Hoover and several newspaper men "what a President should do whose friends had betrayed him."

As he embarked for Alaska the President looked haggard. On his return he showed no improvement. In Seattle, another message sent him into collapse with a heart attack. On August 2nd he died in San Francisco. He had lost the will to live. While his body took its last earthly ride to Washington, and then back to Marion, millions lined the railroad tracks to pay a final affectionate tribute as the funeral train passed by.

3. THE FEATHER-DUSTER TREATMENT

Calvin Coolidge was up in Plymouth, Vermont, vacationing from the fleshpots of Washington society and the partisanship of the Senate, when word arrived that Harding had died. At his happiest when on the farm, the Vice-President was cheerfully doing chores and working in the fields. Reporters journeying to the village made what they saw into homey copy for the inside pages of their newspapers; tourists were warmed at finding so high an official obviously enjoying rural life. The day before the fateful telegram, they had photographed him tending to an ailing maple tree.

In the midst of the nation's grief that picture together with the story of his swearing in by his father—a justice of the peace and notary public after the Coolidgean tradition of "service"—touched the chord of simplicity in the public's heart. After all, the country really knew little of the new President; the Boston police strike had been four years ago, and that single event had given him a prominence now almost forgotten. Washington interpreted him to be a dour, peevish man, averse to the endless parties and apathetic to the everlasting rumors and gossip of scandal that were a staple of the city's conversation. It had no idea whether his silence cloaked a blank mind or a deep one. It could not understand his self-sufficiency. It did not realize how much he prized his personal independence, the independence of a man unneedful of comradeship, talk and advisers.

Those who carefully informed themselves on the inner doings of the Harding Administration knew that Coolidge had, on his predecessor's request, attended all cabinet meetings and said nothing of

what he heard. Among senators and gallery sitters he had built a reputation as a parliamentarian—and justifiably so—from the rule book
methods by which he had disciplined the Farm Bloc. On his succession,
when he issued the usual statement that he would "carry out" the
Harding policies which, he said, had been "begun for the service of the
American people and for meeting their responsibilities," when he
asked all "who have been associated" with Harding to stay on, the
students of politics accepted it for what it was—a disclaimer of arrogance and personal triumph. Coolidge recognized his accidency. But
where were the policies? The gay Ohioan had left little but a set of un-
related negatives. What of the advisers? A man of Coolidge's bedrock
honesty would find appointees like Forbes, the swindler, and Daugherty, the mercurial lawyer, intolerable. Furthermore, in Massachusetts,
there were stories that Coolidge, when he was aspiring to the governor's chair, had purposely refrained from helping John Weeks in a difficult senatorial campaign. Weeks had lost but his service to the Republican party had since been repayed by the bestowal upon him of the
war ministry in Harding's cabinet. Again, Senator Lodge and the new
President lost no love between them. Could they work together?
Would their hostility divide the party councils? Would one attempt to
discipline the other?

Among the first problems of his heritage, Coolidge saw, or was reminded of, the small cloud labelled "oil" that Senator Thomas Walsh
was pointing to. Scant intimations of the story had, as yet, been given
the public; but the New Englander, in his silent attendance of the cabinet meetings, must have concluded that the transfer of the naval reserves from Denby's spiritless control to Fall's hungry authority involved more than administrative legerdemain. Prying investigators
asked if the tracts, set aside for the public welfare and defense, had
been leased for the exploitation of private operators. Fall had tacitly
denied these allegations, but demurred from giving details because of
their "military" nature. For the moment this statement had to satisfy
the questioners. Everyone knew that the Japanese were unhappy over
the short end of the 5:5:3 ratio they had received in the Naval Disarmament Conference.

But the investigators were not put off indefinitely by scare stories
of war with Japan. They noticed Secretary Fall's affluence, unbeliev-
ably large for a cabinet officer with his modest salary as the only acknowledged source of his wealth. They noted drilling operations on the reserves. They traced the devious courses of Liberty Bonds that had gone
from oil companies into his personal accounts. Friendly senators

warned Coolidge what the evidence indicated, how it could not be suppressed. Since Fall had resigned while Harding was still alive and before the story broke, his political fate was out of the President's hands. But there was still the matter of prosecuting the offenders. No advance word came from the White House; "malefactors of great wealth" was a distasteful phrase for a New Englander schooled on the heady doctrine that business and Republicanism were totems for unquestioning worship.

Walsh's revelations made fine ammunition for Democrats and Progressives. Secretary Denby, former Secretary Fall, Messrs. Doheny and Sinclair, the chief bribers and primary beneficiaries of the Interior minister's generosity with the public's resources, cut sorry figures in the searching glare of the Senate investigation. Those ubiquitous Liberty Bonds had traveled strange places; their movements could not be satisfactorily explained—or, more accurately, the reticence of the explanations told clearly why they had traveled where they had. Yet, while this oil-spattered linen of postwar Republicanism was being delectably aired, the other end of Pennsylvania Avenue continued morosely quiet. Strangely quiet too were the defenders of the party honor and the code of business ethics. To them these were matters better left unsaid. Far from being public servants, Senators Walsh and Wheeler were "scandalmongers" and "poison-tongued partisans," the catspaws if not the originators of a Bolshevik conspiracy.

The stark picture of Denby's blundering forced that gentleman to return to private life. A congressional resolution—probably unconstitutional—had been passed demanding that the inert President ask for another resignation, that of his Attorney General. Harry Daugherty had approved Harding's executive order that had transferred the reserves to the Interior Department—an act of seeming illegality because the reserves had originally been granted the Navy Department under law of Congress—and he now failed to show interest in prosecuting the offenders for the patent corruptions now being uncovered. Coolidge drew up at this dictation and for a time retained Daugherty. Under pressure he appointed Owen Roberts and former Senator Atlee Pomerene, an Ohio Democrat, as special prosecutors of the Government's case against Fall, Doheny and Sinclair. By implication Daugherty was not to be trusted; but nevertheless he still went to his Justice Department office.

Coolidge was moving in his own way, cautiously, stubbornly, unspectacularly. He was doing his best to minimize the potential for destruction inherent in the scandals. He eyed the coming presidential election; and he wanted to disperse, as widely as possible, what shot the Democratic politicians would fire. In close phalanx, the Republican party might conceivably come through the ordeal unwounded. To stand uncovered and penitent before the country would be impolitic; the guilt was too recent, and the opposition marksmen, with guns still in hand, were in no temper to grant a magnanimous absolution. So Calvin Coolidge moved quietly, doing nothing to provoke a crisis, awaiting a favorable turn of events.

In March 1924 the wisdom of his strategy was plain to all. Daugherty declined to show Congress some documents it wished to see. The President roughly dismissed him, naming as his replacement an Amherst friend and a capable attorney, Harlan F. Stone of New York. Temporarily, Daugherty's name vanished from the headlines and popular attention. So too with the offenders. Once out of the Senate and into the courts, the legal technicalities involved in proving the conspiracy in oil made dull reading, and faded from the press. Occasionally the case jumped into momentary view, as when news came of the revocation of the leases, of Fall's conviction, of Doheny's acquittal, of Sinclair's imprisonment for tampering with the jury that acquitted him on the greater charge of conspiracy. But, in the main, the public forgot. Calvin Coolidge was sweeping lightly over the accumulated filth. It was as if a chambermaid applied a last-minute dusting to a long unaired room that was soon to be inspected. There was no need for thorough cleaning since the room would again be closed after the inspection. Mere waving of the feather-duster would send the offending particles off the furniture and into the air. They would settle back after the door had once more closed. In his deliberate way Coolidge disturbed the scene of the scandals only enough to enable it to pass muster. To have washed and scrubbed would have meant overhauling business and the party—a piece of work he considered outside the requirements of his job and the dictates of his conscience.

*   *   *

At heart the President felt the oil scandals and later on the exposure of fraud in Daugherty's Justice Department were inconsequential affairs. What mattered to him was the growing prosperity in business circles. This attested the soundness of the country's economic and moral habits. Capitalism, he thought, was solving the nation's problems in its own private ways. The role of Government was that of caretaker, of preservator of the demesne in which capitalism operated.

Without fanfare the chief steward went about simplifying the complexities of the alliance under which business and politics ruled. To a remarkable extent Coolidge agreed with the generalization of Lincoln Steffens that the businessmen were more responsible for the turns American society took than were the politicians. The difference was that Calvin Coolidge believed wealth directed affairs toward achieving the highest good. Thus he proposed to reduce the importance of the political middleman. In Secretary of the Treasury Andrew Mellon, that great Hamiltonian, was personified the wisdom of monopolistic industry and the acumen of finance. Through aluminum and through banks, Mellon had accumulated incalculable millions and the Yankee Chief Executive was dazzled by his cabinet minister's golden sparkle. Mellon's riches, believed Coolidge, were testimony to his insight. His advice carried tremendous if not dominating weight. Its conservatism admirably fitted the President's preconceptions. The same was true of another adviser. Chief Justice William Howard Taft, an Ohio man but also a conservative ex-President and a conservative interpreter of the law, called more often at the White House now than he had when his fellow Ohioan, Warren Harding, lived there. For Taft was an honest and formal gentleman, the type that impressed a puritanical Vermonter.

Naturally, some one had to suffer in this realignment of leadership, and the victims were the Best Minds of the Senate. Harried within by the Farm Bloc and the enlarged Democratic minority, they exasperatedly watched their power slip away while the sour President dickered directly with finance and steel and coal. The "Soviet" was powerless; Congress might be constitutionally bound to enact the laws, but Coolidge held an old ruralistic suspicion of all multiplicity of law. The less legislation, he thought, the better. Where business functioned well in the absence of law, its needs could best be met through consultation with the chief steward in the Executive branch of the government. Such practice was more efficient. Senators fumed; but the logic of the Coolidgean position was inescapable. And private enterprise appreciated not having to calculate on the whims of 435 Representatives and 96 Senators, or worry through public committee hearings where hostile critics like LaFollette and Norris examined motives.

Most maddening to the Best Minds were the orthodox methods Coolidge appropriated from them to grant capitalism the latitude it wished. Through the Federal Reserve Board he and Mellon reduced reserve requirements and untied credit resources that opened the floodgates of "boom" and prosperity. Stock and bond floatations increased enormously; installment sales superseded much cash buying; a stream of dollars crying for speculative opportunity poured into Wall Street. Congress had had nothing to do with it. If the White House reflected the glitter of finance and industry, if it played the moon to capitalism's sun, it also managed to eclipse the Capitol chambers; for the moment, the presidency was no mere satellite of a Republican Congress. Moving in his own orbit Calvin Coolidge was obscuring his party's dogma of legislative supremacy, and its proponents were restrained from altering his path. There was nothing in his actions against which they could protest.

Still, for all the cosmic strength the President drew from his strange antiquarian doctrines and his hidebound individuality, his will was not absolute. Conservative Senators and Representatives felt the old juices of power. Once the issue no longer concerned direct homage to business, they gave him cheerless moments. That they could do so stemmed also from his conceptions of the executive role. His duty, he believed, was to "recommend legislation" and to pass on what came back for signature. Reading the Constitution literally, he assumed to himself no other relationship with Congress. Thus he respectfully advocated American membership in the World Court, and called for tight economies in the government's budget. But having once suggested what he thought beneficial, he started no pressures in motion to force his program into law. He carried no case to the people as Theodore Roosevelt or Woodrow Wilson or Abraham Lincoln had done. Instead he sat icily in the White House while the legislators tore apart his messages. His World Court and taxation requests were denied, and he submitted. He vetoed a soldiers' bonus bill, passed after he had pronounced against it in his first message to Congress. The Best Minds, cognizant of the veteran vote, overrode him.

Later, when Harlan Stone was elevated to the Supreme Court, the Senate refused to confirm Coolidge's nominee for the Attorney Generalship. It was the first time in almost a century that such an appointment had been denied a president; yet, the error was Coolidge's, first for having submitted a name that was unacceptable to the Progressives and uncommendable to the conservatives, second for not generating a movement for approval or, at least, organized support by solid party men. In presuming not to dictate, he also refrained from attempting a minimum of legislative-executive co-operation. When rebuffed he raged privately at the Senators but kept to his frigid, unchanging ways. Again, with no proposals to the depressed farmers other than a faith in their eventual receipt of capitalism's bounties, he twice vetoed the McNary-Haugen bills—a plan which would have given agricultural relief at the expense of the payers of income taxes. Republicans in the Farm Bloc made unkind remarks, but no public retort came from the Chief

Executive. To Chief Justice Taft he gave his close-mouthed opinion: the senators were "a lot of damn cowards!"

Nevertheless, in relation to the whole, these were minor skirmishes. His intention was not to fight Congress but to give it as little to do as possible. His implement for doing his job was not the mop or the brush but the feather-duster. As its wielder Coolidge wanted no upset, no revolutionary laws, no treasury raids, only the slightest change. He swept diligently and carefully; but, after all, the feather-duster makes no deep impress for all the vigor with which it is swung. At best, it tickles the surface; at worst, it does nothing. This was salutary for Calvin Coolidge. He irritated the legislators when he dusted in the vicinity of their self-esteemed prerogatives. But he neither lifted clouds that provoked their permanent irascibility nor disturbed the sheen that gave the business civilization its golden glow. If anything, he attempted to enhance the glow, and this mollified many of the congressmen.

4. COOLIDGE, THE SYMBOL

It was no accident that Sinclair Lewis's *Main Street* and *Babbitt* were best sellers during the Harding regime, or that H. L. Mencken and George Jean Nathan cast jaundiced glances on American culture in the Coolidge era. The materialism of a business society, the shallowness of the contemporaneous ideals, the obtuse morality at the founts of political, economic and social power—all offended the sensitive minds and drove them to revolt. But the majority were rather irked than convinced by the critics. The blustering Chamber of Commerce speeches; the widespread quoting of an unoriginal Harding adage—"boost, don't knock"; the vilification of Walsh and Wheeler for daring to uncover the scandals; all manifested a mind thinly disturbed at the truths of the accusations but patently unwilling to believe them. Seeking relief from its torment, America looked at the model of Vermont honesty, simplicity and thrift in the White House and idealized the man residing there. It pronounced him the American's American and hailed his commonplaces as utterances of the new gospel. Of course, this simply made the President fair game for the Lewises and the Menckens, but it provided for the spiritual needs of the mass of conservative-thinking, money-making Americans who could not admit that the prosperity and existing standards might be false.

Actually, Calvin Coolidge measured to the portrait as the people did not. In reality, they were not like him, and they did not want to be like him. They were expansive while he was crabbed and silent; they were restless in their new automobiles while he sat in his rocking chair on the White House porch; they speculated in the market and bought on the installment plan while he banked most of his presidential salary; they built new gadgety homes and apartments and boomed the Florida swamplands while he contentedly visited Plymouth and maintained an old apartment in Northampton. Verily, Ethan Allen's hill gods had no place on the plains. And Coolidge's gods were more repressed than Allen's, for Coolidge hated rebellion and excitement.

Yet, he was popular, beyond doubt; and within his desires and their limitations he was effective. After the revelations of the Roman holiday during his predecessor's term, his accession was the best thing that could have happened to the Republican party. No one could have accused Calvin Coolidge of violating the Volstead Act, keeping a mistress or standing by men guilty of corruption. Coolidge was incorruptible. He provided business with what it wanted without a price. He believed honestly, as most businessmen believed honestly, that capitalism knew what it was doing. In that faith he was immovable. When counselors with different opinions came to him and told him that the economic superstructure being erected, however well-intentioned its builders, was a monstrosity bound to collapse, he silently registered his contempt for their suggestions. Mr. Mellon and Wall Street thought otherwise; their right to his ear was inherent in the solid piles of dollars they had accumulated. Thus the bubble kept growing; its very size moved the admiration of a country given to applaud as much for bigness as for quality. Though it was not his doing, though he did not comprehend what was happening, the country associated his name with the bubble and called it "Coolidge prosperity." It was only later that men remembered that those mounting figures on their account sheets so cheerfully labelled "credit" can also less tidily go under the name of "debt."

Meanwhile the political side of the President's personality was subterraneously active in revamping the party to his type of guidance. In principle, his attitude toward government's place in human affairs and the breadth of executive power in directing government was essentially negative. But of Republicanism and his own progress he thought in highly positive terms. He recognized the meaning of the party's ascent to the seats of the mighty, and he proposed to keep it there. The apathetic reaction of the public to the Harding administration's sins he rightly interpreted as damaging merely to individual reputations; he understood that most people absolved the Republican party of responsibility for the debacle. If an advantage arose to any Republican from the situation, it properly belonged to him. If, aside from Fall, Forbes,

Daugherty and the rest, blame were to be cast, it would lie upon the Senate cabal that had chosen Warren Harding as its man.

First Coolidge struck at Henry Cabot Lodge, successor to Penrose. That Lodge was aging and having his troubles with the senators of the Farm Bloc contributed to Coolidge's luck. But here the President also called forth his experience on the Massachusetts political ladder. Though Lodge was the party's floor leader in the Senate, Coolidge gave his friendship and respect to Borah and Capper. They, rather than the Massachusetts Senator, received the Chief Executive's confidences; they carried on the President's business on Capitol Hill. In reply, Lodge struck back by killing the World Court proposal, by advocating the pension and bonus bills so offensive to the Coolidgean sense of economy. It was a fruitless sortie. The hard-shelled Puritan, once moving, could not be halted. Lodge and his Old Guard went down, as much to the delight of a rank and file tired of their dictations as to the dethroner.

Early in his administration Coolidge had taken over the Southern "rotten boroughs" by appointing Bascom C. Slemp to a White House secretarial post. Slemp, a Virginia Republican who had been a congressman, knew the trade of politics well. With tireless efficiency he organized for his chief the delegations from the South, in some cases ruthlessly cutting out the senatorial favorites. Meanwhile New England was being pulled from under Lodge's thumb. The state patronage of Massachusetts was given to William M. Butler, who had been Murray Crane's lieutenant and was now the executor of the old boss's political estate. Senator George Moses was charged with retailoring the other Yankee contingents to fit the Presidential standard.

In June, 1924 the handiwork was exhibited for public approbation. Cleveland played host to the Republicans and found them less addicted to smoke-filled rooms and uncertainties than four years before. The senators were present, but only as delegates with one vote apiece. They had no influence in the resolutions committee and no say on nominations or secondings. Not a little pathetic were Lodge and Watson wandering about lost and uninformed. Helplessly, they stood by while Coolidge was nominated unanimously but for the few intractables who clung to LaFollette and Hiram Johnson. In a flurry of excitement Lowden was tendered the vice-presidential niche on the ticket but declined; the bluff Charles G. Dawes was given the place. It was not an Old Guard convention in other respects. Sparing of money and words alike, the President and his managers cut its sessions down to a miserly three days. Spectators and delegates had a dull time; but they saved their cash.

The campaign also seemed drained of emotion and the good noises that are a national tradition. To the repressed glee of the parsimonious Yankee, the Democrats wasted their substance and fury on each other. Governor Al Smith of New York and William Gibbs McAdoo unbudgingly checkmated each other through ballot after ballot while tempers flared. The old grievances of the city machines and the urban immigrant collided with rural provincialism and anti-Catholic and prohibitionist bigotry. On the 104th ballot a compromise agreement was reached on John W. Davis, West Virginian by birth but a New York lawyer for the Morgans by occupation. By that time the organization men were no longer interested. In August LaFollette entered the assizes as an Independent candidate, and drew away the liberal and radical votes that might have made the race a close one. He also attracted a few hundred thousand who had voted for Harding. In the main he provided a Red diversion for Republican orators who now evaded the task of answering the oil charges. Coolidge gave but one speech in his own behalf; he did not have to do even that. Though he received only 54 per cent of the popular vote compared to Harding's 61 per cent four years before, his electoral sweep was enormous. Davis and LaFollette neutralized each other. Extraneous forces had allowed a replacement of the Republican hierarchy without schism; the opposition had done the splitting.

* * *

The victory pronounced Calvin Coolidge a success. Boom and business had won. Yet it was possibly significant that, for a slogan, the Republicans depended for votes on "Keep Cool with Coolidge." Unwittingly, they caught the glacial quality of their candidate's personality. But, even in an adjectival sense, coolness is not the same as safety. And five years later, conservatism demonstrated that it too had panaceas that could explode. Until that time, however, it enshrined the crusty New Englander and decided that his copy-book phrases were common sense. To his credit, he received the adulation modestly, even with embarrassment.

But Coolidge, the success of his times, is a failure in history. The incongruity of eighteenth century puritanism governing a twentieth century materialism finally became unworkable. Herbert Hoover, a twentieth century conservative, suffered the wrath of the voters; Franklin Roosevelt, a twentieth century liberal, was asked to reconstruct the ruins. Calvin Coolidge lived on to see the shambles his version of capitalism had wrought. Observing it, he could not quite accept the judgment that he and Andrew Mellon had been wrong.

IN A POLITICAL democracy the role of the politician is one of constantly courting his electorate so that it will continue to look upon him with favor. This, in itself, is a task requiring the skill of an expert and the distilled knowledge of a professional. For the electorate is ever divided and sectionalized; opponents of the other party and rivals within his own are ever evaluating his actions and decisions in highly critical terms. Their hope is to persuade a voting majority to themselves; it is the politician's business to prevent them from doing so. To do otherwise is to fail. Thus, a large share of his energies must be devoted to defense. But by no means need his program be devoid of idealism or constructive effort. Ultimately, he must present something positive; yet the course he chooses is, of necessity, watered with circumspection and compromise. In maintaining his position over his antagonists, he is still the politician.

Statesmanship, being the consumation of political propositions, is thus more difficult of achievement. Not only must a politician constantly protect himself against his critics, but in advancing his program he must be sensitive to divisions of popular opinion. These rather than the taunts of the back benches cause him to move slowly, if he can move at all. For under the democratic principle the people are charged with defining the purposes of government. Their government can take direction only if they agree on general objectives; or in other words, if the popular and political debate is over methods of implementing precise ends. The ends themselves must have been fixed in advance. Should the people refuse the debate and permit minority pressure groups to tell the government what shall be its ends and what are the proper methods, they are not practicing democracy.

In times of peace the United States has, on different occasions, shown both tendencies. The politician with a broad and integrated policy designed to meet the requirements of a democracy has therefore been hampered. Division, sectionalization and criticism have made its total acceptance unlikely, its chances of fulfillment impossible. Failing to find agreement on a point from which he could start, he has normally offered the expedient of the moment. This may have partially satisfied the need and the majority, but it has seldom solved the entire problem. Above all the practice of expediency has not earned kudos for statesmanship.

It would seem that a democratic people must provide its politicians with common aims before politicians can become statesmen, that there must be common agreement upon basic premises. The ideals of "prosperity," "general welfare," "the common good" and "national interest" are subscribed to by almost all. Yet they are wholly apart from the real matters to be considered; they are desirables, to be sure, but largely irrelevant to the debate. They are asseverations of scant meaning or application. They represent the strivings of men in nearly every modern society, those highest truths toward which mankind is presumably dedicating itself. But in the practice of American government and politics they suggest nothing.

For the United States, the genuine fundamentals to be considered by the public are best stated by posing a series of questions: What kind of capitalism does the United States want? How much free competitive enterprise and how much private enterprise? What shall be the principles of political democracy? Where is the balance between liberty and responsibility? What are the experiences, what is the proper interpretation of the American tradition? Immediate issues like the tariff, the tax structure, public works and soil conservation are related to the answers to these questions. Statesmanship, of course, approaches the immediate issues with careful, sound and popular solutions. But because the electorate disagrees within itself in answering the fundamental inquiries of what it desires and believes in, the chances for a politician practicing statesmanship are reduced. He is thereby seriously handicapped in any attempt he might make to secure that latitude of action he requires to rise above his craft.

In peacetime only rarely does he receive a full-scale opportunity— as under conditions of emergency, or where some extremely eloquent persuasion on his part is particularly effective, or where mass lethargy permits him a free field. In time of war, however, a political democracy has its numbers in agreement on a single overpowering aim—victory. How that victory is achieved is not deeply questioned until after the war is over. If the methods proposed by the incumbent politician are winning, his program is accepted and he is temporarily (at least) recognized as a statesman of the first order. Success becomes the first index of his statesmanship.

It is not surprising that the United States has produced great war presidents in Lincoln, Wilson and Franklin Roosevelt. As wartime officeholders, they were given carte blanche in the pursuit of victory.

They needed to practice the political arts far less to accomplish their purposes than did their peacetime brothers. Their highroad to statesmanship was, in many respects, the road of their own abilities. Circumstances of conflict set them on the road without their having to seek it; they had only to move. In moving, each of them became an undeniably successful Chief Executive and national leader; his policies and contributions were defined as worthy statesmanship.

But, in peace, Wilson and Roosevelt, and most other American presidents, found they had first to travel the devious bypaths of politics before they caught sight of the highroad for which they searched. The dangers of the paths, their necessities of coping with obstacles forced them into far different practices from those they used in war. Pre-eminently, they were politicians; only occasionally did they emerge as statesmen. The same is true of almost every non-presidential figure. In war, unless determinedly obstructive or downright traitorous, these men of lesser office have displayed the higher qualities called for in representatives who govern in the popular interest. In peace they once again seek the advantage, suggest very tentative directions, reverse themselves at the hint of reproach. In a political democracy, even if they willed it otherwise—and probably most of them would—they are creatures of an indecisive public and the unresolved questions of its debate.

1. THE ROOSEVELT AURA

It was perhaps because Franklin Roosevelt raised the importance of the questions into public view and, by his measures, implied certain tentative answers that, during his twelve presidential years, he was indisputably and at all times the first figure of his country. To label him as belonging in one classification or another—liberal, progressive, planner, idealist, pragmatist, aristocrat, Democrat, democrat, "tyrant," "dictator," prodigal, turncoat, politician, statesman—is to elevate one set of facts in utter disregard for many others. If a case can be made for one or several, the matter is minor compared to the position the man himself held in the nation's consciousness. The Roosevelt years call to mind, in a time only a few years after his death, no one who approximates him in his impact upon the country, and in evoking the personal loyalties of the masses. In even short retrospect it is apparent that his opponents were more anti-Roosevelt than they were devoted to any single champion of their own.

He did and was responsible for so much, he said and had written about him so many words, that no one can hope to ingest it all. From his life and deeds, there continues to flow a river of effect on the United

States and the world as well as a stream of reminiscence, criticism, analysis and hypothetical inquiry. The difference is simply that, while he lived, the flow was greater. Since then, the pressures of others have perforce changed, diluted and revised his world and his works. In Roosevelt's lifetime, certainly, most of these same pressures existed, but they were present—both as men and influences—where he was, at least, the dominating single man. He too was bent by forces and movements; but, in the bending, he added his individual turn to their directions. How far or to what course remains to be more fully demonstrated, for, like Franklin Roosevelt, those forces have a resiliency, enormous and potential. They may conceivably snap back to leave nothing but a memory of his hopes and efforts, as they did to Woodrow Wilson's dreams of peace and international order.

The last year of his life found him cast as the leader of an international coalition for victory and the architect of a plan for peace. It was the part he preferred. To the country heading the assault of the western powers on Germany and carrying the burden of the war against Japan, his conduct of the civilian direction over military affairs was perhaps the one largest criterion on which the public judged him. That he was able to overshadow the striking aggressiveness of generals like MacArthur and the winning qualities of those like Eisenhower is significant. In doing so, he maintained a leadership, in the popular mind, that was superior to any challenge that might arise from the spectacular technicalities of those who were experts in warfare. By mid-1944, much of the American military and naval machine had been constructed and trained; its home fabricators of materiél and its supply lines were thoroughly organized and approaching the stage of full functioning; some evidences of the United States' organization for war had been shown in the deliveries of lend-lease goods, in the battles in Africa and Italy, the air war over Germany, the tortured fighting on New Guinea and the Pacific atolls, in naval battles. Credit belonged to many men, and to the people as a whole. But being constitutionally accounted the Commander in Chief, Roosevelt was the man who faced judgment. So too in the slow push toward Rome, the D-Day landings and the sweep across France to Paris, the island-hopping toward Japan, Washington (and specifically, the President) was held to as strict accountability as the field commanders. Success in all these moves reflected favorably upon him; it increased his stature.

Much the same was true of his position in dealing with Great Britain and the Soviet Union, and, to a lesser extent, China. Their military victories provided him a certain prestige at home, if only because so many of his critics were chronic Anglophobes or anti-communists embittered beyond the point of appreciating the British and Russian contributions to the alliance. More evident still was the power he had in negotiation. The unity that came out of the Moscow and Teheran conferences of late 1943 and the promise of world organization that seemed a certainty after Dumbarton Oaks in the late summer of 1944 were the substructure of the edifice he hoped to create. By and large the American electorate approved his hope, and most accepted his conference method and its results as productive. However suspicious many were of his domestic policies and his personality, they believed that he was the best the United States had to enforce co-operation, write the peace, and establish the United Nations on a broader plane than a war entente.

To all appearances, the facility with which Roosevelt pulled together Winston Churchill and Josef Stalin in common cause presaged well. Had this amity been merely military in its scope, there would have been just reasons for doubt of its abiding value. But because their agreements looked forward to a postwar association dedicated to peace, there prevailed a strong confidence in his guidance. Even more abroad than at home, his name became a symbol. A large group of Americans, unaware or at least unimpressed by the actual physical destruction and the spiritual enervation of war, remained dubious of his methods; but few openly disbelieved the desirability of what his methods sought. His influence had been considerable enough to shock a majority out of isolationism and into an acceptance of the necessity for a world organization. What he envisioned was, however, neither clear-cut nor fully expounded. His Republican opposition, the Congress in its resolutions, his own words—in press conferences and public speeches—had collectively pared down and hedged about any full-spoken internationalism that first thoughts summon to mind. There was always a reservation to maintain the sovereignty of the United States—or, as Roosevelt called it, the "integrity"—in its political independence and geographical area.

In a sense, this illustrated his method. For the long future he stated the dream, the ideal. For the shorter future he offered sketchy outlines of what he believed to be generally acceptable or possible of persuasion. In the immediate present he negotiated the first short step; then he explored the *modus vivendi* for a second step soon to follow. Examples abound from his conduct of both foreign and domestic affairs. If part of his ideal of peace was a world rid of Nazi Germany, the moves toward that realization were tenuous and often faltering. From his "quarantine" speech in 1937 through the "unconditional surrender" agreements in 1943 to the Yalta Conference in 1945, his objective was manifestly the same. But the moves toward fulfillment came slowly; one might suggest what the next would be, or it might not; almost never did it project indications of the third or fourth move forward. So also in his program for the United States. The Social Security Act did not imply the Full Employment Bill and 60,000,000 jobs. On appearances, the Agricultural Adjustment Act did not lead inflexibly toward the Ever-Normal Granary.

Franklin Roosevelt was not one to present detailed blueprints of his long-run course. He had seen, at first hand, Wilson's experience with the packaged Fourteen Points and the rigidly defined League of Nations. Consequently, while he announced his ideals, he suggested few full and direct lines to their implementation. His statements on the Four Freedoms and the "Economic Bill of Rights" contained nothing with which most men would quarrel. If they were questioned or attacked, it was their "visionary" nature rather than their aspirational quality that was derided; not many dared to say openly they opposed recognition of the freedoms or the rights. Nevertheless, having enumerated them, Roosevelt's efforts to secure their eventual achievement fit no comprehensive program nor did he leave his heirs a schematic diagram of procedure. The very fact that, in 1948, several disagreeing factions exist—each claiming to be following his lead, each basing its claims on grounds not easily refuted—is another indication that this was his method.

Essentially, he realized that whatever he might try to do toward accomplishing his aims had, in a political democracy, to be accepted by a majority. The confusions that arose in his program reflected the confusions of that majority. Shifting opinions from time to time produced the contradictions inherent in the gulf between the neutrality legislation of the 1930's and the lend-lease policies of the 1940's, or between the RFC loans to big business and the anti-trust prosecutions. There is no question that the public mind oscillates between ideas, toward and away from conservatism, embracing and repelling liberalism; and it was in this mental climate that Roosevelt had to pick and choose. His bent was toward liberalism, but he made his payments to the conservatives. This was the price of his continued leadership. Thus it seemed that occasionally he had to be pushed, while at other times he prodded the people into moving faster along his path. Periodically, he went too far ahead of them, and was brought up short. Of this last, the best remembered instance is the Supreme Court fight of 1937. A more conservative Congress defeated his proposition, but it did not overwhelm his ends; by the conservative means of waiting for the old justices to retire, he finally got the Court he wanted, and in the interval, brought the incumbents to take a suddenly broader view upon those of his measures over which they sat in judgment.

This propensity for constantly switching speeds kept him, on the whole, pretty much abreast with the majority. It enabled him to win over a more stolid Congress in such matters that the legislature, at heart, was indisposed to grant—the extension of selective service in 1941, the demand for an effective price control law in 1942. Another aspect of his technique in adjusting to opinion and congressional stubbornness lay in his quick retirement from untenable ground. Though he suffered setbacks in such proposals as the Administrative reorganization bill of 1938 and his request for a wartime national service law, his tactic of refusing to draw out the battle maintained his prestige and power with a minimal loss. By the time his opponents got around to unlimbering their heaviest artillery for a strong barrage, or when they thought they had encircled him, he had withdrawn, leaving them an empty field on which they poured their shot and pursued their fruitless and protracted countermarches. By so keeping Congress and the conservative foe off balance, he was able to make a quick thrust soon afterward that moved the country closer toward one or another of his ideals. Usually such a move was successful; the opposition had not yet returned from its safari in some different direction.

There is, in all this, the suggestion that Roosevelt was an able politician—a quality his severest critics admitted, generally with maledictions upon all politicians as a class of men. His four victories stamped him an excellent vote-getter. But beyond this hold on the populace was his management of the Democratic coalition—for by 1944, instead of being a party, his political agency was a diverse, inharmonious assembly of denominations. If it had functioned as a party, in the traditional sense, during the campaigns from 1932 to 1938, the importance of its elements had become gradually rearranged. In 1940 the place of the urban industrial labor segment became obvious.

Under so astute a national chairman and Postmaster General as James A. Farley, the shifting had gone on at a comparatively slow rate, undermining the type of control he knew and practiced. After he left the process was accelerated. The influence of patronage declined progressively; groups became bound to the Rooseveltian coalition by sympathy or long-established habit. Those who identified themselves with the lower classes and underprivileged of the cities were unqualifiedly for him, as were the workingmen who thought of themselves as laborers rather than as members of the middle class. Organizationally, this meant the preponderance of the CIO and a smaller proportion of the AF of L. Primarily from the cities, too, came the independents, verging in their thinking from liberal to radical, who composed a portion of the middle and upper income categories. To these were added those traditional northern Democrats, the city machines, which now needed Roosevelt's name because they could not win without it. Of a slightly different circumstance were the Democrats of the South, who varied through all shades of politics and conviction. Theirs were loyalties of everything from devotion to the man and his policies to allegiance to a party label, no matter what its estate. Lastly, there were the northern Negroes, perhaps more solidly Rooseveltian than any but the CIO.

These, then, were the components of Roosevelt's majority. It was his skill in political management and the appeal of his platform and works that molded them into a team. Yet it was a rare time when one or another of the factions was not particularly aggrieved—labor over the rigidity of the "little steel" formula that kept a ceiling on wages during the wartime prosperity, the Negroes at the periodic obeisances the administration made to southern Democracy's prejudices, the machine bosses and party regulars over the appointments of those nonprofessional politicians, the New Dealers. Mostly, a critical event like an election or a vital national measure was needed to reunite them; shortly afterward they would go scattering once more. In the last years, they joined together mainly to further the military prosecution of the war and to provide Roosevelt his mandate in international negotiations. On other matters the tendency was for the large southern conservative wing to agree with the confirmed opposition Republicans.

At bottom, the alliance between southern Democrats and northern Republicans, in their mutual antagonism to Roosevelt's domestic program, spelled the reason for his years of conflict with Congress. With many presidents in the past, executive-legislative tilts had arisen from the argument over which of the two co-ordinate branches of government was to wield the greater power—in other words, which was more properly the representative of the people and the states. In the Roosevelt years much of the verbiage set forth by the proponents of congressional rule still stated the case along these lines. But, in fact, the real source of contention was not so much who should hold power as to what ends its exercise should be directed.

Nothing better illustrates this case than the deeds of the Seventy-eighth and Seventy-ninth Congresses in their independent forays. The passage over presidential veto of the Smith-Connally War Labor Disputes Act was a case in point. In its intention, the law aimed at cutting down labor's power to strike by imposing a "cooling-off" period and permitting the government to seize struck plants; in practice, though unpopular with those it was supposed to regulate, it worked more to labor's benefit than to that of business. With greater deviousness the conservative alliance hit at old New Deal projects—and in 1943, primarily symbols of the Roosevelt policies of older days—like the National Youth Administration and the Home Owners' Loan Corporation by ending their lives through riders to unvetoable war appropriations bills. Or, when it came to New Dealers, congressional purposes were equally obvious. In the same years, a bill of attainder, attached to such an act forbade any payments from the funds it authorized to be made to three men specified by name. Sometime afterward the rider was held unconstitutional, but its purpose had been served. Lacking the independent wealth or inclination to carry on inside government ranks without compensation, the three were forced to resign their posts.

The most ambitious effort to impose strictures on the President and his philosophy of the ends of government came with his appointment of Henry Wallace as Secretary of Commerce in January, 1945. Being ninth on the cabinet seniority list, the office itself had small prestige compared to the vice-presidency Wallace had just relinquished. But tied to the post was the administration of several large governmental lending agencies, including the Reconstruction Finance Corporation. And this provided enormous administrative power to relatively inferior rank in the government, a power to influence the pattern and course of the private enterprise economy of the United States. That Wallace was an experienced and competent administrator was undeniable; that he was loyal to his chief and reflected (and sometimes initiated) Roosevelt's views was to be expected of any man appointed to a subordinate position. But Congress was wrathful. The senatorial alliance hated Wallace's economic views. It prepared to reject him for his ideas—and presumably ideas approved by the President.

An irreconcilable minority of the Senate—thirty-two in the final vote on confirmation—was against Wallace under any conditions. But others were willing to abide him if the "loan powers" were separated from the secretaryship. Senator George of Georgia introduced such a bill. In the committee hearings the conservative alliance listened approvingly to Jesse Jones, the outgoing Commerce Secretary and Loan Administrator, when he stated, with some absence of modesty, that he did not "believe there is another fellow in the world" who could handle both jobs at the same time. Wallace received harsher treatment, but emerged with a compliment from Senator Vandenberg for an "able presentation" of his opinions. Then, the committee made confusion of all by recommending George's bill and reporting unfavorably on the nomination. Parliamentary wrangling, led by the irreconcilables, held up both matters until a delayed note to Majority Leader Barkley from the President at Yalta indicated that the separation measure would be approved by the White House. Finally, after more than a month of struggle, the compromise—in which an emasculated office was given a man deemed philosophically unworthy of its full powers—passed. Within a month, the alliance developed more confidence; it rejected Aubrey Williams as Rural Electrification Administrator after some searching inquiry into his religious thoughts and his political beliefs.

*   *   *

The Wallace-Jones feud was, in microcosm, the feud of the two largest wings of the Democratic party, and of twentieth-century liberalism versus twentieth-century conservatism. Within the party it had been active since Roosevelt's unsuccessful "purge" of 1938. Frequently it had dropped below the surface when foreign relations crises and the demands of electoral victory cemented short-lived coalitions and unity behind the personality of the President and the singularity of the presidency. Under compulsions of party regularity conservatives sided with the administration if such action did not conflict with their basic views. At such times, however, the strife had abated only temporarily. Neither the war nor the need of the Democratic Party for unity could end it.

In part this breakdown of the harmony of the early New Deal came from the President's defeats during his second administration—the Court plan, the reorganization bill, the 1938 elections. These lowered his reputation for political leadership; they demonstrated the success of partial revolt. But certainly after 1940, his increasing preoccupation with international affairs and military details led him into growing impatience at intraparty disputes and domestic problems. In effect he renounced the fascinations of politics for the opportunity of statesmanship. The result was the throwing back of responsibility upon subsidiary leaders of the New Deal and the Democratic coalition. If Wallace, as Vice-President, represented one group, Jones, as Secretary of Commerce, represented another. It was expected that they would resolve their differences without recourse to the judicial settlements handed down by a Chief Executive busily engaged elsewhere.

In the same manner, the calling of James Byrnes from the Supreme

Court to act as "assistant president" in charge of the home front was not only designed to free Roosevelt from all but the most major decisions; it was also supposed to placate the South and those right-of-center Democrats who believed themselves benighted in the President's friendship for the CIO. So too, Postmaster General and National Democratic Chairman Frank Walker was supposed to handle everything in the political sphere aside from the truly extraordinary. War agency heads and regular departmental officials would presumably set aside their internal bickerings, work out their difficulties, and settle their problems without reliance on regular direction from the Chief of the Government.

For the United States and the Democratic party, Roosevelt's deliberate withdrawal from mundane considerations was a test of co-operative leadership. It is clear that the test failed. Under Walker, the party machinery rusted. Byrnes lost stature, alienating labor without gaining appreciable business support. The feuds and disputes over personality, prerogative and power festered—that between Wallace and Jones in 1943 over foreign economic policy was only the sharpest of many. Hostility and ambition set the various factions to building up strength for the day when the coalition would break permanently or when Roosevelt would step down. This is not to say that the administration was breaking down. As long as Franklin Roosevelt remained President, he carried enough authority and magnetism to enforce his wishes and secure the necessary program for success. On the whole, the war was fought according to his plans and the vital powers needed to govern the domestic front were exercised as he wished.

But as he became more inaccessible to all except his diplomatic and war advisers, he lost a measure of his first-hand information and some increments of control over what, in previous years, were simple challenges to his political mastery. His veto of the tax bill of 1944—a courageous act in itself—fell upon Congress without his party's having received sufficient preparation for its impact. Majority Leader Barkley's denunciation of the message, his fiery resignation, and triumphant re-election by the Democratic caucus were, in a single episode, an indication of how far the President had strayed from things political.

In terms of its lasting effect Roosevelt's insulation had its most significant result in the vice-presidential nomination of 1944. Here, he depended upon other eyes and ears. In 1940 he had practically dictated Wallace's candidacy as the contingency of his own acceptance of the nomination for a third term; now, he made no such demand. From early 1943 on, advisers and agents freely predicted that a Roosevelt-Wallace ticket would be defeated. Conservative southern "regulars" were hinted to be planning manipulations of the electoral vote in order to prevent a Democratic victory if the incumbent Vice-President should run for re-election. Others pointed out that Wallace, for all his support and idolization by organized labor, small farmers, agricultural workers and liberals was anathema to the city machines, many middle-class Democrats, and seventy-five per cent New Dealers. They urged the President to nod elsewhere—toward Byrnes, Associate Justice William O. Douglas, possibly Senator Barkley. A St. Louis politician, Robert Hannegan, had been called into the Democratic national chairmanship to resuscitate the party organization; he unqualifiedly urged Senator Harry S. Truman of Missouri. In the face of these pressures and advices, Roosevelt apparently procrastinated. Personally he seems to have preferred Wallace; politically he allowed the contentious factions to start heavy missionary work among the prospective delegates.

Still, the mere political maneuvering in selecting a running mate to secure victory in the assizes must have been only one of several considerations from Roosevelt's point of view. With his knowledge and background he must have recognized that most of those who warned him against Wallace simultaneously promoted someone else. As large an object of his thought as any was the need for a friendly Senate from 1945 to 1949. Those would be years of writing peace treaties and establishing the United Nations in all its huge proportions. A vice-presidential liaison man would be helpful; and Henry Wallace had hardly set a brilliant record in his present office—whatever the reasons.

There is no solid evidence that the possibility of the fourth-term vice-president's active succession to the presidency was weighed seriously. The President and his doctors apparently believed he could live through another four years in office. Some of the importuners may have believed the chances for his death before 1949 to be substantial; if they did, they can, by virtue of several of the names they advanced, be charged with playing fast and loose with the highest office in the country. Certainly, from the electioneering and switching that went on at the Chicago convention, it may be doubted if most of the delegates gave more than passing recollection to the fact that the vice-president is always a potential president. The issue of Roosevelt's health was raised, overtly or by innuendo, by the hostile press and Republican party. The purpose was to hit at him and not at his running mate. Where Democratic politicians introduced the question, their use of it was simply to administer the *coup de grâce* to a second place candidacy already replete with many other objections.

Fundamentally the party's battle over the vice-presidency was a jockeying for position by the various wings. Roosevelt's renomination was a foregone conclusion, and all but a few bitter-end southerners were ready to accept the fact and the candidate. Second place became a symbol of power, its capture an index of relative strength within the coalition. As the forces girded for the struggle, it was clearly a contest of Wallace against the field—the conservative southern favorites, the entries of the urban machines, the "favorite sons." A Gallup Poll taken shortly before the convention showed Wallace the favorite of sixty-five per cent of the Democratic voters; Barkley and Speaker Sam Rayburn followed; Senator Truman was seventh on the list. In the charmed circle of the party politicians, however, there was a far more equal proportioning of sentiment.

A large number of delegates under the influence of liberal convictions or the Political Action Committee of the CIO were for the renomination of the incumbent Vice-President. The South had its sprinkling of local men. Byrnes headed the roster of those half-way supporting the administration. Senator Bankhead was the hope of those against the administration. Truman came to Chicago championing Byrnes. He expected that he might give a nominating speech for the man who had once been his colleague in the Senate; he felt that the South Carolinian deserved recognition for the arduous and gloryless task of pulling the domestic strings while Roosevelt mapped world strategy. The Missouri Senator was aware of Hannegan's persistent efforts to get him convention votes; but he was inactive in his own behalf and more than a shade reluctant. He liked the Senate and wanted to stay there; perhaps Hannegan's work would insure him the empty honor of a favorite son endorsement by his home state.

But Robert Hannegan had an experienced, unsentimental eye for politics. He did not believe Henry Wallace could win and had not hesitated to tell the President so. He found in Harry Truman those attributes of necessary counterpoise and complement to Roosevelt—the common touch, unobjectionable politics, midwestern residence, a degree of public stature, modesty, and acceptability to the party hierarchy. That his candidate was, like himself, from Missouri helped to the extent that Hannegan ruled the state delegation. He talked up Truman to the President. In time he got what he needed—letters explaining that Roosevelt's personal choice was Wallace but that he also felt "Harry Truman . . . would bring real strength to the ticket." During the convention Hannegan published the letters; the ensuing events unveiled his allies—Frank Walker and the local bosses, Kelly of Chicago, Flynn of New York, Hague of New Jersey's Democracy. The support of one conservative labor chieftain, A. F. Whitney of the Railway Trainmen, was utilized to exact secondary endorsements from the powerful leaders of the CIO and AF of L.

Thrust into the midst of this formidable combination, Truman balked ("Bob, I don't want the darned thing") and then gave way to the handshaking, smiling and non-committal platitudes that marked him an active candidate for the nomination. His consent was the last to be secured. All that remained was the balloting. Wallace led on the first roll call with 38 per cent of the delegates to Truman's 28 per cent. Then, during the second vote, while lesser contenders dropped out and the galleries shouted "We want Wallace," Hannegan and the bosses pushed the buttons; machine-controlled delegations vied with southern conservatives to climb on the Senator's bandwagon. Down in the Missouri delegation Truman calmly watched the surge while he chewed a wartime hot dog.

2. PLOWBOY TO PRESIDENT

In describing the Democrat thus nominated, *Time* magazine, with its own standards for selecting adjectives, acquainted its readers with him as "a gray little man," "neat," "mousy-looking," "a likeable plodder," and "a drab mediocrity." Throughout the campaign, when they bothered to report on his strenuous travels, *Time* editors treated Candidate Truman tepidly in their terse, telegraphic terms. When they and the rest of their genre had finished their work on Harry Truman, vice-presidential aspirant, they had presented to the country a picture of a very small man indeed. A few lines limned his small-town, Missouri background. In the main, two feature points of his career were exploited: he had been an honest adjunct of Tom Pendergast's machine and a product of its benefactions; he was chairman of the Senate War Investigating Committee which was generally accounted to be doing excellent work in ferreting out waste, corruption and inefficiency that held back victory, or raised its financial cost. From this second phase of his life in politics, Senate newspaper correspondents had voted him, after the President, the civilian best informed about the war. That some of the first phase lingered as well, was clear from a *soupçon* of philosophy he expounded several times during the campaign. At Kansas City, he gave it its most succinct statement: "A statesman is only a dead politician. I never want to be a statesman."

The Republican candidates, Thomas E. Dewey and John Bricker, ranged back and forth across the country, exploiting the errors of Roosevelt's twelve years and indicating a few they might commit themselves. For example, Bricker unthinkingly welcomed the endorsement of Gerald L. K. Smith, and Dewey, apparently on consultation with the military experts of the party's national committee but not with the Joint Chiefs of Staff, announced that, if elected, he would place General MacArthur in supreme command over the Pacific war.

Meanwhile, the Republican board of strategy did itself something of a disservice by deciding to stake its all on the hypothetical story that Truman's nomination had been "cleared with Sidney" Hillman, chairman of the CIO's Political Action Committee. The tactic probably attracted some votes of the prejudiced, but it palpably showed also a willingness to employ methods that were in the poor taste of pointing derogatorily to a man's origin and religious ancestry. Furthermore, in attacking Hillman, one of the country's outstanding labor leaders, the Republicans implicitly contradicted the pious declarations of their friendship for labor which they had written into their platform. Most of all, they further energized an already alert PAC into still more action in the large cities of the country where heavy Democratic majorities invariably overcame rural preponderances for Dewey.

Two men, Truman and Henry Wallace, carried the heaviest speaking load for the Democrats who otherwise did little enough campaigning as a party. Roosevelt, busy in the presidency while the war approached its climactic stage, sallied out occasionally to repel the sharpest thrusts of his freer-speaking opponents and to suggest, in vague terms, his program for the years of peace. It devolved upon Harry Truman to engage in the day-to-day slugging. On his nomination, he had proclaimed himself "a work-horse"—reminiscent of Theodore Roosevelt's characterization of himself as "strong as a bull moose" in the second McKinley campaign. The active member of the Democratic team had, in his equipment, a number of arrows to shoot into the thick-skinned but tender GOP hide—the failure of Herbert Hoover and its backwash (a Democratic weapon that will, in all likelihood, survive so long as memory of that unfortunate gentleman lives), the glorious works of Roosevelt's three administrations, the obstructive and frequently reactionary tack of Republican congressmen, the magical name of Franklin D. Roosevelt.

Over 8,000 miles and across fifteen states, he sent his shafts flying. His efforts were not pronouncedly successful; Truman was neither an appealing orator nor an effective expositor of issues. Although his broadsides were well prepared and better thought out than the nebulous banalities of Bricker, his high pitched and unemotional delivery were no competition for the booming voice and revivalist atmosphere in which the Republican vice-presidential candidate conducted his meetings. Dewey's assaults on the New Deal were spoken in distinct and measured tones that suggested a careful training for radio; Truman's flat midwestern twang, with its touch of Missouri softness, raced into the microphone, and the words came out slurred over and knotted.

Yet, if he scored few triumphs on the rostrum, he did good work when his train plowed to a halt at the whistle-stops and the small towns. For there, in the hand-shaking, in the colloquies with local politicians, in delivering compliments for local Democratic candidates, in five-minute speeches from the observation platform, Truman was in his element. He typified small-town America. The people who met him at the stations and the politicians who rode to the next stop were his kind. His big-city addresses were on grim subjects—the war, peacetime jobs, the Hoover depression—and were strained performances.

But out in the country, he was an attractive man, cheerful and smiling, modestly and simply seeking votes. Townsfolk liked him; here was no Olympian personage but one of them who had made good. Among them he was humility itself, neither pompous nor dominating nor assertive; his easy manner and wide grin were strong antidotes to the steely coldness and mathematical precision that proclaimed Dewey the product of an urban civilization and a streamlined age. The comparison helped the Democrats; preponderant rural Republican majorities were cut down to a size where they could be overwhelmed by the heavy Democratic ballots cast in the large cities. There, with its doorbell ringing and street meetings, the CIO insured a powerful turnout by labor and the lower classes. There too, Henry Wallace talked indefatigably, going into homes to enlist the housewives, jumping from one crowd to the next, riding between cities in day-coaches crammed with citizens who did not recognize their Vice-President.

In the end Dewey and the Republicans were defeated by many factors—Roosevelt, victories in Europe and the Philippines foretelling the conquest of the Axis, labor and the PAC's vigorous campaign, the Republican record of isolationism, the extreme conservatism and reaction of many of its leading figures, its failure to present a constructive alternative to the New Deal. If the Democrats could be accused of doing most of their fighting on the issues of 1932, Republican leadership, Dewey aside, appeared to have lifted its arguments from the nineteenth century and to have applied them out of context in the twentieth.

For Harry Truman the election meant a slight rise in prestige; he now sat in the chair of the Senate instead of at one of the desks below. He was no longer a chairman of the committee with which his name had become identified, but its members were still his friends. He had a better office and was able to entertain senatorial colleagues on a larger scale; he was still able to enjoy the special camaraderie of the upper house. As a Senator his first teacher of the involved etiquette of the body and the delicate handling of ninety-six dignified and painfully sensitive senior legislators had been Vice-President John Nance Garner. Truman set hmself toward practicing the lessons he had learned. In his room behind the chamber he joked with his associates on earthy matters; after four years of Wallace, who was a teetotaler, Truman's welcome bourbon mellowed frayed tempers and rigid consciences. The unofficial sessions brought back something of the old clubhouse spirit and got him a certain affection that Henry Wallace, with his shyness and novel thinking on politics and economics, never had. Outside too, he found himself suddenly lionized by Washington society and pulled into its competitions; as a Senator, his presence at a party represented a minor triumph for the hostess, but as Vice-President, he was deluged by more invitations than he could possibly satisfy.

If he wanted to do more than preside over the Senate, entertain his friends and fulfill his social obligations, Truman had no chance. Theoretically the vice-president is at the disposal of the chief executive. This may mean he substitutes for the president on formal occasions or he may be given specific jobs like Wallace's chairmanship over the Board of Economic Warfare and his special mission to China in 1944. Or, it may be possible for him to build his peculiar position into that of liaison officer between the White House and Capitol Hill. Such may, as his biographers claim, have been Truman's intention. He was given no time to prove it.

Before Truman was comfortably seated on the dais, Roosevelt had left for Yalta, but not before the upper house was handed the last episode of the Wallace-Jones controversy. Truman, taken by surprise at the sudden nomination of Wallace to the cabinet, tried to promote the administration's request for immediate confirmation; but it took Senator Alben Barkley to steer the final compromise arrangement past the sniping combination of Republicans and southern Democrats. After Roosevelt returned and had delivered his report on the Crimean conference Truman sat in at the few cabinet meetings that occurred. The secrets of international diplomacy and forthcoming military strategy were, however, denied him. He saw the President infrequently; it is doubtful if he was being groomed as a successor for 1948. Then, Franklin Roosevelt went down to Warm Springs, Georgia, to rest.

*   *   *

What Harry Truman's accession meant to the folklore of American political democracy was its reaffirmation of the great dream that any man can still reach the presidency. Perhaps the really astonishing thing about the dream is that it has come true so often, that men like Truman, up from the masses, have come to the White House more frequently than aristocrats like the Roosevelts.

Of his presidential type Truman was, in point of origin, one step above Millard Fillmore and Andrew Johnson, one step below the middle-class beginnings of Chester Arthur and Calvin Coolidge, several flights beneath John Tyler and Theodore Roosevelt. His family had its moderate successes and its moderate failures. It had moved up and down the western tier of Missouri counties and towns. Truman himself was born at Lamar, where his father owned a horse and mule trading business. But before he entered school his parents had set down and pulled up stakes in several places—Harrisonville, Grandview and Independence. On his own he tried ten years of farming and two separate periods of earning a living in Kansas City before he finally settled for good in Independence. The variety of his jobs in his years after leaving school is indicative of a young man's searchings to find himself—timekeeper for a railroad construction gang, bank clerk, bookkeeper, farmer, partner in a haberdashery venture. Perhaps he would have lived out his life as a farmer, plowing straight rows for corn, raising wheat, and caring for cattle, were it not for the first World War.

There had always been a latent feeling for soldiering in him. An uncle had fought for the Confederates and much of Truman's reading in adolescence was devoted to the Civil War. On graduation from high school he had been given a congressional appointment to West Point but was rejected because of his poor eyesight. With that, his dream of a career in the regular army vanished; but, through his life, he has kept a respect, which sometimes appears to approach awe, of the military. In his bookkeeping days he joined the National Guard and stayed with it through his years on the farm. The war took him away from the land, gave him a commission, and ultimately command of a field artillery battery composed mostly of Kansas City Irish. His service was hardly extraordinary, but it was better than average. He received a captaincy, and he turned the battery into a competent fighting unit after it had successfully resisted the efforts of five other commanding officers. At

St. Mihiel, it almost broke under fire, but his calm orders ended the panic. By his discipline and through general luck, its total battle casualties were light, in spite of two months in the heavy offensives that ended the war.

A year with Battery D left him popular with his men and restless to have another try at city life. In the Army he had helped to start and run a prosperous canteen. The boom of 1919, a friend who knew merchandise, and the prospects of profits from the Battery D boys as customers led him into the clothing business in Kansas City. His small savings and a good deal of borrowed money went into setting up the establishment. Had it been able to weather the depression of 1921-22, he might have stayed a storekeeper, playing extremely local politics in the Jackson County Democratic party—as had his father—and working himself into the hierarchy of the newly organized American Legion. As it was, however, the crash of his business forced upon him a debt it took fifteen years to repay. It also sent him, at thirty-eight, looking for a new occupation.

Again the army was his salvation. Before going overseas Truman had met a nephew of Tom Pendergast at Camp Doniphan where the artillery units of the Missouri National Guard had trained. After the war Irishmen from Battery D had gone back to Kansas City, a number of them as subalterns in the Pendergast machine, many of them to lounge around the Truman clothing emporium. The failure of the business coincided with the auspicious days when Boss Pendergast, octopus-like, was spreading his tentacles out of the city over rural Jackson County and across the state. Some of the posts that made the small-town courthouses into satrapies of city hall were the county judgeships. These were not jobs where the incumbent handed down law from the bench; they were rich little enclaves where the "judges" were, in reality, county commissioners dealing principally in public works contracts. What this meant to Tom Pendergast, who owned a cement company, can readily be imagined.

Meanwhile, Harry Truman, the bankrupt haberdasher, had gone back to Independence. In Kansas City, former Battery D men, with their American Legion connections, were urging him on Pendergast for the eastern district, the farm country, of which Independence was the center. The Boss assented, and an unwritten, informal pact was made. Truman would serve his benefactor by rounding up Democratic votes for the machine, but would participate in none of the arrangements the machine had of voting cemeteries and favoring high-bidding contractors. He also demurred from any of the fancier schemes by which Tom Pendergast perpetuated his power and increased his wealth. Pendergast gave his blessing and agreeably patronized the vagary of the small, neat man who was so popular with the Irish boys in some of the ward clubs and who might bring in votes.

The candidate and the organization set to work, and won the election by a bare 500 votes. Two years later, in Calvin Coolidge's landslide, he was trounced. Truman bided his time, eked out a living, and spread his name around the city by building up the local automobile club. In 1926 he planned to run as the Democratic candidate for County Collector, a sinecure worth $25,000 annually in salary and fees. The Boss, however, put him off with a lesser elevation to presiding judge of the county court; and there he stayed until 1934, quietly nursing ambitions for a better place like congressman or governor, but never being able to bring Pendergast over to his persuasion. That he was honest in spending the county's money is beyond dispute. When the federal government concentrated its attention on bribery, corruption and tax evasion in the Kansas City bailiwick, it sent the Boss and a number of his satellites to prison. Among the personal records pored over by the Federal Bureau of Investigation and the U. S. District Attorney was that of the presiding judge. His revealed nothing felonious, doubtful or censurable.

What he could be chided upon was his insensitivity; for Truman, even at the safe distance of the Independence courthouse, must have caught some of the stench that drifted over from the big city. On his trips over to Pendergast's capital, he must have caught a view of the open gambling and unabashed prostitution that made it a mecca for salesmen and cattlemen; during prohibition and afterward, he must have marveled at the widespread drinking of one brand of bourbon, the bottles with Pendergast's White Seal label. But, if he did, he kept his peace. The pact he had with the Boss was working out; Truman pulled in rural Jackson County votes for the machine and Tom Pendergast did not ask that favorite contractors be accommodated. Both men, politicians of the so-called school of realism, respected the code; and, years later, when Pendergast had come upon evil days, Truman as Senator would not denounce him, and Truman as Vice-President walked in his funeral cortege.

There is a tale that, in 1934, Truman again wanted the County Collectorship. Pendergast adeptly put him off with a less profitable offer: "The best I can do for you right now, Harry, is a U. S. Senatorship." Another story says that the presiding judge had his eye on the governor's chair. Nevertheless, that year he entered the Democratic primary contest for the upper house with machine support against the candidate of Bennett Champ Clark's rival machine that had its headquarters in St. Louis. At the crucial point, a third man, Representative John J. Cochran of St. Louis, entered the race. Clark, no mean political mechanic himself, was retaught an elementary lesson he had perhaps forgotten; Cochran split the St. Louis vote. Truman won easily, and in the flush of the New Deal's early popularity, rode into the Senate in the November assizes.

His first term was absolutely without distinction; his committee jobs were about average, but as a junior senator, he possessed little prestige. His friends were drawn from the ranks of the part-time New Dealers like Garner and Burton K. Wheeler, who was his chairman on the Interstate Commerce Committee. Occasionally he was given charge of a subcommittee. His voting record shows him a ninety per cent administration man, one of sixty or seventy senators who habitually lined up with Roosevelt's measures and policies. Several times, however, he stood with the anti-administration minority. He opposed the bumper $4,800,000,000 relief appropriation. In the contest for Senate majority leader when Joseph T. Robinson died while defending the President's court reorganization bill, Truman backed Pat Harrison, the conservative Mississippian, against Alben Barkley, Roosevelt's choice and the eventual victor.

Perhaps the low point of Truman's career was reached in 1938. Bennett Clark had secured the reappointment of Maurice Milligan as federal district attorney for Kansas City; Milligan was beginning to unearth the felonious methods by which deceased residents and very much alive precinct workers worked for Tom Pendergast. In Truman's eyes there was another damning fact in Milligan's history; he was a brother to the Clark candidate in the 1934 senatorial primary, brother of the man who toured Missouri accusing Harry Truman of being the "office boy" of "bossism." In a lonesome minority the junior Senator raged against Milligan's confirmation; his was the only dissenting voice.

By 1940 Milligan had placed the Boss in Leavenworth Prison, and had an eye on Truman's seat with the covert approval of the White House. Also aspiring to replace the obscure Senator was Governor Stark, whose strength was with the farmers. A truce with Bennett Clark kept the opposition Democratic machine in St. Louis neutral; the press of the state divided its preferences betwen Milligan and Stark. On election night, the district attorney led by 11,000 votes with Kansas City still to be heard from; yet the following morning, it was evident that the remnants of Pendergast's empire and the aging men of Battery D had been diligent—Harry Truman had slithered through to renomination by the Democrats. In autumn Franklin Roosevelt's third term drive pulled him in.[1]

Once more the swift pace of war picked him up and carried him beyond what seemed to have been the horizons of his ambition. From Burton Wheeler he had learned the technique of investigation; in his small-town background, there lived a distrust of bigness and a suspicion of the waste that attends gigantic operations.

Having gone bankrupt himself and having scraped for years to clear his obligations, he had developed a sharp sense of economy. The burgeoning federal government and the fabulous contracts being let attracted his attention. Complaints from home of excesses in camp construction and cost estimates set him upon an independent inquiry. He found what he might have guessed, that moneys being poured into war projects were sometimes squandered. Inefficiencies in administration and practice were obvious. Truman's rural honesty was outraged, possibly the more so because he was a member of the Appropriations Committee that had voted the funds being spent. Lacking full information he did not know exactly what was going on; but with judicial impartiality he refused to make broad accusations or insinuations. His evidence was slight, his legal training limited to a short period of attending a night college of law when he had been a county judge. But having discovered corruption he believed that its source should be revealed, and that Congress was the proper agency to undertake the task.

It was with some reluctance that the administration majority allowed him to set up his own investigating committee in the spring of 1941. When the legislature indicates it wishes a hand in directing the country through a national crisis, the memory of Lincoln's toilsome years rendered more onerous by the Joint Committee on the Conduct of the War screams for recollection. A contemporary example of congressional searchings was the House Committee on Un-American Activities, amassing volumes of testimony of no legal usefulness, exploding sensational charges with monotonous regularity and then beating a loud retreat when the charges appeared proved in the reverse. But Truman's committee bent on its own method. It inaugurated its hearings without fanfare; its chairman parcelled out the work and credit to its other members; its investigators attempted to find all facts in any case that was given consideration; its attorney sifted his evidence before he reached his conclusions. Witnesses were treated courteously and fairly; badgering tendencies on the part of several members were

[1] In Missouri, Roosevelt ran 87,000 votes ahead of Willkie. Truman received 28,000 fewer votes than F.D.R. and won by 44,000.

curbed; mountains of fact were studied and evaluated before recommendations were made. The pervading spirit of the committee was one of inquiry, not prosecution; its reports were temperately worded. Its aim was the correction of abuses rather than publicity.

Beginning with a minute appropriation, Truman and his lawyer, Hugh Fulton—who had been selected because of his abilities instead of his political standing—did most of the work. As the value of what they were doing became more appreciated, Congress gave them larger funds to carry on expanded efforts. Gradually the committee became the most important of the many congressional boards of scrutiny. Informal meetings in "Harry's doghouse," the sitting-room behind Truman's office, kept Republican and Democratic members agreed on objectives and procedures. Private hearings with interested officials soothed resentments before they developed into splenetic outbursts and straightened out irregularities before head-chopping became necessary. Though investigators after faults are not benignly approved of by the investigated, the committee won a certain amount of admiration from businessmen and government administrators and a grudging respect from the Army and Navy. It went after corruptions and inferior contract goods; it cut through red tape and exposed inefficiency and conflicts; it broke down walls of military and naval indifference to certain inventions, and examined charges of discrimination against small manufacturers; and it rooted for the causes of shortages in critical war materials.

Every so often, the welcome chimes of its revelations struck a sour note—as when it permitted Senator A. B. Chandler to express his happy surprise that a war contractor had presented him with a swimming pool, and then kept Chandler in his characteristically gleeful frame of mind by opining that neither politics nor ethics was involved in the favor. So too, the Truman investigation got nowhere when it talked about miners' wages to John L. Lewis; and had to be called off when it wanted specifications from General George C. Marshall on why the Manhattan District Project cost so much with no apparent results.

But, over all, where the committee's work or findings came into public view, its calm recitations of what it found and its evident desire to seek the truth made it popular. The press, conservative and liberal alike, had no quarrel with its utility. Whether an administration agency or a private company was criticized, the reasons were clearly stated, and, for the most part, were unarguable. Harry Truman's dark associations with Tom Pendergast faded; his work in the public service brought him the type of praise he had never before received for his political endeavors. If a touch of the politician remained in his loyalty to his old friends in Missouri, it stemmed from his education in a particular school of politics. If Hugh Fulton did a large share of the intelligent correlation of facts and the preparation of the cases, the tone Truman set in the hearings and the control he exercised over his fellow senatorial inquisitors were instrumental in his committee's success. He had appeared in his best light. Undoubtedly this won him the nomination at Chicago.

3. FINISHING THE FIRST JOB

Franklin Roosevelt's methods placed Harry Truman in a peculiarly advantageous position. With Germany's defeat a few weeks off, with major strategies laid down for MacArthur's team in the Pacific, the new President had but to allow the engines of war to roll under the impact imparted to them by his predecessor, and total victory would inexorably arrive. In point of fact the builder of the ensuing peace would be the dead Commander; but Truman would, by the force of circumstances, be around to deliver the invocation.

In the uncertain, longer-range problems of foreign relations, and world organization, Roosevelt's heritage was typically less definite. At Yalta he had helped compose those measures called forth by the promise of Germany's imminent defeat. That being the requirement of the immediate future, it was worked out thoroughly. Had he wanted to do so Truman could not have changed it. Fairly detailed plans and objectives for the occupation of Germany after its surrender were also agreed upon—thereby binding the United States to a policy that could be renounced only at peril to Big Three unity. If any other revisions were to come, they would have to be arrived at in future conferences; if not, the flexibilities in applying the Crimean declaration could arise only from divergent interpretations of words and from varying administrative practices. More sketchily, in the characteristic Roosevelt way, the United States was committed toward working in the creation of the United Nations, roughly on the basis of the previous conversations at Dumbarton Oaks. Tentative moves were announced looking toward America's full participation in helping establish European governments "representative of all democratic elements," and in carrying out "emergency measures for the relief of distressed people." Still more dimly implemented were the plans for regular meetings of the foreign ministers and the expressed hope for unity in peace.

A short sensation raised Russophobes to a feverish heat of denunciation during the last two weeks of Roosevelt's life. It leaked out that the United States would support the Soviet Union's demand for three votes in the General Assembly of the new organization soon to be char-

tered in San Francisco. The Soviet view was that its two extra autono-
mous republics—Ukraine and White Russia—were as independent as
the British Dominions, each of which had one vote. The anti-Russian
objections ranged from the wild accusation that communism was to
be given disproportionate weight to the more sensible one (not really an
objection) that the "secret" arrangement could have been announced
openly when the other Yalta agreements had been given the world.

Actually the fears of domination were quite thin and patently un-
demonstrable as a result of the last major Roosevelt legacy to inter-
American relations—the Act of Chapultepec, signed in March. That
work had no direct relationship to the San Francisco conference six
weeks later. But the reasonableness of Yankee diplomacy brought the
United States a sizable bloc of Latin American votes in the forthcoming
United Nations conferences. Though not so amenable to a steadfast
following of the American State Department as were the three Soviet
votes in their devotion to the Commissariat of Foreign Affairs, the
American contingent more than counterbalanced whatever advantage
Russia was supposed to have won.

That the Act of Chapultepec was signed, and its significance noted,
weeks before the Yalta voting agreements became known, showed
some of the latent anti-Russian tendencies that were beginning to beset
American foreign policy. It is an open question how far this tide could
have been held back, whether or not Roosevelt had lived. When, at San
Francisco, the United States led the sponsoring of Argentina for admission to the United Nations, the dubious procedure was endorsed by
every Latin American country. It proved that if the United Nations
were to be used as a testing arena for national interests or national prejudices, the Americas would stand firm with an initial strength of
twenty-one votes. It also proved that the tempest that had raged over
Russia's small bloc was of teapot proportions.

Until San Francisco Harry Truman's place in all this was extremely
minor. As Senator and Vice-President, his specialty had been the domestic sphere. He had never greatly influenced the country's foreign
policy, and he was certainly uninformed on recent developments. He
had not been at Yalta; he had not been advised of the secret agreement
on voting. There was every opportunity for a strong-willed Secretary
of State to assume a guidance that stopped just short of absolute control over American foreign relations.

But with Roosevelt's death, this major field of governmental activity
was left in inexperienced hands. Particularly after Cordell Hull had
resigned, F.D.R. had found less need for a strong State Department.

Using the full powers of his office to negotiate agreements personally, he had become his own Secretary of State. Hull's successor, Edward Stettinius, had been at Yalta, at Chapultepec and headed the American delegation at the San Francisco conference. Nevertheless his qualities of leadership were small, partly from his uncertainty or his unwillingness to indicate directions toward which the tangled complexities of American diplomacy might steer, partly because he lacked stature in the eyes of the Senate. During the Crimean discussions and after, he had performed as an aide-de-camp to his chief, leaving no stamp of his own on what was done. In Mexico, he had leaned heavily on his advisers and the unofficial congressional delegation.

Thus with Stettinius not measuring to the possibilities of his office and with Truman studying hard to make up for the enormous gap in his knowledge and experience, there existed, at the top of the administration, a vacuum in the creation and direction of diplomacy. At San Francisco, those who would fill this void assumed full control, to hold it at least until the Secretary was replaced or the President felt confidence in himself. It was the career men of the State Department who took the lead in advancing the proposal to admit Argentina into the society of politer nations six months after Roosevelt and Hull had denounced her government as fascistic. The careerists quite openly lined up a Latin American bloc behind Yankee interests, taking care in most cases to see that what the United States espoused first fitted the principles of hemispheric solidarity before receiving broader application. This was not policy in an exact sense; it was simply a continuity of traditional attitudes by a group of men who esteem tradition for its own and their sakes above all else.

The policy illustrating the American approach to the United Nations was developed in other hands—neither in the administration's nor the State Department's. Even before the conference began Senator Arthur Vandenberg emerged as a leader, occupying a suspicious middle ground between bitter-end isolationism and idealistic internationalism. To his voice, as to the fearsome voice of the United States Senate, all of the American delegation deferred and other countries listened. His sole challenger among his countrymen was not Stettinius, but Commander Harold Stassen whose sturdier internationalism appealed to foreign delegates and a sizable portion of American public opinion, and whose incisive judgments cut through inconsequentialities and won admiration.

What came out of San Francisco, after nine weeks of spectacle and discussion and debate and eventual agreement, was the United Nations

Charter. Having been based on the Dumbarton Oaks drafts, it was a document in which the Big Three held most of the power but offered hope to the rest of the world. Its workability manifestly depended upon the co-operation of the United States and the Soviet Union. That the conference had done its work well enough to have the charter signed by all the participating nations was more a tribute to Franklin Roosevelt's vision than to those on the scene. Had Roosevelt lived he would undoubtedly have dominated the proceedings. His successor, still unsure of himself as a diplomat and international planner, had merely delivered two insignificant speeches. The one real impasse—that over the use of the veto power in the Security Council—was solved in Moscow by Harry Hopkins and Stalin on an old Rooseveltian formula. The new directors of American policy had no more to do with the agreement than the Russians they were debating in the Golden Gate city's opera house.

Meanwhile, in Washington Truman was building a fabulous popularity among his countrymen with his unaffected small-town ways. He received serious visitors and mere handshakers and well-wishers by the score. He was photographed in pleasant little acts—presenting medals, taking a brisk walk, superintending from the sidewalk the cutting down of a tree. He smiled often; he was obliging to the press, and though his words were not profound, their simplicity and sincerity temporarily disarmed those who had grown to hate the presidency because they hated Roosevelt. The praise he received was generous; the country was giving him a chance. Most sharp analysts were too polite to note that his speeches cloaked his uncertainties in tremendous appeals to authority—to God or to the memory of Roosevelt—that they seemed to waver when they presented what he, Harry Truman, as President, thought should be said. With V-E Day, he modestly accepted the triumph as one not his own, and pointed toward the defeat of Japan and the end of the war.

At last his ceremonial days were over. He had interspersed them with messages to Congress endorsing pieces of F.D.R.'s program—the Bretton Woods monetary agreements, a request for executive power to reduce tariffs, prolongation of the Fair Employment Practices Commission. In mid-July, after weeks of rumors of such an impending event, Truman went to Potsdam to confer with Churchill and Stalin. For a while, at least, he was finished with meeting the friends "who knew him when"; he was going to his first real task as President; presumably, he would pick up the reins dropped by Roosevelt as chief of foreign relations.

The European junket was a combination of work and play for the new Chief Executive. He reviewed troops, talked with generals, attended and gave dinners, paid visits of state that were models of informality. During one party, with a characteristic absence of inhibition, he followed a concert pianist at the keyboard. His selection, Paderewski's "Minuet," was probably made without thought that the symbolic connection of its composer's name with Polish prewar independence could be stretched, by some active imaginations, into a relationship to the Polish discussions listed on the conference's agenda.

On the whole he seemed to handle himself competently as he rounded out his first hundred days in office. The primary matters for consideration were Russia's entrance into the fight against Japan, a joint agreement on and enunciation of an occupation policy for Germany, the question of reparations payments, general discussions and a statement of broad objectives on the fate of postwar Europe. On each point, what was substantially the American view obtained. Stalin reiterated a pledge first made at Teheran, and set August 15th as the starting date of Russia's active participation in the Japanese conflict. A general plan, which on the surface appeared fairly hard, was worked out for Germany's demilitarization, "re-education," future balance of industry and agriculture, and the trial of her war criminals. Of significance to the future was the agreement that, while the conquered country was broken into four zones during her occupation state, decisions on her economic rehabilitation would treat her as a single unit. Divisions of the reparations she was to pay—in terms of industrial equipment and foreign assets—were made in harmony with American proposals.

Although little was definitely settled on the specific problems posed by Europe, and although much was put off to the future conferences, a satisfactory compromise was apparently reached on the organization of the new Polish state. The Soviet Union's special concern in the region was given recognition by Truman; his was merely a gracious approval of an unchangeable fact. In return Stalin accepted three western aspirations: for "representatives of the Allied press [to] enjoy full freedom" in reporting the news from eastern Europe, for "free and unfettered" elections in Poland, and for a "democratic" Germany.

The sum of the work was heartening, not so much because of the volume of decisions, but because, after seventeen days of conferences, three victors had been able to discover mutual intentions and set them down on paper as an expression of their common efforts and their plans to continue to work together. A blueprint had been drawn; to how it was read and how closely it would be followed in the further construction of the peace were tied the fears and hopes of the world. Certainly, the beginning was auspicious. Truman, at Potsdam, accomplished more than what had been expected of him.

The days Truman spent in conquered Germany marked the end of the transitory period when he held the presidency but the work he did was his predecessor's. As he boarded his ship for Europe, the Gallup Poll reported eighty-seven per cent of the people favored the work of his administration thus far. It was the high point of his popularity. Before he left, Congress passed the Reciprocal Trade Act which permitted him to cut tariff rates up to fifty per cent in negotiating new commercial pacts. While he was gone it approved the Bretton Woods agreements and the United Nations Charter. But as a sign of the future, it allowed a Senate filibuster against the extension of the Fair Employment Practices Commission, meanwhile preventing the appropriation of funds for ten important war agencies. Caught in a vise between offices operating without funds and the adamant refusal of southern senators to countenance "a damnable, Communist, poisonous piece of legislation,"—as Bilbo, the gentleman from Mississippi, called it—the majority sacrificed principle to immediate considerations. With the downfall of the FEPC began Harry Truman's conflict with Congress on matters of domestic policy.

But more portentous of a new era was the coded report he received from Los Alamos, New Mexico, where the explosive power of atomic energy as applied to military weapons had been tested successfully. Here was the consummation of that two-billion-dollar experiment he had been asked to stay away from when as a Senator he wanted to investigate it. With Secretary of War Stimson he prepared the final ultimatum to Japan before loosing the weapon. In concert with Great Britain and China, the warning was issued from Berlin on July 26th. "Unconditional surrender," the no-quarter condition the allies had presented to Germany after Casablanca, though still used as a term, was narrowly interpreted to affect only the enemy's armies. Otherwise, specific promises were made: Japan would retain industries incapable of being transmuted to war purposes; she could organize a non-militarist government; her home islands would be left intact; occupation would last until disarmament was accomplished and a peaceful government fully established. As though left to future determination, or to keep the door open for a peace feeler by the supreme source, no mention was made of the Emperor. The alternative, said the manifesto, was an "utter devastation of the Japanese homeland." While American newspapers interpreted this to mean a forthcoming invasion, Japan's Premier rejected the offer as "unworthy of public notice."

On August 6th, while the President sailed home from Europe, the bomb fell on Hiroshima. Three days later, a second fell on Nagasaki. In between, Russia declared war and began its push into Manchuria. On the tenth the Japanese began negotiating for the best surrender they could get; on the fourteenth they accepted the only one the rampaging allies would grant—one based on the Potsdam terms. Truman was happy in the victory and self-effacing in the presence of the new power unlocked by science. But, in his great moment, signs showed the honeymoon was ending. Congressmen, expansionists and isolationists asked what he meant by his offhand remark at the conference that the United States wanted no territory out of the war. What about those Pacific islands—the Marshalls, the Solomons, Iwo Jima—where we had bases? Businessmen were disturbed at the abrupt two day holiday he ordered to hail the dawn of peace. They still had to pay their help.

The country celebrated. It saw a rosy future—unlimited travel, new automobiles, better gadgets, lower taxes, shorter hours, an end of worry and fevered tension. In the White House Harry Truman suddenly emerged from the lead-strings laid out by Franklin Roosevelt. From that moment the office was his to do with according to his own abilities, his own judgments and his luck.

IN 1943 an interviewing newspaper man, bent upon a scoop, received from Franklin D. Roosevelt the opinion that the "New Deal," as a slogan, had served its usefulness and should be retired, that "Win the War" was its proper replacement. The change of title, if the President could have effected it, would have been a masterful move. For after years of repetition his conservative opposition had finally accepted the term "New Deal," appropriated it, and turned it into phrases of opprobrious description. Having seized it, and having made it a synonym in their own minds with all shapes and forms of deviltry, they would not let it drop. "New Dealism" proved too handy a club for anti-Rooseveltians to permit its retirement from the lexicon of politics. It remained to become an epithet.

But in surrendering the words Roosevelt had no intention of renouncing the deeds. In his last message to Congress on the state of the Union, he had no reason to believe that the group he addressed would be the first to grapple with postwar problems. He expected that Germany would soon collapse and talked about a reduction of taxes after that anticipated event. Necessarily the largest part of what he had to say dealt with the war and foreign policy; but woven delicately into the background were other suggestions that Congress might consider for the day when the fighting ended. Gently, lest he arouse congressional antagonisms that slept very lightly, he requested that the legislators think about a public works program embodying the construction of housing, roads and airports and the development of imaginative projects similar to the TVA. Still reassuring, the President announced his faith in "private enterprise"; but filling in the bare outlines, it could be seen that Roosevelt was still what he characterized himself—a little left of center.

1. RECASTING THE ADMINISTRATION

During his days as a senatorial investigator Harry S. Truman's apoliticality in summoning businessmen, bureaucrats and generals before his committee had led commentators to pronounce him devoid of ideology. They supposed his long record of affirmative votes on Roosevelt's proposals to be the application of the party regularity he had learned as a student in the Pendergast school. They could not mark him a typical southern Democrat, for against the ten per cent opposition he had shown toward Rooseveltian policies and appointments, they balanced his consistent support of poll-tax repeal, a federal anti-lynching law and anti-discrimination measures. Above all they labelled him a politician, and found his politics uninspiring and, aside from the necessities of his trade, uninspired by interested persons or groups. Almost jubilantly, another group of commentators—the outright conservatives—assessed the men who were his friends and the generals and admirals upon whom he would depend for much of his information, and decided that the government under the new President would swing to the right of center.

No one could look at Truman and believe he represented danger from the left. He looked like and spoke the language of the small-town Middle West, a notoriously unreceptive ground for European radicalism. The thick steel-rimmed glasses on his somewhat sharp face retained to him some of the appearance of the farmer he once had been. His carefully fitted double-breasted suits, with four precise points of a handkerchief peeking out the pocket, stamped him the small-businessman he had tried to be. The button from World War I always in his lapel, which he continued to wear after most World War II veterans had discarded theirs, advertised him a man not wholly disillusioned of the fight that had been his, a man who still remembered he had been there and was proud of that memory. The effect of the apparel he chose for himself was one of nattiness and confidence, one that neither accentuated nor softened his medium height, which looked short when one compared him to the taller and burlier westerners who surrounded him. Obviously he was fanatically neat with his clothing and desirous of being correct—though arbiters of fashion once shuddered when he wore a striped bow-tie with a dinner jacket. But the final impression, despite his easy manner, was not one of natural informality; Mr. Truman seemed too conscious of what he was wearing.

Yet this too was in character. The prototype of the American male is not supposed to be fully relaxed or comfortable until he is tieless and in his oldest pair of trousers and his most faded shirt. On his vacation excursions the Missouri President, slightly rumpled, looked his happiest.

At his early press conferences Harry Truman was, to the reporters, a surprise and a relief. He greeted them with a cheerful smile; he fidgeted slightly while he watched them enter the room and as they asked their questions; he gave them concise, earnest answers or politely indicated what he did not care to discuss. After having received a bad press for years from the St. Louis papers and the *Kansas City Star,* he was sensibly making the best of an opportunity to secure a good one. On their side the interviewers had hoped to be enthusiastic. They enjoyed the deference paid them and the President's openness. With Roosevelt it had been different. He had been news, to be sure; but his press conferences were tests of wit. Some of F.D.R.'s remarks were provocative, others purposely enigmatic; he had matched distasteful questions with jokes or jibes; he had been fond of epigrams and allegory. Truman offered sheer reporting, straight answers, no erudition that had to be thought out and assimilated, no involved allusions or tales that had to be interpreted and explained to readers. While Truman made news, just as had Roosevelt, he also made life easier.

As analysts probed Truman's personality, his record and first days, several hopeful predictions were made. From his committee experiences and his friendships with so many men on Capitol Hill, the conclusion was derived that the Executive would work in harmony with Congress. This seemed certain to be borne out when he complimented the Senate by asking its President, Kenneth McKellar of Tennessee, to sit in at cabinet meetings. The House felt a pleasant glow when the Chief Executive proposed, in his request for a new presidential succession law, that the Speaker, as the leader of the chamber more nearly representing the popular will, be placed next in line for the throne. Still, these were mere gestures; the commentators overlooked the difficulties other presidents who had been senators, such as Jackson, Johnson and Harding, suffered at the hands of Congress.

A second optimistic assumption was that Truman, a neat man who liked everything in its place, would put in order the administrative muddles that Roosevelt, both for lack of interest and unwillingness to make a frank decision, allowed to develop. Harry Truman, said the seers, would provide for efficient administration; perhaps his contribution in this limited aspect of the presidency would be almost as great as that of Chester Arthur, whose fine work in keeping his departments and his subordinates in harmonious operation has made him the model for all successive presidents to approximate. Under the Missourian, it was felt, bunglers would receive scant consideration, no opportunity to suggest second chances to cover a first mistake, no "kicking upstairs" to another and less important office; if a man did not deliver, he would go. No more embarrassing policy disagreements like the Jones-Wallace squabble would be permitted; personal animosities like those Harold Ickes held for his fellow men would have to be controlled; jurisdictional disputes between agencies and departments would not be tolerated. Everything would move with certainty; everyone would know where the administration stood on an issue and what it proposed to do.

Finally, expectations ran high that new faces, plain faces, new personalities, unpretentious personalities, would quickly replace the Roosevelt junto. The new men would be down-to-earth Americans like the President, as typical of the country's heartland between the Alleghenies and the Rockies as the man from Missouri, the geographical center of the area. They would be as alike as their conservative blue and grey double-breasted suits. Certainly, men of political ripeness and influence, men matured in the trade, as Truman was, would come to office. A wholesale exodus seemed necessary to effect the change. Those with small party standing like Secretary of the Treasury Morgenthau, Agriculture minister Wickard and Attorney General Biddle, converted Republicans like Stettinius and doubtful Democrats like Navy Secretary Forrestal, old timers like Stimson and Ickes and those who had for a long time wanted to resign like Postmaster General Walker and Frances Perkins would have to be replaced. Others with less specifically defined positions—Harry Hopkins, the ailing confidant and special agent of the late President; the White House corps of Steve Early, Judge Samuel Rosenman, playwright Robert Sherwood; the intellects, the professors, the idea-men—were all marked for departure for one reason or another.

Five days after Truman's accession, the commentators sat back comfortably. Their analyses were being vindicated. The President's press secretary was to be Steve Ross, an old schoolmate from Independence, Missouri, a Pulitzer Prize winner in journalism and head of the *St. Louis Post-Dispatch's* bureau in the Capital. The empty post of Federal Loan Administrator—the place the Senate had refused Henry Wallace—was filled by naming John W. Snyder, also of St. Louis. The two appointments seemed in character. As judge and senator, Truman had been Ross's humble and devoted reader; here was a Missourian for whom the green Chief Executive had infinite respect. For companionship Truman could turn to his old friend Snyder. As artillery captains they had met in France; as reserve officers they had bivouacked together and worked their ways up to colonelcies.

Both had labored in obscurity in the 1920's, Truman in his clothing store and the lower reaches of Jackson County politics, Snyder in his uncle's bank in Arkansas. In the thirties and forties they had risen, Truman to the Senate, Snyder in the RFC, first as a branch manager in

St. Louis, then as executive vice-president of the Defense Plant Corporation. In 1943 there had been a rupture with Jesse Jones, and Snyder returned to St. Louis to a much-improved banking position. His financial connections denoted him a conservative; from his earlier stint in Washington it was also recalled that he was shrewd in handling government moneys and an able man at his desk. Short, plump and serious, he epitomized the average businessman, and gave no hint of the tycoon. He had gone to Chicago in 1944 to help his old buddy from Independence put over Jimmy Byrnes; he had stayed to catch the fever of convention intrigue and work openly for the Missouri Senator. Jesse Jones was quoted to have said the President "could not have made a better appointment."

Then, through the war months, the other nominations came. There was nothing of an avalanche, a ruthless cutting out of the old order; but, as men's names were sent to Congress or announced, a definite trend was noticed. An old friend from Nebraska, once a Battery D soldier, was transformed overnight from the insurance business to the President's chief administrative assistant. Six weeks showed the impropriety of the gesture; the gentleman disappeared from public view into the yawning cave of John Snyder's RFC. An independent oilman from California, Edwin Pauley, who as treasurer of the Democratic National Committee had joined the bosses in the back-room work at Chicago, was given his first reward, appointment to the Allied Reparations Commission, a post with ambassadorial rank. A Rooseveltian economist, experienced in international affairs, had had to step down in the arrangement. A politician had displaced a thinker. Rumors washed over the city and flooded the press. Pauley's elevation was seen as only a stopgap boon until other destinies were settled; it was expected a niche in the cabinet would be opened for him. The Treasury? Commerce? Navy? Interior? Gossips had a holiday with other stories. What about Hugh Fulton, the attorney for the War Investigating Committee, who had breakfasted with Truman on April 13th? What of Jimmy Byrnes, a private citizen ostensibly practicing law in South Carolina but a frequent visitor to the White House?

The next weeks set the pattern. National Democratic chairman Robert Hannegan, the Missourian who plotted the strategy of the vice-presidential nomination, received the Post Office. Two Missouri cronies from World War I, both artillery officers and both reservists, got ceremonial jobs and opportunities for advancement as the President's military and naval aides. Admiral Leahy, Roosevelt's conservative military adviser and liaison officer to the Joint Chiefs of Staff, was retained.

David Lilienthal, the liberal New Dealer in charge of the TVA, was reappointed over the wild growlings of Senator McKellar. Maurice Milligan, the federal attorney responsible for Tom Pendergast's fall, lost his position to the Missouri state Democratic chairman. Some tired Rooseveltians were prevailed upon to remain—Harry Hopkins for a special mission to Russia in order to break a stalemate in Russo-American discussions over the use of the veto power in the projected United Nations Security Council, Judge Rosenman for another year as speech-writer and policy adviser, David K. Niles as the White House assistant on minority and racial problems.

In settling gradually into office, the President apparently had evolved a rule-of-thumb on his selections: to repay the politicians who had helped him and who required stroking for future support, he doled out offices which Roosevelt men vacated voluntarily or could be removed from without too loud an outcry; to assist his Missouri poker set to prestige and power, he planted them in places close to the White House where they might amuse him and themselves and perhaps do good work; to keep the best Roosevelt men in the government he would reappoint some and steer hungry office-seekers into jobs where one expected to find a partisan rather than an administrator or thinker. Summed up, it meant that Truman was pulling his administration away from the Roosevelt type of government by coalition and personality; he was replacing it with the party government he had learned in his apprenticeship.

At the end of May the hitherto slow process of change was speeded up by three new cabinet appointments. The sensitive, high-principled, aristocratic liberal from Philadelphia, Attorney General Francis Biddle, was let out twenty-four hours after he had been assured he would be held in office to continue his program. The new law officer was Tom Clark of Texas, an assistant in the Justice Department, but more important, a protégé of Senator Connally and Speaker Rayburn, and a politician bred from childhood. Clark's reputation had been made not so much in the development of law as in negotiation and adjustment; his collection of gaudy bow-ties suggested a brash, effusive personality. Out of the Labor Department went Madam Frances Perkins, an original Roosevelt appointee from 1933 who had survived despite poisonous criticism and her own desire to resign, meanwhile watching independent executive agencies absorb most of her power. Coming in was Judge Lewis Schwellenbach, formerly a freshman Senator with the President and a thorough-going Roosevelt New Dealer. After begging to be excused, he had bowed to Truman's insistence that he was needed in the ministry. One definite condition attached to his acceptance was that the Department would receive some control over the several unco-ordinated agencies concerned with labor problems; another rumored condition was that Schwellenbach, on completion of his tour of duty, would be raised to the Supreme Court.

The third departure, one heralded before Roosevelt's death, was Secretary of Agriculture Claude Wickard. His successor, Representative Clinton P. Anderson of New Mexico, had, during the immediate weeks before his appointment, been blasting at food shortages in a highly pub-licized campaign. The surprise in this nomination did more than un-nerve Anderson and the critics who agreed with him; it put them to the immediate test of devising a policy to correct what they had criti-cized. For his purposes, Anderson, like Schwellenbach, was given a hand in several agencies that had previously been independent of his Department.

At the time, most significance was attached to the Labor selection. After a few months, however, while the Judge strove helplessly to avert collision between unions and management, the words of the Secretary of Agriculture were to carry heavier weight with the President, more influence in Congress, and turn the administration into new paths. For Anderson, a rancher, was to display far more friendliness to the rural producers of food than the urban consumers; the totality of his deeds and recommendations eventually undermined food price controls. In a number of statements before congressional committees he contra-dicted or disagreed with other administration spokesmen; congressmen liked his thinking better than that of the "bureaucrats." Although they went past his ideas in writing the laws, the absence of solidarity on the administration front, as broken by the Secretary, was all the encourage-ment needed by Anderson's listeners to believe that the "bureaucrats," with their charts and statistics, were dreamers and dunces.

In July the shuffling of offices started once again. The San Francisco Conference over, Stettinius made way for James Byrnes. A man of wide, if not deep, experience on a high level in all three branches of the gov-ernment, the new Secretary of State had the admiration of his chief and knowledge that Truman hoped to tap. Not only had he been along at Yalta where he had met the great and taken down their words in his shorthand notebook, he knew the halls of Congress in their deepest recesses and he understood the minds of the residents. As a past master at compromise he had wrangled and manipulated for the New Deal in the Senate. On the Court his short tenure had been unproductive; but as War Mobilizer or "assistant president" he had fought and whee-dled and persuaded, angered and then calmed most of those who brought him problems of production and prices, allocations, wages and

costs. In the most exasperating job of the war that continuously subjected him to pressures or forced him to make unpleasant decisions, he
managed to survive as a political entity and a somewhat popular one.
But for the CIO he would probably have been Roosevelt's successor.
Brynes's information and his outlook on foreign affairs might have been
foreshortened by his years of working in domestic politics, but the President nevertheless believed his undeniable talents were needed. After
all his high ranking jobs there was no place for Byrnes but the State
Department, unless it be the presidency.

July also brought in the sixth cabinet change—Judge, ex-Congress-
man and War Mobilizer Fred Vinson of Kentucky for Henry Morgenthau, the architect of Bretton Woods, the financier of the war, and
the implementer of the New Deal tax policies. As it proved the prime
beneficiary of the move was neither the new Secretary of the Treasury
nor Truman, but John Snyder who moved up to the Office of War Mo-
bilization and Reconversion fresh on the heels of Vinson's first report
on the accomplishments and prospects of the national economy. Most
of the important policy determinations followed Vinson in his rise up
the ladder; but the operations and administrative procedures were well
laid down for Snyder who had only to follow them.

Of the cabinet appointments only Clark's could be open to question.
The others were all men of proven ability; their party service had rendered them deserving; aside from Byrnes, each was conversant with his
field. Ideologically, there may have been some slight shift toward the
center; yet subordinates like Benjamin Cohen and Dean Acheson
whom Byrnes established with him in the State Department brought
a more liberal air into stuffy conservative corridors. If there was a single
outstanding comparison to be made between the new and the old, it
was that the old were friends of Franklin Roosevelt and public servants; the new were, in addition to all else, politicians of weight.

*   *   *

While Departments changed hands and offices rotated from the
less worthy Democrats to the more worthy, while the war raced to
an end and international conferences discussed and explored unprecedented organizations and devices, Harry Truman interspersed his activities as commander-in-chief and head of foreign relations with
thoughts on the domestic scene. Commencing with a heritage of New
Deal policies and a New Deal team, he fell to using the materials at
hand. In addition to what Roosevelt had mildly suggested in his last
message was the Democratic battle cry of the 1944 campaign—full employment and 60,000,000 jobs.

Since January Congress had spasmodically considered and then banished from its consciousness a Full Employment bill which sought to make the federal government a full partner of private industry in guaranteeing work for all who wanted it. The bill, as originally proposed by four Democratic senators, called for an annual "National Production and Employment Budget" prepared by a committee of experts, a joint committee of Congress to study the estimates and needs set forth in the budget, government spending to create jobs when there was a deficiency in industry. Both parties endorsed the principle; few public figures would openly dare to state that they believed a little unemployment a good thing. The President said it was "must" legislation.

If he meant what he said, if the administration's men who testified in favor of passage understood the measure's implications, the full employment proposal could potentially effect an economic revolution in the United States, not by threatening private property and enterprise but by attacking the business cycle where it struck heavily at those dependent on others for work. If the bill became law it would obviously provide a cornerstone upon which every administration would have to build its domestic economic program. It was straight New Deal—the middle position between unadulterated private capitalism and socialism. Tied to it as integral parts of a "mixed economy" were the other pieces of the program Truman inherited from Roosevelt—increased unemployment benefits, a higher minimum-wage level than the forty cents per hour established in the 1930's, a thoroughly revamped and rationalized taxation structure, plans for extensive public works and housing construction. Internationally too, the system carried implications. If it worked, it would provide America with a stable economy. This, in turn, would underwrite the country's political leadership in the world, enabling it to address itself to problems abroad while prosperity reigned at home, and challenging the Marxian assumption that depressions were unavoidable concomitants of capitalism.

These, then, were the tools to be used in attaining long-run objectives. They were the heart of what Truman advocated, so far as impact upon the United States was concerned. His other recommendations for peacetime conscription and a merger of the armed services into a single mammoth Executive Department were so much fluff. The reconversion program, as formulated by Byrnes and Vinson and as administered by Snyder, was something for an indefinite but—it was hoped—comparatively short interval. So were the matters of controls and the alleviation of shortages.

How successfully the President could push the New Deal for the 1940's and 1950's depended upon a number of factors. A large one was himself—his intensity, his popularity, his ability to persuade and drive others. On the face of it, he was an average man presenting an enormous and intricate mechanism that could not have originated with a county judge from rural Missouri. He was working on borrowed capital; he had to prove he knew what he had and that he knew how to use it.

Executive-legislative relationships, more promising of amity than in the past eight years, provided another gauge for measurement. Personally, the congressmen liked him. They did not fear him or envy him as they did Roosevelt. But, on closer view, his senatorial intimates included men of waning influence like Wheeler of Montana and Guffey of Pennsylvania; one of his closest associates, Carl Hatch of New Mexico, held limited power because of his periodic bolts from party leadership and his independent sponsorship of politically embarrassing bills. The congressional leaders and committee chairmen, however, were only acquaintances, those with whom Truman gossiped about personalities and politics but not issues, those who had regarded Senator Truman as a compliant wheelhorse who voted right on most roll calls.

The strongest of the President's influences in Congress was Les Biffle, secretary of the Senate, not a legislator at all but the theoretical employee of the solons. His experience was enriched by a longer tenure on Capitol Hill than almost every man he served. He knew and had a card file of all that was worth knowing of each member, every lobbyist and any important name in the city. He had a first-rate knowledge of parliamentary tactics and was a master at the manipulation of political consciences. Yet, he was ever the employee, and as such, likely to arouse jealousies and obduracy in senators if called upon to press Truman's wishes too strongly. Thus, in September 1945, Congress and the President were on the most cordial terms. Each felt for the other a nostalgia for the old days and a kind of uncritical affection. Whether the bond was one of true love or sentimental infatuation was still to be indicated.

A third and highly complex factor in Truman's future was the performance of his official family. That its members would be personally loyal to him and play his type of regular politics was to be expected. But, in his administration, the cabinet loomed a more important body than it had in his predecessor's. Instead of a single executive who kept a fairly tight hand on all the reins of power entrusted to his branch, Harry Truman preferred to think of his office in less omnipotent terms. Under him the presidency became a clearing house with a loud-speaker system. The problems the White House received were checked out to the appropriate Departments and agencies for solution.

Also from on high came the occasional presidential speeches and directives. This was the loud-speaker function of the office; these were the words that alerted all on the administration's general policy. Within these utterances were to be fitted the solutions arrived at down below. Consequently, after the President had given his messages and stamped his directions and routing on any piece of business, his concern with a matter ended until it came back to him for signature. Or, in unfortunate instances, it came back as something that had gone unsolved in the echelons beneath, and had, in the delay, grown to expanded proportions.

As examples of how the parceling-out worked, foreign policy became the province of Secretary Byrnes, and became more clearly identified with him than with his chief. The turmoil of postwar labor unrest was unceremoniously dumped on Lewis Schwellenbach. John Snyder, the extremely amateur politician who had risen dizzily in three months from a vice-presidency in a St. Louis bank to responsibility for the reconversion of the nation's economy, was ordered to see through Congress two of the administration's most important legislative interests, the full employment bill and an atomic energy act.

Cabinet government in the United States had done its best work under George Washington. The interval was long. Under Truman, the success of the method was contingent upon how well the Secretaries and agency administrators could operate together as a team, upon how closely they matched their broad grants of power to Truman's general statements. Disagreements or erroneous decisions would prove heavily embarrassing because the President was staking so much on the abilities of his ministry. Having announced his program, he placed himself in the hands of others to secure its enactment and administration. Their conviction in his aims, their willingness to work for his glory became the pegs upon which the neat, smiling President hung his fate. If the pegs held, he could continue his frequent short vacations and the excursions he made into small-town Missouri for homey talk, county fairs, and visits with friends of humbler days. But if the pegs did not hold he would be chained to his office, attempting to sort out and fit together the many pieces of which his mind had only a sketchy and rapidly crammed knowledge.

2. HOME ECONOMICS

To provide government for the United States in peace, President Truman and his ministry might have felt the millenium would arrive if they were allowed to do their jobs and if Congress gave them what they asked. In poll after poll by the measurers of public opinion, the humble man in the White House was enthusiastically endorsed by his country. For a while people were sympathetic because the job that had fallen to him against his wishes was so large. He informed visitors of his shortcomings with disarming candor, he impressed the country as earnest and almost straining to please. Perhaps he took too many short junkets in his desire to escape the tempo of Washington; but he was obviously working harder than he had ever worked in his life. Some liberals were disconcerted when New Dealers began streaming from the public service for less arduous, better paying prospects in private employment. Misgivings arose over certain of the appointments and at the character of his inner circle. Yet the honeymoon lingered on. No matter what was said of John Snyder by the liberals who distrusted him or the conservative congressmen who disliked him, no matter what rumors circulated about George Allen, the man who reputedly advised on politics and the distribution of offices while he regaled the President from an inexhaustible supply of jokes and anecdotes, Harry Truman held the nation's confidence.

On October 10th he delivered his optimistic view of the present and the future. Speaking at a dam dedication in Kentucky after several days of county fairs, church suppers and local courthouse politics, he treated his visible audience and the nation to a kind of crackerbarrel sermon. It was Harry Truman speaking with his easiest informality, attempting to apply the "common sense" words of a rural culture to the problems of an industrial civilization. "We are having our little troubles now—a few of them. They are not serious. Just a blow-up after a let-down from war. . . . Everybody had to blow off steam. . . . Now let's all go home and go to work. Cut out the foolishness and make this country what it ought to be—the greatest nation the sun has ever shone upon."

The President had intended to be soothing. But the press and the critics took him to task for what seemed gross understatement. In Congress, the program he had advocated was stalled; the conservative coalition did not like his proposals or those of his appointees who were drawn from the New Deal legion. All his important recommendations were entombed in committees; even appropriations to which the United States was committed by its pledge, like the country's allotment to UNRRA for relief, were retarded. The full employment bill lay slumbering, certain of defeat if it came up with its provision for government spending in times of depression. A host of atomic energy bills had been prepared by various congressmen and senators, but hearings on them toiled on with no sign of a let-up. The legislature had no program of its own; yet it was neither willing to develop one nor accept that suggested to it.

Across the nation, the "not serious" troubles were a compound of tensions and pulls and stresses that had been accumulating from the beginning of the war. The end of hostilities terminated most agreement about national unity. What had been bubbling beneath the surface erupted in a geyser. Organized labor demanded increased wage rates to compensate for the losses in pay it sustained from the postwar return to shorter hours of work. Its major antagonists, the large corporations, with plentiful accumulations of war profits after heavy taxation, preferred to wait and see, pleading meanwhile they needed what they had for increased costs of operation and materials, and for reinvestment. Local strikes pinpointed the nation; large ones in the basic industries were ominously threatened. In a first reckless moment of victory the War Production Board released most of its controls over materials; plans were laid to curtail drastically the scope of the War Labor Board; the OPA began eliminating the comparatively slight rationing Americans had endured during the war.

With much money waiting to be spent consumers found the goods of peacetime simply not available. Manufacturers had yet to retool and produce in large quantities; with many wholesalers and retailers, they protested that their costs had increased, that they were entitled to higher prices than those permitted under government controls. On the whole, the business community spoke enthusiastically of the next few years; but it held back from action awaiting developments.

Two theories of economics competed for attention: business wanted its own determination of prices based on costs; it was reluctant to grant wage increases until assured that price rises would cover them. If, in the process, prices went up, as they surely would, they would come down again when the production of goods began to flow in large volume and when supply caught up with demand. On the other hand, the government, represented in its argument mainly by Chester Bowles of the OPA, contended that increased prices would dry up the well of purchasing power in consumer hands, that before full production was reached the market would be gone. Rather, if prices were kept down to their established ceilings, greater quantities of goods would be asked for and production would be larger; unit profits might be smaller but total profits would be increased. For the consumers, the upshot was a shortage in almost every necessity—food, clothing, housing—and a widespread patronage of the "black markets" that flouted a government which had not provided for adequate enforcement of the price control laws.

Although Truman had minimized the troubles they were already grown to a size that could not be ignored. The wartime dream for reconversion was a period of peace and plenty; actually reconversion developed into a complex of wage-cost-profit-price-shortage-inflation. Prosperity continued, urged on by consumer buying, by government expenditures, and the outlays of industry revamping itself. But the prosperity was joyless; its survival indefinite. Victory's bright day was marred by overhanging clouds of dread and sudden squalls of dissatisfaction.

The rumblings became more distinct. Seeing a corollary in Bowles's economics, labor—particularly the CIO—argued that wage increases were possible without elevating prices. Strike talk grew general in national industries like coal, automobiles, steel and telephones. A number of federal economists let out opinions that wage raises were possible without price alterations; Snyder's OWMR put the figure at twenty-four per cent, Wallace's Commerce Department at ten. Industry rejected the thought. Management found itself in a strange position; it could afford strikes because Congress was in the process of hammering out a reduction of the excess-profits tax, and because the Treasury would have to refund taxes already paid in if income dropped off, as it surely would when strikes closed factories and mills. Thus, two powerful forces—organized labor and capital management—sparred for an advantage while the national economy lurched on uncertainly.

President Truman met the challenge with a speech and a Labor-Management Conference. The speech sought to placate everyone; it calmed none. According to his view wages could be raised without prices following them; but he named no tentative figure—a sore disappointment to the CIO. He suggested that tax reductions and increased productivity could make up the difference. Price increases would be permitted to those companies which raised wages and then found they could not operate at a "fair profit." Lessons were read to labor that its demands be "reasonable" and that it "strive constantly for greater efficiency and greater productivity." Management was reminded that labor was its "best customer." Both were told the country expected them to "bargain in good faith, with labor recognizing the right of industry to a fair profit, and industry recognizing labor's need to a decent and sustained standard of living." In effect, Truman sent the problem back to each of them, asking one to give wage increases, the other to abide price rises. The solution was a noteworthy attempt at fence-sitting; it offered to pay for industrial peace by permitting the beginnings of an inflation. Neither side liked the idea.

As if the critical reception given his statements were not enough, the President sadly watched his Conference degenerate into a quarrel between Philip Murray and John L. Lewis. If Truman thought agreement could come out of a meeting of the CIO, the AF of L, the National Association of Manufacturers and the United States Chamber of Commerce, he was badly mistaken. The Conference broke up amid NAM cheers for Lewis when he called for a rapid end of all controls. "I want free enterprise and free collective bargaining" was an utterance of the miners' chief that appealed to those present who represented craft labor and industry. Industrial labor and the public representatives, seeking a definition of policy that the assembly could recommend to the government as acceptable to all, were in a minority. Whatever policy any one group urged was opposed by the others. Points of view were so far apart and so fixed in the minds of those who held them that no compromise was possible. In the White House the Chief Executive watched the dissolution of another dream.

The reverberations were amplified when General Motors and the United Automobile Workers fell out, and a long strike began. Once again economic theories conflicted, this time with an additional emphasis on different concepts of underlying ethics. The union contended that the company open its books so that labor and management might arrive at a wage scale computed upon "ability to pay"; the company refused to discuss the proposition, holding it an invasion of management's rights. Negotiations stopped completely, each side accusing the other of bad faith; General Motors called the union's strike tactics a "conspiracy," the UAW charged the corporation with being a monopoly.

In early December the President re-entered the labor scene. Secretary Schwellenbach's earlier efforts as a government conciliator attempting peaceful solution had been fruitless. Talk having failed, the Chief Executive asked for a law. "It becomes the duty of the government," he said, "to act on its own initiative." He requested, therefore, that Congress authorize him to step into any industrial dispute adverse to the public interest that could not be settled by the Labor Department. To deal with threatened strikes he proposed the creation of a fact-finding board empowered to investigate the conflict—if necessary to inspect company books—and make recommendations for settlement. Though the board's suggestions would not be legally enforceable, he believed public opinion, thus informed by publicity, would demand acceptance of the findings by both sides.[1] During thirty days, when investigations, recommendations and discussions were to take place, no strike or lock-

[1] Truman's proposal was not original, but was based on the conditions outlined in the Railway Labor Disputes Act of 1926 under which no strike had taken place since its inception. Only a very few months were necessary to open eyes to the faults of the model he chose; in May, 1946, a railroad strike drove the President into making a far more stern request.

out or change of pay status was to be permitted. As an assurance to the public, Truman added that if Congress gave him the mechanism he would apply it to the General Motors strike; in reassurance to labor, he promised to use the law sparingly.

Thus Harry Truman advanced another of his moderate solutions, one that would split the difference. But, in this case as in others to follow, he found that moderation was not the key to settlement. Industry disliked the inspection proposal; labor denounced the recommendations scheme as an end to collective bargaining. In Congress the House was bent on more stringent curbs of its own construction, while the more liberal Senate showed no inclination to pass any bill unfavorable to labor.

But the President was undaunted. He appointed a fact-finding board to deal separately with the automobile strike. Hearings began. In the midst of them Truman heated managerial tempers at General Motors and throughout the NAM by endorsing the "ability to pay" theory. Shortly afterward, General Motors walked out of the hearings. Several weeks later, when the board announced findings that a 17.5 per cent increase (the union asked for 30 per cent) would be equitable, the corporation rejected the recommendation within twenty-four hours. By that time Harry Truman had another war on his hands, one between the steel industry and its unionized workers. His prestige had slipped badly. In cavalierly disregarding the positive findings of the board without securing so much as a hard rebuke, General Motors, which two months later accepted a figure less than one per cent lower, demonstrated the suspected notion that the presidency was weakening.

* * *

Meanwhile all was not harmonious within the administration. After a few months its conglomeration of personalities, living in close quarters, watched one another with deepening suspicion. Secretary of War Patterson, who had replaced the elderly Stimson at the war's end, listened approvingly while his generals talked of the merger of the armed services; Secretary of the Navy Forrestal, sharing the separatist views of his admirals, confuted the testimony of his opposite cabinet number by condemning the plan before interested congressional committees.

Lewis Schwellenbach, having been unable to expand his Department fast enough to catch up with the runaway problems in industrial relations, was also losing out as the President's labor adviser; the prerogatives of his position if not his title were being usurped by John

Steelman who was closer to Truman's ear. Toward Steelman, the usually judicial Labor minister was beginning to have most uncomplimentary thoughts. Secretary Byrnes and Admiral Leahy disagreed on matters of foreign policy and on the superiority of the State Department to the War Department in carrying out and interpreting the President's general dicta. But, on the domestic front, the storm center was Truman's personal friend and companion, John Snyder, the man who had been brought from Missouri because his old artillery buddy believed the banker's views to be profoundly correct. Yet Snyder, however much he had his chief's confidence, was less than a genius to others. Hannegan thought his conservatism a baleful influence, one that would draw Truman away from the liberal and labor votes he needed in 1948.

More wrathful was Chester Bowles whose attempts to keep prices from rising were undercut by the effects of the Reconversion director's policies. That Snyder was a superior officer in the government and better able to get his views across to his friend in the White House, either in official conversations or over the poker table, made little difference; Bowles, a former advertising man, knew how to bring his side of the story before the public. Combining his skill with convictions drawn from the newer economic theory of Keynes and Alvin Hansen, he expounded his position attractively. His opponent, handicapped by a less lustrous personality, was at a disadvantage; when Snyder drew from his banker's experience and presented older and more conservative doctrines, economics seemed once again to fall into its old classification as the "dismal science."

Nothing better illustrated the Bowles-Snyder incompatibility, and the President's helplessness between them, than the steel strike and its issues. This time, with Philip Murray calling the tune, the question was simple: the workers wanted more money; the industry's management would not give them as much as they wanted. Although it meant forswearing his earlier methods of admonition or fact-finding boards, Truman again jumped into the discussions as a direct arbitrator. The implications of a long strike in steel were far more serious than of that which was simultaneously tying up General Motors; a basic industry would be shut down and fully 15,000,000 wage-earners affected by a halt in steel production. The President offered 18½ cents as the hourly increase he thought fair; the rate was 6½ cents below the union's original demand and one cent below its compromise demand; it was 3½ cents above the industry's offer. Murray accepted it; Benjamin Fairless of United States Steel, speaking for management, rejected it. On January 21, 1946, 750,000 steelworkers struck and 800 plants closed.

The problem passed into the administration's hands for final decision; if steel were given a higher OPA ceiling price, said the industry, the wage increase would be granted. For a month the President's advisers labored toward a solution, something that might provide a formula for the coming wage-price arguments and contingencies in other industries. Chester Bowles, whose campaign to "hold the line" had infected the consuming public with a fear of inflation, held that any price increase allowed must be a low one. Snyder favored giving steel management most of what it asked for. Bowles threatened resignation if Snyder's plan obtained, and then reconsidered. Truman, uncertain of which policy to adopt, delayed in taking action. He could not afford to let go of Bowles—at the moment the most popular man in the administration. On the other hand, he wanted the strike settled.

But it was not in the President to repudiate his crony from Missouri. When Truman announced the granting of a price increase in steel along the lines advocated by Snyder, and when the parties to the dispute accepted the solution, his formula elicited slight praise from either the newspapers or labor or capital. After a month of studying and politicking and indecision he presented what was merely the most obvious expedient. In his own words, it was a "bulge in the old line"; if everyone co-operated, he felt, "there will be no break-through." Most others took a dimmer view; as the indicator of a new "general pattern" for wages and prices, the line might never be breached, but it could be pushed back progressively until there was nothing left to defend. New demands for price increases in commodities dependent upon steel were a certainty. Somewhere near the bottom of the feared inflation spiral forces began moving to push prices upward. Only a miracle of rapid production could stop them.

What little comfort there was to the general public rested in the emergence of Bowles as the central figure in command of the country's domestic economy. In the private argument over economics he had lost the White House decision to Snyder. But he was elevated to the post of Economic Stabilizer in charge of administering the new formula. Theoretically, Snyder was still his superior with power to overrule his directives; but Bowles had become the hero of the masses. He had developed into that extreme oddity, the bureaucrat with an immense popular following and political potency, the storm-tossed appointee who thrived on publicity instead of anonymity. Temporarily, at least, with Henry Wallace maintaining an unhappy silence, he supplanted Truman as the spokesman of the liberals of the country.

Bowles needed all the strength he could muster. The President's popularity with the public was plunging downward at a precipitous rate—according to *Fortune,* from 82.1 per cent in January 1946 to 52.1 per cent in June. In Congress, the administration's program of social legislation—increased minimum wages, a long-range housing plan, health insurance, anti-discrimination laws—had no hope of passage; by filibuster and by committee rules the conservative majority prevented action. Through persistent pressure an Employment Bill was finally adopted; but not before "Full" had been excised from the title and the authorizations largely reduced to fact gathering. As the measure stumbled through House and Senate, provisions to charge the government with responsibility for jobs were shorn. The legislative product was a skeleton. In the fourteen months it had been debated, critics constantly condemned the entire proposal as unworkable; in enactment, opposition congressmen, with their amendments and remarks, showed a clear intent to guarantee that it would be. Their object was to preserve the private nature of the capitalist economy. Any thoughts Truman or his advisers may have had of using full employment as a basis of an economic program or as a political asset were impossible of fulfillment.

By that time many in the nation had lost interest in Truman. Almost fatalistically they saw more strikes coming—to coal and the railroads. Meanwhile the conservatives girded for their next battles in the campaign to eliminate the remnants of Harry Truman's New Deal. Their congressional coalition having refused him the future, they resolved to begin work on wiping out the present and immediate past. One of his requests was an extension of the price control law for another year. Against this the opposition concentrated its drive. As the opinion polls showed in May, two-thirds of the people favored price control in some form or other. Yet this made no difference to those who wished to end it. The movement started; Truman was timorous at meeting the attack. Snyder was glum about OPA's utility, and was half-hearted in defending his chief's policy before congressional committees. Secretary of Agriculture Anderson wanted increased farm prices, and, under questioning, admitted that he thought controls might have to be lifted.

In the face of this dim encouragement from his administration superiors, Bowles fought grimly. To the conservatives, he became a villain; the OPA was represented as embodying all forms of dastardy and inefficiency. Lobbyists for farm, industry, trade and property interests fastened themselves upon Congress. They shouted their wares: OPA was responsible for the shortages and the black market; it was holding down production by its restrictive practices; it was preventing profitable operation. Just give them freedom from the bureaucrats and, they promised, shortages would cease; even prices would fall. From one side trade association pamphlets obliquely charged Bowles with dishonesty and a lust for power. From another, southern senators, some of whom were speculating in cotton futures, made threats that amounted to blackmail; OPA would be struck dead, they averred, unless cotton ceilings were raised substantially.

From the time the President had permitted the "bulge" in the line, prices had become increasingly more difficult to administer. Cost-wage-price relationships were slightly out of focus; the cost of living was slowly going up. Bowles was to be credited for having held things in line as long and as well as he had; he argued valiantly against repeal, assuring all who would listen that such action would begin a runaway inflation. The legislators scoffed. In deference to public opinion they charitably enacted something they called an OPA extension law; but as one looked into its provisions, it was quickly evident that all similarity to the existing form of price control ceased with the title. The House had appalled even the lobbyists. One after another, Representatives held up their credentials of beef or cotton or oil or textiles or automobiles or hogs to introduce decontrol amendments for favorite products. In the best tradition of such displays, one log-rolled for the other. The only major amendment voted down was one expressing "sympathy to the American people"; the House was not in a merciful mood.

In the Senate, however, there was more circumspection. The politically astute conservative, Senator Robert Taft, had led the fight against control by more polished methods than his House allies. Instead of exempting individual items, he argued through provisions that took much of the power to administer prices from Bowles and his agency and placed it in the less zealous hands of the Secretary of Agriculture and a "decontrol" board. He sponsored an amendment that would set a higher base for price determinations and required that increased costs be added in computing new ceilings. With this, and an amendment by Senator Kenneth Wherry that, in effect, passed any additional increases on to the consumer, the bill went to the White House. It had been purposely held back until a few days before expiration of the old law so that the President would either have to accept a weak law or have not even the shadow of price control. Bowles resigned in disgust at the "booby-trap" amendments. Truman, against the advice of those closest to him, sent in a veto that shook Congress into rage. Not only did he state "fundamental" objections to the bill—in other words, rebuking Congress for its behavior—but he made the issue a personal one by mentioning Taft twenty-two times and accusing the Ohio senator of evolving a "sure formula for inflation."

The veto left the country suddenly deprived of controls. Prices shifted upward with a sudden but tentative jerk; in the main, increases were held back awaiting legislative decision. Congress had to act; yet, having been angered by the barbed message and driven into extended session during the peak of the midsummer heat, it sullenly declined to retract those sins of which the President said it was culpable. The Senate moved slowly while Barkley sounded out the areas of compromise. By using his most genial persuasion he finally created another bill that satisfied no one, but that could be accepted by a majority. It temporarily exempted a number of farm products, subjected them and industrial goods to the discretion of the decontrol board, set a new base—one lower than Taft's—and preserved the Taft formula of base price plus increased production costs, and preserved rent controls intact. Barkley thought the compromise "workable"; Truman reluctantly signed it and promised to call Congress into special session if the law failed.

When a special session did finally meet seventeen months later with the problem of inflation on its agenda, it paid more attention to political maneuvering than economic needs. Despite the alarming rise of the index of basic commodity prices, it postponed the matter to the regular session during the election year of 1948. But then, if the conservatives had done away with price control by legislating it into a coffin while the body was still warm, Truman's adherence to the "bulge" theory in February of 1946 had initiated the disease that led to the grave.

* * *

While Chester Bowles was becoming a four-month hero, Harry Truman continued his plodding in the field of labor relations. Unlike his days on the farm, he was not plowing straight rows. Prematurely, he had ended the life of the War Labor Board, thus leaving himself without the government's best mechanism for settling strikes. In order, his next expedients—exhortation, the Labor-Management Conference, fact-finding and personal intervention—had proved ineffective.

By April tumultuous strikes in the coal fields and on the railroads fanned the warm flames under Truman's chair. The miners quit first and stayed out the longest; under the leadership of John L. Lewis they got essentially what they wanted—an increase, a welfare fund supported by a royalty on each ton of coal mined, and paid vacations. The agreement was made under the federal auspices and the government assumed operation of the soft-coal mines; but Lewis forgot his Republican words of "free enterprise" and "free collective bargaining." For him and for his union, the settlement, no matter how arranged, was a victory.

With the railroad trainmen and locomotive engineers, the case was different. They had negotiated under the law for a long time. They had indicated a willingness to accept the settlement outlined by John Steelman, the President's representative. At Truman's request, they postponed the strike for five days. But the railroad managements refused the terms suggested. The strike call went out; members of two of the most conservative of American labor unions quit work, asking for higher wages and changes in the book of rules governing their jobs.

The labor leaders were stubborn. They believed they had just grievances; they thought they had a right to the President's support. Less than two years before, at Chicago, their endorsement of Harry S. Truman for Vice-President had been useful to the Democratic party's bosses in persuading the CIO and AF of L to back the little Senator from Missouri after Henry Wallace's bubble had burst. President Harry S. Truman, however, had recently seen too many newspaper cartoons and editorials and received too many White House callers asking why he didn't do something about the strikes. The inner circle was suggesting that his slipping popularity would jump if he put the unions in their places. John Snyder was convinced that labor was ruining reconversion; he wanted strikes stopped for six months. The President, after months of frustration, was tense.

On the second day of the strike, while the life of a highly mobile nation stalled to a literal walk, the newspapers juxtaposed black headlines of the railroad tie-up with a picture of the Chief Executive happily eating ice cream at an official reception. With negotiations still deadlocked, his tension mounted to anger; he moved toward swift, relentless action. To the public, he delivered a radio address castigating "these two men" —A. F. Whitney and Alvanley Johnston, the union leaders—for stifling the country's economy and aiding inflation.

The next day, he went to the House to address a joint session and ask for a law. He wanted temporary power, lasting only so long as the other war powers delegated by Congress, to deal with strikes. He asked for permission to take over struck industries vital to the nation's economy, to put the profits of government operation into the Treasury, to deprive strikers of their seniority rights if they would not go back to work, to draft them into the Army. No president had ever asked for so stringent a labor law. In point of legislation, on that Saturday afternoon of May 25, 1946, the United States came its closest to totalitarianism.

To make the trains run on time, though proclaiming he would "always be a friend to labor," Truman had somehow overlooked a serious ethical question: can one segment of the population be forced to work, against its will and under conditions it deems intolerable, for the convenience of the majority?

During the speech to Congress, a note was handed to Truman stating that the strike had been settled on his terms. He passed the information on to his listeners and the radio audience amid wild cheering by the congressmen. There is reason to believe he knew of the union's capitulation in advance. That morning Whitney and Johnston had sent such a letter to the White House; two senators, Morse of Oregon and Pepper of Florida, had assisted in its composition. But the dramatic announcement from the speaker's rostrum helped.

Without thinking, the House whooped through the President's request. In the Senate, the rampage ended abruptly. Barkley, without heart for his task, started the measure going. Liberal Democrats were against the legislation; Republicans were prepared to torture the last iota of political advantage from the Majority Leader. The real leadership passed to Taft. Questions on civil liberties probed at the unhappy Barkley. The "draft labor" clause became the cross he bore. He was asked about courts-martial and firing squads; legal arguments, constitutional arguments, ethical arguments taunted him. The administration forces sunk to a record low. For one strange moment in American politics, Harry Truman had succeeded, as the *Nation* pointed out, in uniting almost every shade of opinion against himself—Republicans, most Democrats, Communists, Socialists. Only the White House circle, a small group of southerners, a loyal servant like Alben Barkley and a few party regulars stayed with him.

The reasoning of Taft knocked out Truman's plan. The atmosphere Truman created was turned to other purposes. Lying dormant was the House-approved Case labor bill, written by a Republican congressman from an agricultural district. It contained no conscription clause or reversions of profit to the Federal Treasury. But it provided a permanent code, one that would outlast any granting of emergency powers. In its provisions it foreshadowed the Taft-Hartley law of 1947. The Ohio Senator hammered this bill through the upper house. A remorseful Harry Truman vetoed it, and saw his veto hold. He had the excuse that this was permanent legislation, while his own would have been temporary.

Still, the damage had been done. The large industrial labor wing of the Democratic party developed a suspicion of him it never lost. The confidence of the liberals was shaken; second-thoughts by the country perceived the dangers of his request. The ineptitude of advisers who were also Presidential poker companions and jesters was thrown into bold relief upon the background of the shifting struggle. Politically, too, the request had been a mistake. For, though the first cheers in the House had come from both sides, the Republican cheers lasted longest; the President was asking his fellow Democrats in Congress to give him a law their Democratic constituents did not want. In effect, he was giving them a choice between himself, as the nominal chief of the party, and the party itself. When they rejected him he lost stature.

Finally, he blundered on the tactical side. He diverted attention from his own permanent solution, the fact-finding commissions, and he turned the major body of price-control supporters from an offensive to preserve OPA to a defensive in beating off labor legislation. On his side, he lost both battles; on theirs, they won an impermanent victory in fighting against the proposed labor laws, but they lost the campaign for the economics of control. More still, Truman gave encouragement to those elements toward which he was basically unsympathetic, the conservatives. Probably at that point, the conservative faith secured a majority of adherents in the electorate. Certainly, in Congress, conservatism's ranks gained the strength necessary to push through its measures and to ruin the Executive's legislative program.

Two months later, when Congress adjourned, only one-third of Truman's proposals had become law; the more important two-thirds had been discarded. It has been pointed out by Professor Wilfred Binkley that while .333 is a good batting average in baseball, in politics it is below mediocrity. The public's reaction to Harry Truman was in agreement with that of Congress. In July, 1946, only forty-three per cent thought he was doing a competent job.

3. ATOMIC POLITICS

The scientists who probed and utilized the enormous strength of the atom also presented to the public a natural force that required control by a society that only dimly understood the meaning of what had been discovered. The bombs that fell on Hiroshima and Nagasaki demonstrated not only the most destructive weapon men had yet devised to fight their wars; they also raised greater fears and questions that both blurred and accentuated national sovereignties.

In the first months after the practical examples of atomic energy's uses, the general public seemed numb to its possible consequences. Scientists and philosophers were thoughtful and doubting of the benefits of their contribution. Diplomats, at first, consigned it to the unmentionable. They spoke of peace, but. . . . Economic prophets spoke of the prospects of postwar production, postwar trade, postwar inventions and commodities; they spoke brightly and cheerfully. But. . . . In the War Department, there was a deep appreciation of the revolution that impended upon strategy and of the new weapon's value. In the House of Representatives, the first reaction of politicians was a carelessly drawn bill demanding the death penalty for anyone divulging the secrets of the bomb. Among others, any thoughts which related the new force to international affairs hung on a pendulum that oscillated between impractical vision and terrible fear.

The first two positive ideas—those of the military and of the congressmen—became the first to be joined in a positive approach to the new problem. The War Department developed a plan; Representatives May and Johnson gave it their names and the backing of the Military Affairs Committee of which May was chairman. None of the committee members had read the official Smyth report on atomic energy when they approved the plan. They had heard only the most indefinite testimony from War Department spokesmen and conservative scientists when they gave the bill to the country. Atomic energy development, of course, was to remain the possession of the United States government, but control would rest in military hands; "free" research would be stringently restricted; and secrecy would be enforced severely.

Naturally, among scientists, the men perhaps best qualified to understand the implications of the discovery, there was strong dislike for the May-Johnson bill. But their protests were largely ignored by the House committee. They were treated curtly, even brusquely, and upbraided because they had given the politicians a problem that appeared to have no roots in political experience. The amateur scientific approach to the politics of governing natural force was brushed aside by the professionals who conducted the hearings; as a last resort, the legislators told themselves and the public that the scientists were "radicals," that scientists' notions on politics were untrustworthy.

By inference, the committee was helped rather than hindered by the President. In early October he handed to Congress the sole responsibility for developing a national policy on atomic energy and spoke of negotiations for international control. While he added some words on the possibilities of directing the new power into channels of private enterprise through a system of licensing, and while he emphasized the dictum of the scientists that theoretical knowledge of nuclear physics was international, the total effect of his statement was—by giving Congress its head—a kind of left-handed endorsement of Andrew Jackson May's proposals.

A few weeks later, on his vacation tour of Missouri, Kentucky and Tennessee, he seemed to reinforce his approval of what was happening in the House. For, in the informal surroundings of a fishing lodge, where the chief staple of conversation had been small-town courthouse politics and the chief diversions poker and moderate bourbon drinking, Harry Truman told an astonished press conference (and did not himself catch the significance of what he said) that the United States would keep its "know-how" on the making of bombs to itself. Adding these statements to the fact that Secretary of War Patterson, the only member of the administration who had testified before the House committee, plainly liked the May-Johnson formula, the conclusion to be drawn was that the President, however much he eschewed policy-making by himself and donated it to Congress and international commissions, would accept, without protest, a law providing for military control.

In the Senate, however, the case was wholly different. Senator Brien McMahon, a freshman from Connecticut, had drawn up a bill that looked toward a civilian commission in charge of developing atomic energy for both war and peace. His plan envisioned not military direction but merely military advice. Like the House proposal, its application stopped at the nation's boundaries, as was its constitutional limit, but it presented a law that could more easily be fitted within the framework of any international controls that might be developed in the future. So too, McMahon's provisions for research were broader and his injunctions of secrecy looser. But where comparisons became most evident were in the methods his committee used in developing a law. Months were spent by the members in private study; witnesses of all kinds were heard at considerable length, and some recalled to amplify conflicting testimony. Problems were explored from the points of view of science, politics, ethics and economics; amendments were drawn where one of the committee, like Senator Vandenberg, for example, wished to tighten the security clauses or clarify wordings.

Finally, McMahon showed the qualities of his generalship. At one crucial point he secured a letter from the President that applauded civilian control, and thereby dealt a sharp blow to the generals, particularly General Leslie Groves of the Manhattan District, who were lobbying for military rule. At another time when the press ballooned an international atom bomb scare from the size of a pea to that of a basketball, the Senator held out against the proponents of army control until they subsided into accepting a military liaison committee, without power on the commission that was to establish policy.

Amended and clarified, the McMahon bill passed the Senate after only two hours of debate; with five months of committee testimony behind it and available for reading, there were few grounds for argument. In the House, however, Representative May seized it and would not release it. It seemed doomed to languish in the Military Affairs Committee indefinitely. Important as the bill was, a combination of rules and the powers of a chairman would have prevented its reappearance. The President, having scrupulously turned atomic energy over to Congress and being caught, in his diminishing prestige, in the angry debates over strikes and OPA, made no moves to force action.

Light broke through unexpectedly when Truman's old War Investigating Committee, now under Senator Mead, delved into evidences of corruption in war contracts that involved May's illegitimate use of office and illegal acceptance of money. Suddenly at a disadvantage, the Kentucky Representative released the Senate's atomic energy bill stuffed with May-Johnson amendments. In as much confusion as its committee members, the House passed the amended bill amid dark accusations that McMahon wanted to give the bomb to Russia or "to the scientists." By the time a joint conference committee met, however, the disclosures on May, complete with pictures, broke the resistance of the lower chamber. In its final version, the Atomic Energy Law placed control in a five-man civilian commission, placed research in the hands of the scientists, who were freed of all but necessary security measures, and encouraged work on potential peacetime usages. The President's appointment in late 1946 of David Lilienthal to head the commission was in the spirit of the Act, as was the announcement in September of 1947 that radioactive isotopes would be made available for international experimentation on cancer.

* * *

The performance of Harry Truman in the political problems called forth by the scientific harnessing of atomic energy was typical of much of his approach to the presidential office. The McMahon bill was but an example. Being a strong respecter of the conception that Congress made the laws, he passed the entire problem over to legislative discretion. Months later, when civilian versus military control was a subject of debate, his bare endorsement of the Senate measure was more in the form of a personal opinion than a guiding expression of Executive leadership. There was no denying that, at the beginning of the debate, he was respectful of the position the War Department advanced and seemed prepared to accept the law the generals wanted.

That Congress was constitutionally charged with writing the law in no way diminished the President's responsibility for advising on what kind of a law might be desirable. Ultimately, by the nature of the problem, once the general conditions of control had been set down in a statute, the Executive's place in administering the law would be broader and necessarily freer than is usually the case. Furthermore, since the public owned the process and because atomic energy was a national resource capable of working a technological and economic revolution as well as a military one, its rather full discussion before the public was in order.

Much of the attention of the people and the press was centered on the immediacies of strikes and prices. Yet, the disposition to be made of atomic energy was unquestionably the more important long-run issue. The prestige of the presidency offered its holder the leadership of public opinion. It carried a responsibility for defining issues, for clearing away the myth and rumor and misapprehension that surround a secretive subject. The control of atomic energy was an issue upon which the first man in the government was required to have a point of view. By contributing little to the discussion Truman removed himself from it. He stood not above the debate, but to the side of it. If he had conclusions, he studiously avoided presenting them; if he was aware of the significance of the question, he communicated little of that feeling to the public. That the country got the law it did was largely the work of McMahon and Vandenberg.

This tendency of permitting others to appear to lead the administration became more and more striking as the country moved away from its war psychology, and as the memory of Roosevelt faded. At Potsdam, Truman had performed pretty much in the manner of the one-man government to which the country had grown accustomed. But after Potsdam, little in the conduct of American foreign relations bore evidence that his hand was doing the guiding. Secretary of State James Byrnes not only represented the United States at diplomatic conferences and spoke his country's words; he appeared to be a member of an informal board of strategy that charted America's policy. Others with almost as much power in determining direction were Senators Vandenberg and Connally and a number of men in the State Department. In exploring the untried forest of the international control of atomic energy, leadership came from such men as David Lilienthal,

Dean Acheson and Bernard Baruch. At the United Nations, when Byrnes himself was not doing the speaking, American delegates were beating a path somewhere between their own convictions and their respect for the wishes of the Senate and the State Department.

Thus, coming after a man who kept a tight hold on the reins of government and policy, Truman's abrupt shift to another method and different men brought on a speedy revision of American foreign policy. Not one of those to whom he delegated his leadership could be considered an heir of Franklin Roosevelt. The Republicans on the board of strategy were men of fairly fixed ideas, and although F.D.R. showed indications of granting them concessions in his postwar diplomacy, it may be doubted that they would have been given quite the voice they attained. Certainly, under Truman, the words of Vandenberg and John Foster Dulles were regarded as near-official.

Almost without obtruding, the Chief Executive permitted his board of strategy to handle foreign affairs. Occasionally he spoke publicly; usually, what he said was couched in extremely general terms. For instance, in early October 1945 he told a county-fair audience at Caruthersville, Missouri, his orientation to international relations: "We are going to accept [the] golden rule, and we are going forward to meet our destiny, which I think Almighty God intended us to have—and we are going to be leaders." It is true the occasion was one of revelry and the audience was composed of Truman's type of people—small-town Legionnaires and home folks. Still, it was on this same trip that he announced his decision to keep the atomic bomb secret, and his speeches throughout the tour were well covered by the press.

Coming on the heels of the first unsuccessful Foreign Ministers Conference at London, his remarks were a combination of that religious righteousness and righteous nationalism that had previously made American diplomacy unpopular in European capitals. It would certainly breed little good will in Moscow. Interpreted by the American mind, Truman's statement meant little but a reassertion of those platitudes American politicians habitually use to fill up speaking time; to the Russian mind, it sounded like a simplified version of what Byrnes had been telling Molotov.

A few weeks later the occasion was decidedly formal as Truman spoke on Navy Day, before 1,000,000 people in New York's Central Park and over four radio networks and television. This was to have been his great speech on foreign policy; he and his assistants had worked on it carefully; it had been advertised as a major address for the times. Instead, it was a disappointment—to the listeners because its thoughts were pedantically unoriginal, to the President because of its unenthusiastic reception. The generalities were the old ones, said not only by the incumbent Chief Executive but by many before him; they pronounced for freedom of the seas, the Monroe Doctrine, hemispheric co-operation, the peaceful intentions of the United States, and all the rest. There was little quarrel with what he said or the sincerity he gave to expounding the traditional maxims his country applied to international relations. But it had been expected that current policy would be suggested or outlined. If the maxims were the steel latticework that supported foreign policy, the people nevertheless desired to see the brick and concrete that surrounded them to give the policy character. This Truman had not provided.

From the New York speech until March, 1947, the President, on the whole, held aloof from direct involvement. Periodically, he asserted at press conferences that James Byrnes's policy was the administration's policy; when pressed, he added testily that without administration endorsement there would be no policy. When he reported to Congress or remarked briefly on world conditions, his contributions were generalities outside the day-to-day events. His unwillingness to discuss future plans and directions was marked. Aside from hopeful comments on "collective security," on the success of the United Nations, on peace and prosperity, he ventured no opinions.

*   *   *

It is, of course, too soon to evaluate either the achievements or failures of Truman's method. Nor, at any one point in time, is it fair to stamp final judgment on how closely the means coincide with the stated objectives, especially when the means are in the process of evolution. But it is possible to identify some of the turns made by the policy and to chart some of its attitudes.

Perhaps one of the most revealing characteristics of the period was the confident heralding of a "bi-partisan" foreign policy, a notion presumably based on the fact that both Democratic and Republican politicians were in nominal equality on the board of strategy; and that, therefore, policy was removed from the realm of politics. In reality, bipartisanship had nothing to do with basic formulations. It did possibly cut down a certain amount of marginal carping by those Republicans included among the directors, but it did not nor could it reasonably have been expected to still the criticisms of large segments of either party—the isolationist wing of the Republicans, the internationalist or "anti-imperialist" or "pro-Russian" wing of the Democrats. Actually, party politics stop at the nation's boundaries because that is where their meaning ends. Neither party has held a monopoly on a particular view of foreign policy. Each may have tendencies that pull it toward one side; but in power, each accommodates to the other, forging its direction out of a complex of necessities, external circumstances, popular demands, unassailable facts, and interpretations of national interest.

Thus, the Truman foreign policy—to give it a title, for the sake of convenience—stemmed not from the American party system but from the influences of the times as interpreted by and implemented by a number of men who were essentially conservative. It is unnecessary to dissect the anatomy of conservatism in order to discover its underlying assumptions as they related the United States to the world. They are visible and on the surface. They include a conviction of America's righteousness, a profound belief in capitalism and its glorious future, a high degree of nationalism tempered by certain concessions to a highly integrated globe. As such, the assumptions provided a point from which conservatism started to develop a policy that could meet the responsibilities of the United States in rationalizing the control of atomic energy, in leading the United Nations, and in working out a relationship with the Soviet Union, the only other country that nearly approached it in resources and political power.

But Russia quickly became the hinge upon which all other policy turned. And though the construction of the peace depended upon the concord of the two countries, the breach was opened with the first meeting of foreign ministers at London in September 1945. From then on it widened. Some diplomatic necessities, like writing peace treaties with the defeated satellites of the Axis, were accomplished. In spheres of major responsibility, however, a stalemate developed with each country using all but its military resources to hold off the other. In a world where, in 1945, scientists predicted that another sovereignty could develop an atom bomb in three to five years, and engineers conceded the same possibility in ten to twenty years, neither the United States nor the Soviet Union seemed able or willing to swing away from a mutual antagonism that was following a familiar and predictable pattern toward war. An event in Yugoslavia irritated the United States and was interpreted as a Red move toward global domination; an event in Italy or occupied Japan exacerbated the Soviet press and diplomats into viewing all as a piece of an anti-communist design by imperialist capitalism. Six thousand miles apart, the presses of the two powers copied and further colored the inelegant charges of their governments. In conferences, the cry of "you're another" raised clouds of protest and stubbornness; the accusations of obstructionism and illegal unilateral action ended initial amiability.

The Truman policy took shape in fits and jerks. As it moved on, it picked up in its baggage larger and larger increments of anti-communism. Anti-communism was readily transmuted into anti-Sovietism as the Russians gave what Americans took to be evidences of intransigence. (Though, from the Soviet view, its demands were reasonable claims for recognition of its newly won position as a world power and of its right to share equally in establishing the pattern of postwar life.) It should be noted that the pressures toward anti-communism were not impelled by Russia's attitude alone, although the foreign policy spokesmen found it convenient to say so. Anti-communism is a latent attitude in the American consciousness, and one held close to the surface. It not only antedates the Russian Revolution, but since then has been a theme steadily played upon by a number of opinion-makers. Although there can be no doubt that many honest conservatives and not a few honest liberals can give valid reasons for their opposition to the doctrine, it is equally true that a large section of the public, without respect to its partisan beliefs, has neither a knowledge of the system nor information and understanding of the Soviet Union. That body has only a hatred which, at the proper time under proper prompting, is easily inflamed.

The domestic restlessness of the postwar era projected such an atmosphere. Communism, different and execrable to the huge majority, became immediately suspect. It strained the limits of toleration, and in some cases the limits of rationality. To an extent not precisely measurable, it received the blame for troubles at home. It served the same purpose it had in the 1920's—that of an alien scapegoat on which could be diverted the rancor brewed by economic worries, political uncertainties and ethical confusions. The emergence of Soviet Russia as a great power and that country's position as the fount of communism exaggerated the fears; in turn, the size of the fears obscured the fact that, to most Americans, the original basis of anti-communist feeling is, at bottom, emotional and arises not from international problems but out of a home-grown attitude.[2]

When restlessness was heightened at the slow going in the council of foreign ministers and the United Nations, the blame naturally

[2] Because this book is a study of the United States and the courses of some of its presidents, no comparable space can be given to exploring Russian anti-capitalism and Russian irrationalities in Soviet attitudes toward the United States. It seems, however, that the obverse of the American case can be applied to the Soviet Union. Yet, if a moral conclusion is to be drawn, just as two wrongs do not make a right, two ignorances do not make the beginning of wisdom.

shifted to Russia. When Molotov's or Gromyko's ideas taxed the patience of conservatives or collided with the premises of the conservative faith, anti-communist beliefs flared into an anti-Soviet fire. James Byrnes, fundamentally a conservative but also a politician's politician and a compromiser, essayed to apply his famous senatorial technique to international relations, and failed. His trading at Moscow in December 1945 satisfied him, and apparently the Russians, but not the Senate or the press feeding on anti-communist oats. Sensitive to his sometime colleagues' thoughts and the straws of American opinion, he reluctantly passed to harder bargaining. Senator Vandenberg, whose recent conversion to internationalism contained the deepest suspicion of the Soviet Union, approved the Secretary of State's new line.

The "get tough" policy was born. Designed to combine "patience with firmness," it slowed rather than speeded the settlement of postwar problems. The Russians, too, got tougher. Byrnes, no longer a compromiser, was out of his element; his torrid speeches and reports fitted well into the atmosphere at home. But his effectiveness as a diplomat decreased.

How much Truman understood the implications of "firmness" is unknown. He is not a man who enjoys hating or likes being hated. During most of 1946 he was mainly concerned with domestic matters; his rare statements on foreign policy were too general for either identification with immediate negotiations or to define a trend. Possibly he was hedging.

But three circumstances demonstrate his acquiescence in the policy. First, his growing dependence upon military men in diplomatic posts manifested both his profound respect for soldiers and his appointment of men who are, by and large, intensely nationalistic. Second was his journey to Westminster College in Fulton, Missouri, where he and Winston Churchill received honorary degrees—a type of ceremony the President seems to enjoy immensely. This time the distinction was a double one; for not only was he, a man who had not gone to a real college because he could not afford the cost, given recognition for his rise, but the hero of England's resistance shared the platform with him. Harry Truman, pleased at having arranged this brilliant event for a small college in a small Missouri town, introduced his guest with enormous respect: "I know he will have something constructive to say."

Whether constructive or not, what the old warrior did say on that March afternoon reverberated beyond the confines of the college's gymnasium. He hit at Russia with every verbal rock that could be thrown. A by-product of the speech was his contribution of the phrase "iron curtain." Having called for continued secrecy on atomic power "in this still agitated and un-united world," having presented his evidence and expressed his doubts on "the limits, if any, to [Russia's and the Communist International's] expansive and proselytizing tendencies," he advocated that Britain and the United States preserve the "intimate" military co-operation they had developed under the stress of World War II. He asked that a "special relationship," perhaps looking toward the "principle of common citizenship," be effected between the English-speaking peoples. The overtones were somber in the extreme. With his magnificent command of rhetoric, Churchill did not request but practically demanded the closest kind of military and political alliance against communism.

On the platform Harry Truman applauded. But outside Fulton, the clarion call jarred rather than mobilized. Much of the press on both sides of the Atlantic showed greater disturbance at the Churchillian proposals than at the diplomatic stalemate. Back in Washington the President lost only a little of his jauntiness; he said he had not known what his illustrious visitor was going to say. Technically, this might have been correct, although mimeographed copies of the speech were given to the newspaper reporters the previous evening. Yet, even if Truman had not seen a draft, he must have known Churchill's opinions and received indications of Churchill's forthcoming remarks from their conversations. Furthermore, after the event, *Newsweek* reported the ideas to coincide with those the President entertained and spoke of in private.

Within the State Department, the earth under Byrnes trembled. Just back from Paris after a session of profitless debate with Russia, he was in an uncomfortable position, that of following Vandenberg's insistence on firmness and having to explain away the extreme Churchill advocated while Truman sat listening. Congenitally the Secretary did not like his task; a compromiser moves slowly from one step to the next; he purposely lingers over each, and does not omit a single tread. He assumes nothing to be inevitable; he puts his faith in men's equanimity rather than their processes of systematic logic. What Winston Churchill suggested, no matter how logical as the end result of firmness, was, to Byrnes, a headlong rush. He therefore scotched talk of an alliance with either Britain or Russia. "We propose," he said, "to stand with the United Nations." His nervousness, his irritation and his words disclosed a worried attitude to which Harry Truman, the delegator of power, seemed immune.

In September 1946 the President, after a summer of OPA troubles, became involved once more. Byrnes had grown appropriately granite-like during the intervening months. His relations with Truman had developed tension, but the Secretary still had his office and assumed that his chief supported him, whatever the difficulties of the policy being carried out. But inside the official family there was discontent. Secretary of Commerce Henry Wallace, the last surviving New Dealer in the cabinet, had kept a long official silence. His thoughts, however, had been active. He believed stern words were neither the proper way of dealing with Soviet Russia nor an insurance of lasting peace; he was convinced that the Baruch-State Department plan for international atomic controls was faulty and could be improved. To the President, he confided his misgivings, in cabinet meetings, in conversations and in a letter dated July 23rd. He decided to speak out on the Russian issue to a pro-administration political rally of liberals and radicals in New York on September 12th. The decision was approved by Truman and Hannegan, both of whom understood the worth of the votes Wallace could hold to the Democratic party.

Then followed a fantastic series of happenings—highly comic to Republican observers, extremely disconcerting to the foreign policy-makers, undoubtedly painful to the major participants. On September 10th, Wallace and Truman reviewed the speech together. On the afternoon of the 12th, with the talk already released to the newspapers, the President told a press conference that he agreed with it in its entirety, that he saw no conflict between Wallace's remarks and Byrnes's actions in Paris. In the evening, the Secretary delivered his oral message to a crowd, part of which hissed his words against Russia's expansionism in louder decibles than it cheered his criticisms of the American type of firmness. The 13th saw editorial comment rage at Henry Wallace for what he said about toughness; half-heartedly or not at all was mention made of Wallace's criticisms of the Soviets or the mixed reception with which his words were received.

On Saturday, September 14th, President Truman, smiling and physically relaxed, called in the press to say there had been a "natural misunderstanding." His answer on Thursday had connoted something he had not meant to convey; what he really intended to give was a mere approval of his Secretary's right to make the speech. In reassurance to the fulminating newspapers and to the stunned American delegation in Paris, as well as to those Americans who really thought there was significance in his comment of two days before, he announced, "There has been no change in the established foreign policy of our government."

This stumbling in search of a prescription for relief served to content only the President. Rumblings of anger came in from overseas, from Senators Vandenberg and Connally, from sources close to a suddenly quiet James Byrnes. At home, the transparency of the President's dodge still fascinated minds and tongues.

Tuesday piled crisis on crisis. Word came that Drew Pearson, the widely syndicated columnist, had secured a copy of the July letter and would publish it. In a frenzy, the White House and the Commerce Department released the document first. It was more closely reasoned than the speech and consequently did more damage. If the speech and the first press conference had pulled the props away from Byrnes and left him apparently negotiating for himself alone, the letter opened a trapdoor under Harry Truman. It took away the possible excuse that he had been inattentive to Wallace's ideas. Furthermore the letter included criticism of the atomic energy proposals and of the military influence in foreign relations. Bernard Baruch, Secretary of the Navy Forrestal and Secretary of War Patterson all cried aloud. On Wednesday, Wallace and the President conferred for two hours and issued their joint statement: the Secretary of Commerce was not to speak until after the peace conference had ended. Wallace also said he expected to remain in the cabinet. Forty-eight hours later, the office was empty and Henry Wallace, private citizen, was relieved of his pledge.

In the interval, Truman and the United States delegation had traded words by teletype. While it may be doubted that Byrnes and the Senators actually demanded the Commerce Secretary's head—if only because such demands are not made of presidents—there was a pointed request from Paris that Washington give the delegation positive backing, and not simply approval for the duration of the conference. Otherwise, to Truman's horror, Byrnes stated he would resign immediately. That night Truman wrestled with his problem. The next morning, in a two-minute telephone conversation, he asked Wallace to resign.

If Truman salvaged the policy of firmness he nevertheless had made life miserable for his delegates in Europe and had made their work more harrowing. At the same time, he had managed to explode a political bomb in Democratic ranks, a bomb that shattered more than the public career of Henry Wallace. In the showdown, those who agreed with the Commerce Secretary and those distrustful of the conservatism of Byrnes and the senators lost heart. Nothing could cover the sheer clumsiness of the episode. Wallace's exit from the government was dignified, but Truman's continued presence in office was hardly an index of his prestige.

Again, Harry Truman turned away from the sour apples of foreign relations. The sweet ones of domestic politics that he knew and liked were ripening. The mid-term elections were two and one-half months away.

JUST as cabinet government had, in George Washington's presidency, been unable to hold within a single administration the contrasting points of view of Alexander Hamilton and Thomas Jefferson, so cabinet government under Harry Truman proved unable to comprehend the divergent elements of the Democratic coalition. For at both ends of American political history it was to be found that while pieces of work may be parceled out to individual officers of the administration, the scope of the problems thus attacked may transcend a government department or the concern of the man entrusted with the work.

All presidents have relied, to a greater or lesser extent, upon their official families. That Harry Truman turned to his was not unusual. Plainly the times required that government play a large part in directing the traffic in domestic and international affairs. While it may be mooted whether the President should have assumed the dominant role, there can be no doubt that a unitary policy was needed. If Truman chose to place the creation of policy in other hands, that need for unity remained unchanged. Heretofore strong cabinet governments had usually existed when Congress was dominant. At such times the legislature set down policy and jealously watched its administration. Secretaries of State were continually bedeviled by the Senate; Secretaries of the Treasury performed under the surveillance of the House. During Washington's years, when the cabinet members laid so many of the foundations of the American republic and when the working relationships of the major branches of government, established under a separation of powers theory, had yet to be defined, the first President was nevertheless the chief figure in his administration, both by virtue of his personal prestige and the unity of purpose he demanded in establishing a national government.

When Truman declined to assume all the vestments of presidential power left by Franklin Roosevelt he was still faced with a need for policy. When he broke down power and allotted some of it among his cabinet members and tendered the rest to the Seventy-ninth Congress, he inaugurated a unique experiment in American government. As events turned out the Congress rejected the executive program and formulated none of its own. In essence it kept that negative constitutional power it had maintained throughout the New Deal. It disdained the offer of positive responsibility. By the process of elimination, therefore, positive government passed to Truman's ministry—Byrnes, Snyder, Hannegan, Bowles, Wallace and Schwellenbach; to Steelman, Allen and the other men of the courthouse set. It was incumbent upon them to fashion a unified policy. Their disagreements on a price-wage formula, on OPA and controls, on labor problems, on the conduct of foreign affairs show they did not. Rather, numerous viewpoints flourished in contradiction to one another. The President, either oblivious to the differences or fondly hoping to preserve some sort of coalition, seemed hesitant in choosing among them.

In a parliamentary government such indecisiveness and absence of unity would undoubtedly result in the fall of a ministry. Under the American system it resulted in faltering efforts, an impression of ineffectiveness and the flight of leadership from the Executive branch—out of government, in fact, and into the hands of labor and business and the pressure groups. A sorry light was cast upon the Truman administration. The spectacle raised questions of the men selected by the President to act in his stead; it raised questions of their methods. Eventually it raised questions of their policies.

1. REPUBLICAN RESURGENCE

Henry Wallace's protest was merely the most pointed example of the difficulties of government by cabinet. In its timing and execution—both of which could hardly have been more poorly staged—it gave the critics all the resources they needed in hitting at the administration and diverting the public's thoughts from the type of issues that are nominally supposed to be discussed in campaigns. From Truman's standpoint the episode was unfortunate in all its implications. By September his popularity had slipped well below the fifty per cent mark. Now, it fell further. Aside from the impossible situation the President got himself into by his offhand endorsement and his bumbling retraction, the circumstances surrounding Wallace's departure caused a queasiness among some liberals and a portion of the CIO, both of which had not yet fully recovered from the "labor draft" proposal and the loss on OPA. Politically Truman could not afford to lose them. In disavowing his Secretary of Commerce he may not have thought he lost many votes, but he did lose a particularly active group which, under other conditions, would have worked enthusiastically in the autumn elections.

A second consequence to Truman and the Democratic party was

the use to which the conservative press put the explosive communist issue. Having satisfied themselves that Henry Wallace was an advance agent of the Kremlin who had sat in the councils of two presidents, it followed, by some twist of logic, that those with whom he had been in contact were rendered leprous. How many votes were made by this kind of argument cannot be accurately ascertained. But the Republicans and the press supporting them shouted Red Russia long and loud; the very persistence with which they used the cry suggests that they were confident of its effect, whatever its truth. That Wallace's position was most assuredly not Truman's nor the administration's was beside the point. The aim of the Republicans was to win the country. In that primary business, the legitimate education of the electorate by the contending political parties was left to chance. For a decade conservatism had denounced Roosevelt's New Deal as "radical" and "communistic"; at last, it had an atmosphere in which it confidently believed the label would stick.

Yet, the Red charge, when applied side-long to Harry Truman and full-face to some of his crew (usually unspecified), counted definitely with only a fringe. For most speakers and most voters the anti-communist barrage served as a generator that heated minds to receive other impassioned criticisms. It was here that conservatism made its telling points.

Actually, by virtue of combination with the southern Democrats, the Republicans had held a negative control of the federal government on certain issues since 1938. Their objective in 1946 was, as in previous campaigns, positive control—that is, the power to write all the laws and pass on all appointments. Still, in 1946, there was a difference. The same predictions of victory came out of GOP headquarters, but this time Republicans believed those statements were accurate analyses, not the usual empty releases that in previous years had been sent out to bolster the courage of the rank and file. They perceived sure signs of national unrest, not only in the strikes but in the public reaction to them. They heard the mutterings of housewives over shortages and prices, and of small businessmen at the cost of labor and the scarcities in materials and goods. They listened as veterans criticized the postwar United States for retaining some of the defects noticeable before they left and for seemingly having added some others prior to their return, particularly a dearth of well-paying jobs and a housing shortage.

To meet all these protests with a fully integrated national program would have taxed the greatest ingenuity. The Truman administration had addressed itself to the problems; but with the dissenting choir sounding ever louder and as the problems obviously remained, the method employed and the solutions offered were manifestly unsatisfactory. Yet the Republicans, though vociferous in the ranks of the protestants, advocated nothing that could be construed as alternative policy. In all likelihood they could not, without serious division among themselves. By Vandenberg's presence on the foreign relations team they neatly escaped the dilemma posed by the unrepentant or unchanged isolationism a majority of the party in Congress had indicated since the end of the war.

Nowhere was internal contradiction more eloquent than in the case of the non-partisan Wagner-Ellender-Taft Bill. Passed by the Senate, this proposed long-range program for low-cost housing was kept trussed up in procedural knots tied by Republican members of the House Banking and Currency Committee. The party was unable to decide between a moderately liberal plan of federal spending and the assertions of the real-estate and construction lobbies that exclusively private enterprise could do the job better. The same was true of almost every piece of domestic legislation introduced with the blessing of the White House. Thus in the case of the OPA, where the Republicans obstructed passage as long as they could, they riddled the original law with amendments which were later found impossible to administer; then, they muddied the waters by voting overwhelmingly for the bill and thereby claimed credit for supporting price control.

It was not in the Republican strategy to point with pride to the party's conservatism. That record could speak for itself, if anyone was interested in it. The keynote of the campaign was destructive criticism. They simply asked the cryptic question, "Had enough?" In the sense that the offices being sought were local, they had an advantage. A candidate denounced the deeds of the Democratic administration with impunity; the President was powerless to answer the charges of every Republican House and Senate aspirant. In each district, therefore, and in each state, Republicans fired blast on blast at the Democrats. And the Democrats, bearing the weight of the mixed record of the Seventy-ninth Congress where they had held a titular majority and the confused record of the Executive, were called upon to make too many explanations.

Having leveled an all-out attack, the GOP made no pretense at defense. Having estimated that the temper of the country was against the government both for what had been done and what had not been done, Republicans determined to funnel the blame toward the direction it could be most easily centralized—the White House. Their tactic was to wait for the President to make mistakes, to goad him into as many political blunders as possible. Their wait was not long.

Every political lever on which Harry Truman put his hand seemed to function in reverse. During the summer he endorsed Enos Axtell, a regular party man, running in the Democratic primary of Kansas City's Fifth Congressional District against Representative Roger Slaughter, a conservative. Slaughter, as a member of the House Rules Committee and by his votes on roll calls, had been invaluable to those who helped scuttle the President's domestic recommendations and make life at the White House unpleasant. In announcing his decision to enter the purge actively, Truman said of the congressman, "If he's right, I'm wrong." The CIO's Political Action Committee already thought the Chief Executive was right and was working hard for Axtell, a circumstance that led Slaughter to pronounce Truman its "prisoner." But labor's individual efforts were insufficient. Worried, the President called on Jim Pendergast, the nephew of Boss Tom, to resurrect the decayed power of the old machine in Axtell's behalf. One last time the old bunch got out a large enough vote in their "regular" wards to defeat the obstructive incumbent. But in victory, they had reverted to tricks Missourians had grown unaccustomed to and become moral about since Tom Pendergast's decline. On election day, the machine creaked too loudly; its workings awoke accusations of fraud which, though never proved legally, brought back memories of Harry Truman's associations with the Pendergasts, memories that would better have been kept undisturbed.[1]

The pyrrhic victory in Kansas City paled in comparison to the hot potatoes Congress had thrust on the President in its act extending the OPA. During the six summer weeks of 1946 without the agency, prices had jumped toward inflation. The United States, which through the mouths of its congressional spokesmen had voiced ungenerous words about giving food to others while it reluctantly donated funds to UNRRA, enjoyed an orgy of meats and other foods that had previously been short—that is, unavailable at OPA price ceilings. August 20th

[1] Another Truman pat on the back, granted on less tenable grounds, had also been accorded Senator Burton Wheeler. Wheeler's opponent in the Montana primary was a liberal Democrat committed to the President's program and was the favorite to win. On the other hand, Wheeler had consistently fought the administration's foreign policy, was erratic in his support of the domestic line, and was certain to be a liability in any future Senate session where the Democrats counted their votes closely. But to Harry Truman Wheeler was an old friend in need, and on that basis he received the presidential accolade. The magnitude of the error grew from the day of the Senator's resounding defeat. Montana liberals were disheartened, Wheeler Democrats encouraged toward Republicanism instead of party regularity. Within the state Truman's popularity fell another notch.

became a deadline date when the Decontrol Board, created under the new law, would have to decide whether a number of food products would go back under control. While meat packers and the farm lobby worked against reinstatement, while consumer lobbies labored for a re-application of ceilings, and while organized labor threatened another wave of demands for wage increases if prices went up further, the Board and the administration grimly tried to find a method of executing a law that had been unpopular with the legislators who passed it. Mean-while the truncated OPA worked overtime granting increases in a host of consumer goods—household appliances, automobiles, cotton tex-tiles, and so forth.

On the 20th the Board rendered its decision. Meats, which had risen between 35 and 80 per cent, were again to be placed under ceilings; so were edible oils, which had shown increases ranging from 25 to 40 per cent. No one, including the Board members, was happy—labor, be-cause it thought not enough control had been restored; business, be-cause it thought the board had done too much. Secretary Anderson attempted to appease the packers by overruling Paul Porter, the OPA administrator. Porter wanted to roll back prices to June 30th. The Agri-culture minister granted increases all along the line. Only rents, as a major item in the consumer's budget, were held at their old level.

While this went on in Washington, the President was off sailing and fishing on an eighteen-day vacation cruise in the Atlantic. He returned to the Capital as meat left its butcher shops, as a maritime strike tied up the country's shipping, and as Henry Wallace prepared to speak in New York. The strike was settled in seventeen days; the Wallace episode will continue to rage as long as America has free speech. The meat problem, however, became a political undertow; the victim of its pull was Harry Truman.

With recontrol, meat production fell to one-fourth of what it had been one year before when OPA was flourishing. Slaughterhouses, wholesalers and retailers closed their doors; even the black market was strangled for lack of supply. Democratic politicians, hearing their con-stituents first raise pitiful cries and then angry ones, asked the White House to suspend price ceilings for sixty days—until after the elections. The trick was political and the President refused to condone it. He stuck doggedly to his point that controls were not the cause of the shortage, that ceilings would remain in effect. Out on the range cattle fed contentedly; in feeding pens, hogs fattened on the record corn crop. The Meat Institute, which since March had been campaigning and lobbying for the abandonment of controls, heatedly denied accusations that it had deliberately inspired the shortage to get higher prices with their resultant higher profits. "Had enough?" the Republicans shouted to the voters.

Six days after standing up for controls, the President went on the radio to speak to the nation. His week had been one of conferences and bad news. The Gallup Poll revealed that only 32 per cent of the people—bedrock Democrats—would vote for him if he were a candidate. In Chicago the AF of L flayed price and wage controls. With these signs, and with what the inner circle and the party chieftains told him of Democratic chances in November unless meat somehow got to the electorate, he made his decision. As in the Wallace affair, three weeks previously, one Harry Truman met another Harry Truman coming down the road. To his nation-wide audience he announced a policy for speeding up the removal of all controls. Meat ceilings were to go immediately. Although rents were singled out as an item that would remain controlled the new policy was a full retreat. Naturally, in this about-face, the harried Chief Executive tried to pass the onus off the shoulders of his own party. "The real blame," he said, "lies at the door of the reckless group of selfish men who, in the hope of gaining political advantage, have encouraged sellers to gamble on the destruction of price control." He placed—in his address, at least—responsibility for future performance and prices on the "representatives of the livestock and meat industry."

Before the nation heard his speech the Republicans were already shrugging it off as a "political gesture." With his announcement they accused him of "playing politics" with the nation's diet—an interesting objection in that a political campaign was being fought and that the Republicans, as politicians, had not been exactly silent on the subject of the meat shortage. "Had enough?" they asked once more.

In between they took time to popularize what was implicit in national chairman B. Carroll Reece's favorite slogan, "End Controls, Confusion, Corruption, Communism." Without thought of the original source they hit at the administration's record on housing with "Vote for Truman—Two Families in Every Garage."

Meanwhile the Democratic party as a whole was permeated with "defeatism"—the term *Newsweek* applied. It had only 4 per cent of the press on its side, in contrast to the 22 per cent it had had in 1944. Its candidates were campaigning in an atmosphere of every man for himself; on the stump, few made prolonged efforts to defend the party chief in the White House. The best statement the national committee could evolve spoke of "Peace, production and progress . . . under the inspired leadership of Harry Truman." Utterly on the defensive, speakers seemed unable to exploit the indisputable facts that, for all the shortages and unrest, the country's employment was at a record high and its national income exceeded any previous peacetime year. Though they mentioned the facts they appeared wholly unconvinced that this situation had anything to do with a Democratic administration.

One last trouble hit the administration and the party. John L. Lewis, a Republican with but slight affection for the government's presence in industry, demanded that negotiations for "new arrangements affecting wages, hours, rules, practices, differentials, inequalities and all other pertinent matters" be opened by November 1st. His timing could not have been shrewder. The date was four days before the elections. The government, which had been operating the mines since the last strike, had a sorry choice: if it refused to negotiate, a winter coal strike was inevitable; if it agreed, the cry of Democratic "coddling" of labor would sweep the land. Interior Secretary Krug was for resistance to Lewis and no discussions. But Truman, weighing heatless homes against heated newspaper editorials, agreed to the talks.

With the postponement of this crisis the President went home to the polls in Missouri. Fighting all his desires to mix politics with the duties of citizenship he stayed out of the local campaign. On election night he heard the worst. For the next two years there would be a Republican Congress to pass on his recommendations and to send him its own variety of legislation. Most of the Democratic liberals were defeated. The alliance of Republicans and conservative Democrats would have about two-thirds of each house.

But what was the mandate? The Republican campaign, though vigorous, had neglected to specify what that party would do on the labor problem, on the price problem, on the production problem, on foreign relations, or on atomic energy. In view of the protests at shortages and high prices perhaps the most inexplicable aspect of the election was the evident apathy of the public. Contrary to enthusiastic cheers about the size of the vote, the turnout in the first peacetime elections was small, about 13,000,000 lower than 1944 and almost 30 per cent below 1940. This is not to say that the Democrats would have won if the vote had been larger; every public opinion poll showed them destined for defeat. But because large turnouts tend to favor the Democratic party as small ones do the Republicans, the consequences of apathy can be illustrated in some of the failures of the losers. For example, Missouri, the President's home state, in casting only two-thirds its previous vote, unseated one senator and four representatives, all Democrats. In Utah, where the margin of Republican victory was narrow, the winners gained 2,000 votes over 1944 in the senatorial race while their opponents lost 52,000. Instances like these as well as the spiritless manner in which the city machines and the PAC functioned spell out how ineffectual was the Democratic coalition.

A subdued but still smiling President waited six days before issuing his statement. Asking for co-operation he laid down a "simple formula" for his own conduct in all future conflicts with the Republican Congress. "Without regard to narrow political considerations," said Truman, he would do "what seems to me to be the best for the welfare of all our people."

2. THE ORDEAL OF HARRY TRUMAN

The first post-election shock that came to Harry Truman was generated by a member of his own party, Senator Fulbright of Arkansas. Before Republican editorial writers had finished polishing their paeans to victory they were driven to comment on the Senator's idea that the President should appoint a Republican Secretary of State and resign, thereby turning the government over to the winning party. Loyal Democrats and suddenly worried Republicans jumped on Fulbright for having the temerity to advance such a scheme. Each had reasons other than the objection that the President would be picking his own successor. Democrats would lose federal patronage; Republicans would have total responsibility thrust upon them when many of them did not want it—not to mention the scramble that would take place in a party where every second senator believed himself qualified for the presidency. Publicly Truman stood on his dignity and refused to discuss the proposal; privately he let it be known that he was not one who quits a job.

After that he began to enjoy himself with his stealing of Republican thunder. While his opposition majority wrangled and put together the organization of the Eightieth Congress Truman began to make headlines. Four days after the election he killed wage controls and all price controls but those on sugar, rice and rents. Then he came to grips with John L. Lewis.

There was a thirty-seven-day coal supply on hand. Lewis, though he was receiving his usual bad press, possessed the unmistakable support of his men. The United Mine Workers had as its motto, "No contract, no work." Unless the union came to an agreement with an employer, whether the employer was the government or a private owner, coal would not be mined. And coal being a basic commodity,

Lewis held a considerable fraction of the economic and political life of the nation in his hands. Another protracted strike would paralyze the country. Yet in demanding collective bargaining or the consequence of its absence, the miners' chieftain represented a large body of the electorate that Democratic administrations depended upon for votes. Furthermore, as a Republican, he had a powerful voice in deciding who would get his miners' support in the coal districts. There were many politicians who condemned him in oratory but made certain they did not offend him in fact. There were others who spent off-election years silently detesting him but in election years bargained for his approval.

It is astonishing how little confidence the press had in the government's chances of humbling Lewis and getting coal produced. Nor can this weak faith be charged to the single fact that Harry Truman was the adversary. Lewis had not been bested by the government in twenty-seven years; there seemed no reason to believe that in the choice between coal and principle the administration would not choose coal. Several in the White House circle favored negotiations, notably John Steelman and, for a period, Tom Clark. But Interior Secretary Krug and Clark Clifford, the President's legal adviser, favored stern measures; after a while the Attorney General switched to their side. And Harry Truman, the underdog who had lost a good many battles recently, decided on firmness.

Why he did so is clear; he had no alternative. If Lewis defeated him the presidency would have been reduced to cipher. Thus the Chief Executive decided to oppose the union. Considering the mood of the country—even organs like the newspaper *PM,* the *Nation* and the *New Republic* expressed editorial doubt on the wisdom of the miners' course— the Chief Executive had only to make his decision and give over the technicalities of the fight to his subordinates. In view of the breadth of the common law and the exigencies of the situation they could find a way to victory. That they did, defeating John L. Lewis in the courts after his men had left the pits, is not a part of Truman's story. Having set the policy he retired from the scene. When Lewis finally capitulated, however, and called the miners back to work, the President's prestige took its first upturn in eighteen months.

*   *   *

So far as the administration and American jurisprudence were concerned the prosecution of the United Mine Workers and its leader set no precedents. The injunction secured by the Justice Department's attorneys was predicated on the fact that the government was acting as operator of the mines. With the end of emergency war powers the right of the government to seize struck plants ended. Nor does certainty attach to the method employed. Though a majority of the Supreme Court upheld the conviction of Lewis for contempt of court in ignoring the injunction, the diversity of the opinions filed by the Justices and the reduction of the fines assessed against the guilty showed a reluctance on the part of the high tribunal to approve as standard procedure the kind of action taken.

But the men Truman used in winning his victory and the means he selected illuminated a trend within the administration. In listening to Clifford and Krug he appeared to be moving away from his Missouri courthouse counsellors. In going after Lewis he was not so much attacking organized labor as looking for a way to rebuild his administration.

In December the last of the New Deal program and the last of the New Dealers were abandoned. Paul Porter, who had been called from the Federal Communications Commission to run OPA as it gasped out its last ten months, resigned. Wilson Wyatt, who had been urged to enter the government a year before in order to expedite low-priced housing, found his policies were being axed by men closer to the White House. He had asked the RFC to grant a large loan to a manufacturer of prefabricated housing. George Allen, on the lending agency's board of directors, refused. It proved no jest; Wyatt quit in disgust, his program a failure. With this the administration let down the bars to the construction of costlier homes. Unable to get its own program through Congress and unable to build emergency houses rapidly enough, it tossed the ball back to private enterprise. One year later the ball was still bouncing.

Krug's appearance as a front-page personality was only temporary, an aspect of the cabinet government Truman continued to practice. Since the Interior Department was the other party to the Lewis case, Krug as its Secretary naturally took the headlines. But when the strike ended public attention strayed from the man who had gone out to "get" John L. Lewis and succeeded. The emergence of Clark Clifford as the man at the President's elbow was of greater moment.

Although Clifford was a Missourian and got where he was because of wire-pulling by one of the President's cronies, he was a new type of influence in the White House circle. He was a bright young man, the kind that outshone the older bodies and less agile minds of those who had come from Missouri to help Harry Truman in his hour of need. The hour of need still existed and so did the men. But they had all been bedded down in comfortable jobs—Snyder as Secretary of the Treasury,

Harry Vaughan as a Major General and aide, James K. Vardaman on the Federal Reserve Board. The non-Missourians were also well placed—George Allen in the RFC and John Steelman as a presidential assistant. Postmaster General Hannegan, who had become the liberal hope after the departures of Bowles and Wallace, was only an infrequent caller.

That gave Clifford his opportunity. He had slipped into the palace guard as naval aide to the President, meanwhile doubling as speechwriter after the retirement of Samuel Rosenman. Gradually he moved into Rosenman's other function, that of policy adviser. By the post-election coal strike he had eliminated the other competition. A lawyer with a mind for legal reasoning instead of political manipulation, he had seen a way through the Lewis impasse when the Attorney General wavered in doubt. Previously he had disclosed a knowledge of economics in writing the President's OPA veto and in counseling the process of decontrol. Appealing also to Truman, who liked to stand in the middle of the road as far from the shoulders as possible, was the fact that Clifford considered himself a "liberal—despite the abuse that term has taken," and believed in the Democratic party as a liberal party. Particularly was the man from Independence pleased that Clifford, a handsome and once highly social young man in St. Louis, was retiring, preferred anonymity, and worked loyally and deferentially for "the Boss" without an eye on a bureau chairmanship or a committee post. Best of all he did not make blunders that rebounded on the President, nor, in his shyness, did he appropriate publicity from the Chief Executive.

This constant taking away of the play from the President had been one of the weaknesses of Truman's incumbency. It prevented his reaching the public effectively. Opinion was led by those who spoke the sharper phrases but who possessed neither the ultimate responsibility for propounding the administration's program nor the constitutional power for insuring its success. Under Roosevelt, the administration was, in the public's eyes, centralized in the presidency. Under Truman the definitions of issues flew out of Washington centripetally; the President's words and ideas frequently commanded less attention than those of his subordinates. In discussing foreign relations any one of a dozen of the "bi-partisans" was considered to speak with greater authority than he. Bowles, in carrying the administration's side of the fight on OPA, had overshadowed him. Anderson on agriculture, Steelman or even Schwellenbach on labor—these had acted as official spokesmen for their own fields. Harry Truman, in the country's eyes, simply lived to perform the ceremonial functions of the presidency; otherwise, people waited for him to make mistakes.

After the elections this hydra-headed determination of domestic policy changed. The hydra still existed but for its residence it moved to Capitol Hill where the Republicans held sway. Instead of the ministry laying down rulings that constituted policy, Republican committee members decided that, with a Democratic Executive branch, it was time to reinstate congressional government. John Snyder could still express himself about fiscal procedure, but the congressmen would act in accordance with their own minds and consciences. The annual budget was submitted. But without deep study or serious hearings, and despite the warnings of Vandenberg that appropriations had to be analyzed carefully and related to the policies and commitments of the government before a final total was computed, both House and Senate set a top figure on what they were going to allow the President to spend. Incidentally, the two chambers disagreed between themselves on the figure. In the end they granted Truman more money to operate the country than either said they would, and came closer to his estimate than their own.

All along the domestic front congressional Republicans gathered to themselves the reins of power. Senators Taft and Vandenberg and Speaker Martin laid down the rules for the party's conduct in the business of legislation. Wilder predictions that Congress would pass "ripper" bills—that is, measures momentarily terminating an agency's life and then re-establishing it immediately thereafter—for the purpose of securing Republican appointees on the Federal Trade Commission, the Federal Communications Commission, the SEC and the ICC proved unfounded. So too were the stories that only nominations of Republicans would be confirmed. Rather, in the first few months, the party seemed loath to do anything.

Controls, the first of the four C's so detested by Republican Chairman Reece, were all but eliminated a few days before Congress met. On December 31, 1946, Truman declared that hostilities with the Axis powers were ended. Out of the window went the Smith-Connally Act, a number of minor statutes and, temporarily, the heavy excise taxes on luxury goods and services. The farm price-support program was, by the action, limited to operation until the end of 1948. In order to keep up a source of revenue and to prevent losses to business in the luxury lines (people would have held off purchases for six months until June 30th when the tax laws would expire), the Republicans discovered the necessity to re-enact this part of the heavy wartime taxation. They were also left to wrestle with rent controls.

To fulfill the promise of ending corruption Republicans banded together to prevent the seating of Bilbo of Mississippi after a committee had compiled testimony that showed he had openly advocated the abridgement of civil rights of Negroes and had been ostentatiously venal in accepting gifts from war contractors. Unfortunately for GOP prestige, leadership in the fight fell to a Democrat; but unfortunately for Democratic prestige, the southern bloc filibustered until formal expulsion was abandoned, and Bilbo given his pay but not his desk. Hunting further, Republican auditors discovered that the accounts of the Democratic appointee who had been the House's sergeant-at-arms could not be balanced in any but an illegal sort of way. Criminal action was taken with righteous headshaking, and the search for "corruption" was over until the session's end.   •

Communism also received much attention. The Committee on Un-American Activities led by Representatives Thomas and Rankin burrowed through the government to unearth an occasional person they "exposed" as a communist. They also pulled several undeniable communists out of civilian life. But communism not being a felony, a number of men were convicted of passport violations and contempt of Congress. An economy-minded House appropriated $11,000,000 to enable the Department of Justice to search the federal employment rolls for disloyal persons. No precise definition of disloyalty was evolved; yet some more ambitious souls, reckoning the price of "radicalism" at $5.50 per head and desiring their money's worth, wanted a large number of the two million federal workers thus inspected to be found guilty. The Senate Committee on Atomic Energy listened while Senator McKellar interminably rehearsed his claims that David Lilienthal and the TVA were either communistic or too tolerant of communist ideology. Although the members eventually tired of the aged Tennessean's diatribes, enough clouds of doubt and insinuation seeped onto the floor of the upper house from the committee room for extreme conservatives of both parties to mutter nebulously of the nominee's "temperamental unfitness." Vandenberg's eleventh-hour plea for "logic, equality, fair play and a just regard to public service" carried into the minds of a number of his colleagues; it prevented, in his words, a "political lynching." After three months of delay Lilienthal was confirmed.

It was a delusory hope if Carroll Reece really believed his party could end confusion. In power the Republicans suffered the fate of all parties which are essentially coalitions. Each wing or group sought to promote its own special ideas and satisfy its individual desires. In reorganizing Congress to fit the needs of the new majority the Republican command aroused enmities in the parceling out of committee posts and chairmanships. Later on an incipient revolt of freshmen legislators

disputed Robert Taft's leadership. At least three schools of Republican foreign policy contended for a voice—Vandenberg's internationalism, Taft's neo-isolationism (in reality the word to describe his position has not yet been minted), and the old-guard isolationism. House committee chairmen like Knutson and Taber made tax reduction and economy their respective cardinal points. Representative Hartley thought in terms of his labor bill. A fair number of others were aroused to action by mention of "communism" and "New Dealism."

So long as the question revolved around exclusive fields like taxation or labor relations or communism, the members were willing to follow the party leaders and vote en bloc. But where there were overlapping jurisdictions like the problems called forth by foreign relations—where every man was his own expert—the party divided into atoms. Yet, in its major works, aside from the economy promised, the majority leaders—Taft in the Senate and Walcott in the House—held their teams together. When beaten by Truman's vetoes, they lost because they were unable to bring over enough southern Democrats to make up the necessary two-thirds.

A second source of difficulty to Republican rule was the divided nature of the government. The President's wistful disclaimer that he would act without "narrow political considerations" occasionally came through as when he reluctantly signed the bills that ended portal-to-portal pay suits and permitted "voluntary" rent increases. Normally, however, partisan politics guided the destiny of the government. After the GOP machine began disgorging its measures from legislative committees, Congress and the Executive were plainly busy compiling records for 1948. The spectacle of the Legislature repassing substantially the same tax bill after it had once been vetoed by the President recalled the days of Andrew Johnson. The measure, widely advertised as one reducing the burdens of the taxpayer, would have granted, in terms of the dollar, far larger relief to the wealthy than to those with moderate or low incomes. Such is bound to be the case in any plan for cutting taxes on a percentage basis alone.

This emphasized a double confusion in Republican ranks. Pushed through by tax-reduction advocates, the bill would, if enacted, have unbalanced the budget by cutting estimated receipts below estimated expenditures and added to the federal debt. Obviously, economy—which is a relative term—would have been junked. Secondly, by directing the benefits of the proposed reduction primarily at high-income taxpayers, the party, while proclaiming a conversion to new thought, was actually reviving the old theories of Andrew Mellon. On the other

hand the presidency displayed its own contradictions. In postponing reduction to 1948 Truman and his advisers offered no relief to the lower-income group which was being squeezed by higher prices. Instead of presenting a tax reform program for 1947 they apparently hoped to use the election year as a time when the GOP plan could be profitably propagandized as a scheme to "soak the poor."

Yet tax reform was in order. The multiplicity of governmental activities had been growing since Roosevelt's first days. Although a number of the war functions were shaved away under Truman it is probable that the simplicity of the twenties or even F.D.R.'s first term will never be recaptured. It seemed a requirement that the federal government retain its increased place as both a regulator of and participant in the nation's economic system. Not only would it have to oversee the conduct of business and commerce and act as a major agency in facilitating foreign trade; it would have to step into the breach in such things as loans and investments. Furthermore, it was headed for a new era in supervising labor relations. The incidence of taxation would and did exacerbate the difficulties of administering each of these functions. To eliminate functions merely for the purpose of eliminating costs would be to produce chaos. But Congress, in its economy drive, would necessarily have cut down the role of government without heed to those causes that had first demanded its increase. And the Executive absently fell back on defending the applications of the taxing power as they had been before the impact of government had grown so enormously.

Comparatively speaking, the system of taxation in 1947 favored large corporations over small ones and partnerships and individual proprietaries. In striking at large personal incomes it unquestionably cut down possibilities for reinvestment and chances for the establishment of competing plants. In short, bigness was assisted by making life more difficult for the small enterpriser and new business. The result was still private enterprise; but it was not free enterprise or a competitive economy. Neither political party willingly faced the problem.

The same was true of the law that became known as the Labor-Management Relations Act of 1947. A regulatory act, it directly affected the livelihoods of 15,000,000 members of organized labor and their relationships with their employers. As the single most important bill of the session, it ran a curious course through the legislature. Here was the conservative effort to assimilate the labor problem and rationalize the extra-governmental power of unions within the national fabric. Most of the country agreed the problem had to be tackled. And

for the purpose of writing the law and generalling its passage, Taft allotted himself the chairmanship of the Senate Labor Committee. Nevertheless, whatever the virtues and defects of the eventual law, its process of manufacture was decidedly hit-or-miss. In his annual message Truman asked for an outlawing of jurisdictional disputes and secondary boycotts, for his own fond remedy of fact-finding boards, a strengthening of the Labor Department to handle mediation, and a twenty-man commission to study the problem. It would have been too much to expect a Republican Congress to enact his program. But the outright rejection of all but the first (and least important) of his requests was indicative of the spirit in which the law was shaped.

Labor, like foreign relations, is a field in which every man, upon consultation with his conscience, his prejudices and a little reading, proclaims himself an expert. The Eightieth Congress had its labor experts, real and fancied; but, on the whole, the committee hearings banished expertism. The starting point of the legislation was the once-vetoed Case bill. New proposals that can be described only as vindictive were added. The work of the committees was to expunge some of the most egregious of these while preserving as strong a measure as possible.

This method allowed no dispassionate study of the problem in its entirety—as the President had suggested or as the Senate Atomic Energy Committee had previously demonstrated to be practical. In several instances the Republican high command overruled the advice of two of its authorities, Senators Ives and Morse. That huge majorities countermanded Truman's veto in no way improved the questionable features the majority had wrought. A simulated fury was directed at the White House. Because the Chief Executive's exposition of the law's faults closely followed the CIO's brief he was excoriated. Probably there was more political inspiration than reason in the assault. In rejecting the congressional point of view Truman was constitutionally asserting his own; Congress had done the same thing in a wholly constitutional manner when it refused to consider his recommendations.

Something of the atmosphere in which the law passed was emphasized in the first months of its life. Labor attempted to sidestep its provisions and some sections of management abetted the move. Portions of conservative opinion came around to seeing the ban on communists as "ill advised." Strictures on political activities by unions and the labor press were openly violated in the hope of provoking a test in the courts. Senator Taft spoke some general words on revising the prohibition against the closed shop. Many quarters criticized the single-handed power of the General Counsel of the National Labor Relations Board. In sum the act had not solved the labor problem. Passed in omnibus form it was a catch-all for numerous changes of the older Wagner Act; but it imperiled its own life and workability by loose verbiage and constitutionally doubtful clauses. Its immediate beneficiary was the legal profession. Taft received an increased reputation among Republicans for having seen through Congress a piece of legislation substantially as he wanted it. For his veto Harry Truman received the bolstering support of labor and forgiveness for his bad manners of the previous year.

*   *   *

Unaccountably, while the Republicans ruled Congress, the President gave appearances of feeling comfortable in the job he once had not wanted. Moreover, in spite of the implied "no" that was thundered at the White House in November 1946, the idea of a second term began to have its attractions. In January 1947, James Farley said he thought Truman "dead political timber"; in February, Robert Hannegan started the renomination bandwagon rolling by calling for his chief to remain in office until the work of "leading us to peace and plenty . . . is done."

As usual, the analysts got busy on predictions. A large element in their fare was that, with the New Deal repudiated at the polls, Truman was free of his inheritance and could strike out in his own non-Rooseveltian direction. Samplings of public opinion were encouraging. The upswing begun with the prosecution of John L. Lewis proved the start of a trend. By February, according to Gallup, one per cent more people had confidence in Truman's leadership than in the Republican Congress, though neither had a majority. In March he regained the sixty per cent mark.

This rising presidential popularity was accompanied by a major change in Truman's exercise of his powers of office. He perceived the omen of Republican disunity. Probably, he also foresaw the extremely conservative record the Congress would establish. Cleverly, after delivering his message and his budget, he kept a respectable distance from domestic affairs. If he cherished certain aspects of the Roosevelt program that the Republicans would now scrutinize and amend and perhaps repeal, he also determined to leave the burden of defense upon the congressmen of his own party. Rather than become involved in what would be essentially futile debate with the Republican hierarchy and possibly the ultras of the southern Democratic wing, he temporarily abdicated the sphere. Later, when necessary, as has been described, he came back with his vetoes. Occasionally he threw a spear at Taft, reminding the Senator of the rising price level and the high cost of living. But in this and in the whip-lashes he directed at the Republican fiscal program, he displayed far more agility than had seemed possible in the man who had conducted the Wallace affair and listened to his Missouri cronies in 1946. Having made a provocative utterance and baited his quarry he retired swiftly, much as Roosevelt had done, and thereby let his opponents howl without the satisfaction of stirring from him an answering bark.

In compensation for his loss of the home market Truman blossomed into a world diplomat. On a series of visits of state, he labored at improving hemispheric solidarity. His first large jump in prestige accompanied the replacement of Secretary of State Byrnes. Though tale bearers had spoken knowingly of the strained feelings between the two, this withdrawal came about without the hippodrome extravagances that had so enlivened the passages of Ickes[2] and Wallace to private employment. James Byrnes went back to South Carolina for reasons of "health." Probably this was the largest single factor in his retirement. So long as he and his chief worked together they held their differences of personality under control.

The surprise that greeted the nomination of General George C. Marshall was exceeded only by the praise. The President himself humbly believed his new Secretary of State the "greatest living American." Coming back after a year in China where his predecessor, General Patrick Hurley, had been ornamental with his bristling moustaches and a liability besides, Marshall evidenced a candor and incisiveness unusual in a public figure. Where Hurley listed excuses and threw roundhouse swings at "communists" in the State Department, Marshall, in admitting the failure of his mission and of American policy to achieve peace and stability in the Orient, provided solid reasons. The first soldier ever to be entrusted with the direction of American foreign relations, he

[2] The departure of the self-styled "curmudgeon" came during February of 1946, when the Truman popularity was starting to plummet downward. The entire affair in all its high-spirited name-calling could have been avoided if the President had recognized the impropriety of appointing his good friend and political backer, Edwin Pauley, as Under-Secretary of the Navy. To Ickes, the gesture smelled not only of courthouse politics but oil, an odor to which the old, dyspeptic cabinet officer was particularly sensitive. In his inimitable language, he was quick to tell Congress of his opinions on the nomination and Pauley's integrity. Truman, incensed at this dragging of his friend's name through an oleaginous slime, sought a retraction from the gruff Interior Secretary. He got a resignation. By now thoroughly aroused, the President asked incredulously if Ickes questioned *his* honesty as well as Pauley's. In a fabulous press conference, the former officer implied that he did. His was the last word, except for the committee's. It forced a withdrawal of Pauley's name.

had, nonetheless, excellent qualifications for his position. His work on the Combined Chiefs of Staff and as head of the Army gave him experience and knowledge that were easily transferable to international negotiations. Though somewhat overlooked at the time, the fact of his military rank halted the noisier aggressions of generals and admirals who had crossed frontiers of protocol by advancing plans and ideas contrary to the wishes and intentions of Byrnes. With Marshall in charge of foreign relations army talk of massed flights of B-29's around the world and navy talk about the fleet going anywhere it "damned pleased" ceased.

Nothing changed in American relations with Russia. "Patience and firmness" were still the keynote. A common policy with Britain in occupied Germany had been arranged, not without Soviet protest but without serious objections. During January relations with Russia eased slightly—although readers of much of the American press would not have known it. Little that the Kremlin could consider provocative came out of Washington. In the United Nations the resignation of Bernard Baruch led to the virtual abandonment by the United States of its *quid pro quo* atomic disarmament in exchange for abandonment of the veto power. Russia, reported the *Atlantic Monthly,* was awaiting the crackup of the western bloc over Britain's growing unwillingness to follow American policy and American unwillingness to continue spending money for the salvage of foreign regimes. As a corollary, the Soviet Foreign Office was supposed to be counting upon increasing liberal criticisms and non-communist unrest in Europe and in countries like China, Turkey and Iran where the United States was supporting rightist non-democratic governments.

But while the Secretary of State studied for the forthcoming Moscow conference on the German peace treaty and familiarized himself with the Department and while the President played unobtrusively at minor tasks around the White House and journeyed down to Mexico in a gesture of good will, the British Empire's economic and political difficulties made a dramatic crossing of the Atlantic and landed in the New World. In a note on February 27, 1947, London told Washington of an inevitability that had been only a matter of time. Britain had to pull out of Greece; the United States would have to assume the cost and worry of keeping Greece out of Russian hands.

This situation provided Harry Truman his signal opportunity. Before Marshall's departure the administration evolved a formula which it hoped would save the eastern Mediterranean for western power. On March 12th, with the General discussing peace treaties in Russia, the Truman Doctrine was announced to the Senate and the world. Deferring to the etiquette of diplomacy, the Missourian named no names; but his language was easily construed. Russian expansion was to be contained. Short of war, here was another advance in "firmness." Aid to Greece and Turkey was to be taken on as anti-Soviet policy. The aid would be both military and economic.

Although the Chief Executive asserted that "we [have to be] willing to help free peoples to maintain their free institutions and their national integrity against aggressive movements that seek to impose on them totalitarian regimes," the picture was not one of blacks and whites. Turkey, which was to receive $150,000,000, was a police state; Greece, with its anti-communism budgeted at $250,000,000, had an unrepresentative government composed largely of antidemocratic reactionaries and defended by an army staffed with a considerable number of former collaborationists. Furthermore, despite the protestations of the administration to the contrary, America's rapid action had bypassed the United Nations. In view of subsequent developments it is possibly true that settlement could not have been attained through this slower, alternative course. And while it cannot be said positively that the world organization was thereby weakened, it is certain that there was little in the method the Doctrine employed that harmonized with our stated objective of making the international agency stronger.

In its own terms the Doctrine posed a serious question. Aside from the ethics of upholding antidemocracy on the right as a bulwark against antidemocracy on the left, it was a restricted effort of dubious soundness. Greece's economic recovery was tied to the recovery of Europe and to broad internal reforms; her military security depended not on her army but on the determination of others to defend her. As an isolated case she could easily become what the Republican isolationists said she would be—"operation rat-hole."

Undoubtedly she needed relief. Undoubtedly too, civil war had decimated her political center and divided her people between the left and right. Probably, without the use of anti-communism as a persuader, the $400,000,000 appropriation would not have been granted by Congress. As it was, passage came about four months after Truman's deadline of March 31st. Yet popular as the President's program was at home it became ephemeral within a matter of months. By September, even before she had used a fraction of her dollars, Greece was calling for increased emergency aid. Other cries were heard from the continent. Some merely asked assistance. Others weighted their pleas with fearsome prophecies of the infiltration of communism and the Soviet Union's expansionist ambitions. But Truman made no more sensational speeches to Congress; by then he had sent it too many vetoes. By then also, General Marshall, for all his respect of the chain of command, had taken charge of foreign relations.

Perhaps a definition of the fundamental American foreign policy should have been enunciated in advance of the Truman Doctrine. In any case the President's bold words and strident demands on Greece provoked Russia into reprisals. Hungary was snatched into the Soviet sphere before American work commenced in Athens.

On June 5th, Secretary Marshall, on receiving an honorary degree at Harvard, supplied what was lacking in the President's exposition in March—universal application and positive expression. Four sentences contained the core of his idea. "Our policy is directed not against any country or doctrine but against hunger, poverty, desperation and chaos. Its purpose should be the revival of a working economy in the world so as to permit the emergence of political and social conditions in which free institutions can exist. . . . [Assistance] must not be on a piecemeal basis as various crises develop. Any assistance that this Government may render in the future should provide a cure rather than a mere palliative." Though the entire speech was composed of generalities, admittedly capable of widely variant interpretations, it passed the initiative for calculating needs to Europe and made its point that the United States would not develop a program unilaterally. It was here that the "plan" represented a considerable change from the Truman Doctrine. In naming no villains—nor heroes—among nations, Marshall's policy opened the way for a joint program, "agreed to by a number of, if not all European nations."

If the offer appeared generous, some interpreted it otherwise. At the first European conference called to reply to the Secretary's proposal, Molotov presented his three-pronged criticism: that the plan included resuscitating the Ruhr and thereby would afford Germany a chance to rearm, that the United States Congress would never grant assistance to the Soviet Union and its friendly neighbors (a probably correct assumption), that the United States, in needing Europe fully as much as Europe needed it, would not be able to stand the economic burden if a domestic depression overcame American capitalism. Rather than prolong conversations he thought futile, the Russian Foreign Minister withdrew.

Yet the Marshall Plan, from the American point of view, was not so much a sugar-coating of American "imperialism" as it was a tentative return to an older policy. It could, as the Truman Doctrine could not, be utilized for wholesome relief and economic reconstruction. It could be utilized toward the legitimate end of sustaining America's domestic prosperity. In its broadest terms it coincided with the postwar foreign policy Franklin Roosevelt seemed to have settled upon—a continuation of lend-lease for economic rehabilitation and of UNRRA for humanitarian assistance. That it took almost two years and a deterioration of friendships to come back to this line suggests that American diplomatic thinking was swimming around uncertainly for a long time.

At that, the plan had an uncertain future. It might be a political weapon or an economic benefaction. As presented to Congress in December 1947 it emphasized rehabilitation. Rechristened the European Recovery Program, it asked that seventeen billions be allocated over sixteen nations for four years. In his message Truman barely referred to its usefulness as an antidote to communism. Instead, he dwelt at length on other aspects; seemingly he was more interested in arguing the case for European prosperity.

Ultimately, however, the program depended upon the will of the American people. Very possibly the fate of the world hung on that will and on the method by which the people wanted the ERP implemented.

*   *   *

Any estimate of Harry Truman is probably an estimate of the Main Street, U.S.A., that he personifies. He exhibits its virtues and its faults and those characteristics that cannot perhaps be evaluated on a moral level. He is personally honest, does not possess immense guile and is well intentioned. A number of hand-burning experiences have given him increased caution and an unwillingness to act drastically, however urgent the demand may seem. He is no longer the man he was in April of 1945. Although he preferred the old life, and by his background and limitations was perhaps better equipped for it than the new one, he has made enormous adjustments to the presidency.

Occasionally he has had his relapses, as with his leisurely voyage home from Brazil in September 1947, while the world waited for American action during an economic crisis in Europe. If he has outgrown the black anger that provoked his "draft labor" request, he nevertheless still retains his characteristic of not weighing all the effects of his actions. Thus his doctrine on Greece and Turkey was expressed in language that caused alarm in an unwarlike Western Europe as well as in the Soviet Union's sphere. His executive order on loyalty in the government service, issued in the spring of 1947, was so haphazardly drawn that almost everyone to the left of center could be driven from his job. In this, and in other instances, Truman, like the folks on Main Street, appears a trifle hazy on the virtues of broad civil liberties. In compensation, however, it can be said that he has a totally consistent record in respecting minority rights and in supporting the concrete aspirations of Negroes for economic, political and legal equality.

As President he has delighted in the ceremonial functions of his office. At times he has stretched the privilege of appointment to reward his friends. In consequence the reflections of their shortcomings have fallen upon him. At other times he has unthinkingly committed actions without an adequate preparation of public opinion or a sampling of its potential support. His administration has been marked by periodic confusions and by an inability to fulfill its plans on housing, prices and production. This suggests that Mr. Truman is not the administrator nor chief of government he was predicted to be. On the other hand, more than any president since Rutherford B. Hayes, he has tried to be the Chief Executive of all the people, beyond partisan considerations. Though ever the Democrat when the political chips were down, he has taken counsel from almost all shades of Republican.

But it is as a politician and chief of his party that the President will determine his future. Under his reign the New Deal coalition broke. In the sense that the CIO's political arm became weaker than it was in 1944, the Democratic party also became weaker. Nor did other elements gain positively in strength. The southern wing grew more vocal and demanded greater power because it had lived through the disaster of 1946 untouched. But by the nature of the American electoral college and the party system, the southern Democracy, in its regional supremacy, is in a poor bargaining position. It has only one place to go. The Democratic party's strength and hope remains, as it did under Roosevelt, in the northern urban centers and the independents. Republican power depends upon Democratic weakness with these groups. The success of either party rests with the number of factions it can attract to its side.

After the 1946 elections Harry Truman tried to stand above factionalism. He wanted to become identified with no single wing. He hoped for some amalgam that would give his party unity. After Hannegan delivered his praises in February 1947, mention of a successor was heard no more. Like F.D.R., Truman seemed averse to designating his political heir. The reason was to be found in a question. In December 1946, Harry Woodring, once a Secretary of War and a perennial hope of the Democrats in Republican Kansas, emerged from a White House conference to tell reporters that he believed the President would be a candidate for re-election. To prove his point, he asked, "Who else is there?" The Republicans hoped they could answer him.

WRITING at the end of 1802 while Jeffersonians agitated to change the electoral system, Gouverneur Morris felt that, except for the outright abolition of the vice-presidency, any change would be for the worse. If men were separately and distinctly nominated for the two offices he predicted, two strong rivals would seek the presidency and a multitude of lesser men would contend for second place. As a result the major candidates would pander to local leaders, holding out the minor post as "bait to catch state gudgeons."

The next year, during the furious debate on the proposal to amend the Constitution, Senator William Plumer, a New Hampshire Federalist, took an even less sanguine view of posterity's usage of the office. While Jeffersonians sat watching Aaron Burr in the chair, Plumer told them that their amendment would put an end to the high character of the vice-presidency. In the future such candidates, he asserted with startling foresight, "will be voted for not as President of the United States but as President of the Senate, elected to preside over the forms of this House. In electing a subordinate officer the Electors will not require those qualifications requisite for supreme command. The office of Vice-President will be a sinecure. It will be brought to the market and exposed to sale to ambitious, aspiring candidates for the Presidency. Will his friends and favorites promote the election of a man of talents, probity and (general) popularity for Vice-President, and who may become his rival? No! They will seek a man of moderate talents, whose ambition is bounded by that office, and whose influence will aid in electing the President."

1. THE SEVEN AT THE BAR

It is clear that, of the seven accidental presidents, only Theodore Roosevelt approaches the stature of the giants who held the office. Perhaps, in more strenuous times, he might have been the equal of Andrew Jackson, Woodrow Wilson or his distant cousin, Franklin. But he had no wars in which to lead the nation. He thought of himself as a crusader; but through much of his incumbency the conservative Republicans were a millstone around his neck. Even without them, however, Roosevelt, the man of action, was held in check by the American

353

people. They were feeling restless, but were undecided on direction. Often he had to kindle his own flame. Yet even his immense vitality could not always keep it burning. Occasionally the cold breath of the public extinguished it. Nevertheless he performed one service that puts him deservingly into the group of capable chief executives. Governmentally, as well as chronologically, he introduced the United States to the twentieth century. Considering the attitude of the country when he succeeded McKinley this in itself was no mean feat.

Coolidge, on the other hand, would have wiped out the interval, and made over America into the pattern of the 1870's. There could be no greater contrast between men, the one expansive of emotion, life and deed, the other parsimonious and crabbed. Nevertheless, each in his day was the picture of the successful politician and the figure of his times. Both trod many of the same rungs on the ladder—the state legislature, the governorship, the vice-presidency, the presidency. Both owed their nominations to revolts against the party hierarchy and to personal popularity. In each case the popularity was somewhat misplaced—Coolidge's because he did not actually settle the Boston police strike, Roosevelt's because he was not really a war hero. That they are the only two of six to have won renomination and re-election places them above their companions-in-accident in the practice of the political arts. It also places them above a number of regularly chosen presidents. The reasons are almost elemental. Both maintained their appeal to the electorate and both maintained control over their parties. If Calvin Coolidge rejected practically everything else in the Rooseveltian success story he understood the wisdom of these Rooseveltian techniques. That the Vermonter is finally counted on the side of failure is not his own fault but the fault of his decade. The twenties apotheosized Coolidge's economics and his aphorisms. He existed as a public figure by permission of his society. When the society decayed his reputation fell.

The mark of failure was on four others before they left office. Harry Truman may yet prove a special case, depending not only upon his own future conduct but also upon that of his successor. Until that time, however, the record is against him. All five received a vote of "no confidence" when their parties or men were defeated in the mid-term elections. All had unhappy dealings with Congress, were refused their own programs and—in four instances—received laws of which they disapproved. Tyler, Johnson and Truman made full use of the veto power. In so doing they illustrated that what strength the presidency had during their tenures was defensive. Together with Arthur and Fillmore they saw leadership seized by other chieftains—by Clay, by Calhoun, by Stephen Douglas, by Thaddeus Stevens, by Blaine, by Robert Taft. They seemed helpless to head off the interlopers.

Tyler, Fillmore, Arthur and Truman found it impossible to use the cabinets they inherited. While they gained in some replacements—as did Truman from the inclusion first of Byrnes and then of Marshall— only Arthur was able to use his ministry to anything approximating optimum effectiveness. Johnson, on the other hand, in attempting to retain the Lincoln cabinet, sealed his doom. Roosevelt and Coolidge, through selective cutting, saved what they needed and discarded what they did not want. In view of the results, theirs seemed the sounder method. Certainly the mass resignations under Tyler and Fillmore and the summary departure of at least four men (with a narrowly averted threat by a fifth—Byrnes) under Truman were not easy shocks for the Executive branch to bear. A cabinet officer, it is true, holds his place by the sufferance of the president; but, if he is competent or has been in office over a period of time or represents a faction, he gives his department a certain character and the administration a particular aspect. Rapid shifts in personnel impair the working of a department. Thus Johnson's difficulties with Stanton in 1867-1868 kept a most important executive agency in turmoil. The procession of Secretaries of State between 1945 and 1947 unsettled the foreign ministry's policy-making divisions when the country needed stability.

There is another side to cabinet relationships. Basically, the members of the official family possess degrees of power without responsibility. They influence and make policy that affects the people, but they are answerable only to their chief and, in the limited areas of appointment and impeachment, to Congress. It is therefore necessary that they act in harmony with the desires of the President and serve his interests. At the same time they have a right to expect preferential treatment or defense from the Chief Executive. While it is perhaps too much to ask that the ministers be mutually compatible among themselves and with the president as well, it is important that they subordinate personal differences to the requirements of working toward the same purposes.

This was not the case during the Tyler, Fillmore, Johnson and Truman administrations. Webster outstayed his usefulness to Tyler and worked to secure the presidential nomination Fillmore also wanted. Tyler sought to avoid Calhoun's presence in the cabinet, and distrusted him after the appointment had been forced by circumstances. For like Webster, John C. Calhoun was too strong and ambitious a man to be satisfied by secondary position in another's administration. Johnson's inability to deal with his cabinet or without it is a classic case. His incredible toleration of a disloyal Secretary of War not only contributed greatly to the wreckage of the presidency but nearly brought personal ruin on its incumbent.

Truman's cabinet troubles rendered his administration all the weaker because he placed so much reliance upon the advisory circle. He was right in demanding the resignations of Ickes and Wallace after they opposed his policies and practices. Yet he showed no consistency. His Secretary of Agriculture repeatedly disagreed with other officers of the government and with the President. He remained nevertheless. Byrnes and Truman were distant in their personal feelings and only a loss of face by the Chief Executive averted open rupture. Presidential temporizing over whether or not to call Congress into special session to deal with the European political and economic crisis of the autumn of 1947 virtually overrode Secretary of State Marshall's warning that immediate action was necessary.

With regard to unofficial advisers, the unsuccessful five demonstrated questionable wisdom, although some had plain bad luck. Tyler, in selecting his Williamsburg set, chose men outside the stream of the times. He then found it impossible to get along with Beverley Tucker and lost Upshur through an accident. Others ground their own axes. Fillmore listened to men who counseled a break with Weed, and therefore with the northern wing of the Whig party. Johnson early lost Preston King and, because he had the mountaineer's suspicion of everyone around him, was burdened with numerous minor tasks. Arthur, who never had a chance for success, was unable to attract first-rate men. Truman used the dubious method of government by crony. Afterwards when looking for better-trained men, he found them shy of both low salaries and the pedestrian attitude of Washington toward national and world affairs. None of the five created an inner circle that resembled, in talent and ingenuity, the "Kitchen Cabinet" of Andrew Jackson or the "Brain Trust" of Franklin Roosevelt. None could muster loyal men like those who labored for Washington and Jefferson. None could go it alone like Lincoln or Wilson.

*   *   *

The relationships of the seven to their times, their dealings with Congress, their problems with advisers, are pragmatic measures of their stature and success. A more absolute yardstick is their usage of the constitutional and the customary powers of the presidency.

Four of them thought of performing as Commander-in-Chief. Truman alone held the power in wartime, but his sparing use of it followed the pattern laid down by F.D.R. His independent and prodigious request that Congress permit him to draft striking workers and operate struck industries for the profit of the state was wisely denied. Johnson's military prerogatives were attenuated on the one hand by Stanton and on the other by Congress. At one point the legislature ordered the commanding general of the armies to receive his orders directly from itself and forbade the President to give him instructions. By means of that probably unconstitutional act Johnson became Commander-in-Chief without a command. Fillmore thought he might use troops to force New England into compliance with the fugitive-slave law; he also warned that the Army might be ordered to pacify the Texas-New Mexico border. But both times he declined to use the power.

Considering Theodore Roosevelt's affinity for the parade ground and his devotion to the warlike spirit, his applications of force and command were limited. On the whole he seems to have used them more widely in his imagination than he did in fact. Perhaps mercifully, the Army was not ordered into the coal fields during the 1902 strike. Since the 1920's, historians have been discounting his claim that he ordered Admiral Dewey to stand ready to meet the German threat on Venezuela; Roosevelt apologists have seldom risen to the defense.

How the seven employed the power of appointment and the power of recommendation to the legislature is fairly well explored in the foregoing text. Here again Roosevelt was successful and the others trailed far behind. Arthur got his men but not his program, and the men proved loyal. Andrew Johnson has the poorest record. Not only was his policy on southern reconstruction toppled but he suffered acute embarrassment in dealing with a number of generals he appointed as military governors under the congressional laws. To date Harry Truman stands a few niches above the Tennessean in this particular. His program has been largely denied him; but for his purposes, the men he has chosen as lieutenants—both inside and outside the cabinet—have, with a few notable exceptions, supported him.

As heads of the country's foreign relations, six of the seven have been practically the captives of their Secretaries of State. Even Roosevelt, for all his personal participation in international affairs and the establishment of policy, was more dependent upon John Hay and Elihu Root than he cared to admit. Nowhere in the stories of the accidental presidents is there anything like the degree of independent direction Lincoln, Wilson and Franklin Roosevelt maintained in relating the United States to the world. Yet these too had Foreign Secretaries of either great capacity or strong conviction.

Two other founts of presidential power—party leadership and the influencing of public opinion—provide tests of achievement and effectiveness. Once more Roosevelt stands above the others. After the death of Hanna he came close to remaking the Republican party in his own image. It happened that the image blurred when he designated William Howard Taft his heir apparent. Nevertheless, in dictating Taft's nomination, the irrepressible Teddy demonstrated an unusual strength that carried almost to the end of his presidency. And just as surely, Roosevelt showed how great was his popular appeal when he cracked the party in the Progressive revolt of 1912, four years after his supposed abdication of power. Similarly, in his popular appeal, probably no president was more effective in taking his case to the people and watching their demands rebound on Congress. His closest rival was his cousin Franklin, but TR had no such setbacks as the Court fight and the elections of 1938 and 1942. The first Roosevelt was indefatigable, a wizard at manipulating the press, and, with no radio to assist him, a brilliant platform personality.

In spite of the strains imposed by his course Harry Truman comes second to Roosevelt I as a political chieftain. A comparatively minor figure in his party's hierarchy when he took office, he soon became its first man, nominally and actually. Local leaders deferred to him; booms for other candidates in 1948 were suppressed. Though he did not dominate the Democrats as Theodore Roosevelt dominated the Republicans, Truman secured undisputed control of the party machinery—something none of the remaining five was able to accomplish. Where he falls short as a politician is in the breakup of the New Deal coalition Franklin Roosevelt found indispensable. He has lacked the fire to draw independent voters unimpressed by the dogma of party regularity. Since 1946 this group of indefinable size has been shopping around.

But the far more serious weakness to his party and his program and to himself as a politician and a president has been Truman's inability to lead public opinion. Aside from the Truman Doctrine speech and proposal, when he seemed to have caught the temper of the majority, his efforts to carry the masses with him or to point a direction were consistently unavailing. When he defended price control or attacked the Taft-Hartley bill, others on his own side led him. When he advanced his own recommendations for labor legislation he could not evoke enthusiasm from the country. When he put forward the several food conservation programs he was unable to dramatize the urgency that he claimed required them. Often, he has spoken after the fact. He has given the appearance of waiting until all the returns are in and then endorsed what might be the most popular or the least damaging position.

By varying degrees downward the remaining five were either indifferent party leaders or showed no leadership at all. They were either indifferent molders of public opinion or did themselves positive harm by what they said or essayed to promote. Coolidge controlled the Republicans but did not rule them. He was in the White House, and the Republican Old Guard—itself failing—could not dislodge him, while the new hierarchy kept him there as a symbol. Though his glacial personality was patently at odds with the madness of the twenties, his frigidity was mistaken for sanity. The boom that bore his name was mistaken for genuine prosperity.

Tyler, Fillmore, Johnson and Arthur all contributed to destroying the coalitions that elected them. None of them had it in him to rebuild. Perhaps nothing could have saved the Whigs, for together with the Jacksonian Democrats, they could not face slavery as an issue nor could they find the formula to evade it after Clay and Webster died. Nevertheless Tyler and Fillmore were as important as any two men in contributing to the destruction of the party. Ambition and stubborness in the one case, sheer ambition in the second, cost the party its only two chances. Neither Johnson nor Arthur had national followings within party ranks. Neither could reconstruct their organizations to fit their needs. The hard-driving Tennessean alienated rather than warmed when he went out proselytizing. The urbane New Yorker was a poor speaker and though a lucid writer, was much too much the conservative in habit and outlook to project himself beyond the caricatured notion the public had of him when he took office.

Nevertheless, in achievement or in failure, in leadership and in impotence, each thought he deserved a second term. That each of them revised and even reversed the conduct of affairs charted by or expected of his predecessor made no difference. The seven, in concert with every other president the United States has had, believed their courses proper. Yet Johnson could only assume that he was following Lincoln's plan. Roosevelt, Fillmore and Arthur blatantly reversed that which had gone before them. Coolidge rudely turned out Harding's "Ohio Gang" and cleared away the most glaring eyesores. Tyler performed as though William Henry Harrison had never lived and as though Henry Clay had no stake in Whig policy. Harry Truman often seemed most assured when eliminating a relic of the New Deal or denouncing something that had once been a tenet of the New Deal's philosophy. Thus not only in men but in administration did the accidental seven give the electorate a government for which it had not asked. It is no wonder that four of six were never permitted a second opportunity.

2. THE STAGE REVISITED

If, on the whole, the presidential careers of five of the seven were largely unfortunate, it might still serve to place the men in perspective before drawing final judgment on the system that raised them to office.

Judged on the single criterion of experience, few presidents could match the lifetimes of public service of Tyler, Johnson and Coolidge before their successions. Together with Roosevelt each had been governor of a state. Six had legislative experience of varying nature and four were well grounded in the workings of Congress. All had worked as administrators in government. Arthur excepted, none had fewer qualifications than Generals Harrison and Taylor. Chester Arthur included, all came to the White House after a more prepossessing career than Abraham Lincoln's. On the whole all had a wider acquaintance with the practical matters of politics than did Woodrow Wilson or George Washington.

Again, on the presidential record, if none achieved place among the truly great, none can be numbered with the least worthy. For sheer corruption, crudeness, and enthronement of the commonplace, nothing equaled the administrations of Grant and Harding. Technical bungling appeared to be studied policy under Franklin Pierce. James Buchanan, a busy and seemingly competent public servant in his pre-presidential years, was almost derelictly inactive during his stewardship. Although the magnitude of the disasters that befell Johnson place him close to Buchanan, and some of the consequences of Millard Fillmore and Calvin Coolidge—and perhaps John Tyler—set them near or below the danger line, none rendered quite so poor an account of himself as the four others. In addition, once more aside from Andrew Johnson, the heroes considered here were no less successful as Chief Executives than were six chosen by the standard elective process—the two Adamses, Van Buren, Hayes, Benjamin Harrison and Taft. If, of the seven, Theodore Roosevelt alone stands out, most of his colleagues in coincidence would seem to belong in the middle bracket of all American presidents.

This, however, is insufficient cause for rejoicing in the infinite wisdom of the founding fathers, the framers of the Twelfth Amendment, or the delegates to national party conventions. It need only be recalled that most of the successions occurred when there was a demand for better than average statesmanship and a requirement of intelligence as well as adroit politics. Nor can it be said that in these several times of crisis, the need for leadership went unrecognized. Other men saw it and other men took it. That leadership was somewhere else than in the presidency—where it belonged—or that it was permitted to slip away is more an indictment of the men than of the law. Nevertheless, that only one of seven was an unqualified success indicts the law and its operation.

In almost every instance, the political conventions that nominated John Tyler *et al.* considered other candidates. But there is no indication that the alternatives would have given more outstanding service, though Hamlin probably would have had an easier time with the Radicals than Johnson. When one reviews the list of prominent men who, from time to time, would not allow their names to be considered for the vice-presidency—names like Webster, Clay and Borah—and when one recalls a restless but helpless John Calhoun watching in exasperation while Andrew Jackson led a political revolution, it is evident that the fault lies more with the office than the party conclaves. From the first, politicians ignored the original conception of the post. They found it more realistic to use the place to shelve an annoying ambition, to "catch state gudgeons," to buy off a faction. They did not cause the vice-presidency to become that way. Those qualities were there for exploitation, and perceptive men used them.

But because vice-presidents do periodically become presidents, it might—unless one is satisfied with the record—be worth shoring up the office or abolishing it altogether. The latter step has been seriously proposed several times. Because under the Senate rules, the president *pro tem* votes as a senator from his state and because the chair can be rotated readily, the inconvenience to the upper house would be minor. On the death of a president an interim appointee, either selected by Congress or established under a succession law, would exercise the "powers and duties" of the office until a special election was held.

The plan has several drawbacks. First, under the party system, it normally takes more than a year between the planning of a nominating convention and election day. While, in emergencies, the period could be shortened appreciably, the longer stretch of time is not without advantages. It permits a considerable number of men to become candidates for nomination. It also weeds out a good number of the unfit who enjoy a short boom and gradually fade. Though this method is not infallible in separating the wheat from the chaff, it has a certain virtue in winnowing the grades of chaff. Furthermore, a relatively long period of campaigning by actual nominees acquaints the voters with the men and provides a hint of what they stand for.

A second objection arises where Congress and the Executive branch are controlled by different parties. On the sudden death of the president this could cause a drastic reversal of policy and a thorough rotation of personnel. Such would be especially the case if the temporary replacement owed his job to Congress or if he arrived under the provisions of a law like the recent Presidential Succession Act. There would always be the possibility that Congress would wholly dominate the Executive during the hiatus. Moreover, the chance that a special election would keep the two branches divided between parties would produce a second wave of reversals and dismissals.

Another proposal would do just the opposite to abolishing the vice-presidency. Instead of subtracting it would add another for a total of two. Because the presidency is now too large a job for one man, this plan would give the Chief Magistrate an executive assistant with duties as great or greater than those of James Byrnes during World War II. This would be the First Vice-President of the United States. Because of the scope of his job it is presumed that proved ability would constitute a standard in his selection. The Second Vice-President would handle the Throttlebottom functions. If anything, he would have less to do than the current nature of the office requires. Here, an objection may be raised that such services are not worth the annual $25,000 the public pays for them. But this complaint had more validity before the era of multibillion dollar budgets.

A stronger disadvantage in the suggestion rests with the more important first vice-presidency. Executive policy must be unitary. And while presidents may listen to criticism by cabinet members and bow to the pressures of party in cabinet appointments, they nevertheless reserve the right of dismissal. A subordinate goes if he will not conform on major issues or if he high-handedly promulgates contrary policies. But with an elected executive vice-president a chief of government would have no such power. To illustrate this weakness, it is only necessary to picture Hannibal Hamlin administering Lincoln's policies or John Nance Garner tied to carrying out Franklin Roosevelt's program. A second weakness would occur upon accidental succession. Throttlebottom would step into the executive vice-presidency.

A more elastic, if less specific, reworking of the office is also possible. It would give the vice-president what some have enjoyed, cabinet status without portfolio. It would allow, subject to final presidential approval, direct supervision over several executive departments—say Agriculture, Interior, Commerce and Labor. It might also permit ex-officio membership on all or the most important Senate committees. He might work on special presidential projects or act as an envoy extraordinary after the manner in which Wallace investigated China for Roosevelt II in 1944. None of these tasks are constitutionally definable. In this there is some advantage. For to enlarge the purview of the office by strict clauses in the nation's organic law is to subtract from the presidential power, divide the Executive, and break down responsibility. An informal building up of vice-presidential functions permits greater diversity of action for the incumbent and greater freedom for his chief.

In time these enlarged duties would become customary, expected adjuncts of the second office. No post of any consequence has remained within the limits first prescribed for it. As the scope of government has grown the offices of the government have broadened their powers. Additional growth in the vice-presidency would not only enhance the office but provide relief for overworked presidents. Furthermore, the vice-president would have a greater share in the administration to which he was elected. In the event of his succession there would be greater continuity.

Objections may be raised that his presence in committees, even without a vote, would cut across the lines of a government based on the theory of separation of powers. This would be so. But in reality the lines are clearer in theory than in practice. Each major branch carries on operations in the spheres of the other two. Executive agencies are both quasi-judicial and quasi-legislative in their interpretations of broad grants of power. Congress hears evidence that might easily be presented in the courts and directs the judiciary to hear certain cases. It also lays down conditions for administering laws. So far as the presidency of the Senate goes, no one pretends that a vice-president is impartial. He is a party man striving to win the most for his own side by parliamentary legerdemain and by refined lobbying in his quarters. He is, at present, more a man of Congress than of the administration. Should more duties be required of him, he would move toward identifying himself with the Executive branch where he properly belongs. To the extent that he did his work well he could enhance his party prestige. In time, because of these added responsibilities, parties would be forced to select better running mates on their national tickets. Involved would be considerations of the social interest as well as those of political advantage or personal reward.

This throws the problem back upon men. It places responsibility on politicians and on the electorate. It tends to minimize mechanical solution. For mechanical solution seldom provides a full and complete answer. A machine, whether in a factory or in government, requires human operation. In a free society men are responsible for governing the machine. A vice-president is one of the agents the electorate chooses to act for it. Perhaps it is not too much to ask that he be given work commensurate with the presidential potentialities of his office. Perhaps it is not too much to ask that the electorate follow with more attention those it elects as its agents.

Omitted from the list below are collections of letters, printed speeches, pamphlets, newspapers, articles in magazines and learned journals, memoirs, public documents, congressional debates and some specialized monographs. In the research on this book, they were, however, consulted. I have kept them out of the bibliography on the assumption that they would be either unavailable or uninteresting to most laymen. I ask the indulgence of those who would have wished them included as more solid evidence of work on my part.

Because of the breakdown in the listing, some books are useful in more than one category. A reading of the appropriate chapters will disclose them to anyone. They are, therefore, entered but once. Those books that are starred might be of special interest to the lay reader.

P. R. L.

GENERAL

Alexander, D. S., *Political History of the State of New York*.
*Bailey, T. A., *Diplomatic History of the American People*.
*Beard, Charles A., and Beard, Mary R., *Rise of American Civilization*.
*Bemis, Samuel F., *Diplomatic History of the United States*.
———., ed., *The American Secretaries of State and Their Diplomacy*.
*Binkley, Wilfred E., *American Political Parties, Their Natural History*.
*———., *President and Congress*.
*Brogan, D. W., *Government by the People*.
Channing, Edward, *History of the United States*.
*Corwin, Edward S., *The President: Office and Powers*.
Flick, A. C., ed., *History of the State of New York*.
*Gabriel, Ralph H., *The Course of American Democratic Thought*.
*Hacker, Louis M., *The Triumph of American Capitalism*.
Hart, A. B., ed., *Commonwealth History of Massachusetts*.
Hatch, L. C., and Shoup, C. L., *History of the Vice-Presidency*.
Hesseltine, W. B., *The South in American History*.
Hicks, John D., *A Short History of American Democracy*.

Kent, Frank R., *The Democratic Party*.

*Laski, Harold, *The American Presidency*.

Latane, J. H., *A History of American Foreign Policy*.

McClure, A. K., *Our Presidents and How We Make Them*.

*McLaughlin, A. C., *A Constitutional History of the United States*.

McMaster, John B., *A History of the People of the United States*.

Myers, W. S., *The Republican Party, a History*.

Milton, George F., *The Use of Presidential Power*.

*Morison, Samuel E., and Commager, Henry S., *Growth of the American Republic*.

Oberholtzer, E. P., *History of the United States since the Civil War*.

*Parrington, Vernon L., *Main Currents in American Thought*.

Rhodes, James F., *History of the United States*.

Richardson, J. D., *Messages and Papers of the Presidents*.

Stanwood, Edward, *A History of the Presidency from 1788 to 1897*.

*Swisher, Carl B., *American Constitutional Development*.

ORIGINS

Alexander, Holmes, *Aaron Burr, the Proud Pretender*.

*Beveridge, Albert J., *The Life of John Marshall*.

*Bowers, Claude G., *Jefferson and Hamilton*.

*———., *Jefferson in Power*.

Farrand, Max, ed., *The Records of the Federal Convention of 1787*.

Parton, James, *Life and Times of Aaron Burr*.

*Schachner, Nathan, *Alexander Hamilton*.

*Warren, Charles, *The Making of the Constitution*.

HARRISON AND TYLER

Adams, Samuel H., *The Godlike Daniel*.

*Brooks, Van Wyck, *The World of Washington Irving*.

*Chitwood, O. P., *John Tyler, Champion of the Old South*.

*Cleaves, Freeman, *Old Tippecanoe, William Henry Harrison*.

Cole, A. C., *The Whig Party in the South*.

*Dodd, W. E., *Statesmen of the Old South*.

*Fraser, Hugh R., *Democracy in the Making*.

*Fuess, Claude M., *Daniel Webster*.

Goebel, Dorothy B., *William Henry Harrison*.

Green, James A., *William Henry Harrison; His Life and Times*.

*Hunt, Gaillard, *John C. Calhoun*.

*James, Marquis, *The Life of Andrew Jackson*.

*Johnson, Gerald W., *America's Silver Age.*
Lodge, Henry Cabot, *Daniel Webster.*
Meigs, W. M., *John Calhoun.*
Poage, George R., *Henry Clay and the Whig Party.*
*Schlesinger, Arthur M., Jr., *The Age of Jackson.*
Schurz, Carl, *Henry Clay.*
Stephenson, G. M., *The Political History of the Public Lands, 1840-1862.*
*Turner, Frederick J., *The United States, 1830-1850.*
Tyler, Lyon G., *Letters and Times of the Tylers.*
*Van Deusen, G. G., *The Life of Henry Clay.*
Wise, Henry A., *Seven Decades in the Union.*
Wellington, R. G., *Political Influence of the Public Lands, 1828-1842.*

TAYLOR AND FILLMORE

Barnes, T. W., *Memoir of Thurlow Weed.*
Bent, S., and McKinley, Silas B., *Old Rough and Ready.*
*Beveridge, Albert J., *Abraham Lincoln.*
*Dyer, Brainerd, *Zachary Taylor.*
Griffis, William E., *Millard Fillmore.*
Sandburg, Carl, *Abraham Lincoln, the Prairie Years.*
*Van Deusen, G. G., *Thurlow Weed, Wizard of the Lobby.*
Weed, Harriet, ed., *Autobiography of Thurlow Weed.*

LINCOLN AND JOHNSON

Abernethy, T. P., *From Frontier to Plantation in Tennessee.*
Allen, James G., *Reconstruction: the Battle for Democracy.*
*Beale, Howard K., *The Critical Year.*
Bowers, Claude G., *The Tragic Era.*
Charnwood, Lord, *Abraham Lincoln.*
*Current, R. N., *Old Thad Stevens.*
*Dubois, W. E. B., *Black Reconstruction.*
*Hendrick, B. J., *Lincoln's War Cabinet.*
*Henry, Robert S., *The Story of Reconstruction.*
Hesseltine, W. B., *U. S. Grant, Politician.*
*Josephson, Matthew, *The Politicos, 1865-1896.*
*Miller, Alphonse B., *Thaddeus Stevens.*
*Milton, George F., *Age of Hate.*
*———., *Conflict.*
*Randall, J. G., *The Civil War and Reconstruction.*

*Sandburg, Carl, *Abraham Lincoln, the War Years.*
Stryker, L. P., *Andrew Johnson, a Study in Courage.*
*Welles, Gideon, *Diary.*
Winston, Robert W., *Andrew Johnson, Plebeian and Patriot.*

GARFIELD AND ARTHUR

Caldwell, R. G., *James A. Garfield.*
Chidsey, Donald B., *The Gentleman from New York: A Life of Roscoe Conkling.*
*Eckenrode, H. J., *Rutherford B. Hayes.*
Hamilton, Gail, *Biography of James G. Blaine.*
*Howe, George F., *Chester A. Arthur.*
*Muzzey, David S., *James G. Blaine.*
Smith, T. C., *James A. Garfield.*

MCKINLEY AND ROOSEVELT

*Beer, Thomas, *Hanna.*
Bishop, J. B., *Theodore Roosevelt and His Time.*
Charnwood, Lord, *Theodore Roosevelt.*
Croly, Herbert, *Marcus Alonzo Hanna.*
*Dennett, Tyler, *John Hay, from Poetry to Politics.*
Dennis, A. L. P., *Adventures in American Diplomacy.*
*Dumond, F. L., *Roosevelt to Roosevelt.*
Dunn, Arthur W., *From Harrison to Harding.*
*Einstein, Lewis, *Roosevelt, His Mind in Action.*
Hill, H. C., *Roosevelt and the Caribbean.*
*Jessup, P. C., *Elihu Root.*
Kohlsaat, H. H., *McKinley to Harding.*
Lodge, Henry C., *Selections from the Correspondence of Theodore Roosevelt and Henry Cabot Lodge.*
Olcott, Charles S., *The Life of William McKinley.*
*Pringle, Henry F., *Life and Times of William Howard Taft.*
*———., *Theodore Roosevelt, a Biography.*
Rhodes, James F., *The McKinley and Roosevelt Administrations, 1897-1909.*
Rippy, J. F., *Latin America in World Politics.*
*Roosevelt, Theodore, *An Autobiography.*
*Steffens, Lincoln, *Autobiography.*
*Sullivan, Mark, *Our Times.*
Thayer, William R., *John Hay.*

————., *Theodore Roosevelt.*
*White, William A., *Autobiography.*

HARDING AND COOLIDGE

*Adams, Samuel H., *Incredible Era.*
*Allen, Frederick L., *Only Yesterday.*
* Coolidge, Calvin, *Autobiography.*
————., *Have Faith in Massachusetts.*
Fuess, Claude M., *Calvin Coolidge.*
*Griswold, A. W., *Far Eastern Policy of the United States.*
Slosson, Preston, *The Great Crusade and After.*
*White, William A., *A Puritan in Babylon.*
————., *Calvin Coolidge.*
*————., *Masks in a Pageant.*

ROOSEVELT AND TRUMAN

*Byrnes, James, *Speaking Frankly.*
Clemens, Cyril, *The Man from Missouri.*
————., ed., *Truman Speaks.*
Coffin, Tris., *Missouri Compromise.*
*Flynn, Edward, *You're the Boss.*
*Gregory, C. O., *Labor and the Law.*
Helm, William P., *Harry Truman, A Political Biography.*
*Lord, Russell, *The Wallaces of Iowa.*
McNaughton, F., and Hehmeyer, W., *This Man Truman.*
*McNeill, William, *The Greek Dilemma.*
*Perkins, Frances, *The Roosevelt I Knew.*
*White, T., and Jacoby, A., *Thunder out of China.*
Wish, Harvey, *Contemporary America.*

INDEX